AUSTRALIA
Law Book Co
Sydney

CANADA AND USA
Carswell
Toronto

HONG KONG
Sweet and Maxwell Asia

NEW ZEALAND
Brookers
Wellington

SINGAPORE and MALAYSIA
Sweet & Maxwell Asia
Singapore and Kuala Lumpur

ENGLISH LEGAL SYSTEM— THE FUNDAMENTALS

ENGLISH LEGAL SYSTEM

FIRST EDITION

By

JO BOYLAN-KEMP
Principal Lecturer in Law, Nottingham Law School

LONDON
SWEET & MAXWELL
2008

First edition 2008

Published in 2008 by
Sweet & Maxwell Limited of 100 Avenue Road, London NW3 3PF
http://www.sweetandmaxwell.co.uk
Typeset by
Interactive Sciences Ltd, Gloucester
Printed and bound in Great Britain by
Ashford Colour Press, Gosport, Hants.

No natural forests were destroyed to make this product;
only farmed timber was used and re-planted.

British Library Cataloguing in Publication Data

A CIP catalogue record for this book
is available from the British Library

ISBN 978-1-84703-402-1

DEDICATION

For Shorty & Spike

PREFACE

If the Law section of any good bookshop is perused then there will be found a number of textbooks that are dedicated to explaining the English legal system to their readers. Some are large heavy tomes that take forever and a day to read but provide the reader with an in-depth and highly intellectual view of the system once they have read it; others aim to explain the basic law but provide little insight into the issues that have arisen or can arise in this area. This textbook aims to be slightly different to those others found as it aims to do 'what it says on the tin' (so to speak) and explain the 'fundamentals' of the English legal system, whilst also highlighting and addressing the issues that can be found within it. The text is primarily focused towards undergraduate law students but it would be of equal interest to those studying A-level law, ILEX, a law module in another discipline or simply to those who are interested in discovering about the English legal system for personal reasons. To aid understanding there is found within each chapter a number of visual aids (flowcharts, graphs and grids etc.) so that the complex or important information is broken down into a user-friendly format. At the end of each chapter a number of Self-Test Questions will be found so that understanding and retention of information can be evaluated.

It is at this point that I would like to take the opportunity to thank those who have helped and supported me in my endeavour to complete this text. My thanks go to those at Sweet & Maxwell, especially Constance Sutherland, who have put up with my rather haphazard approach to deadlines with saint-like patience; to my colleagues and dear friends Rebecca Huxley-Binns and Shani Cassady for all of their advice, support and proof reading (I shall await to return the favour!) and finally to my loving family, especially my husband Robin, who have provided endless amounts of encouragement, tea and love, and managed to keep the children amused whilst 'mummy wrote her silly book'.

The writing of this text has not been an easy task. The law is not a static creature and the landscape of the English legal system has in parts noticeably changed over recent times; as a result if there are any errors or omissions then I apologise. The law is stated as I believe it to be on May 16, 2008.

Jo Boylan-Kemp

CONTENTS

LIST OF FIGURES

TABLE OF CASES

TABLE OF STATUTES

TABLE OF STATUTORY INSTRUMENTS

TABLE OF INTERNATIONAL AND EUROPEAN CONVENTIONS AND LEGISLATION

1 Introduction to the English legal system

The English legal system is a wide and varied topic that covers everything from how the courts work through to how to use and interpret the law. The aim of this text is to explain the main principles of this system so that a basic understanding of the fundamentals can be gained. There is little to no black letter law found within the covers of this book as the substantive law is left to other more suitable topics (such as Criminal Law and Contract Law), what will be covered is a consideration of the main driving doctrines and the common procedures found within the justice system as a whole.

A comprehensive understanding of the legal system is vital for any person coming to the law; be they a law student, a student studying another discipline (such as architecture or medicine) or even a layperson who simply has a personal interest in the law. Students often wonder why they have to study the English Legal System and it is sometimes perceived as a 'non-topic', or not 'proper law'. However this perception is dangerously flawed, as it is essential for an understanding of the system to be properly developed at an early stage, as the law does not occur in a vacuum. It is all well and good learning the academic legal rules as to what constitutes an assault but it is also necessary to know how an allegation of assault would be dealt with by the justice system; for example who would prosecute, what court would hear the case and what would happen if the defendant were convicted. If these procedures are not understood then there is very little point in knowing the substantive law.

To hold a basic understanding of the English Legal System will provide a student with the necessary foundations so that a clear understanding of the objective and workings of the substantive law can then be achieved. This text will follow a logical pathway through the whole justice system, explaining the processes but also analysing them along the way, and it will also spend time considering the potential changes that may occur in the near future. The law is never static but always changing depending on the societal needs of that time. In this first chapter we will consider the different sources of law that can be found within the English Legal System.

1.1 The constitution

The United Kingdom, unlike the majority of the civilised world, does not have a written constitution but rather it has an unwritten one. A constitution is most commonly described as a system of governance, which details the structure, powers, and duties of the government and the rights that are to be conferred on the citizens living within the state. The Oxford Concise Dictionary defines the term 'constitution' as meaning:

> A body of fundamental principles or established precedents according to which a state or organisation is governed.

Essentially a constitution is constructed of the customs, institutions and laws which have been combined to create the government and to which all of those who live within the community are required to accede. However, the term 'constitution' does not just apply to the government, as any political entity can have a constitution that sets out their fundamental political principles, amongst other things.

A constitution is normally a written document that sets out the structure of the government and the institutions within it. It is a codification of the laws of the land that can be turned to and relied upon by any person who falls under its reach. A codified constitution provides a range of benefits, in that it can be simple to identify and access, as well as being easy to understand by all of those who come to it. The problem however with a codified constitution is that it is a rigid and generally unflexible source. If the law needs to be modified to reflect the changes in society then this can be quite a difficult task to achieve. It involves amending the original constitution and to do this it means that special procedures must be undertaken, such the calling of a referendum.

As stated above, the United Kingdom does not have a written constitution but it possesses an unwritten one, which is constructed from the wealth of rules that regulate the state. These rules can be found within statute law, case law, custom and conventions. The United Kingdom's constitution is entrenched in the fabric of the country's historical development and although it cannot be easily pinpointed it is an accepted form of governance. The problem that comes with an unwritten constitution is that it can often be difficult to find the principle that is being relied upon as the legal and democratic make up of the country has developed in a rather piece-meal fashion over a prolonged period of time. The benefits, however, are that the rules of law are flexible and can be easily remoulded so as to develop in a way that matches with the development of society. If a problem occurs that cannot be dealt with by the law as it is at that time then new legislation can be drafted so as to combat the problem at an early stage. This flexibility is generally heralded as a positive benefit; however, this positive can easily be turned into a negative due to the fact that the law can be changed quickly and therefore often without due consideration as to the ramifications of the amendments.

1.2   Why the 'English' legal system?

The 'British Isles', the 'United Kingdom', or 'Great Britain'; all of these names are used to refer to the territory of which England is a part, so why therefore is the legal system referred to as the 'English' legal system and not the 'United Kingdom' legal system or the legal system of 'Great Britain'? Each of these jurisdiction titles (which are often used interchangeably and not very accurately) actually denote a different composition of the variety of countries and islands that could potentially be included as part of that jurisdiction. If a person were asked to make a list of the countries and islands to be included within any of these above titles it is suggested that the main ones stated would be England, Wales, Scotland and Ireland (with the latter possibly being split down further into Northern Ireland and Eire). The above nomenclatures do generally involve these listed countries, but each one also has its own individual membership of a myriad of other islands found within the 'British' state.

For instance the term 'Great Britain' is taken to include England, Wales, Scotland and the outlying islands of Orkney, Shetland and the Hebrides. The title 'United Kingdom' covers Great Britain (so England, Wales, Scotland, Orkney, Shetland and the Hebrides) and Northern Ireland. The 'British Isles' is cited as including the United Kingdom, the Channel Islands (Jersey, Guernsey, Alderney, Sark) and the Isle of Man. Ireland, or more correctly, the Republic of Eire, is a separate jurisdiction all together.

As there are so many different combinations of geographical locations it would be difficult (if not next to impossible) to bring all of the individual territories together underneath one single umbrella of a legal system. As a result the British Isles is split into a number of separate jurisdictions, these being England and Wales, Scotland, Northern Ireland and the Channel Islands; each one with its own legal system. Originally England, Wales, Scotland and Northern Ireland had their own individual legal systems but in the 15th Century, under the rule of Henry VII, Wales was absorbed into England, whilst Scotland (who retained its own judiciary and church) and Northern Ireland remained largely independent but were subject to the laws made by the English Parliament and could not create their own primary legislation. England and Wales were viewed as one unified jurisdiction and this is to what the term the 'English legal system' relates, whereas Scotland and Northern Ireland were viewed as having separate jurisdictions. In 1998 both Scotland and Northern Ireland were granted powers (under the Scotland Act 1998 and the Northern Ireland Act 1998 respectively) to create legislation that was applicable only in those separate jurisdictions. Wales has also begun to become more independent in recent times due to the devolution of powers and the creation of the Welsh Assembly Government which has, since 2007, been permitted to enact a degree of primary legislation, although it is likely to be a long time yet before it is viewed as a legal jurisdiction in its own right and so for the foreseeable future the term the 'English legal system' will be taken to cover both England and Wales.

1.3 Who makes the law?

There are four predominant sources (or makers) of the law within the English legal system, which are:

- Parliament
- The Courts
- The European Union
- The Council of Europe

1.3.1 Parliament

Parliament is the English legal system's principal law making body. It consists of the House of Commons, the House of Lords and the monarch. They are responsible for passing the laws that will then govern the lives of everyone who comes within its jurisdiction. One fundamental doctrine of the English legal system is that of Parliamentary sovereignty, which means that Parliament is viewed as supreme (the highest source) in respect of the creation of laws. In 1885 the now famous British jurist and constitutional theorist Albert Dicey stated that:

> The principle, therefore, of parliamentary sovereignty means neither more nor less than this, namely that 'Parliament' has the right to make or unmake any law whatever; and further, that no person or body is recognised by the law of England as having a right to override or set aside the legislation of Parliament.
>
> (A. Dicey, *An Introduction to the Study of the Law of the Constitution*, 1885)

Effectively this means that Parliament has the right to make any law that it so chooses (even if it were completely absurd) and that if Parliament creates a law (no matter how absurd) then those who live within the jurisdiction must abide by it, whether they disagree with it or not. Even the courts are not allowed to go against legislation enacted by Parliament and they are required to apply and enforce it regardless of their views upon it. The reason as to why it is accepted that Parliament holds this supremacy is due to the fact that Parliament is democratically elected. Every person who lives within the jurisdiction (and who is eligible to vote) has the right to have a say in the constitution of Parliament and as a result this allows Parliament to be taken as the superior law making body in respect of regulating the lives of the citizens who live under its powers. Although Parliament is the principal law making body that has the power to make any law that it deems appropriate, there is a degree of limitation to these powers. If Parliament was to make a law that was wholly unacceptable to the society that it serves then the individuals responsible within Parliament could be removed from this position of power through the democratic process. When composition of Parliament changes then the successors are not bound to follow the laws left behind by their predecessors.

The true extent of the supremacy of Parliament has been challenged over recent years due to the joining of the European Union (EU) and the enactment of the Human Rights Act 1998 (HRA 1998). The EU has the power to make law that is applicable to all of its member states (as the UK is) and each member state is then duty bound to follow and apply this law under its terms of its membership of the EU. Therefore if a law enacted by the EU is considered to be incompatible with the domestic law (the laws of the UK as enacted by Parliament) then the law made by the EU will take precedence. This new hierarchy of precedence has significantly eroded the supremacy of Parliament and has received much criticism by political parties and certain factions of the public alike. Another perceived 'blow' to the status of Parliamentary sovereignty has come about due to the enactment of the HRA 1998. The HRA 1998 requires the UK to ensure that its legislation is compatible with the European Convention for Human Rights and Fundamental Freedoms (1950) (ECHR) and if there is an alleged breach of the ECHR then under the HRA 1998 the matter can be dealt with by the domestic courts as opposed to having to resort to the jurisdiction of Strasbourg. Britain was one of the initial signatories to the ECHR in 1950 but simply being a signatory did not require Britain to set aside any of its domestic laws in preference of the ECHR. Rather if a citizen of the UK wished to rely upon a Convention then they were required to take the case to the European Court of Human Rights

(ECHR) in Strasbourg. The UK attempted to abide by the ECHR as best it could but if any issues of incompatibility arose (between the ECHR and domestic law) then the matter was resolved outside of the domestic jurisdiction and it did not impinge upon the domestic rule of law.

The implementation of the HRA 1998 changed the way in which the ECHR impacted upon the domestic law. Section 3(1) of the HRA 1998 sets out that:

> So far as it is possible to do so, primary legislation and subordinate legislation must be read and given effect in a way, which is compatible with the Convention rights.

It can be argued that the requirement to try and interpret domestic legislation in a way that is compatible with the ECHR has further eroded the principle of Parliamentary supremacy, as by attempting to ensure compatibility the courts may effectively go against the original intentions of Parliament in enacting the legislation; thereby inadvertently proclaiming that the ECHR is actually more superior to that of domestic law. Even when new legislation is being considered Parliament is required (under s.19 HRA 1998) to consider whether the legislation is to be compatible with the ECHR and to make a declaration to this effect. However, the HRA 1998 did not declare the ECHR to be supreme and there are a number of safeguards found within it that allow domestic law to take precedence (even if only for a limited time) over the Convention rights. Under s.4 of the HRA 1998 the court are not permitted to overrule domestic law in favour of the ECHR. If an issue of incompatibility does arise then the courts are required to apply the domestic law in question and then make a 'declaration of incompatibility', from which it is envisaged that Parliament will review the incompatible legislation and make suitable amendments to the law. In respect of the requirement to consider proposed legislation in line with the ECHR, it is not mandatory for any new legislation actually to be compatible with the ECHR (and if it is deemed as incompatible then a declaration must be made to this effect) but it is highly unlikely that new legislation would be enacted if considered incompatible as it would simply be challenged through the courts at a later point in time.

1.3.2   The courts

The courts do make law, not in the way that Parliament does, but rather they can change the ways in which the law is applied (due to their interpretation of the legislation) and they can further develop the law by way of the common law (see 1.4.1). They are entirely independent of Parliament and the government, and in some ways they can act as a control mechanism to these other powers.

1.3.2.1   The separation of powers

The great political philosopher Montesquieu, to describe the method employed by democratic states to govern their affairs, coined the phrase the 'separation of powers' in the 18th Century. Montesquieu's philosophy was that 'government should be set up so that no man need be afraid of another' and he considered that the arrangement of a state's administrative system by way of the separation of powers was a method which would help to ensure that this philosophy was achieved.

The separation of powers model is tripartite in form and it involves the separating of the state into three individual elements, these being the executive, the legislature and the judiciary. The executive is comprised of the government and governmental servants, such as local authorities and the police. The legislature is Parliament (as described above), and the judiciary involves the authority that can be exercised by the judges. Each individual element must work together to ensure that the state functions properly but as they are all independent of each other it means that no single one can become too powerful or dominant. The English system is heralded a great success in maintaining a separation of powers but realistically there can never be a complete separation as each limb must work closely with each other and there will inevitably be overlap in the responsibilities and duties.

Figure 1.1 The separation of powers

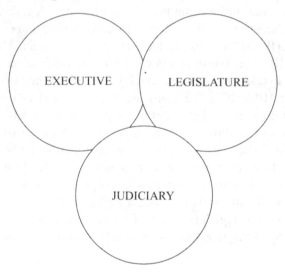

1.3.2.2   The Rule of law

Another fundamental doctrine of the English legal system is that which is known as the 'rule of law'. The principle behind this rule is that no person is above the law. Paine, an 18th Century British revolutionary, summarised this belief when he commented in his widely read pamphlet *'Common Sense'* that:

> For as in absolute governments the king is law, so in free countries the law ought to be king; and there ought to be no other.

Dicey later set out three principles, which he felt encompassed this doctrine. These being:

> (1) the absolute supremacy or predominance of regular law as opposed to the influence of arbitrary power;

6

(2) equality before the law or the equal subjection of all classes to the ordinary law of the land administered by the ordinary courts; and

(3) the law of the constitution is a consequence of the rights of individuals as defined and enforced by the courts.

The definition found within *Halsbury's Laws of England*: *Constitutional Law and Human Rights*, para.6, provides us with a much more detailed definition as to what this rule of law is perceived to entail.

The legal basis of government gives rise to the principle of legality, sometimes referred to as the rule of law. This may be expressed as a number of propositions, as described below.

"The existence or non-existence of a power or duty is a matter of law and not of fact, and so must be determined by reference either to the nature of the legal personality of the body in question and the capacities that go with it, or to some enactment or reported case. As far as the capacities that go with legal personality are concerned, many public bodies are incorporated by statute and so statutory provisions will define and limit their legal capacities. Individuals who are public office-holders have the capacities that go with the legal personality that they have as natural persons. The Crown is a corporation sole or aggregate and so has general legal capacity, including (subject to some statutory limitations and limitations imposed by European law) the capacity to enter into contracts and to own and dispose of property. The fact of a continued undisputed exercise of a power by a public body is immaterial, unless it points to a customary power exercised from time immemorial. In particular, the existence of a power cannot be proved by the practice of a private office.

The argument of state necessity is not sufficient to establish the existence of a power or duty which would entitle a public body to act in a way that interferes with the rights or liberties of individuals. However, the common law does recognise that in case of extreme urgency, when the ordinary machinery of the state cannot function, there is a justification for the doing of acts needed to restore the regular functioning of the machinery of government.

If effect is to be given to the doctrine that the existence or non-existence of a power or duty is a matter of law, it should be possible for the courts to determine whether or not a particular power or duty exists, to define its ambit and provide an effective remedy for unlawful action. The independence of the judiciary is essential to the principle of legality. The right of access to the courts can be excluded by statute, but this is not often done in express terms. A person whose civil or political rights and freedoms as guaranteed by the Convention for the Protection of Human Rights and Fundamental Freedoms (the European Convention on Human Rights) have been infringed is entitled under the Convention to an effective right of access to the courts and an effective national remedy. On the other hand, powers are often given to bodies other than the ordinary courts, to decide questions of law without appeal to the ordinary courts, and sometimes in such terms that their freedom from appellate jurisdiction extends to their findings of fact or law on which the existence of their powers depends.

7

Since the principal elements of the structure of the machinery of government, and the powers and duties which belong to its several parts, are defined by law, its form and course can be altered only by a change of law. Conversely, since the legislative power of Parliament is unrestricted, save where European Community law has primacy, its form and course can at any time be altered by Parliament. Consequently there are no powers or duties inseparably annexed to the executive government."

These three principles essentially set out that a person should only be regulated by the settled law; that they should only be punished according to the law; and that everyone, no matter who they are, is subject to the law. No person should be punished or tried arbitrarily or, punished or tried due to arbitrary laws. The extent to which the modern day English legal system holds true to these principles can be said to be under some doubt, as in recent times (especially in relation to the 'war on terror') the law has permitted the authorities to detain individuals for significantly long periods of time without charge (although this has been successfully challenged in the court in *A & X v Secretary of State for the Home Department* [2004] UKHL 56) and the UK has recently been forced to apologise for being complicit with America in the practice of extraordinary rendition. Extraordinary rendition occurs when an individual is kidnapped by state representatives and transferred between states, with the aim of their detention being without recourse to the legal system. A number of detainees in Guantanamo Bay are believed to have arrived at that location by way of this procedure and it is often associated with the use of torture and inhuman treatment. Britain has always vehemently denied having any involvement with the practice of extraordinary rendition but on the February 21, 2008 the government had to formally apologise after it was discovered that a number of rendition flights had stopped on UK territory to re-fuel in 2002.

1.4 Sources of law

Figure 1.2 Sources of law

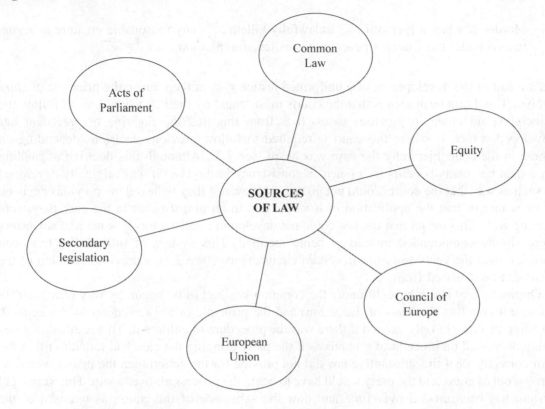

1.4.1 Common law

Prior to the Norman Conquest of 1066 there were many different rules of law found all over the country. The law being applied at this point was custom law which varied depending on the local customs, for example in the Midlands area Mercian law was used, whilst in the north Dane law was predominant. William the Conqueror realised that these different systems were difficult to manage and would be a bar to obtaining effective rule over the country as a whole. So as to bring uniformity to the land William decided to set up a central system of government that would include the justice system. Initially the king and his representatives travelled the length and breadth of the country to discover the local customs and to listen to and resolve the disputes of his subjects. This system of justice became known as the *Curia Regis* (King's Court) and it was the very beginning of the common law system. From the workings of the *Curia Regis* evolved a uniformed law that applied to everyone within its jurisdiction; the law was common to everyone and it became known colloquially as the 'common law'.

The common law is still a fundamental principle of the English legal system today and it works alongside the law of equity (see 1.4.2) and the legislation created by Parliament. An example of the common law can be seen by the fact that killing someone is a crime. The offence of murder is not found within any statute, but the fact that it a crime is entrenched within the common law by way of *Coke's* case (*Coke's Institutes* 3 Co Inst 47) which states that:

> Murder is when a [person] . . . unlawfully killeth . . . any reasonable creature *in rerum natura* under the Queen's peace, with malice aforethought . . .

As a result of the development of a uniformed justice system there arose the principle of *stare decisis*. This Latin term means that the courts must 'stand by their decision' and so follow the principles laid down in previous cases. It is from this that the doctrine of precedent has developed, which is where the court is required to follow previous decisions depending on where in the court hierarchy the case was heard (see 2.3). Although this doctrine of binding precedent has many benefits to it (such as consistency in the law) it was originally developed in such as way that the courts could not go against it even if they believed the previous decision to be wrong or that the application of it would end in an unjust result in the case they were dealing with. This meant that the law could not develop in a satisfactory manner and any errors were simply compounded instead of being rectified. This system of inflexibility has been softened over the years and now, in certain circumstances (see 2.3), a previous decision of the court can be departed from.

Originally any claim brought under the common law had to be begun by way of a 'writ' (a document detailing the basis of the action) and the principle of *ubi remedium ibi ius* applied, meaning that a right only existed if there was the procedure to enforce it. This resulted in cases being dismissed on procedural grounds as if the party bringing the case had failed to fill in the writ correctly, or if the substantive law did not provide for the action then the matter would be thrown out of court and the party would have to begin the process all over again. This very rigid system has been eroded over time and now the substance of the claim, as opposed to the content, is taken to be the most important factor by the court.

Despite there being certain flaws within the common law system it was heralded as an overall success and transported to all the countries within the British Empire, which became known as the 'Commonwealth'. Even though the British Empire has been disbanded these countries (for example Australia, Canada and Hong Kong) still have a common law system in place and largely follow the same principles at the UK (even though the individual laws may be different). This system can be contrasted with the civil law system found throughout the majority of Europe and associated countries.

1.4.2 Equity

There is a well-known maxim that is often recited in relation to the concept of equity and that is:

> "He who comes to equity must come with clean hands".

Equity is all about the idea of fairness and natural justice. It is often viewed as plugging the gaps and loopholes of the common law so that the strictness of the substantive law does not stand in the way of achieving what is essentially right and just. Equity developed alongside the principles of the common law as a result of its failings and it originally helped to achieve a suitable outcome where the one provided by the common law was viewed as inappropriate. The only remedy that was initially available to an aggrieved party under the common law was damages. Damages could be highly satisfactory in some cases, for example where the claimant's property had been destroyed or they had been swindled out of some goods or money, but where a claimant had a situation such as the defendant running a brothel next to their house or the defendant's animals constantly eating all of their crops (we are going back many, many years here) a financial remedy would not help to rectify the situation. What the claimant would want in these examples is for the nuisance to stop, not just to be compensated and then have to continue living with the problem.

The state of the law and the limited possibilities of redress resulted in a large volume of claimants being unhappy with the remedy that they achieved. As a result these disheartened litigants began to petition the king in the hope that he would provide them with a remedy. Initially the king took a personal interest in the plight of his subjects, but as time went on and the volume of petitions increased the king (at some point during the 15th Century) handed the responsibility of assessing the petitions over to the Lord High Chancellor (whose role later evolved into that of the Lord Chancellor today). Due to the high number of referrals the Lord High Chancellor created a specialist court to deal with such matters and the court was named the 'Court of Chancery' (now the Chancery Division of the High Court). The court was run by the Lord High Chancellor and he would make judgment based on his opinion of the merits of the case put forward by the parties, the participants were truly at the Lord High Chancellor's mercy as there was no hierarchy of case precedence established for this court.

As the Court of Chancery developed the common law judges became increasingly dissatisfied with the state of affairs, as they viewed the court to be a method of overriding and usurping their authority; if a litigant was unhappy with the remedy provided for by the common law court then they could turn to the Court of Chancery for a more favourable one. This rivalry between the two courts came to a climax in the *Earl of Oxford's Case* (1616) 1 Rep. Ch. 1 where the two courts came into direct conflict. The common law court held that the law dictated one outcome, whilst equity dictated the exact opposite (and threatened to imprison those concerned unless they acted as directed). The case was referred to the king who was requested to rule upon the matter, he held that where there was a conflict between the common law and equity, equity would prevail. Logically this decision was correct as if equity could not prevail over the common law then it would not be able to fulfil its purpose of providing justice where the common law could not.

Although the matter was settled as a principle of law there could still be found a degree of contention between the two court structures and this persisted until equity began to evolve into a more formalised set of rules and the doctrine of precedent began to take effect. The Judicature Acts of 1873–75 succeeded in alleviating the remaining antagonism between the two systems by restructuring the entire court system so that the common law and equity were working together (and could be administered by all courts), as opposed to against each other. Under these Acts all courts are now able to turn to both common law and equitable remedies depending on

11

which is deemed to be the most appropriate in respect of the individual case, although equity will still always prevail where there is a conflict between the two systems.

1.4.2.1 Equitable remedies

As alluded to above, equity provides an increased selection of remedies that the court can turn to so as to satisfactorily remedy the specific issues at hand. The remedies that can be found under the rules of equity are:

- **Injunction**—this requires the defendant to either cease a certain action or, in certain cases, it can require the defendant to undertake a certain action. (e.g. cease making noise after 11pm, or undertake necessary repairs to a dangerous building).

- **Specific performance**—this requires the defendant to fulfil an obligation that they had agreed to undertake (e.g. completing the building of a new house after there had been a dispute as to payment).

- **Rescission**—this returns the parties to the position they were in prior to a contract being made (e.g. if the contract was to supply goods in return for payment and the payment was withheld rescission can ensure that the goods (or their value) are returned to the supplier).

The granting of an equitable remedy is a matter of discretion for the courts. A successful claimant will always receive the common law remedy of damages (if appropriate) but the court does have to taken into consideration the justness of their actions when considering equitable remedies. For example, even if an equitable remedy would be of great benefit to one party (take the granting of an injunction so as to abate a noise nuisance) if it were to disproportionately disadvantage the other party (so the injunction to stop the noise would detrimentally affect the other party's business) then the court would be unlikely to grant such a remedy. Equity is always about fairness and natural justice and this is in respect of all parties to the matter, not just the party bringing the claim.

1.4.2.2 Modern day equity

So far the discussion has been focused on the historical development of the doctrine of equity, but it is also necessary to consider the way in which the modern day courts approach equity. If we return to the equity maxim quoted above of 'He who comes to equity must come with clean hands' then the current approach can be analysed. In the case of *D & C Builders v Rees* [1966] 2 Q.B. 617, D & C Builders (a small building firm) had been contracted to undertake some building work at the defendants' (the Rees) house. The Rees had already paid D & C Builders part of the monies for the work (£250 out of a £732 total) but then refused to pay the remaining balance due to their decision that the standard and quality of the work was not acceptable. D & C Builders were in serious financial difficulties at this time and were near the point of bankruptcy and the Rees were aware of this fact. The Rees then approached D & C Builders and offered £300 in full and final settlement of their bill for the building works. D & C Builders reluctantly accepted this offer. Under contract law the decision to accept such an offer would be held to be the end of the matter but D & C Builders then brought proceedings against the Rees to recover the outstanding amount. The Court of Appeal held that the Rees were liable to pay D & C Builders the remainder of the money owed as they had not 'come to equity with clean hands'; they were aware of D & C Builders' financial situation and had attempted to take advantage of it. To hold in their favour would have resulted in an injustice being performed and it was a potential injustice that equity could remedy.

The equitable maxim stated above is not the only maxim that has been created by the doctrine of equity and there are a number of others which are as equally well-known, such as 'equity is equality', 'equity will not suffer a wrong without a remedy' and 'he who seeks equity must do equity' etc. Each maxim is an accepted principle of equity and has associated cases that can be used to illustrate their workings.

1.4.3   Legislation   (parliament   + Queen)

legislation = statute = Acts of parliament

Legislation is created by Parliament (as discussed above), which consists of the Houses of Parliament (the House of Lords and the House of Commons) and the monarch (currently the Queen). Legislation is the formal enactment of rules into a document containing the law. Legislation can be referred to in one of three ways; these being 'legislation', 'statute' and 'Acts of Parliament', and it does not matter which name is used as they all mean the same thing. For legislation to be created it must go through a thorough process which aims to ensure its suitability, appropriateness and robustness, and there will generally be a reason behind why an attempt is being made to legislate on a certain issue (e.g. the Dangerous Dogs Act 1991 was enacted in response to the number of incidents where children were seriously injured or killed by aggressive dogs).

Often (but not always) legislation starts out as a consultation paper known as a 'Green Paper' where the initial proposals are set out by government with the purpose of them being commented upon by interested parties. After the initial consultation process has taken place the Green Paper will then be formally drafted into a more detailed document called a 'White Paper', which sets out the clear basis of the intended legislation. This again will be put out for consultation for a set period of time (generally three months) so as to gather further views and recommendations on the proposals.

1.4.3.1   Bills

All legislation (whether it went through the consultation process or not) will begin life as a Bill. A Bill can arise from one of three sources, these being:

- Public Bills
- Private Members' Bills
- Private Bills

A public Bill is one that is drafted by Parliament and the proposed law within it will have the intention of becoming part of the law of the country so as to govern all who live within the jurisdiction. Parliamentary legislative draftsmen whose main occupation is to draft the laws of the country will draft a public Bill.

A private member's bill is a draft Bill prepared by a backbench MP and the Member will often have a personal reason for proposing the new legislation. The Member does not have to produce a full version of the draft Bill but rather must provide its short title (what it will be called) and long title (provides a brief description of what it involves) (see 3.4.1 for a fuller explanation of these terms). A private member's bill can be introduced into the House of Commons by one of three ways; the first is the ballot where the Member has to enter a ballot and the first seven drawn will then be afforded a days debating time in the House. A private member's bill selected by ballot will stand the best chance of becoming law as it will receive a substantial amount of debating time. The second method is known as the 'ten minute rule' where the Member is provided with ten minutes to outline the idea of the Bill to the House and although it is unlikely that a Bill will go on to become law through this process it does allow the Member to raise awareness of the issues contained in the Bill. The final method that can be employed is by way of a presentation. The Member will be allowed briefly to present on the Bill, but the presentation actually involves doing little more than introducing the name of the Bill into the House and as a result very little else generally follows on from such a presentation.

An individual or a body, such as a local authority, brings a private Bill, and it has the aim of conferring a specific benefit upon the party, or affording them relief from another law or wrongdoing. If the Bill is enacted into legislation then only the party who has made the application will be subjected to its powers. For example there is currently a private Bill lodged with the House of Commons by Broads Authority, which sets out that its purpose is to confer further powers upon the Broads Authority in relation to the maintenance of the navigable waters and banks that make up the Norfolk Broads.

For a Bill to become legislation it has to pass through a long and quite complicated process that is described below. The flow chart at Figure 1.2 should provide a useful aid in understanding this process (begin by following the dotted line to its logical conclusion before considering the route of the black line).

Figure 1.3 Enactment of legislation

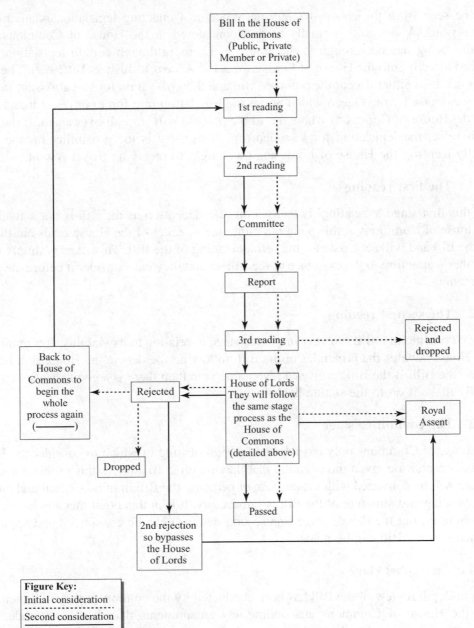

1.4.3.2 The enactment of legislation

As can be seen from the above diagram the process of enacting legislation is anything but straightforward. A Bill will normally be first considered in the House of Commons before potentially being passed through to the House of Lords (although certain legislation can be introduced directly into the House of Lords as was the Access to Justice Act 1999). The House of Lords can then either accept the proposed Bill and then pass it on for Royal Assent (a rubber stamping exercise by the Queen which brings the legislation into force) or reject it and send it back to the House of Commons where the whole process will start all over again. If the House of Lords reject the legislation for a second time then there is the possibility for the Bill to essentially leapfrog the House of Lords and go straight to receiving Royal Assent.

1.4.3.2.1 The first reading

Calling this first stage a 'reading' is really a bit of a deception as the Bill is not actually read by the House of Commons at this point but rather the Speaker of the House reads out the short title of the Bill and will set a date for the second reading of the Bill. This stage is simply to alert the Member's attention to the existence of the Bill so that they can consider it before the second formal reading.

1.4.3.2.2 The second reading

The second reading of a Bill is a very important stage in relation to its viability. It is at this point that the House debates the principles of the Bill, following the debate the House will be asked to vote on the Bill. If the Bill receives a favourable vote then there is a good chance that it will eventually make it on to the statute books.

1.4.3.2.3 The committee stage

As the House of Commons only has a limited period of time in which to consider the Bill the finer details cannot be given the attention that they require. To address this problem a specific committee will be convened with the purpose of perusing the Bill in minute detail and ensuring that the wording and structure of the Bill is satisfactory. It is at this point that any issues which came to light during the debate stage (the second reading) can be considered and appropriate amendments to the Bill can be made.

1.4.3.2.4 The report stage

After an in-depth review of the Bill has been conducted by the committee they will then report back to the House of Commons and outline any amendments that they have made. These amendments will then be debated upon and a vote will be taken in respect of each amendment.

1.4.3.2.5 The third reading

This is the final stage for a Bill to be considered by the House of Commons on its first (and possibly only) passage through it. The third reading will involve the amended Bill being presented to the House and then it will be opened up for a short debate. As all the amendments have been made by this point the debate is generally concerned once again with the general principles of the Bill and it is usually a relatively short debate. The House will then vote upon the acceptance or rejection of the Bill.

1.4.3.2.6 The House of Lords

If the House of Commons rejects the Bill then the matter goes no further, if however it accepts the Bill then it will be passed up to the House of Lords for further debate and scrutiny. The House of Lords will follow the same three stage reading process as the House of Commons did. If the House of Lords accepts the Bill then it will be approved and passed to the Queen for Royal Assent. If the House of Lords rejects the Bill then it will be returned to the House of Commons for the whole process to start all over again.

If the House of Lords reject a Bill on the second consideration of it then it does not necessarily mean that the Bill has received a death sentence as there are certain instances provided for by legislation that mean the House of Lords approval is not required and the Bill can move straight to receiving Royal Assent.

Prior to the Parliaments Acts of 1911 and 1949 proposed legislation required the approval of both Houses of Parliament. This requirement of double approval lead to a number of Bills being rejected by the House of Lords and never becoming law, as the House of Lords had the power to block any legislation with which it disagreed. The 1911 Act removed some of the House of Lords' powers to restrict the development of the law by only permitting it to delay the enactment of legislation for a two-year period before it would automatically receive Royal Assent on the condition that it had been approved by the House of Commons in three successive sessions. Where the Bill was a 'money bill' (meaning that it concerned matters of taxation) the maximum delay that could be caused by House of Lords was a period of one month before it proceeded on to gain Royal Assent. The 1949 Act further reduced the delay that could be enforced by the House of Lords in respect of general bills down to one-year (as long as it was passed by the House of Commons in two successive sessions).

The Parliaments Act 1911 was only used on three occasions and one of those was for the passing of the 1949 Act (which further eroded the House of Lords' powers) and the 1949 Act has since only been used four times to pass the:

- War Crimes Act 1991
- European Parliamentary Elections Act 1999
- Sexual Offences (Amendment) Act 2000
- Hunting Act 2004

After the passing of the controversial Sexual Offences (Amendment) Act 2000 (which lowered the age of consent for male homosexual activity to 16) and the Hunting Act 2004 (which prohibits the hunting of wild mammals (foxes) with dogs) the validity of the Parliaments Act 1949 was challenged by the Countryside Alliance in the case of *R. (on the application of Jackson and others) v Attorney-General* [2005] UKHL 56. Their submissions were that as the

Parliament Act 1911 was used to amend the law and pass the 1949 Act without the Lords' approval then the later Act was unlawful (or at the very least secondary legislation) as the 1911 Act did not contain the provisions for such an action. The House of Lords (sitting in its judicial capacity) held that the 1949 Act was lawful as the 1911 did not provide for making any major constitutional changes but as the amendment enacted by the 1949 Act (reducing the delay time down from two-years to one-year) was effectively only an administrative change then there was no major constitutional reform and therefore the law and the decision (the Hunting Act 2004) could stand.

1.4.3.2.7 Royal Assent

As stated above the process of receiving Royal Assent is now really an administrative one. Traditionally the monarch was required to give their considered consent to any new legislation before it would come into force. Nowadays the Queen must still give her consent to the legislation but this will not be 'considered' consent (she will not sit down and read every proposed Act of Parliament). Consent will never be refused by the monarch and it has been mooted on many an occasion that if they were presented with his or her own death warrant they would still be obliged to sign it (although this theory has yet to be tested!) Once legislation receives Royal Assent it is viewed as being immediately in force (and therefore law) unless a later date has been specified for its enactment.

1.4.4 Delegated legislation

Delegated or secondary legislation occurs when Parliament provides a certain body (normally a local authority/government) with the ability to make the law. Effectively Parliament will pass an Act (described as the 'parent Act'), which sets the basis and scope for the particular law, and then it will pass this on to the nominated body who will then add the necessary detail to the framework of the parent Act by producing appropriate delegated legislation.

Delegated legislation can be made by one of three ways:

- Statutory Instruments
- Byelaws
- Orders of Council

1.4.4.1 Statutory instruments

Parliament can confer the power to make a statutory instrument upon a governmental department or Minister. Parliament will pass a parent Act and then the Minister will draft a statutory instrument (SI) to implement the requirements of the enabling Act. The SI will have the same status as an Act and will not be viewed as inferior legislation. An example of an SI is the

Footballer Spectators (2008 European Championship Control Period) Order 2008, which amended the exercise of the powers conferred by ss.14(6) and 22A(2) of the Football Spectators Act 1989. SI 1165/2008 (this reference number indicates the fact that it is the 1165th SI made in 2008) relates to the control that can be exercised over football supports to prevent violence and disorder in respect of a competition that is being held outside of the UK. The Football Spectators Act 1989 provides that any person who is subject to a banning order must report to a police station at specified times and surrender their passport for a period of time beginning five days before the first match and continuing until the tournament finishes. In respect of the 2008 European Championship SI 1165/2008 extends this control period to one of ten days before the commencement of the first match and to continue until the end of the competition. Football hooliganism and violence is unfortunately rife within the British football culture and these provisions are part of the control mechanisms to reduce such behaviour.

Statutory Instruments

2008 No. 1165

Sports Grounds And Sporting Events, England And Wales

The Football Spectators (2008 European Championship Control Period) Order 2008

Made   24th April 2008
Laid before Parliament   25th April 2008
Coming into force   19th May 2008

The Secretary of State makes the following Order in exercise of the powers conferred by sections 14(6) and 22A(2) of the Football Spectators Act 1989(1):
    The Secretary of State considers that the provision made by article 2 of this Order is expedient in order to secure the effective enforcement of Part II of that Act.

Citation, commencement and interpretation

1.—(1)This Order may be cited as the Football Spectators (2008 European Championship Control Period) Order 2008 and shall come into force on 19th May 2008.
    (2) In this Order—
'the Tournament' means the external tournament known as the UEFA (Union of European Football Associations) EURO 2008 European Championship finals tournament in Austria and Switzerland, and
'Part II' means Part II of the Football Spectators Act 1989.

Control period

2. Section 14(6) of the Football Spectators Act 1989 shall have effect in relation to the Tournament as if, for the reference to five days, there were substituted a reference to ten days.

3.—(1)In relation to the Tournament, the period described in paragraph (2) below is a control period for the purposes of Part II.

(2) The period referred to in paragraph (1) above is the period beginning on 28th May 2008, being ten days before the day of the first football match which is included in the Tournament, and ending when the last match included in the Tournament is finished (which, subject to postponement, is due to be on 29th June 2008) or cancelled.

Vernon Coaker
Parliamentary Under Secretary of State

Home Office
24th April 2008

EXPLANATORY NOTE

(This note is not part of the Order)

This Order describes the control period under the Football Spectators Act 1989 for the UEFA (Union of European Football Associations) EURO 2008 European Championship finals tournament in Austria and Switzerland. The control period begins on 28th May 2008, being ten days before the first match in the tournament, and ends when the last match in the tournament is finished or cancelled. The last match is due to be played on 29th June 2008.

During a control period the powers contained in sections 19 (requirements for those subject to banning orders to report to a police station and surrender passports) and 21A and 21B (summary powers to detain and refer to a court with a view to making a banning order) of the 1989 Act are exercisable.

1.4.4.2 Byelaws

A byelaw is passed by a body such as a local authority, or a public or nationalised body (e.g. British Rail) to regulate certain behaviour under their area or control. For example Gelding Borough Council in the area of Nottingham have passed a byelaw to be able to fine people who allow their dog to foul and then not clean it up a maximum of £1,000 (although they normally impose a fixed £50 penalty notice).

1.4.4.3   Orders of council

An order of council is more formally known as an Order of the Legislative Committee of the Privy Council and they are essentially another form of a SI. This method tends to be reserved for passing the most important pieces of secondary legislation, or in times of emergency. So for example, on April 9, 2008 an Order was made by the Privy Council under the Royal Marriages Act 1772 to allow Peter Phillips (who is the son of Princess Anne and currently eleventh in line for the throne) to marry Autumn Kelly.

1.4.4.4   Why the need for delegated legislation?

There are a number of benefits for allowing the creation of legislation to be drafted by parties other than Parliament.

Speed—it takes a long period of time for a Bill to pass through Parliament and become law (months or even years) and so if the legislation is required urgently the Parliamentary process is unable to facilitate this. Other bodies (such as the Privy Council or local authorities) have more time available to deal with such matters so that the legislation can be brought into force at the time that it is needed. Allowing other bodies to pass law also alleviates some of the burden from Parliament, which then permits them to spend more time debating the more important or complex laws.

Knowledge—as byelaws can be passed by the local authority concerned then they will have the local knowledge necessary to determine whether such a byelaw is required, and if so what should then be contained within it. The same can be said of the byelaws passed by an organisation such as British Rail, as their work is based in the railway system they are best placed to appreciate what legislation is needed. Parliament are often too removed the situation to determine what is and what is not appropriate.

Flexibility—appropriate legislation can be created and amended as required depending on the circumstances at the time. Not every possible scenario can be envisaged by Parliament and this allows for the law to change with the unforeseen.

1.4.4.5   Control

It would obviously not be ideal if local authorities or Ministers could go around making any law that they felt like as this could result in a small area of the country or a small group of people being subject to draconian laws. Therefore there are procedures in place to stop the power to make legislation being abused.

1.4.4.5.1   Parliamentary supervision

Parliament will often require (by way of the parent Act) that any delegated legislation be laid before them for approval before it can be brought into force. There are two ways that this can be done, one is by way of affirmative resolution and the other is by way of negative resolution. Affirmative resolution requires the proposed secondary legislation to be put before Parliament so that it can then be voted upon. Negative resolution again requires the draft legislation to be put before Parliament but this time if no opposition to the proposed legislation is raised within a specified period of time (normally 40 days) then the draft legislation becomes law.

1.4.4.5.2 Committee supervision

There are a number of Parliamentary committees that are charged with scrutinising secondary legislation (i.e. the Joint Committee on Statutory Instruments (reports to both the Commons and the Lords) and the Commons Select Committee on European Secondary Legislation). The Committees are mainly there to act as a safeguard and they have no powers to act themselves. The Joint Committee on Statutory Instruments, for example, considers proposed statutory instruments (although they are concerned with the technicalities of the legislation, not its merits) and they will then report back to both Houses as to the practicalities and viability of the proposals.

1.4.4.5.3 Judicial control

The judiciary cannot ignore or overrule secondary legislation (as they equally cannot with primary legislation) but the court can undergo a process known as judicial review (see 13.4) to ensure that it is appropriate. If the court concludes that the legislation is not appropriate then they can declare it void by way of it being ultra vires (beyond the powers of the body who enacted it). There are two forms of ultra vires, procedural and substantive. Procedural ultra vires is where it is held that the procedures, as laid out under the parent Act, have not been complied with. Substantive ultra vires is where the secondary legislation goes beyond what was intended by Parliament when they enacted the enabling Act.

1.4.5 The European Union

The EU and European law as a topic is covered by numerous other textbooks so only a brief overview will be provided here so that the links between the EU and the English legal system can be identified.

The EU was established in 1951 by the creation of the European Coal and Steel Community (ECSC) by France, West Germany, the Netherlands, Belgium, Luxembourg and Italy. In the aftermath of the Second World War it was recognised by those nations that such a war should never happen again and, to try and establish a political alliance and help with regeneration of the countries, the ECSC was developed. The ECSC was an agreement to encourage greater co-operation and freedom in the areas of trade and energy, and in 1957 the Treaty of Rome was signed by the six states, which created the European Economic Community (the EEC). This later became the European Community (EC), following the Treaty of Maastricht in 1993, under which the European Union was also created. Over the years many other states have joined the

EU (the United Kingdom joined on the January 1, 1973) and to date there are 27 member states.

Figure 1.4 The member states of the European Union

Austria	Germany	Netherlands
Belgium	Greece	Poland
Bulgaria	Hungary	Portugal
Cyprus	Ireland	Romania
Czech Republic	Italy	Slovakia
Denmark	Latvia	Slovenia
Estonia	Lithuania	Spain
Finland	Luxembourg	Sweden
France	Malta	United Kingdom

In general the law contained within treaties does not affect the everyday lives of the citizen's living within the states that the treaties cover, as treaties are normally charged with the regulation of conduct between different states. However the law of the EC works in a way that is different to the norm described above. The European Communities Act 1972 provides for the law of the EC to be absorbed into domestic law, as s.2(1) of the Act states:

> All such rights, powers, liabilities, obligations and restrictions from time to time created or arising by or under the Treaties, and all such remedies and procedures from time to time provided for by or under the Treaties, as in accordance with the Treaties are without further enactment to be given legal effect or used in the United Kingdom shall be recognised and available in law, and be enforced, allowed and followed accordingly.

Upon being ratified EU law becomes automatically part of our domestic law and neither the government nor Parliament need do anything to achieve this. An example of the effect of this automatic application of EU law can be seen in the case of *Marshall v Southampton Health Authority* [1986] 2 All E.R. 584, ECJ. In *Marshall* the appellant (a woman aged 62) was told by her employers (Southampton Health Authority) that she must retire. The domestic law at that time set out that a woman should retire at 60 and a man at 65 and the issue of retirement age did not fall under the remit of the Sex Discrimination Act 1975. However European Law had been passed, namely the Equal Opportunities Directive 1976, which did cover the issue of retirement age and so the appellant took her case to the European Court of Justice (ECJ) alleging a breach of this directive. The ECJ held that Mrs Marshall should succeed in her case as the UK had not implemented the directive correctly and she was entitled to use the provision against her employer to stop them forcibly retiring her. Even though the directive had not been properly transposed into domestic law it was still regarded as being part of the law. A similar case occurred again in 1994 but this time the issue did not involve the question of retirement age but rather the matter of part-time working. The fact that many part-time employees were subjected to reduced employment rights under UK law (Employment Protection (Consolidation) Act 1978) was challenged in the House of Lords in the case of *R. v Secretary of State for Employment Ex p. Equal Opportunities Commission* [1995] 1 A.C. 1. The Court held that the domestic legislation was incompatible with the European law on the basis of equal rights as the majority of part-time workers are female and therefore there was an unacceptable element of discrimination between the sexes. The domestic law was subsequently changed to reflect this decision and improve employee rights.

Where domestic law is held to be incompatible with European law the domestic law must be suspended until the matter is remedied. The leading case on this point is the well known case of *R. v Secretary for Transport Ex p. Factortame (No.3)* [1991] 3 All E.R. 769, ECJ, which involved the granting of shipping licences under the Merchant Shipping Act 1988. A number of Spanish fisherman were refused fishing licences under the Merchant Shipping Act 1988 as the Act set out that such licences should be granted to predominately British crewed fishing boats. The Spanish fishermen challenged the validity of the Act arguing that it was incompatible with European law. The Divisional Court who first heard the matter referred to the ECJ for a reference upon the matter and in the interim they granted an injunction, which had the effect of suspending the Act in question until the matter was resolved. The case went up to the ECJ and it was contended there that the domestic courts had no power to suspend an Act of Parliament. The ECJ held that the Divisional Court had decided correctly and that a domestic court was entitled to set aside domestic law where it conflicted with European law and that the Merchant Shipping Act breached the EC Treaty.

1.4.5.1 EU legislation

The European legislation has both primary and secondary legislation. Primary EU legislation is found within Treaties (as described above) and there are five types of secondary legislation, these being:

- Regulations—similar to UK Acts of Parliament and come into force in all member states on enactment.

- Directives—sets out the objectives intended to be achieved but each member state then has to enact specific legislation to achieve these objectives.

- Decisions—a decision is addressed to a particular member state, company or person upon whom it is binding. It does not have wider application.

- Recommendations—not strictly legislation but is a recommendation that, although not strictly binding, should not be ignored by to whom it is addressed.

- Opinions—again not strictly legislation but is a recommendation that, although not strictly binding, should not be ignored by to whom it is addressed.

1.4.5.2 The European Court of Justice

As the EU has a large number of member states who each speak different languages and have different systems of law there can at times occur confusion as to how the legislation from the EU should be interpreted in a member state. So that any such confusion can be remedied a member state can make a reference to the European Court of Justice (ECJ) under Article 234 of the Treaty of Rome. Article 234 provides:

> The Court of Justice shall have jurisdiction to give preliminary rulings concerning:
>
> (a) the interpretation of this Treaty;
> (b) the validity and interpretation of acts of the institutions of the Community and of the ECB;
> (c) the interpretation of the statutes of bodies established by an act of the Council, where those statutes so provide.
>
> Where such a question is raised before any court or tribunal of a Member State, that court or tribunal may, if it considers that a decision on the question is necessary to enable it to give judgment, request the Court of Justice to give a ruling thereon.
>
> Where any such question is raised in a case pending before a court or tribunal of a Member State against whose decisions there is no judicial remedy under national law, that court or tribunal shall bring the matter before the Court of Justice.

The ECJ acts in a supervisory capacity in relation to the enactment and interpretation of EU legislation so that the law is interpreted consistently by all member states. Such a reference must be made where there can be no further appeal from within the domestic courts and the lower courts have the discretion to make a reference in certain situations. Once a reference has been made on a certain point no other reference on the same point can be made and any decision made by the ECJ becomes binding on all member states.

1.4.6 The Council of Europe

The effect of the ECHR on domestic law has been described above at 1.3.1 but where the ECHR comes from and why it is so important will now be discussed. The Council of Europe introduced the ECHR in 1953. The Council of Europe is a separate entity to that of the EU (even though it is also based in Strasbourg where the EU Parliament is) and it is mainly concerned with the concept of basic human rights as opposed to political matters. The UK permitted its citizens to be able to rely upon the rights held under the Convention in 1966 but if they wished to do so they were required to travel to the ECtHR in Strasbourg as the domestic courts were unable to deal with such matters until the enactment of the HRA in 1998. To be a member of the Council of Europe the state has to ratify (sign) the ECHR and at present 47 states (far more than belong to the EU) have done just this.

The ECHR contains a number of basic human rights, each set out in a protocol. Each right is not an absolute right and can be qualified in certain circumstances. The brief overview of the main rights is set out in the table below and full details can either be found in the ECHR or Sch.1 of the HRA 1998.

Figure 1.5 Articles of the ECHR

Article	Title	Details
Art 2	Right to life	Protects the right of every person to his or her life. Contains exceptions for the cases of lawful executions, and deaths as a result of acting in self-defence.
Art 3	Prohibition of torture	Prohibits torture, and "inhuman or degrading treatment or punishment". There are no exceptions or limitations on this right.
Art 4	Prohibition of slavery	Prohibits slavery and forced labour.
Art 5	Right to liberty and security	Everyone has the right to liberty and security of person, should only be subject to lawful arrest and detention and should be informed of arrest in a language that is understood and should have access to the judicial system.
Art 6	Right to a fair trial	Everyone charged with an offence or in determining civil matters has the right to a public hearing before an independent and impartial tribunal within a reasonable time. Everyone is presumed innocent until proven guilty.
Art 7	No punishment without law	Prohibits the retrospective criminalisation of acts and omissions so no person may be punished for an act that was not a criminal offence at the time of its commission.
Art 8	Right to respect for private and family life	Everyone has a right to respect for one's "private and family life, his home and his correspondence". This is a broad Article in the situations it can cover.
Art 9	Freedom of thought, religion and conscience	The freedom to change a religion or belief, and to manifest a religion or belief in worship, teaching, practice and observance.
Art 10	Right to freedom of expression	The freedom to hold opinions, and to receive and impart information and ideas.
Art 11	Freedom of assembly and association	Protects the right to freedom of assembly and association, including the right to form trade unions.
Art 12	Right to marry	Provides the right for men and women of marriageable age to marry and establish a family in accordance with domestic laws.
Art 14	Prohibition of discrimination	Protects against discrimination based on grounds such as sex, race, colour, language, religion, etc. The right is limited in scope only to discrimination with respect to other rights under the Convention.

1.5   Law review and reform

The law is always changing and evolving with the needs of society. To ensure that the law develops appropriately and remains fit for its purpose there are a number of bodies that review the laws of the land and make recommendations as to how they could be improved and reformed.

- **Parliament**—the members of Parliament will review and introduce new legislation (by the methods discussed above) so that the needs of society are meet. The change in legislation will be dependent on the political stance of the government at that time.

- **Judiciary**—the judiciary can, to a certain degree, reform the law through the doctrine of precedent but this is rarely a quick process.

- **Law reform agencies**—such as the Law Commission, who is charged with the objectives of simplifying and codifying the law. The Law Commission write consultation papers that the government may then act upon and draft a proposed Bill for new or amended legislation.

- **The media**—public outcry can have a significant effect on the direction that legislation can take and if there is enough noise from the media (which allegedly reflects the feelings of the nation) then Parliament (as a democratically elected body) may listen and implement appropriate changes. The enactment of the Dangerous Dogs Act 1991 (discussed above) is evidence of the influence of the media upon the law making process.

- **Academics**—legal academics who specialise in a certain area of law can provide insightful and authoritative commentary on the law. Increasingly academic writings are being cited in court as authority and are having an impact upon the development of the law.

- **Europe**—both the EU and the ECtHR have an impact on the reform of the law within the UK as the laws need to be compatible with these sources.

- **Royal Commissions**—created by the government to investigate matters of general public concern. Examples of Royal Commission reviews include the Woolf Report (see chapter 8 on the Civil Justice System) and the Auld Review (see chapters 9 and 10 on the Criminal Justice System).

- **Pressure groups**—groups such as the NSPCC and Fathers for Justice can also have an impact upon the way in which the government and Parliament reform the law.

1.6 Summary

(a) The British constitution is an unwritten one made up from case law, legislation, Conventions and custom. This is diametrically opposed to the majority of the rest of the civilised world who have written constitutions, which codify their laws. An unwritten constitution brings with it certain benefits, such as flexibility.

(b) The English legal system holds jurisdiction over both England and Wales. Scotland, Northern Ireland, the Republic of Eire and the Channel Isles have their own independent legal jurisdictions.

(c) Parliament is the English legal system's principle law making body and the law that they enact is applicable to every person within that jurisdiction. Parliamentary sovereignty means that Parliament's will is supreme, however this doctrine is being slowly eroded away due to the UK's membership of the EU and due to the introduction of the HRA 1998.

(d) The courts develop the law through case law and they act as a control mechanism to the other limbs of the state administration system; these being the executive and the legislature.

(e) The doctrine of the rule of law ensures that a person should only be regulated by the settled law; that they should only be punished according to the law; and that everyone, no matter who they are, is subject to the law.

(f) The common law has developed over time through the system of case law. The principle of *stare decisis* means that previous decisions of the court have to be followed and that through the doctrine of precedent the courts are duty bound to do so. The doctrine of precedence helps to ensure that there is consistency in the law although the strict application of it has been more flexible overtime to allow the development of the law.

(g) Equity was developed to fill the loopholes in the common law and provide appropriate and effective remedy where the common law could not. The remedies provided under equity can now be bestowed by all of the courts.

(h) Legislation is the enactment of rules and regulations into a document (an Act of Parliament or statute) that is applicable to everyone in the jurisdiction. The creation of legislation involves a long and complex process, first through the House of Commons and then through the House of Lords. Originally the House of Lords could block any proposed legislation that they opposed but now the House of Lords approval can now be circumnavigated in certain circumstances. For legislation to be deemed as in force it must first receive Royal Assent.

(i) Delegated legislation is statutory law created by a body other than Parliament. This secondary legislation can be created by a statutory instrument, byelaws or an Order of Council. Parliament will enact a parent or enabling Act conferring the power to create legislation upon a specific body. Secondary legislation is not inferior to primary legislation and so to control the abuse of this power Parliament is generally required to approve any drafted delegated legislation before it comes into force.

(j) The EU has had a large impact upon the supremacy of Parliamentary law as if there is a conflict between European and domestic law then European law will take precedence. The domestic courts can make a reference to the ECJ to gain clarity on how to interpret and apply EU legislation.

(k) The European Council is predominately responsible for the ECHR. The ECHR sets out the basic rights that are afforded to any citizen of a signatory state. The UK incorporated these rights into domestic law by way of enacting the HRA 1998.

(l) There are a number of different agencies that continuously review the law so as to ensure that appropriate amendments are made and so that the law does not become stagnant and lacking in suitability.

1.7   Self-test questions

1. The 'English legal system' encompasses:

   (a) England
   (b) England and Scotland
   (c) England and Wales
   (d) England, Scotland and Wales

2. Parliamentary sovereignty means that Parliament is:

   (a) supreme to any other law-making body in the UK
   (b) supreme to any other law-making body in Europe
   (c) supreme to any other law-making body in the world
   (d) supreme to any other law-making body in the universe

3. Equity developed due to failings in:

   (a) the civil law system
   (b) legislation
   (c) the European Union
   (d) the common law

4. If the House of Lords reject a Bill on two successive occasions then:

   (a) the Bill is dropped
   (b) the Bill returns for a third passing through the House of Commons
   (c) the Bill bypasses the need for House of Lords' approval and receives Royal Assent
   (d) the Bill has to be re-drafted entirely

5. Delegated legislation is:

    (a) superior to primary legislation
    (b) inferior to primary legislation
    (c) equal to primary legislation
    (d) subordinate to primary legislation

1.8 Further reading

A. Albi and P. Van Elsuwege, "The EU constitution, national constitutions and sovereignty: an assessment of a European constitutional order" [2004] 29(6) E.L. Rev. 741–765.

N.W. Barber, "Against a written constitution" [2008] P.L. Spr, 11–18.

Lord Bingham, "The rule of law" [2007] 66(1) C.L.J. 67–85.

V. Bogdanor and S. Vogenauer, "Enacting a British constitution: some problems" [2008] P.L. Spr, 38–57.

L. Claus, "Montesquieu's mistakes and the true meaning of separation" [2005] 25(3) O.J.L.S. 419–451.

Mark Elliott, "Parliamentary sovereignty under pressure" [2004] 2(3) I.J.C.L. 545–554.

J. Laws, "The rule of law: form or substance?" [2007] 4(1) J. 24–40.

J. Laws, "The constitution: morals and rights" [1996] P.L. Win, 622–635.

J. Laws, "Law and democracy" [1995] P.L. Spr, 72–93.

A. Lester, "The Human Rights Act 1998—five years on" [2004] 3 E.H.R.L.R. 258–271.

C. Timmis, "Conflicting interests", Counsel 2007, Sep, 8–10.

Helen Wildbore and Francesca Klug, "Breaking new ground: the Joint Committee on Human Rights and the role of Parliament in human rights compliance" [2007] 3 E.H.R.L.R. 231–250.

2   Judicial reasoning

2.1   Do judges make law?

> [the judge] being sworn to determine, not according to his private sentiments . . . not according to his own private judgment, but according to the known laws and customs of the land: not delegated to pronounce a new law, but to maintain and expound the old one.
>
> *Blackstone's Commentaries 69*

The English jurist and professor Sir William Blackstone authored (between 1765–1769) what became known as one of the authoritative guides to the English law. As part of his thoughts on the legal system and the role of the judiciary within the law making process he developed what is described as the declaratory theory, the basis of which being that the role of the judge is to discover and declare the law, but not to make the law. It could be argued that Blackstone had a very two dimensional view of the role of the judge and of the law, and his theory has been criticised by a number of academic writers (such as Dworkin (1986) and Kairys (1998)) who have submitted that the role of the judge (to declare the law) is not as simplistic as made out by Blackstone. If a judge's role were only to state the law as it is written then there would be little need for the judiciary or lawyers, as any layperson could come to the law, read what was there and apply it. The role of a judge, it appears, is to apply the laws as set out by Parliament, but in doing so they also have the responsibility of moulding and developing the laws of the country, creating legal principles along the way that work together with the statutory provisions of Parliament and which ultimately try to follow the ebb and flow of the needs of the society at that specific point in time.

The judiciary are not the primary lawmakers but they do have a significant effect on the law and they predominately do this by the methods and doctrines that they employ whilst interpreting these laws. There are two key ways in which the judiciary can influence the evolution of the law and these are by the doctrines of precedent and statutory interpretation, which will be discussed below.

2.2   Precedent

There is a highly entrenched and rather fundamental doctrine within the English Legal System that helps to develop and mould the direction that the law takes. This doctrine is known as 'judicial precedent' and it stems from the principle of *stare decisis*, which comes from the legal Latin term of '*stare decisis et non quieta mover*' meaning 'stand by decisions and do not move that which is quiet'. The doctrine works by requiring judges to follow the decisions that have been made in previous cases, thus ensuring that there is a consistency in the law and that people coming to the law (or their lawyers) will be able to make an educated guess as to the potential success and likely outcome of their case. By being able to refer back to previously decided cases the courts are able to ensure that the law develops in a fair and just manner, and it also means that a great deal of time is saved as a judge does not have to start from scratch but can make reference to what is already there and then use this to assist them in their own decision making process.

One point to note is that the principle of *stare decisis* differs from that of *res judicata*, which is another Latin term often found within the law. *Res judicata* translates as 'the thing has been judged', meaning that the court has already decided the issue between the parties and that the decision should not be changed. For example if a man has already been judged by a court in Lincoln to be the father of a child then he is prevented from re-opening the case in another court in Bristol to try and achieve a more favourable decision, such as a finding that hc is not the child's father and therefore not liable to pay child maintenance. The matter has been settled (subject to the usual appeal routes) and cannot be reheard. This doctrine is in place to prevent disgruntled litigants attempting to re-litigate on the same point, as this would prove unfair and costly to the other party to the case.

There are two types of precedent found within the English legal system; one is binding precedent, meaning that it must be followed, and the other is persuasive precedent, which means that the courts may follow it depending on whether they find it persuasive in relation to the matter in front of them.

2.2.1   Binding precedent

Binding precedent can be found in the *ratio decidendi* of the case. This Latin term (*ratio decidendi*) translates as the 'reason for the decision' and is often just shortened to *ratio*. Where there is more than one *ratio* in a case the plural is *rationes decidendi*. Essentially the *ratio* is the reasoning behind why the judge came to the conclusion that he did (see 3.3.3 for how to identify the *ratio*). The *ratio* is the binding element of the case and it is the principle of law based on the facts of the case that can then be applied in future cases.

The *ratio* however is not the decision in the case. The decision in a case is specific to that individual case and need not be followed in future cases (even if the facts seem identical). The decision is the judgment as to who is successful or, as to whether the defendant (in a criminal case) is guilty or innocent. The decision in the case will be of vital importance to the parties involved but will be of little or no interest to the lawyers. Conversely the *ratio* of the case will probably be of little or no interest to the parties but they will care vehemently about the result and how it affects them.

The *ratio* of a case and its effects can be illustrated by reference to the infamous case of *Donoghue v Stephenson* [1932] A.C. 562, the *ratio* of which has proved to be highly influential upon the development of the law of torts. In *Donoghue v Stephenson* the plaintiff's friend brought her a drink of ginger beer, which was in an opaque glass bottle; she poured out half of the drink into a glass and drank it. She then poured out the remainder of the contents of the bottle and in doing so out fell a decomposed snail. The plaintiff then claimed to have suffered a stomach upset and emotional trauma as a result. As the plaintiff had not brought the drink herself there was no contractual relationship between her and the vendor so instead she brought a claim in torts against the manufacturer of the ginger beer, alleging that they owed her a duty of care. At first instance the case was dismissed but the plaintiff appealed to the House of Lords and Lord Atkin delivered the now famous judgment, which contained the legendary 'neighbour principle'. Lord Atkin (at page 580) stated:

> There must be, and is, some general conception of relations giving rise to a duty of care, of which the particular cases found in the books are but instances. . . . The rule that you are to love your neighbour becomes in law you must not injure your neighbour; and the lawyer's question: Who is my neighbour? receives a restricted reply. You must take reasonable care to avoid acts or omissions which you can reasonably foresee would be likely to injure your neighbour. Who, then, in law, is my neighbour? The answer seems to be—persons who are so closely and directly affected by my act that I ought reasonably to have them in contemplation as being so affected when I am directing my mind to the acts or omissions that are called in question.

The decision in the case was that the manufacturers were to pay the plaintiff damages in respect of the injuries suffered. This is the point that the plaintiff and the defendant were primarily concerned with. The *ratio* of the case however produced a legal principle that dramatically changed the face of torts law. The *ratio* propounded by the case of *Donoghue v Stephenson* is that where an established duty of care does not already exist, a person will owe a duty of care not to injure those who it can be reasonably foreseen would be affected by their acts or omissions. This decision had far-reaching implications; a car driver now owes a duty of care to everyone on the road and all pedestrians, a manufacturer is responsible to ensure that no harm comes from their goods and an individual must ensure that they do nothing which could result in the harm of another.

Not every case is reported and only those which are published can be relied upon as precedent (chapter 3 explores how cases are reported) as it is impossible to rely upon an authority if the material facts and the precise *ratio* cannot be identified. Further, not every statement of law is to be deemed to be authoritative *ratio* and there may be principles created by a case that are superfluous to the actual decision but nevertheless become persuasive (but not binding) precedent in their own right.

2.2.2   Persuasive precedent

Persuasive precedent can come from many sources and it can be just as valuable to the courts as that of binding precedent. The most often cited form of persuasive precedent is that which is known as *obiter dicta.*

2.2.2.1 Obiter dicta

The Latin term *obiter dicta* (or *obiter* for short) translates as 'things said by the way' and it can be found within the part of the judgment in a case that does not go directly to the *ratio*. Strictly speaking there are two types of types of *obiter*. The first is where a judge in a case makes a statement of law that is not linked to the materials facts of the case (thereby not being part of the *ratio*). Examples of this type of *obiter* can be found in the discussions of the judiciary when they are considering hypothetical cases or facts whilst considering the decision in a case. It may be that they state what they would have decided if the facts of the case had been different (so if the facts were X they would have decided Y, but as the facts are actually A they must therefore decide B). This type of precedent is not binding but it can be highly persuasive, especially where the hypothetical scenario given is the basis of a later case under consideration.

The second type of *obiter* is where a judge discusses the facts of the case and makes a statement as to the law based on those facts but that statement does not become part of the *ratio*. An example of when this can occur is where there is a dissenting judgment in a case (where a judge does not agree with the decision of the majority in the case and gives his reasons for doing so).

2.2.2.2 Other sources of persuasive precedent

Persuasive precedent does not have to just come from the judges and there are other sources that can be cited as persuasive that are important to know about as a law student. The most common sources of persuasive precedent are listed below.

- *Obiter dicta*
- A dissenting judgment
- A minority judgment (where the judge agrees with the overall majority decision but has different reasons for doing so)
- The Privy Council
- Lower courts
- Academic commentary
- Law reform agencies

2.3 The hierarchy of judicial precedent

2.3.1 The European Court of Justice

The ECJ is supreme to domestic law. The principles created by the court in relation to the interpretations of Treaties and other European Union legislation must be followed within the

English legal system. As a result European precedent binds the domestic courts. The ECJ however, is not bound by itself and can depart from earlier decisions where appropriate.

2.3.2 The European Court of Human Rights

As the ECtHR is concerned with matters involving an individual's basic human rights it is difficult to instil a set rule of precedent. The UK is required to try and ensure that domestic legislation is compatible with the provisions of the ECHR so far as is possible. If all domestic legislation were compatible then the need to bring a case under the ECHR would be greatly reduced, however compatibility is not a mandatory requirement but rather a goal to be achieved wherever possible. When the HRA 1998 was being passed by Parliament the then Lord Chancellor opined that by insisting the domestic courts were bound by the ECtHR would produce results that would be inconsistent with the very spirit of the ECHR. Lord Irvine stated that:

> The United Kingdom is not bound in international law to follow that Court's judgments in cases to which the United Kingdom had not been a party, and it would be strange to require courts in the United Kingdom to be bound by such cases.
> (583 HL Official Report. 5th Series col.511, November 18, 1997)

However, the House of Lords in *R. (on the application of Alconbury) v Secretary of State for the Environment, Transport and the Regions* [2001] UKHL 23 further considered the matter and concluded that although not bound domestic courts should try to ensure that they followed ECtHR decisions whenever possible, primarily to prevent the case in question being referred on the ECtHR for judgment on the matter.

2.3.3 The House of Lords

The House of Lords is the final appellate court in England and Wales and until 1966 it was bound by its own previous decisions as establish under the principle in *London Tranways Co Ltd v London CC* [1898] A.C. 375. The rationale behind the court being bound was that there had to be a final point where there could be no further litigation brought in a matter. This obviously meant that the law could not develop with the changing times as a decision made by the House in the 1700s could still be binding upon it in the 1900s even if the reasoning and decision in the case was no longer appropriate; nor could mistakes in the law be rectified. So as to remedy this defect the House of Lords, in 1966, issued a *Practice Statement* ([1966] 3 All E.R. 77), which set out that the House of Lords was no longer bound by itself.

> Their Lordships regard the use of precedent as an indispensable foundation upon which to decide what is the law and its application to individual cases. It provides at least some degree of certainty upon which individuals can rely in the conduct of their affairs, as well as a basis for orderly development of legal rules.

Their Lordships nevertheless recognise that too rigid adherence to precedent may lead to injustice in a particular case and also unduly restrict the proper development of the law. They propose, therefore, to modify their present practice and, while treating former decisions of this House as normally binding, to depart from a previous decision when it appears right to do so.

In this connection they will bear in mind the danger of disturbing retrospectively the basis on which contracts, settlements of property, and fiscal arrangements have been entered into and also the special need for certainty as to the criminal law.

This announcement is not intended to affect the use of precedent elsewhere than in this House.

This Practice Statement gave the Lords the power to depart from previous decisions where it was deemed 'right to do so' and this was to be decided by the Lords on a case-by-case basis. The House did not employ this power until two years after the release of the *Practice Statement* and the first case where it was used was that of *Conway v Rimmer* [1968] A.C. 910, which overruled the earlier decision of *Duncan v Cammell Laird & Co* [1942] A.C. 624. In *Duncan & Cammell Laird & Co* the House had held that the Crown did not need to disclose certain information under the principle of 'public interest immunity' due to the fact that the country was at war at that time. The later case of *Conway v Rimmer* occurred in a time of peace and so the reasoning behind the decision in the earlier case was no longer relevant. As a result the House of Lords felt that it was therefore right to depart from the decision in *Conway v Rimmer* and it invoked its powers to do so under the *Practice Statement*.

The power to depart from a previous decision has been used infrequently by the House and there are only a handful of cases where it has been employed. In *Murphy v Brentwood BC* [1991] 1 A.C. 398 the court overruled the previous case of *Anns v Merton* [1978] A.C. 728 holding that a local authority could be liable for not remedying known defects in property before any damage occurred. In *Shivpuri* [1987] A.C. 1 the case of *Anderton v Ryan* [1985] 2 All E.R. 355 was overruled, despite it only being made a year earlier. In *Shivpuri* Lord Bridge, at p.23, stated in relation to the use of the *Practice Statement* that:

> Is it permissible to depart from precedent under the *Practice Statement (Judicial Precedent)* [1966] 1 W.L.R. 1234 notwithstanding the especial need for certainty in the criminal law? The following considerations lead me to answer that question affirmatively. First, I am undeterred by the consideration that the decision in *Anderton v Ryan* was so recent. The Practice Statement is an effective abandonment of our pretention to infallibility. If a serious error embodied in a decision of this House has distorted the law, the sooner it is corrected the better. Secondly, I cannot see how, in the very nature of the case, anyone could have acted in reliance on the law as propounded in *Anderton v Ryan* in the belief that he was acting innocently and now find that, after all, he is to be held to have committed a criminal offence.

In this case the House of Lords set out its reluctance to overrule criminal cases due to the need for certainty within the criminal law. However, only a year after the case of *Shivpuri* the Lords were again back to considering whether or not to overrule another criminal case. In the case of *Howe* [1987] A.C. 817 the House was required to consider its previous decision in the case of *DPP for Northern Ireland v Lynch* [1975] 2 W.L.R. 641, which set out that duress could be a defence for murder. The House in *Howe* determined that the case of *Lynch* had been wrongly decided and that the development of the law had taken a wrong turn. It overruled *Lynch* and asserted in *Howe* that duress could never be a defence to murder.

In fact within the handful of cases where the power to depart from previous decisions has been invoked by the House a large number of them have been criminal cases. For example in the case of *R v G* [2003] UKHL the House held that the longstanding case of *MPC v Caldwell* [1982] A.C. 341 should be overruled due to the unjust results that its principle created. In *Caldwell* it was held that where a person caused criminal damage they would be liable if a reasonable person could have foreseen that such damage would have resulted, even if the defendant did not or could not have seen that possibility themselves. This principle was applied by the courts in criminal damage cases for over 23 years, resulting in decisions such as that in *Elliott v C* [1983] 1 W.L.R. 939 where the court held, applying the case of *Caldwell*, that a young girl of 14 years old with learning difficulties was liable for criminal damage through burning down a shed, despite her lack of understanding or foresight of the consequences of her actions, because such a result would have been foreseen by a reasonable person. This was obviously not a satisfactory state of affairs as liability was imposed where the defendant was not morally culpable. When the case of *G* came before it the House took the opportunity to rectify the situation. *G* involved two young boys (aged 11 and 12) who were convicted of causing criminal damage after a fire that they had started resulted in damage equating to almost a million pounds being caused to the surrounding properties. The boys had lit a fire in a wheelie bin and, thinking that it would burn itself out, left whilst it was still alight, but unfortunately the fire took hold. The boys were convicted at first instance as the court was bound by the case of *Caldwell*. Upon reflection the House, whilst quashing the boys' convictions, determined that the *Caldwell* principle was wrong and that a person should only be liable if they personally foresaw the possibility of the harm being caused. It used the powers prescribed by the *Practice Statement* to remedy a defect in the law.

Despite the use of the *Practice Statement* in the cases described above (and there are also other examples not considered here) the House is still cautious in respect of using this power and its reluctance to apply it can be seen in the case of *R. v Kansal (No.2)* [2001] UKHL 62. In *Kansal* the House stated that it had probably got the law wrong in the earlier case of *R. v Lambert* [2001] UKHL 37 but it applied the law in *Lambert* nevertheless as it was of the opinion that the matter under discussion in both cases, and the decision taken in the earlier case (that the HRA 1998 would not have retrospective effect on appeals where the original decision in the case had been made before the Act had come into force), would have little effect on the law in the long-term. Overruling the earlier case would simply not have achieved anything in terms of creating worthwhile legal principle as the matter was one that was likely to not come before the courts again.

Overall the House will only depart from previous decision where it is felt it is right to do so and as there are other methods available to the House to avoid previous precedent such as distinguishing, rejecting a case due to it being made *per incuriam* (see below) or having to depart to ensure compatibility with the HRA 1998, then there is often no need to invoke the *Practice Statement* powers at all.

2.3.4 The Privy Council

The Privy Council is the final court of appeal for Commonwealth countries and although the judicial composition is the same of the House of Lords (the Law Lords sit both in the House and in the Privy Council) the Privy Council is not binding upon the domestic courts. It is however extremely persuasive upon the courts of England and Wales and the decisions will generally be followed by the House of Lords and the lower courts (if there is not a binding House of Lords authority already on that point of law). Obviously if the Law Lords were to make a certain decision in the Privy Council upon a point of law it would then be very unlikely for them not to follow it when they later sat in the House of Lords and heard a case on the same point of law.

The sheer persuasiveness of a decision of the Privy Council can be illustrated by reference to the effect of its decision in the case of *Attorney-General for Jersey v Holley* [2005] UKPC 23. Under English law the House of Lords in *R. v Smith (Morgan)* [2001] A.C. 146 had held that whilst considering the defence of provocation to murder (under s.3 Homicide Act 1957) the court was entitled to take into account the specific personal characteristics of the defendant when considering whether the provocation was such that it would have made the reasonable man lose his self control and act in the way that the defendant had done. This opened up the defence of provocation to being used in cases where the defendant was suffering from depression or another mental illness (a situation which has been legislated for under s.2 of the Homicide Act 1957 as the defence of diminished responsibility). The same issue then arose again in the case of *Holley.* Here the defendant was a chronic alcoholic and he had killed his girlfriend whilst under the influence of drink. He submitted evidence to the court that his alcoholism was a disease and so should be taken into account when assessing his level of self-control in relation to the provocation suffered. At first instance the evidence of his alcoholism was disregarded by the court, but on appeal it was accepted that the evidence was such that the jury could have taken it into account and consequently his murder conviction was reduced to one of manslaughter. The Attorney-General appealed to the Privy Council (on an undertaking that he would not seek to restore the defendant's original conviction), which held on allowing the appeal that characteristics such as alcoholism (those which would affect the defendant's level of self-control) should not be attributed to the reasonable man (who the defendant was to be judged by) as Parliament had not legislated for this under the defence of provocation but rather the defence of diminished responsibility had been enacted to cover such circumstances. This decision was obviously contrary to that decided by the House of Lords in *Smith* and the Privy Council had refused to follow that decision as it was thought to be wrong in law (the Privy Council are not bound by domestic law).

The question now arose as to whether the Privy Council case was to be binding upon the English Courts due the composition of the court that heard it (nine Law Lords sat on the panel!). Professor Ashworth commented on the matter in *Appeal: precedent—Privy Council decision overruling decision of House of Lords* [2005] Crim. L.R. 966:

Is *Holley* binding on English courts? There may be a purist strain of argument to the effect that it is not, since it concerns another legal system (that of Jersey). However, the reality is that nine Lords of Appeal in Ordinary sat in this case, and that for practical purposes it was intended to be equivalent of a sitting of the House of Lords. It is likely that anyone attempting to argue that *Morgan Smith* is still good law in England and Wales would receive short shrift, and the Court of Appeal in *van Dongen* [2005] 2 Cr. App. R. 632, para.61 assumed, without deciding, that *Holley* now represents English law.

The issue was then addressed by the Court of Appeal in the case of *R. v James and Karimi* [2006] EWCA Crim 14. The rules of precedent dictated that the Court of Appeal was bound to follow the decision of the House of Lords but in this particular case it went against the decision of the House in *Smith* and followed the preferred decision of the Privy Council in *Holley*. Judgment was given by Lord Phillips of Matravers C.J., and on the point of precedent he stated (at para.42) as follows:

> The rule that this court must always follow a decision of the House of Lords and, indeed, one of its own decisions rather than a decision of the Privy Council is one that was established at a time when no tribunal other than the House of Lords itself could rule that a previous decision of the House of Lords was no longer good law. Once one postulates that there are circumstances in which a decision of the Judicial Committee of the Privy Council can take precedence over a decision of the House of Lords, it seems to us that this court must be bound in those circumstances to prefer the decision of the Privy Council to the prior decision of the House of Lords. That, so it seems to us, is the position that has been reached in the case of these appeals.

In essence what the Court of Appeal did in the case of *James and Karimi* was to overrule the House of Lords and state that the Privy Council should be followed as authority instead. This action did raise some questions as to whether the status of the precedent of the House had been eroded, but Lord Phillips, in the case of *James and Karimi* explained the reasoning behind the court's decision, stating (at para.43) that:

  (i) All nine of the Lords of Appeal in Ordinary sitting in Holley's case agreed in the course of their judgments that the result reached by the majority clarified definitively English law on the issue in question.

 (ii) The majority in *Holley*'s case constituted half the Appellate Committee of the House of Lords. We do not know whether there would have been agreement that the result was definitive had the members of the Board divided five/four.

(iii) In the circumstances, the result of any appeal on the issue to the House of Lords is a foregone conclusion.

It appears that the Court of Appeal took the decision that it did so as to avoid further unnecessary litigation; if the matter could be finalised in the Court of Appeal due to highly persuasive authority then what was the point of the matter progressing to the House where the

Law Lords would simply come to the same decision. The Court of Appeal however did acknowledge that the circumstances in the case were highly unusual due to the comprehensive composition of the court for the hearing in *Holley* and it would be very unlikely that such a situation will arise again.

2.3.5   The Court of Appeal—Civil Division

Despite the anomaly discussed above in relation to the cases of *Holley* and *Smith (Morgan)* the Court of Appeal is bound by the House of Lords as the House is a superior court to it in the hierarchy. The Court of Appeal (both civil and criminal divisions) binds the courts below it in the court hierarchy, and it is normally bound by its own previous decisions, this principle being known as the 'self-binding' rule.

There are however exceptions to the self-binding rule where the court can depart from a previous decision and these are set out in the case of *Young v Bristol Aeroplane Co Ltd* [1944] K.B. 718 by Lord Green M.R. There are three exceptions to the rule and they are as follows:

1. Where there are previous conflicting decisions of the Court of Appeal. In such circumstances the court may choose to follow whichever authority it deems to be most appropriate. In practice the court will often follow the latest decision although they are not obliged to. The case that is not followed is then taken to be overruled. It may seem strange that the same court can create conflicting decisions but it is entirely possible, as there may be differently constituted Court of Appeal hearings occurring on the same day and they may end up dealing with the same issue of law but come to differing conclusions.

2. Where a previous Court of Appeal decision conflicts with a later decision of the House of Lords but that decision has not expressly overruled the Court of Appeal decision. When this occurs the Court of Appeal is obliged to follow the House of Lords decision under the normal rules of precedent, even if they are not in agreement with the decision.

3. Where the previous decision of the Court of Appeal has been made *per incuriam*. The Latin term '*per incuriam*' translates as 'made through lack of care' but this does not just mean that the court can ignore the decision because it thinks it was wrongly decided, it has a far more specific meaning than this and how this principle should be approached was set out in the case of *Morelle v Wakeling* [1955] 2 Q.B. 379.

In *Morelle v Wakeling* the court were charged with determining what was meant by the term *per incuriam* and the conclusion of the court as to this question was that:

As a general rule the only cases in which decisions should be held to have been given per incuriam are those of decisions given in ignorance or forgetfulness of some inconsistent statutory provision or of some authority binding on the court concerned: so that in such cases some part of the decision or some step in the reasoning on which it is based is found, on that account, to be demonstrably wrong.

(Per Evershed M.R. at 406)

This principle has been extended slightly in later cases such as *Williams v Fawcett* [1986] Q.B. 604 to cover where there has been a 'manifest slip or error' which has had an affect on the liberty of the subject and that the case was unlikely to reach the House of Lords for the error to be corrected.

Lord Denning M.R. was not overly pleased with the self-binding rule imposed on the Court of Appeal and in a number of cases (for example *Gallie v Lee* [1969] 2 Ch. 217, *Broome v Cassell & Co Ltd* [1971] 1 All E.R. 801 and *Rookes v Barnard* [1964] 1 All E.R. 367), he championed the propositions that the Court of Appeal should be subject to the same *Practice Statement* as the House of Lords and so could depart from its own previous decisions, and that the Court of Appeal should not be strictly bound by the House of Lords and consequently should be able to declare its decisions as *per incuriam* where appropriate. This debate continued until the case of *Davis v Johnson* [1979] A.C. 264 where the House of Lords clarified the matter and asserted its authority over the Court of Appeal.

In the Court of Appeal Lord Denning M.R. directly questioned the appropriateness of the Court of Appeal being strictly bound by the House of Lords and he put forward a voracious argument as to why, in his opinion, the state of affairs was wrong (p.278).

On principle, it seems to me that, while this court should regard itself as normally bound by a previous decision of the court, nevertheless it should be at liberty to depart from it if it is convinced that the previous decision was wrong. What is the argument to the contrary? It is said that if an error has been made, this court has no option but to continue the error and leave it to be corrected by the House of Lords. The answer is this: the House of Lords may never have an opportunity to correct the error: and thus it may be perpetuated indefinitely, perhaps for ever. [. . .] an erroneous decision on a point of law can again be perpetuated for ever. Even if all those objections are put on one side and there is an appeal to the House of Lords, it usually takes 12 months or more for the House of Lords to reach its decision. What then is the position of the lower courts meanwhile? They are in a dilemma. Either they have to apply the erroneous decision of the Court of Appeal, or they have to adjourn all fresh cases to await the decision of the House of Lords. That has often happened. So justice is delayed—and often denied—by the lapse of time before the error is corrected.

The arguments put forward as to why the Court of Appeal should be allowed to depart from a previous House of Lords decision seem to contain logic and substance and the conclusion reached by Lord Denning M.R. (at p.282) on the matter was that:

So I suggest that we are entitled to lay down new guidelines. To my mind, this court should apply similar guidelines to those adopted by the House of Lords in 1966. Whenever it appears to this court that a previous decision was wrong, we should be at liberty to depart from it if we think it right to do so. Normally—in nearly every case of course—we would adhere to it. But in an exceptional case we are at liberty to depart from it.

When the case was heard on appeal in the House of Lords Lord Diplock addressed the issues raised by Lord Denning M.R. in the lower court and provided a firm answer to the suggestions made.

> [t]he rule as it had been laid down in the *Bristol Aeroplane* case [1944] K.B. 718 had never been questioned thereafter until, following upon the announcement by Lord Gardiner L.C. in 1966 [*Practice Statement (Judicial Precedent)* [1966] 1 W.L.R. 1234] that the House of Lords would feel free in exceptional cases to depart from a previous decision of its own, Lord Denning M.R. conducted what may be described, I hope without offence, as a one-man crusade with the object of freeing the Court of Appeal from the shackles which the doctrine of stare decisis imposed upon its liberty of decision by the application of the rule laid down in the *Bristol Aeroplane* case to its own previous decisions; or, for that matter, by any decisions of this House itself of which the Court of Appeal disapproved. . . .
>
> In my opinion, this House should take this occasion to re-affirm expressly, unequivocally and unanimously that the rule laid down in the *Bristol Aeroplane* case [1944] K.B. 718 as to stare decisis is still binding on the Court of Appeal.

Lord Diplock effectively shot down in flames the campaign that Lord Denning M.R. had mounted against the hierarchical nature of precedent within the courts. As the House of Lords could itself rectify any previous error made in law it was of the opinion that the Court of Appeal need not concern itself with correcting such errors, it was an intermediate court and its role was not to correct its superiors but to concentrate on applying the law as it was.

The status of the Court of Appeal in the precedent stakes has not since been overly queried by the court and the rule that the court is bound by the House of Lords and binding on itself still stands firm. One does however have to wonder whether Lord Denning M.R. was on to something with his campaign as if a case could be dealt with satisfactorily at a lower court level than the House of Lords then surely this could only be of benefit to the justice system as a whole.

2.3.6 The Court of Appeal—Criminal Division

The Criminal Division of the Court of Appeal is subject to the same rules as the Civil Division described above (*Young v Bristol Aeroplane*) however as the court is dealing with matters of liberty as opposed to simply civil remedies (which are often financial in nature) the Criminal Division of the Court of Appeal is slightly more flexible in its interpretation of the rules. In the case of *R. v Taylor* [1950] K.B. 368 at 371, Lord Goddard C.J. set out the approach to be taken by the criminal court:

> This court, however, has to deal with questions involving the liberty of the subject, and if it finds, on reconsideration, that, in the opinion of a full court assembled for that purpose,

the law has been either misapplied or misunderstood in a decision which it has previously given, and that, on the strength of that decision, an accused person has been sentenced and imprisoned it is the bounden duty of the court to reconsider the earlier decision with a view to seeing whether that person had been properly convicted.

The court is not willing to be ruled so strictly to the settled principles and is more concerned with ensuring that justice is done. This principle of flexibility was reaffirmed in the case of *R. v Simpson* [2003] EWCA Crim 1499 where the court held that that the rules as to precedent reflected the practice of the courts, and were of considerable importance because of their role in achieving the appropriate degree of certainty as to the law, but they should not be regarded as so rigid that they could not develop in order to meet contemporary needs.

2.3.7   The High Court

The High Court can be split into two distinct sections, the Divisional Court of the High Court and the High Court.

2.3.8   The Divisional Court of the High Court

The Divisional Court of the High Court works in an appellate capacity very similar to that of the Court of Appeal. It hears appeals from the High Court and the decisions made by it can be appealed direct to the House of Lords (see chapter 13). As a result the Divisional Courts are bound in the same way as the Court of Appeal; they are bound by the House of Lords and the ECJ, they are self-binding and the principles established in *Young v Bristol Aeroplane* apply, and they bind all inferior courts.

2.3.9   The High Court

The High Court is a court of first instance. It is bound by all courts superior to it and its decisions are binding to all courts below it in the hierarchy. It is not however bound by itself. A Chancery Division judge will not be bound by a decision made by a Family Division judge (although it would be a rare occasion for them to be considering the same issue anyway), and a Family Division judge will not be bound by the decision of another Family Division judge. That being said previous decisions by other High Court judges will be viewed as extremely persuasive due to the idea of judicial comity. It could be quite awkward for a judge to completely take to pieces a colleague's carefully crafted judgment on a matter and then walk out of court and sit and have a drink with the other judge. The idea of judicial comity is that the judges will follow previous decisions made by other judges as a sign of respect.

2.3.10   The Crown Court

As a court of first instance and towards the bottom of the hierarchy the Crown Court is bound by all of the courts above it and it has no binding effect itself (although the decision of a High Court judge sitting in the Crown will certainly be quite persuasive). The Crown Court is not self-binding and there are two main reasons behind this fact (which apply equally to the High Court above), the first being that the court deals on a daily basis with a person's liberty and it would be unjust to apply strict precedent in such circumstances. The second being that the majority of Crown Court cases are not recorded and so it would be nigh on impossible to be bound by a decision that could not be referenced. Those Crown Court cases that are reported can sometimes have a persuasive effect depending on the individual facts of the cases.

2.3.11   The magistrates' court and the county court

All other courts are superior to these courts and they are viewed as being the most inferior courts in the hierarchy. They are bound by every court above them and they are not binding on themselves or other courts.

2.3.12   Tribunals

Tribunals are very much like the inferior courts in that they generally do not bind each other or any other court. They are however bound by superior courts (Court of Appeal and House of Lords).

Figure 2.1 The hierarchy of precedent within the court system

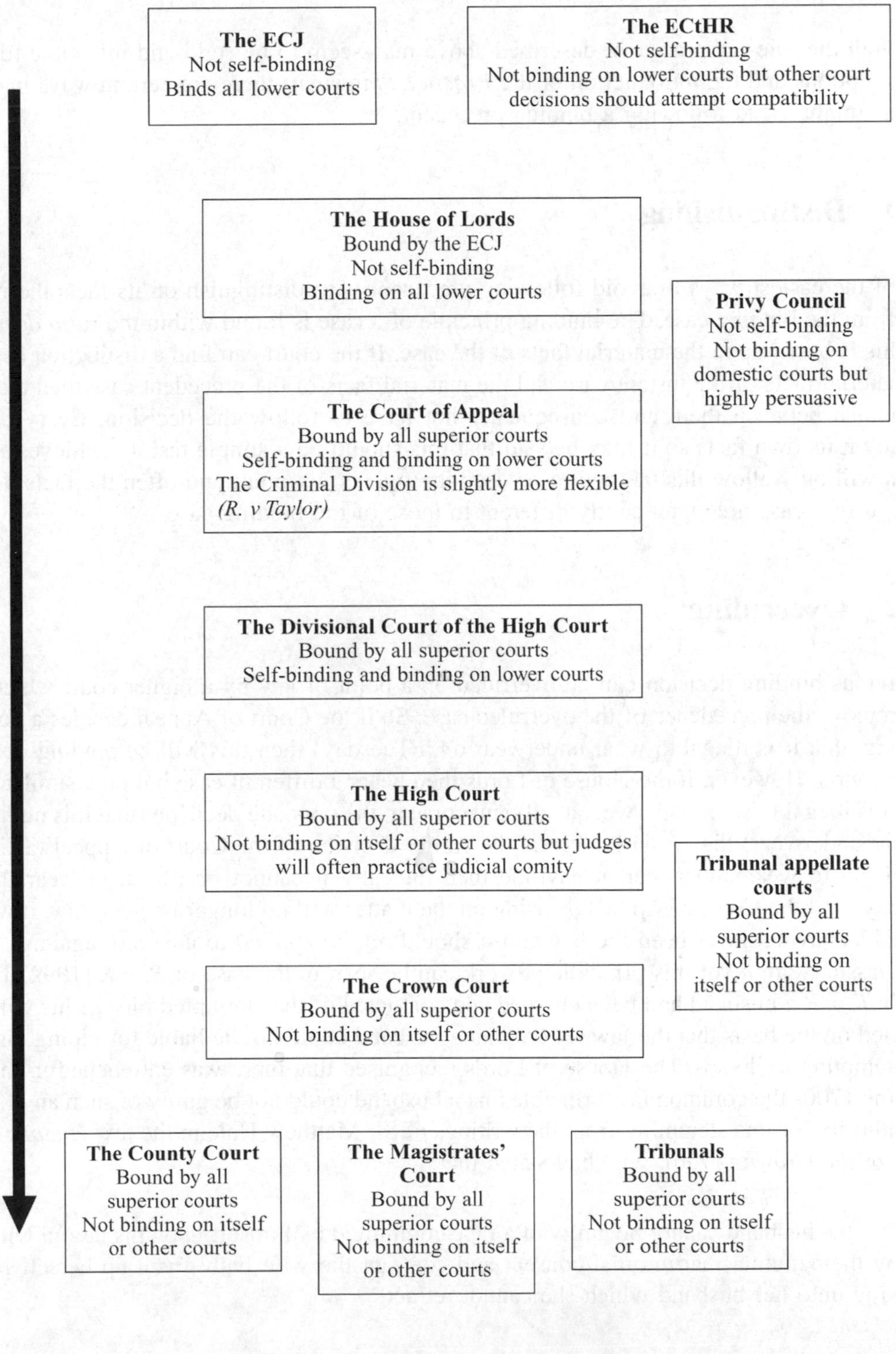

The ECJ
Not self-binding
Binds all lower courts

The ECtHR
Not self-binding
Not binding on lower courts but other court
decisions should attempt compatibility

The House of Lords
Bound by the ECJ
Not self-binding
Binding on all lower courts

Privy Council
Not self-binding
Not binding on
domestic courts but
highly persuasive

The Court of Appeal
Bound by all superior courts
Self-binding and binding on lower courts
The Criminal Division is slightly more flexible
(R. v Taylor)

The Divisional Court of the High Court
Bound by all superior courts
Self-binding and binding on lower courts

The High Court
Bound by all superior courts
Not binding on itself or other courts but judges
will often practice judicial comity

**Tribunal appellate
courts**
Bound by all
superior courts
Not binding on
itself or other courts

The Crown Court
Bound by all superior courts
Not binding on itself or other courts

The County Court
Bound by all
superior courts
Not binding on itself
or other courts

**The Magistrates'
Court**
Bound by all
superior courts
Not binding on itself
or other courts

Tribunals
Bound by all
superior courts
Not binding on itself
or other courts

2.4 Precedent in practice

Although the rules of precedent described above may seem to be rigid and inflexible (despite the exceptions and the introduction of the *Practice Statement*) there are certain ways in which a court might avoid following a binding precedent.

2.4.1 Distinguishing

One of the easiest ways to avoid following precedent is to distinguish on its facts the instant case from the binding case. The binding principle of a case is found within the *ratio decidendi* and this is based upon the material facts of the case. If the court can find a distinction between the material facts of the instant case and the material facts of the precedent case then they can distinguish between them and consequently not have to follow the decision. Every case is unique on its own facts so it may be said that this should be a simple task to achieve, but the courts will only allow this method to be used up to a certain point and often the facts used to distinguish a case are significantly different to those of the binding case.

2.4.2 Overruling

A previous binding decision can be overruled on a point of law by a higher court which will then remove the precedence of the overruled case. So if the Court of Appeal decides a point of law (e.g. that it is illegal to wear underwear on a Tuesday) then this will be binding upon all lower courts. However, if the House of Lords then hears a different case but on a similar point (that it is illegal to wear underwear at all) and come to the opposite decision (that it is not illegal to wear underwear) then it will overrule the earlier decision of the Court of Appeal (as if it is not illegal to wear underwear at anytime then logically it cannot be illegal to wear it on a Tuesday) and the Court of Appeal decision on the matter will no longer be good law, it will be viewed as having never been the law and it should not be applied to any case again.

A classic example of this principle at work can be seen in the case of *R. v R* [1992] 1 A.C. 599. In *R. v R* a husband had been charged and convicted of the attempted rape of his wife. He appealed on the basis that the law set out that a husband could not be liable for raping his wife (or attempting to do so). The House of Lords recognised that there was entrenched in the law from the 1700s the common law principle that a husband could not be guilty of such an offence, the authority for this stemming from the writings of Sir Matthew Hale in the text *History of the Pleas of the Crown* (1736), who had stated that:

> . . . the husband cannot be guilty of a rape committed by himself upon his lawful wife, for by their mutual matrimonial consent and contract the wife hath given up herself in this kind unto her husband which she cannot retract.

This is not the most politically correct or acceptable statement ever to be made but nevertheless it was settled law that a husband had the right to rape his wife without facing criminal liability. The Lords appreciated that this view did not sit well with modern societal views (remember this was only 1992—not that long ago) and therefore they took the decision to overrule the common law and hold that a husband could be held liable for the rape, or attempted rape, of his wife.

An overruled case therefore has what is known as retrospective effect, this means that it is deemed to have never have been law in the first place and that any person who was convicted under that principle should then be able to appeal their conviction. For example, in 1980 Mr X was convicted of manslaughter due to supplying the victim with a drug which they then self-injected and overdosed on. In 1988 Mr Y was convicted of the same offence, with the case of Mr X being cited as binding precedent. In 2000 Mr K is then tried and convicted of exactly the same offence but, on appeal the House of Lords decides that a person cannot be guilty of manslaughter for simply supplying the drug, as the victim decided to take the drug autonomously and was not forced to do so by the defendant. The court quashes Mr K's conviction and states that the principle of law from Mr X's case is overruled and is now to be considered as bad law. What does this then mean for Mr Y? As the effect of the overruling is retrospective it means that Mr Y can now appeal his conviction on the basis that it was decided on an incorrect principle.

The English law does not allow at present the doctrine of prospective overruling (as is favoured in America). Prospective overruling occurs whereby the court will decide to overrule a principle of law in respect of all future cases but that they will still apply the (soon to be bad) principle of law to all cases or transactions that have already commenced by the date of the judgment in question. The overruling cannot be relied upon by any settled cases. This may seem very unfair to the defendant in the case but the principle seems to be applied in mainly money cases, or where there is a business transaction that would result in unjustness occurring in respect of the parties involved if the law were to be changed at that point in time. The use of prospective overruling in English law has been mooted as a possibility but it is unlikely that it will ever become an accepted principle of the English legal system.

Precedent can also be overruled by statute law. If Parliament were to enact a new piece of legislation that was at odds with a principle found within the common law then the legislation would take precedence due to the doctrine of Parliamentary supremacy and the case law would therefore become obsolete.

2.4.3 Reversing

As a case passes through the appeal process the appellate courts may do one of two things; it may either dismiss the appeal, whereby the original decision of the lower court stands, or it can allow the appeal and reverse the decision of the lower court. Reversing means that the decision of the lower court is changed, and this will be done in circumstances where the higher court believes that the lower court interpreted the law incorrectly. By reversing a decision the higher court effectively overrules the lower court's decision and thereby any principle established by the lower court is then to be viewed as bad law.

2.5 Precedent and human rights

The introduction of the Human Rights Act 1998 (HRA 1998) had a significant effect upon the doctrine of precedent in that the court could, if it felt that previous binding precedent was incompatible with the ECHR, ignore the binding precedent and establish a new principle of law that was compatible with the HRA 1998.

Section 2 of the HRA 1998 provides that:

(1) A court or tribunal determining a question which has arisen in connection with a Convention right must take into account any—

(a) judgment, decision, declaration or advisory opinion of the European Court of Human Rights,

(b) opinion of the Commission given in a report adopted under Article 31 of the Convention,

(c) decision of the Commission in connection with Article 26 or 27(2) of the Convention, or

(d) decision of the Committee of Ministers taken under Article 46 of the Convention,

whenever made or given, so far as, in the opinion of the court or tribunal, it is relevant to the proceedings in which that question has arisen.

The most important word in s.2 as to the doctrine of judicial precedent is the word 'must'. The court does not have the option to ignore the ECHR or decisions made under it and this applies to both superior and inferior courts alike, so if the Court of Appeal were bound by a prior precedent of the House of Lords but they deemed it to be incompatible with the ECHR then they must follow the Convention and declare the superior court's decision as bad law.

This is exactly what happened in the leading case on this point of *Ghaidan v Godin-Mendoza* [2002] EWCA Civ 1533. In *Ghaidan v Godin-Mendoza* Mr Mendoza had, from 1972, lived in a flat with his homosexual partner, over which his partner had a protected tenancy. Sadly Mr Mendoza's partner died in 2001 and the landlord tried to repossess the flat. The court at first instance granted Mr Mendoza an assured tenancy, which was not as secure as the protected tenancy, as Mr Mendoza was not taken to be within the meaning of the term 'surviving spouse' as set out in the Rent Act 1977. Mr Mendoza then appealed to the Court of Appeal on the grounds that, since he and the original tenant were partners in a longstanding homosexual relationship, the court were obliged to read the 1977 Act in a way which was compatible with his Convention rights (namely art.8 and art.14), and so he should be treated as the spouse of the original tenant and therefore be granted statutory tenancy.

The Court of Appeal were bound by the earlier House of Lords precedent of *Fitzpatrick v Sterling* [2001] A.C. 227 which set out that a homosexual partner cannot be viewed as a surviving spouse but would rather be viewed as a member of the deceased person's family. The court acknowledged that Mr Mendoza would be discriminated against if the decision in *Fitzpatrick v Sterling* were applied and so they granted Mr Mendoza statutory tenancy and held that the words 'as his or her wife or husband' in the Rent Act 1977 should be read as meaning

'as if they were his or her wife or husband'. By doing so the Court of Appeal e₁.
overruled the House of Lords decision in *Fitzpatrick v Sterling* by invoking the ₁
provided under s.2 HRA 1998, although the court did not directly state that that was what
had done.

The effect of this is that the lower courts can now overrule the superior courts decisions if
it is incompatible with Convention rights. This does not however, mean that the hierarchy of
precedent has been destroyed but rather that the rule of Parliament is to be taken as supreme.
The HRA 1998 is domestic legislation and as such it will always take precedence over case law
(as does any legislation passed by Parliament) and therefore in such a case the lower court will
only be enforcing the will of Parliament.

2.6   Arguments for and against the doctrine of judicial precedent

Arguments for	Arguments against
Time saving The judge does not have to start from scratch but can consider past precedents to help with the decision.	**Promotes laziness** As a judge only has to refer to previous decisions he does not have to fully consider the matter personally.
Certainty The law is settled so that a person coming to the law or a lawyer advising on the law can assess the likely outcome of the case based on past decisions.	**Stagnation** The law stagnates as the judiciary can refer to past precedent and need not consider new and innovative ways of dealing with a case.
Justice It would be unfair and unjust for a decision to be taken in one case and then the same set of facts arise again and the opposite decision be taken instead.	**Difficult to remedy mistakes** Any errors in the application of the law can only be remedied if the same issues arise again in a later case that is heard by a higher court.
Consistency Links into certainty and justice. By providing consistency then different courts throughout the country will apply the same law.	**Backwards looking** Links into stagnation. Precedent involves looking back at how the law was decided as opposed to looking forward as to how the law should be decided.
Flexibility Precedent allows the courts to develop the law with the changing times and so reliance on Parliament changing the law is not required.	**Unconstitutional** Parliament should be the only law makers in the country and by developing case law in this manner the courts are taking this function away from Parliament.

2.7 Statutory interpretation

As we have discussed in the previous chapter Parliament makes legislation, but once it is has been passed by Parliament that is not the end of the matter. In fact it could almost be said to be the beginning as laws are not just made to keep Parliament busy, but are rather designed to be used and implemented by members of society and the courts, and this is where the real problems start. Parliament passes a phenomenal amount of legislation per year, for example in 2007 they passed 31 Acts of Parliament, and in 2006 55 Acts were passed, and these figures do not include the thousands of statutory instruments that were also created. As so many new laws come on to the statute books and because there are statutes that date back so many years (to name but a couple of the problems that can be encountered) it is inevitable that problems will arise as to what the statutes actually mean and how the laws within them are to be applied. Uncertainty as to the law is a very unsatisfactory state of affairs (in fact art.7 of the ECHR requires there to be certainty within the law) and uncertainty in law and how to deal with this appropriately is a fact that the courts have had to battle with for a long time. In the remainder of this chapter we will consider why such uncertainty can arise and then go on to analyse the methods that the courts have employed to deal with this uncertainty by way of a method known as 'statutory interpretation'. A quick point to note before considering this matter in detail is the difference between the terms 'statutory interpretation' and 'statutory construction'. Statutory interpretation involves the consideration of what is meant by the word in question; what does it mean? Whereas statutory construction involves the application of the word once it has been defined. Essentially statutory construction means how should the courts then apply and use that word.

2.7.1 Why is there uncertainty in the law?

Uncertainty in the law can arise through a number of factors that are identified below (although there are probably more reasons which have not yet even been identified by the courts).

2.7.1.1 Automatic implications

Human beings, not robots, draft legislation and therefore the legislation has the potential to be as fallible as the draftsman who drafted it. Obviously the draft Bill is normally passed through both the House of Commons and the House of Lords where it is repeatedly scrutinised by a variety of different people and any major errors or omissions will be spotted, but there may be situations where a specific word is omitted from the statute as everyone who considered it came to the conclusion that its meaning was implicit in the statute. For example if a statute sets out that 'it is illegal for a person with a child or a dog to enter a restaurant' then how would this apply to a person who had with them both a child *and* a dog? The legislation does not expressly say that a person with a child *and* a dog would be committing an offence if they entered the restaurant but it would be implied from its meaning. Where a situation arises that is not expressly legislated for then complications and uncertainty may arise.

2.7.1.2 A broad term

Where the word in a statute can be said to have a broad meaning then problems can arise. A draftsman may try and capture a number of possibilities within one statutory provision so that it is all encompassing, but by doing so this may raise uncertainty as to its full extent. Take for example a statute that states that 'it is an offence to keep any domestic animal within a residential house'. What does the term 'domestic' mean here? Does it mean any animal that is a common household pet, such as a cat or dog? But if so does it then cover animals such as a pig or a llama? Some people keep both of these animals as pets. Or does it mean animals domestic to the UK? What then about tropical fish, an iguana or a tarantula? All of these animals are regularly kept as pets within residential houses in the UK but they are certainly not domestic to the UK. A broad meaning may not provide the level of specific detail actually required.

2.7.1.3 Ambiguity

A word within the English language can have more than one meaning and it may be difficult to determine which meaning was intended, so for example the word 'bear' can mean:

- an animal (a big grizzly brown one)

- to carry (a weight either physically or emotionally)

- to support something (the chair could bear her weight)

- to accept or tolerate (you must bear the responsibility)

- to produce (a mother can bear a child, or a tree can bear fruit)

- to change direction (bear north east at the big tree)

The meaning of the word used can have a dramatic effect on a sentence and sometimes it is difficult to identify which meaning was intended by Parliament. In the case of *R. v Allen* (1872) L.R. 1 C.C.R. 367 the meaning of the word 'marry', as found in s.57 of the Offences against the Person Act 1861 (OAPA 1861) was under consideration. An offence under s.57 was committed if a person was 'to marry while one's original spouse was still alive' (and they had not gotten divorced). The question was raised as to whether the term meant that a legally binding marriage ceremony must have been undertaken or whether it could just mean going through a ceremony of marriage. If it were the former interpretation then that would mean that the offence of bigamy could never be committed, as any subsequent marriage where the person is already legally married is not held to be valid. If it meant the second option, that only a marriage ceremony had to be performed, then this would mean that the offence of bigamy could be committed. The court held that the word 'marry' in s.57 was to mean the latter so as to give effect to the aim of the statute.

2.7.1.4 An error

Errors do occur, even in important legal documents such as an Act of Parliament. It is easy for a person to make a mistake that other people then do not then notice until it is too late to rectify.

2.7.1.5 Unforeseen events

Not every development in society can be foreseen, even by the most forward-thinking and imaginative person. For example 50 years ago the concept of email would have been hard to grasp by the majority of laypeople. This issue of unforeseen events occurred in the case of *Ireland and Burstow* [1998] A.C. 147 where the defendant was tried under s.47 of the OAPA 1861 for causing psychiatric harm to the victim (he had made a number of silent phone calls to her and as a result she suffered from a psychiatric illness). The problem arose as s.47 is the offence of 'assault occasioning actual bodily harm' and this then left a question as to whether or not 'bodily harm' also included 'psychiatric harm' as the statute was drafted in 1861 when psychiatric harm was not contemplated. The Lords held that psychiatric harm was to come under the term of bodily harm and that the Act should be construed in the light of the scientific knowledge current at the time of the offence as opposed to the knowledge that was had at the time of drafting. The statute was to be viewed as a living one that could be adapted to keep up to date with the changing times and new developments.

2.7.1.6 Changing language

The English language is not static. Words become redundant or their meaning can change over time. The language used in the times of Chaucer would make little to no sense to most people in the 21st Century, but it was at one time the accepted form of the English language. Nowadays txt speak (sorry, text speak) is becoming more common and (quite worryingly) more accepted as a version of the English language. A good illustration of the ways that the meaning of words can change over time is by considering the word 'gay'. It now has very different connotations as to what it did 40 years ago. Language therefore can change and this can leave the judiciary with a degree of confusion when the word that has changed is found within a statute. In the case of *Cheesman v DPP, The Times,* November 2, 1990 the word 'passengers' as in s.28 of the Town and Country Planning Act 1847, was under consideration. The meaning of the word 'passengers' was of critical importance to the case as the offence the defendant had been charged with under s.28 was that of 'wilfully and indecently exposing his person in a street to the annoyance of passengers'. The defendant had been apprehended by two policemen for masturbating in a public toilet, and it was under dispute as to whether or not the policemen were passengers under the Act. The court investigated the meaning of the word as in 1847 when the legislation was drafted and discovered that it then meant 'a passer-by', whereas under the modern interpretation it meant someone who is carried in a vehicle (so a car or a bus). The same word but with two completely different meanings due to the development of the language. Whether Mr Cheesman was found guilty or not is considered below at 2.9.1.

Figure 2.2 Common causes of statutory uncertainty

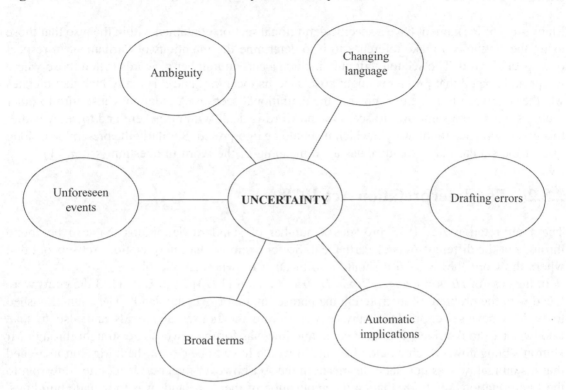

2.8   Applying the (uncertain) law

It is the role of a judge to apply the law as enacted by Parliament to the instant case in front of them. In a straightforward case this is quite simple. If the statute states that X would be guilty of theft if he stole some money and X then steals some money it would be an easy task for the court to come to conclusion that X is therefore guilty of theft. However, if X had stolen some bars of gold, that were technically not money, what is the court to do? He has obviously committed an offence as he has stolen something and it has quite a high financial value to it but the item is not money. Should the courts interpret the law by giving meaning to the words that Parliament has used, so that 'money' would mean legal tender (coins and notes), or should it interpret the law in such a way that it seeks to give the words Parliament's intention, so 'money' could then mean anything that has a financial value. The way in which the court chooses to interpret the meaning could have a significant effect on the case (here whether X is guilty or innocent of the offence) and so the court have to be careful as to which interpretation it chooses to employ. To help them in its task of applying often uncertain law the judiciary have developed a number of techniques to aid interpretation, which will be considered below.

2.8.1 The Act

Many Acts of Parliament have a specific definitional section contained within them so that those using the statute can make reference to it to determine the intentions of Parliament in respect of a specific word. The section will only include a certain number of words (often those where it was anticipated that problems might arise as to its meaning) and it is really luck that dictates whether the word in issue is defined in the definitional section. A judge may also turn to other sections within the same Act to see how the word is dealt with elsewhere and to see whether this gives guidance to the way in which it should be interpreted. Similarly the pre-amble or long title of the statute may provide clues as to meaning of the word in question (see 3.4.1).

2.8.2 The Interpretation Act 1978

The Interpretation Act 1978 provides a number of standard definitions that can be found throughout the different Acts of Parliament. So for example the Interpretation Act sets out that where the word 'he' is used it should also mean 'she' where applicable.

In the case of *Hutton v Esher Urban District Council* [1973] 2 All E.R. 1123 the court were faced with the problem of interpreting the phrase 'in, on or over any land'. The council wished to build a new sewer to drain surface water from the houses and roads and also to take floodwater from the river. The most economic line was for the sewer to go straight through Mr Hutton's bungalow, which would mean that it would have to be demolished. Mr Hutton argued that his bungalow was not 'land' as meant in the Act however the court held, after referring to the Interpretation Act 1978, that on the application of the Act 'land' was to include buildings. Mr Hutton's bungalow was duly demolished.

2.8.3 Explanatory notes

Since 1999 all new Acts have been accompanied by explanatory notes that explain the purpose of the Act and individual sections in that Act in detail. Their preparation is required to aid the passage of the Bill through Parliament and now they are commonly being cited within the courts as an aid to statutory interpretation (see 3.4.3 for further details on explanatory notes).

2.9 Rules of interpretation

Where a judge has considered the sources discussed but has still not found a resolution to the interpretation of the word they may then look to one of the rules of interpretation that have been developed by the judiciary over time. There are four mains rules of interpretation and they are:

- the literal rule

- the golden rule
- the mischief rule
- the purposive approach

Each one considers the word and its meaning in a different way and each can produce a very different result when applied to the same word. The individual judge in a case will decide which, if any, rule they wish to employ and many judges will have a preferred rule that they return to using time and time again. Obviously as the choice of rule to be used is left to the discretion of the individual judge it means that one judge may interpret the word (by the use of a certain rule) in a different way to how another judge would have done so (by them employing a different rule). However, once the meaning of a word is defined, and it does not matter by which technique this occurs, then that will be taken to be the meaning of the word in later cases by way of the doctrine of precedent. The way in which the judiciary view the use of the rules on statutory interpretation was commented upon by Lord Reid in the case of *Maunsell v Olins* [1975] A.C. 373, when he stated:

> They are not rules in the ordinary sense of having some binding force. They are our servants, not our masters. They are aids to construction, presumptions or pointers. Not infrequently one 'rule' points in one direction, another in a different direction. In each case we must look at all relevant circumstances and decide as a matter of judgment what weight to attach to any particular 'rule'.

2.9.1 The literal rule

The literal rule is often the first rule that a judge will employ when attempting to interpret a statute and it works by way of the judge construing the words to their ordinary and grammatical meaning, whatever the end result. The fact that a completely ridiculous result could come from using the literal rule should not deter a judge from employing it as can be evidenced from Lord Esher's statement in *R. v City of London Court Judge* [1892] 1 Q.B. 273.

> If the words of an Act are clear, you must follow them, even though they lead to a manifest absurdity. The Court has nothing to do with the question whether the legislature has committed an absurdity.

It is often quite easy to identify whether a judge is using the literal rule or not as they tend to use words and phrase such as natural, ordinary and literal, and they may look to what the dictionary definition of the word is so as to identify the common everyday meaning of the word. The literal rule can work very well in some cases and can result in some ridiculous conclusions in others. An example of the literal rule ending in the absurd can by seen by the case of *Whiteley v Chappell* (1868) L.R. 4 Q.B. 147.

In *Whiteley v Chappell* the defendant had been convicted of the offence of impersonating a person entitled to vote. The defendant had impersonated a person who had been entitled to vote at the time of registration but who had subsequently died before the election. On appeal the question for the court was whether the legislation covered the situation where the defendant was impersonating a dead person. The court held that he could not be guilty of such an offence as the person whom he had impersonated was dead at the point of impersonation for the purposes of voting and therefore he was not a person who was entitled to vote—due to being dead. Hannen J., acknowledging the result, stated that:

> I regret that we are obliged to come to the conclusion that the offence charged was not proved; but it would be wrong to strain words to meet the justice of the present case, because it might make a precedent, and lead to dangerous consequences in other cases.

Another case where the use of the literal rule ended in a result that could not have been intended by Parliament when enacting the legislation in question was that of *Fisher v Bell* [1960] 3 All E.R. 731. In this case a shopkeeper had placed for sale in his shop window a flick knife. He was charged with an offence under s.1 of the Restriction of Offensive Weapons Act 1959 of offering a knife for sale. An issue arose as to whether the defendant was making an offer to sell or merely an invitation to treat (where a person comes and makes an offer to which the seller can then accept or reject it but makes no offer themselves). Under the law of contract the displaying of goods in a shop window (or offering them) is taken to only be an invitation to treat and so the Court of Appeal held that the defendant could not be guilty of the offence charged.

Despite the court recognising that such a situation could not have been outside of the intentions and minds of Parliament when they enacted the legislation the judge in the case, Lord Parker C.J., refused to fill in any of the 'gaps' left by Parliament in the drafting of the legislation, stating that to do so would:

> [a]ppear to me to be a naked usurpation of the legislative function under the thin disguise of interpretation.

If we return now to the case of *Cheeseman v DPP* (cited above) the court were left with a dilemma as to whether the term 'passengers' should apply to the policeman who had arrested Mr Cheesman in the public toilets. Taking the 1847 meaning of the word to be a passer-by the court decided that they would not have any difficulty with stretching that to a member of the public who had wandered into the public toilets, but that because the policemen had stationed themselves in the public toilets waiting for Mr Cheesman (a number of complaints had been made to them by the public alerting them to Mr Cheesman's activities) then they could not be strictly described as 'passers-by' or 'passengers' and therefore his conviction was quashed.

The use of the literal rule can be a very straightforward no nonsense way in which to resolve an issue concerning interpretation and its application does respect the supremacy of Parliament in regards to it being the primary law-maker. However, its application does result in some ridiculous and often very harsh decisions being made. In *London & North Easter Railway Co v Berriman* [1946] 1 All E.R. 255 a widow failed in her claim for compensation after her husband had been killed whilst maintaining a train track. The legislation only covered situations where the death occurred whilst the victim had been relaying or repairing the train tracks, not maintaining them, and the court when applying the literal rule to the wording of the legislation dismissed the widow's claim.

2.9.2 The golden rule

The golden rule can be explained best as an extension of the literal rule that is to be applied where the literal rule results in absurdity, as in the cases above. The literal rule should be applied initially and the words should be construed according to their ordinary plain meaning wherever possible, the golden rule then only being turned to as and when necessary. One of the first examples of the golden rule can be seen in the case of *Mattison v Hart* (1854) 14 C.B. 357, where it was stated that:

> We must, therefore, in this case have recourse to what is called the golden rule of construction, as applied to Acts of Parliament, viz, to give the words used by the legislature their plain meaning unless it is manifest from the general scope and intention of the statute, injustice and absurdity would result.

A judge is not obliged to employ the golden rule if they believe that to do so would be to go away from the intention of Parliament. An example of a case where the golden rule was used was in *R. v Allen* (1872) L.R. 1 C.C.R. 367 (see above) where the literal interpretation of the word 'marriage' (in s.57 OAPA 1861) would have required there to be a legally binding marriage undertaken, but this could not occur due to the offence in question being bigamy, (which already required the offender to be legally married before they could commit the offence and so any subsequent marriage would be automatically void) and so the court applied the golden rule instead so as to avoid an absurdity occurring.

The golden rule can also be applied by the courts where the application of the literal rule would result in a completely unacceptable decision, as occurred in the case of *Re Sigsworth* [1935] Ch. 89 where a son who had murdered his mother would have inherited his mother's estate had the court not decided to apply the golden rule to stop him benefiting from his ill gotten gains.

In *Adler v George* [1964] 2 Q.B. 7 the golden rule was used to halt a rather ingenious but also rather ridiculous submission from the appellant. The appellant had been convicted of obstructing a member of Her Majesty's armed forces whilst in a prohibited vicinity. The statute that he was charged and convicted under set out that it was an offence to obstruct someone 'in the vicinity of a prohibited place'. The appellant submitted that as he had actually been in the prohibited place then as 'in' could not be construed to mean the same as 'in the vicinity', which it was argued denoted being outside but near to the prohibited area, then there was consequently no evidence against him. The court applied the golden rule so as to avoid the appellant being acquitted and held that the term 'in the vicinity of' was to be interpreted as meaning 'in or in the vicinity of'.

The golden rule is often described as being similar to the purposive approach (discussed below) and it can be quite difficult to identify at times, especially when the judge does not specifically state that they are employing the golden rule or that they do not clearly identify what they view as being the absurd result. What is an absurd result is also open to wide interpretation in itself and it can mean different things to different people, for example in *Allen* the absurd result was that the statutory offence would have been unworkable if the rule had not been applies, whereas in *Re Sigsworth* the golden rule was used to stop what the court viewed as a completely unacceptable result due to the moral behaviour of the defendant.

2.9.3   The mischief rule

(looking back at the problem that needed remedying)

The very old case known as *Heydon's Case* (1584) Co. Rep. 7a sets out the principles of this rule of statutory interpretation. The four keys elements are:

- ① • What was the law prior to the Act?
- ② • What was the mischief (problem) that needed to be remedied?
- ③ • What was the remedy that Parliament wanted to impose?
- ④ • What was the purpose behind the remedy?

The mischief rule requires a judge to perform some detective work in respect of determining what the Act is actually all about. It is very different to the literal rule, which is only interested in applying what is on the statute books, as the mischief rule looks to the will and intention of Parliament and then interprets the law in a way that is compatible with this.

For example in the case of *Smith v Hughes* [1960] 2 All E.R. 859 two women had been convicted under s.1 of the Street Offences Act 1959, which made it an offence "for a common prostitute to loiter or solicit in a street or public place for the purposes of prostitution". The women were aware of the offence and so they carried out their profession from upon a balcony and through a first floor window, banging on the window or calling from the balcony to attract the attention of the passing men. They were convicted under s.1 but appealed on the grounds that they were not 'in the street or public' when they had been calling out to the men. Lord Parker C.J., whilst dismissing their appeal stated that:

> The sole question here is whether in those circumstances each defendant was soliciting in a street or public place. The words of section 1(1) of the Act of 1959 are in this form: "It shall be an offence for a common prostitute to loiter or solicit in a street or public place for the purpose of prostitution." Observe that it does not say there specifically that the person who is doing the soliciting must be in the street. Equally, it does not say that it is enough if the person who receives the solicitation or to whom it is addressed is in the street. For my part, I approach the matter by considering what is the mischief aimed at by this Act. Everybody knows that this was an Act intended to clean up the streets, to enable people to walk along the streets without being molested or solicited by common prostitutes. Viewed in that way, it can matter little whether the prostitute is soliciting while in the street or is standing in a doorway or on a balcony, or at a window, or whether the window is shut or open or half open; in each case her solicitation is projected to and addressed to somebody walking in the street.

The court considered the purpose of the legislation and what mischief it intended to remedy (prostitutes being on the streets) and although the statute itself did not expressly satisfy the situation before the court the judges in the case were of the opinion that the use of the mischief rule so as to ensure the liability of the women was appropriate.

The mischief rule was again employed in the slightly later case of *Royal College of Nursing v DHSS* [1981] A.C. 800. Here the issue involved the interpretation of s.1(1) of the Abortion Act 1967, which provides that ' . . . a person shall not be guilty of an offence under the law relating to abortion when a pregnancy is terminated by a registered medical practitioner . . . ' When the Act was initially passed all terminations were carried out surgically by a qualified doctor but as medicine had advanced it had now become possible for an abortion to be conducted quite easily by the way of taking certain drugs. This procedure could be carried out by a registered nurse and did not require a doctor present. The DHSS sent out a circular specifying that a nurse could lawfully carry out such a procedure so long as it was conducted under the supervision of qualified medical practioner (a doctor). Upon consideration the House of Lords held that the directions set out in the leaflet were lawful and therefore a nurse could carry out such a drug induced abortion provided it was carried out under appropriate super-vision. The decision was a rather controversial one and only achieved by a narrow majority. The Lords considered the mischief rule when interpreting the section and they came to the conclusion that the mischief considered by Parliament when enacting the legislation was to prevent backstreet abortions occurring. Therefore by allowing the abortion to be carried out in an appropriate medical setting under the care of a nurse was, in respect of the purpose of the legislation, an achievement. Lord Wilberforce and Lord Edmund-Davies preferred the literal approach to interpretation and voiced their opinion that by deciding as the House did they were effectively rewriting legislation, which was the role of Parliament and not the judiciary.

2.9.4 The purposive approach الطريقه الغايئه (منتنيه)

Not so much a true 'rule', but rather more like a philosophical approach (as its name suggests), the purposive approach is at the opposite end of the statutory interpretation spectrum to that of the literal rule. Instead of a judge simply saying what they see (as they do with the literal rule) the purposive approach involves the judge considering what the intentions of Parliament were when they enacted the legislation. It is often confused with the mischief rule as they both do consider the will of Parliament, but the mischief rule could be described as looking back at the problem that needed remedying, whereas the purposive approach looks forward to discover what Parliament were trying to achieve (there may not even have been a mischief present but Parliament simply wanted to legislate for something new). A good example of the purposive rule in action can be seen in the case of *R. v Registrar General Ex p. Smith* [1991] 2 W.L.R. 782.

In *Ex p. Smith* the appellant had been adopted as a young baby and as he grew up he began to show signs of severe mental disturbance, which resulted in him expressing hatred towards his adoptive parents. He was then convicted of murder and whilst in prison he committed a further murder and as a result of this he was subsequently moved to Broadmoor hospital. The appellant then applied under s.51 of the Adoption Act 1976 for a copy of his birth certificate. Section 51 provided that:

> Subject to subsections (4) and (6), the Registrar General shall on an application made in the prescribed manner by an adopted person a record of whose birth is kept by the Registrar General and who has attained the age of 18 years supply to that person on payment of the prescribed fee (if any) such information as is necessary to enable that person to obtain a certified copy of the record of his birth.

The application was denied on the grounds that the psychiatrist had reported that he believed that the appellant might well have hostile feelings for his birth mother. The court held that s.51 should be interpreted in a purposive way and that if it was thought that the appellant would use the information to commit a crime in the future then there should be no discretion to allow the appellant access to this information. Lord Justice Staughton, when handing down the judgment of the court commented that:

> If it be the law that Parliament, even when enacting statutory duties in apparently absolute terms, is presumed not to have intended that they should apply so as to reward serious crime in the past, it seems to me that Parliament must likewise be presumed not to have intended to promote serious crime in the future. That is consistent with the growing tendency, perhaps encouraged by Europe, towards a purposive construction of statutes . . .

The purposive approach can be quite difficult to differentiate from the mischief rule (and many commentators will say that they are one and the same thing) but over recent times has become one of the more favoured approaches to statutory interpretation and can be frequently identified within case law when the judges have been considering the meaning of the legislation in question.

2.10   Aids to interpretation

As well as using the statutory interpretation techniques described above a judge can also turn to a number of 'aids' to interpretation to help them in their quest to understand what is meant by the statute. Aids to interpretation can be split down into two types 'intrinsic' aids and 'extrinsic' aids.

2.10.1   Intrinsic aids

Intrinsic aids are aids found within the Act itself and the most commonly used aids are the ones described at 2.8.1 (other sections within the Act) and 2.8.3 (the explanatory notes). There are also certain rules of language that can be used to aid statutory interpretation. The rules considered above (at 2.9) have generally focused on a specific word within the statute, but it must be remembered that the word is not in a vacuum as it sits in a sentence, and the meaning of that sentence can only be understood if it is read in full. The rules of language encourage the consideration of the words surrounding the word in question so as to try and glean an idea as to its true meaning. They all have (rather hard to pronounce) Latin names but their concepts are actually quite easy to understand.

2.10.2   Rules of language

2.10.2.1   The *ejusdem generis* rule

This means that when general words follow particular words then the general words are limited to the thing considered by the particular words. For example if the Act contained the words 'chocolate, candy, butterscotch and other confectionary' then the 'other confectionary' would include other sweets and would not include items like crisps or fruit.

In the case of *Lane v London Electricity Board* [1955] 1 All E.R. 324 the *ejusdem generis* rule was applied. The plaintiff was an electrician who had been instructed by his employers to install extra lighting at their substation. In checking the lighting that was already there prior to him starting to install the new lights, the plaintiff slipped and fell, injuring his knee. He brought his claim under The Electricity Regulations 1908 (reg.26), which provided that:

> All those parts of premises in which apparatus is placed shall be adequately lighted to prevent danger.
> 'Danger' is defined by the regulations as meaning danger to health or danger to life or limb from shock, burn, or other injury to persons employed, or from fire attendant upon the generation, transformation, distribution, or use of electrical energy.

The question in the court was whether the words, 'or other injury' could include the fact that the claimant's foot slipped whilst he was inspecting the lighting which then caused the harm. The court held that in this context the regulation must be read ejusdem generis with 'shock' or 'burn'. In other words, it is to be taken to mean 'or other injury due to electrical energy' and therefore could not be extended to a fall.

2.10.2.2   *Expressio unius est exclusio alterius*

This rule of language is ever so simple to understand and apply. It effectively means that the expression of one thing implies the exclusion of another, so where specific words are used and are not followed by general words the Act only applies to the specific words mentioned.

For example if an Act set out that it was an offence to keep 'guinea pigs, gerbils and rabbits' it would mean that keeping a hamster is perfectly allowed as a hamster is not specifically named in the Act.

2.10.2.3   *Noscitur a Sociis*

This phrase means that the meaning of a word can be gathered from its context. In *Muir v Keay* (1875) L.R. 10 Q.B. 594 the defendant had been convicted of keeping a refreshment house

61

without a licence under s.6 of 23 & 24 Vict c.27 (Refreshment Houses Act 1860), which provided that:

> ... all houses, rooms, shops, or buildings, kept open for public refreshment, resort, and entertainment, during certain hours of the night, are to be deemed refreshment houses and require a licence.

The defendant owned premises known as The Café. It opened during the night and on the night in question there were 17 females and 20 males there, all of whom were supplied with cigars, coffee, and ginger beer. The defendant appealed against his conviction contending that the words 'and entertainment' required there to be musical or other public performance on the premises. The court dismissed the appeal, and held whilst applying the *noscitur a sociis rule*, that other entertainment did not have to involve music or a public performance, but rather it could include simply providing a reception for customers to congregate in, as was the case at The Café. The meaning of the term 'and entertainment' was to be taken from the other words within the section so 'public refreshment' and 'resort' did not imply any form of musical entertainment and therefore the word entertainment within that section did not either.

2.10.2.4 Presumptions

Another intrinsic aid to statutory interpretation is that of presumptions. Presumptions as to the law can be made by a judge in certain circumstances. If there is nothing to say that the presumption should not stand then it will be accepted by the judge, however, if the statute states something that goes against the presumption then it will be rebutted and cannot stand. The most common presumptions are listed below:

Statute does not change the common law—this means that unless a statute expressly states that the common law has been changed then the common law will remain as it is.

There is a presumption in favour of *mens rea* in a criminal case—this presumption means that a person will not be convicted of a criminal offence unless it can be proved beyond reasonable doubt that they meant to commit the offence. If an Act is silent on the *mens rea* (the mental element of the offence) then the court should read into the Act an appropriate *mens rea* for the offence in question. There are certain offences where this presumption can be rebutted and these are known as strict liability offences. This means that a person will be guilty of the offence for simply carrying out the prohibited act, they did not have to mean to do so. An example of an offence where the presumption of *mens rea* is rebutted is that of speeding. A person does not have to intend to speed to be guilty of the offence; they simply just have to go over the speed limit. Even if the driver did not realise they were speeding they will still have committed the offence.

Legislation does not apply retrospectively—legislation will normally only apply from the date it is brought into force, it will not apply to circumstances that have occurred before the legislation was enacted. To illustrate this point consider the following example. Jim likes kicking dogs and cats, every dog or cat he sees he kicks (or at least tries to). On Monday it was not an offence to kick animals and Jim had a great day as he kicked twenty cats and three dogs. On Wednesday Parliament enacted a law that set out that kicking any animal would result in a criminal conviction. Jim cannot be prosecuted under the law for his actions on the Monday as the law does not apply retrospectively, however if Jim then went and kicked a dog on Thursday he would be guilty of the offence, even if he was not aware that this behaviour had now been criminalised. The presumption that the law does not apply retrospectively can be rebutted, but only by the Act of Parliament expressly stating this fact, or in the case of revenue laws that can apply retrospectively regardless of whether it is expressly stated in the Act or not.

The monarch is not subject to the provisions of any statute—meaning that the Queen could go around breaking any law that she wished as there is a presumption that she is not bound by any statute unless it expressly states that she is.

2.10.3   Extrinsic aids

Extrinsic aids are aids that a judge refers to for help with interpretation but which are outside of the Act. Some common extrinsic aids to interpretation are:

- Historical setting
- Other Acts of Parliament
- Case law
- Dictionaries
- Textbooks/academic commentary
- *Hansard*
- Reports
- Treaties and international Conventions

Many of these extrinsic aids are quite self-explanatory but one does warrant further consideration.

2.10.3.1   *Hansard*

Hansard is a documentary record of the daily debates that take place in Parliament. Originally the use of *Hansard* as an aid to statutory interpretation was prohibited by the courts, as reference to it was thought to promote confusion, not clarity, and that it was an unreliable source. Lord Denning however was very much of the opinion that *Hansard* could be a valuable aid to interpretation and in the case of *Davis v Johnson* [1979] A.C. 264 he admitted to having referred to it before delivering his judgment (although this action was swiftly condemned in the House of Lords).

The rule against referring to *Hansard* was overturned in the landmark case of *Pepper (Inspector of Taxes) v Hart* [1993] AC 593 where the House of Lords set out that it could be referred to as an aid to statutory interpretation, but only in certain circumstances. The circumstances were set out in the speech of Lord Browne-Wilkinson, where it was stated that *Hansard* could properly be referred to when:

- The legislation was ambiguous or obscure or lead to an absurdity.

- The material relied upon from *Hansard* consisted of one or more statements by a minister or other promoter of the Bill together if necessary with such other parliamentary material as is necessary to understand such statements and their effect.

- The statements relied upon were clear.

If then the legislatory provision is not ambiguous, or the statements that are wished to be relied upon are not clear then *Hansard* will not be permitted as an aid to statutory interpretation. The use of *Hansard* was confirmed and even extended slightly in the later case of *Three Rivers DC v Bank of England (No.2)* [1996] 2 All E.R. 363. This case was concerned with the introduction of a European directive into English law and the court held that *Hansard* could be relied upon where the provision concerned was not ambiguous but that it was important to interpret the statute so as to give effect to its obligations, therefore *Hansard* could be referred to so as to discover the purpose of the legislation.

The use of *Hansard* is now an accepted aid to statutory interpretation and it has been used effectively in many cases. It seems that Lord Denning was right to champion the use of *Hansard* and his comment in *Davis v Johnson* that:

Some may say—and indeed have said—that judges should not pay any attention what is said in Parliament. They should grope about in the dark for the meaning of an Act without switching on the light. I do not accede to this view.

appears to have been an innovative and logical view to have of such a potentially valuable source.

2.10.4   Human Rights Act 1998

The HRA 1998, as discussed at 2.5, also allows the ECHR to be used as an extrinsic aid to statutory interpretation. The courts are required to ensure that domestic legislation is interpreted in a way that is compatible with Convention rights (s.3 HRA 1998) and in doing so they are permitted to consult the individual rights of the Convention as an aid to discover how to interpret domestic law. This is what occurred in the case of *Ghaidan v Godin-Mendoza* [2002] EWCA Civ 1533, as discussed above.

Another example of where the law of was interpreted a way so as to be compatible with Convention rights can be seen in the case of *R. v A* [2001] UKHL 25. In *R. v A* it was alleged that the defendant had raped the complainant. The defendant's case was that sexual intercourse had taken place but that the complainant had consented. The defendant made an application to the trial judge to cross-examine the complainant about her previous sexual behaviour.

Section 41 of the Youth Justice and Criminal Evidence Act 1999 provides for an embargo on the cross-examination of the complainant's previous sexual history without the leave of the court. Leave (permission) to cross-examine on this topic will only be given in limited circumstances (s.41(3) and (5)). The defendant was denied leave to conduct the cross-examination. On an interlocutory appeal to the House of Lords he contended that the embargo on undertaking such question was a breach of his right to a fair trial under art.6 of the ECHR as art.6(3) sets out that:

> Everyone charged with a criminal offence has the following minimum rights . . .
>
> (d) to examine or have examined witnesses against him . . . .

The House was required to consider whether s.41 should be read in accordance with s.3 HRA 1998, so as to make it compatible with the defendant's art.6 rights, meaning that cross-examination of the complainant should have been allowed.

Lord Steyn, when delivering his opinion on the matter stated that:

> In my view section 3 requires the court to subordinate the niceties of the language of s.41(3)(c), and in particular the touchstone of coincidence, to broader considerations of relevance judged by logical and common sense criteria of time and circumstances . . . [the] test of admissibility is whether the evidence (and so the questioning in relation to it) is nevertheless so relevant to the issue of consent that to exclude it would endanger the fairness of the trial under article 6 of the Convention. If this test is satisfied the evidence should not be excluded.

Essentially what Lord Steyn was saying (and what the House held) was that s.41 should be read in a way that is compatible with Convention rights and that the embargo on questioning a complainant about their previous sexual history should be lifted where the questioning is relevant to a fact in issue in the case and such questioning is necessary to ensure that the defendant receives a fair trial.

2.11 Summary

(a) The doctrine of judicial precedent stems from the principle of *stare decisis*, which means that previous decisions of the court should be stood by and followed in later cases. This doctrine helps to ensure that there is consistency and fairness in the law and it also aids in the deciding of a case as the judge does not have to start from scratch but can refer back to past cases for assistance.

(b) Precedent can either be binding (that which must be followed) or persuasive (that which can be followed) depending on which court decided the case. The general rules of precedent are that the higher courts bind the lower courts, a court on the same level of the hierarchy (e.g. the Court of Appeal) will be self-binding and the lower courts do not bind any other court.

(c) Binding precedent is found within the *ratio decidendi* of a case. The *ratio* is the reason for the decision in the case and it is the principle of law based on the facts of the case that can then be applied in future cases. Persuasive precedent is known as *obiter dicta* and this can be found within the part of the judgment in a case that does not go directly to the *ratio*. Dissenting judgments, points made that are not directly related to the material facts of a case and Privy Council opinions, are examples of persuasive precedent.

(d) The doctrine of precedent follows the hierarchy of the court system. The European Court of Justice is binding upon all lower courts (even the House of Lords) on matters of interpretation of European Union law.

(e) The House of Lords is no longer self-bound following the 1966 *Practice Statement*. The House will normally follow previous precedent unless it is of the opinion that it is right to depart from it. The House is normally quite reluctant to depart from settled law but will do so where there is a need to do so, such as to rectify a mistake in the law or to develop the law in line with that of society.

(f) The Privy Council is not binding on the domestic courts, nor is it self-binding. However, Privy Council decisions will be highly persuasive precedent and will most likely be followed by the House of Lords.

(g) The Court of Appeal is self binding and is not permitted to depart from its own previous decisions unless one of the exceptions as set out in *Young v Bristol Aeroplane Co Ltd* [1944] K.B. 718 is satisfied. These conditions are that 1) there are two conflicting Court of Appeal decisions, 2) there is a conflicting House of Lords decision, or 3) that the decision was made *per incuriam*. The Court of Appeal Criminal Division has slightly more flexibility in respect of departing from previous decisions due to the fact that it is considered with a person's liberty.

(h) The Divisional Court of the High Court is bound in the same way as the Court of Appeal. The High Court (first instance court) is bound by all superior courts but is not self-binding.

(i) The lower courts (Crown, magistrates' and Tribunals) are not self-binding nor are they binding on any other court. They can however be persuasive.

(j) To avoid a binding precedent the court may seek to distinguish the case on its facts, overrule it (if it is a higher court) or reverse it (which means that no other court will be bound by any precedent created by the part that was overruled).

(k) The Human Rights Act 1998 must be taken into account when considering the precedent of cases as the court, under s.2, is required to ensure that ECHR decisions and principle are taken into account when considering domestic law.

(l)   If the court is uncertain as the meaning of a word or phrase in a statutory provision then it will be obliged to interpret the word so as to give application to the law. There are a number of different rules developed by the judiciary so as to aid them in this task.

(m)   The literal rule is where the word in question is given its ordinary, natural and plain meaning no matter what the end result is. Often a dictionary will be used to discover the everyday meaning of the word in question.

(n)   The golden rule is where the literal rule is applied but the end result by way of its application is absurd. If this is the case then the judge can interpret the word in a way to avoid such absurdity.

(o)   The mischief rule is where the judge will look to the mischief (or wrong) that Parliament was trying to remedy when it enacted the statute. The words will then be interpreted in a way that is consistent with that aim. The mischief rule is very close to the purposive approach.

(p)   The purposive approach is where the judge will look to the purpose of the legislation; essentially what Parliament was trying to achieve.

(q)   The judiciary can also turn to aids to interpretation to help them. Aids can either be intrinsic or extrinsic. Intrinsic aids will be those found within the statute itself, whereas extrinsic aids will be those from outside of the case, i.e. case law, law reports, academic commentary and *Hansard* etc.

2.12   Self-test questions

1. Persuasive precedent can come from:

   (a) the Privy Council
   (b) academic commentary
   (c) lower courts
   (d) all of the above

2. The Court of Appeal can depart from one of its own previous decisions when:

   (a) it does not agree with the decision
   (b) the decision is made *per incuriam*
   (c) the decision is *res judicata*
   (d) it wants to develop the law

3. The term 'reversing' means:

   (a) the facts of the case are different
   (b) the court declares a previous case as bad law
   (c) the court changes the outcome of the instant case

(d) the court changes its own mind

4. To avoid an absurd result a judge will employ which technique of statutory interpretation:

(a) the literal rule
(b) the golden rule
(c) the mischief rule
(d) the purposive rule

5. Which source below is not an extrinsic aid to interpretation:

(a) case law
(b) *Hansard*
(c) another Act of Parliament
(d) the *Noscitur a Sociis* rule

2.13   Further reading

R. Clayton, "The Human Rights Act six years on: where are we now?" [2007] E.H.R.L.R. 1, 11–26.

T. Hickman, "The courts and politics after the Human Rights Act: a comment" [2008] P.L. Spr, 84–100.

J.C. Jenkins, "*Pepper v Hart*: A Draftman's Perspective" (1994) 15 Stat. L.R. 23.

R. Reed, "Foreign precedents and judicial reasoning: the American debate and British practice" [2008] 124 L.Q.R. (Apr) 253–273.

G. Williams, "The Meaning of Literal Interpretation" [1981] N.L.J. 1128.

3 How to find the law and use it

3.1 Introduction

The focus of this text is not particularly a skills based one; the primary purpose of it is to explain the English legal system as it is at the time of writing. However, there are certain skills that it is felt would be beneficial to spend some time considering. These skills include the art of being able to find the law and then being able to use it effectively once it has been found, which is what will be the focus of this chapter.

It is surprising how many undergraduate law students can explain the theoretical basis of the law, such as what a legal issue is or what is meant by a *ratio decidendi*, but on being asked to identify them from a law report, they have no idea of how to actually find these principles, or where to even start looking. This chapter will aim to explain how to find the law, be it case law or statute, and then how to go ahead and use it once found. Case law and statutes are the tools of the trade for a lawyer, just as a hammer and a blowtorch are for a plumber, or a screwdriver and electrical tape are for an electrician. It would be a very worrying moment when a supposedly qualified plumber picked up a blowtorch and then asked what it did, the same could be said if a lawyer stood up in court and asked the judge what the law was. To illustrate and aid in the understanding of these skills an edited version of the case of *R. v Cockburn* [2008] EWCA 316 (below at 3.3) will be used.

3.2 Finding case law

3.2.1 Online

The first thing to know is where to find the law. On being asked to find either a case or a statutory provision most law students will immediately refer to one of the online databases, such as Westlaw UK and Lexis Nexis. These legal databases are a veritable treasure trove of legal materials; they stock the majority of cases, legislation, journals and other legal sources, and they are relatively easy to use. It is not an objective of this chapter to explain in detail how to use these databases, as there are many other textbooks available that are more directed towards developing these skills (see Further Reading at the end of the chapter), so only a brief explanation will be given here. To illustrate how a case can be found by way of an online resource, reference will be made to the Westlaw UK online database. The case that will be searched for is a very famous criminal law case known as *R. v Ireland;Burstow*. At present it is assumed that we do not have the case citation available for the case and that we only know the case name.

On entering the Westlaw UK site it is advisable to go to the link entitled 'Cases' as that is what we are searching for, and will limit the scope of the electronic search to judicial decisions only. On clicking upon the link for Cases the following screen will appear.

(SOURCE: Westlaw UK)

The search box allows the input of either 'Free Text', which is used when either the case name and/or citation are unknown but the area of law is known (e.g. assault or police powers and judicial review). The 'Party Names' search box should be completed where the names of those involved in the case is known, and the 'Citation' search box can be used when the exact citation of the case is known. A case citation is the numbers and letters found after the case name, i.e. [2006] 2 All E.R. 66, (see 3.2.5 below for further details). As the case being searched for is that of *R. v Ireland;Burstow*, the name Ireland has been typed into the 'Party Names' box. Clicking on the 'Search' button will result in the following being shown:

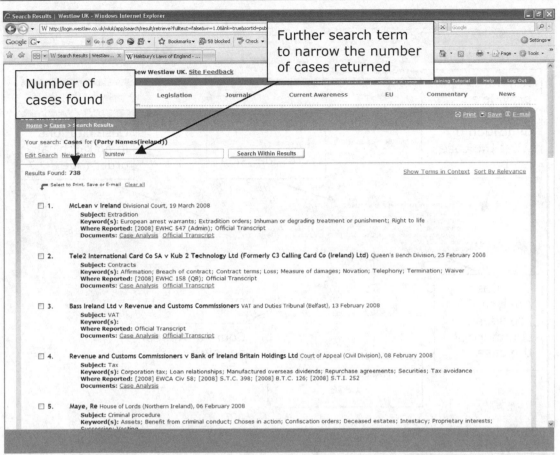

(SOURCE: Westlaw UK)

The search term 'Ireland' has returned 738 potential matches, which is a large volume of cases and therefore needs to be pared down further so that the specific case we are looking for can be found. To do this the legal database provides for a further search to be conducted within the limits of the first search results, and it is here that the term 'Burstow' (the other party name in the case) can be entered. The results that this returns can be seen in the box below:

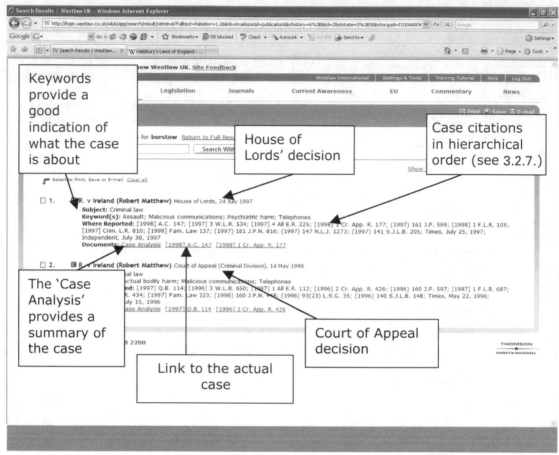

(SOURCE: Westlaw UK)

There are now only two results left, both relating to the same case but they are the decisions from different courts (the Court of Appeal and the House of Lords). As the House of Lords is the highest court within the domestic court hierarchy (refer to 9.4.5 for further discussion on this point) then this will be the latest decision in the case and, therefore, it will also be the most authorative in terms of precedent. If the case citation [1998] A.C. 147 is then clicked on, the House of Lords' opinion in the case will appear (as shown below).

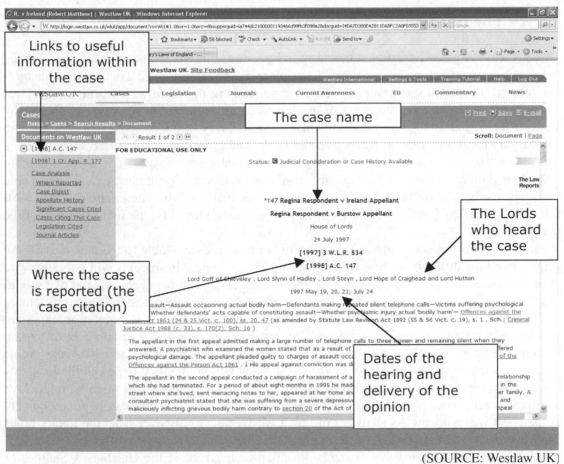

(SOURCE: Westlaw UK)

This screen now shows the actual case decision. As students it is imperative to not only know how to find a case, but also understand what is included in the document once it has been found. Set out at the top of the case is what is known as the 'head note'. The head note is a summary of the case facts and the decision in the case; the case facts are normally set out in a couple of paragraphs and it is a very brief overview of the case and what it was about. A summary of the court's decision will also be detailed here (normally under the paragraph entitled '**Held**').

The head note provides the essence of the case, but that is all it provides. The head note should never be relied upon as the definitive guide to the case as it is only a signpost as to what can be found within the actual decision. Head notes are good to use for determining whether or not a particular case may be of use; they are a quick reference point. They should not, however, be used or relied upon as authority. The authority comes only from that found within the decision of the court (as set out in the judge's speech).

3.2.2 The library

There is another place though that the law can be found, and this is unfortunately a place that students are frequenting less and less. This place is the library. The law libraries in most institutions are well stocked and easy to navigate, and are therefore well worth a visit. Over recent years due to the development of the Internet and online resources it seems that many students have quickly lost the vital skills that using a library develops. By actually going into a library and walking around, picking up the books and Law Reports from the shelves etc., a student will become more aware of what the law actually involves, as it will become more tangible and more understandable than just words on a screen or a print out. Actually being able to visualise what the different Law Report series look like and what the citation [2002] 3 All E.R. 456, or [1975] 1 A.C. 186 relates to will have a huge impact on the understanding of the law a whole.

Many students are not aware of the vast array of resources available to them as they do not get to see all the different sources whilst working online; generally students will only be aware of the resources that they regularly use and this can result in them being cheated out of a wealth of other sources that will aid them in their studies and develop their understanding to a more in-depth level. Being able effectively to use the hard copies of the Law Reports is an important skill to learn because when in practice if a lawyer is required to find a certain case or journal to help in the preparation of their case they will normally not have access to the online resources, such as Westlaw UK and Lexis Nexis. They will be required to search the local law library, either in their firm or set of Chambers, or at the court; and it will often be imperative that the lawyer knows precisely where to look so that the relevant report can be found quickly as the court will not wait. As a student of law it is advisable to discover what the library holds and how to use the hard copies of the sources held by them.

An example of a source that students are often unaware of is the Halsbury's Statutes of England and Wales, and the Halsbury's Laws of England and Wales. Both of these sources are invaluable to the law student and the professional lawyer. Halsbury's Statutes contains up-to-date versions of all the statutes in England and Wales, and Halsbury's Laws is essentially a comprehensive encyclopaedia of the law with details of relevant authority and statutes. Lexis Nexis publishes the Halsbury's series and so it can also be found online, but it cannot be stressed enough that students should aim to use the hard copy sources in the library at least for some of their research during their time studying law; even if this only entails finding one case per week (or even per month) in the library as this will still help the development of these essential skills.

3.2.3 Case names

The name of a case is a good initial indicator as to whether the case is a criminal case or a civil one, and who the parties to the case are. Criminal cases are quite easy to identify as (for example) the most common format is either *R. v Brown* or *Regina v Brown*. The *R.* or *Regina* (or *Rex* if the monarch at that time is a King) stands for the Crown (the King or Queen), and they are named first as they are the party who are bringing the proceedings (prosecuting). The defendant (in this example Brown) is then named second as they are the party whom the proceedings are against.

A quick note needs to be made in respect of both the '*R.*' and the '*v*' in the case name. The '*R.*', as noted above, stands for 'the Crown' and this is how it should be orated (simply saying 'R' should be avoided at all costs). The term 'King' or 'Queen' should only ever be used in the Privy Council and no other forum. Similarly the *v* is not to be said out loud as 'versus', this is the America style and should not be used within the English courts. The *v* should be said as either 'and', or 'against'. So the case name of *R. v Brown* would be said orally as either, 'the Crown and Brown', or 'the Crown against Brown', with the latter being the preferred option.

Another style of criminal case name that can be found frequently within the law reports is that of (for example) *Green v DPP*. Here the case name indicates that Green is appealing by way of case stated (see 13.2.2.1.3) against the Director of Public Prosecutions (the DPP) who is the head of the Crown Prosecution Service (see 9.2.1). Green is the party bringing the proceedings and the DPP is the defendant in the matter. The name of the case would therefore be orated as 'Green against the Director of Public Prosecutions'.

A final commonly found criminal case name is (for example) that of the *Attorney-General's Reference (No.1 of 2008)*. This case name indicates that the Attorney-General has made a reference to the court to clarify a point of law (a form of appeal (see 13.2.1.1 for further details)) following the acquittal of the defendant or due to the imposition of an unduly lenient sentence.

In civil matters the case name will include the names of those involved in the dispute and their named order will indicate what their roles in the dispute are. So, for example, the case name of *Green v Brown* would indicate that Green was bringing a cause of action against Brown (e.g. suing him for damages for personal injuries caused by a car crash). If, in the same case, the names were switched so that the case name become *Brown v Green*, this would then show that at first instance Green was successful and that Brown had subsequently appealed the decision. Brown has therefore become the person bringing the proceedings (by way of appealing) and Green (now second named) has to defend the appeal. These case names would be orated as 'Green and/against Brown' or 'Brown and/against Green'. This procedure of first naming the party bringing the particular proceedings may well change in the near future as it has been mooted that the party names should remain consistent throughout so as to avoid any confusion or doubt as to the roles of the parties and stage of proceedings. If this practice were removed then people coming to the law would need to refer to the case chronology (it is always good practice to do this anyway) to determine the stage that proceedings had reached.

3.2.4 Case chronologies

Each case will set out the history up to an including the point that the case is reported in what is known as the 'case chronology'. The chronology of a case can be found by reading past the head note of a case to the part where the court hearings and decisions are listed. This is sometimes entitled 'Case history' and at others it is not bestowed with any particular title. Case chronologies provide invaluable information to any person reading a case (especially when new to the law) as it sets out what has happened so far, which then makes understanding what is going on in the instant case easier. It is often assumed that if a case is being heard on appeal then the defendant must have been acquitted (or unsuccessful if the matter is a civil one) and be the party bringing the appeal. This however is not always the case. It may be that the prosecution or claimant are lodging an appeal to clarify a point of law or are asserting that the decision was erroneous due to a failure by the court. Or the circumstances may be that a defendant (or the prosecution) have had one appeal already refused and are appealing further on that point, or that an appeal has already been allowed by the lower court and a further appeal to this decision is being sought. Who is appealing and against what is a vital fact to know and the case chronology is the source from which to identify this information. The importance of the case chronology will dramatically increase if the proposals to keep the case name order the same from the start to finish do become the norm. To illustrate what information is included in a typical case chronology consider the case chronology of the case of *Ireland;Burstow* below.

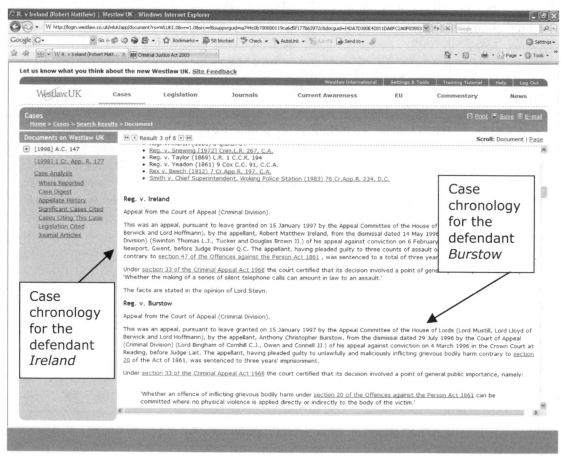

(SOURCE: Westlaw UK)

3.2.5   Citations

Students are often baffled about the meaning and letters that follow a case name, and many will only use the case name to search for the case that they need. Getting to grips with the meaning of case citations is imperative as a law student. If a lawyer is required to refer to a case in court (or if a student is required to refer to a case during a moot or mock trial) then the full correct case citation needs to be given. Judicial reasoning is reported in a number of different sources and these sources have a hierarchical structure of their own. If a case is to be cited then it is important that the most appropriate citation is given.

Case citations contain all the necessary information for the individual case to be located. The citations can be easily broken down into four component parts, these are:

- The year the case was reported in (although this is not required if the case citation has round brackets)

- The volume number (if appropriate) of the law series

- The standard abbreviation of the law series

- The page number upon which the case starts or the case number of that year (when a neutral citation (see 3.2.6))

So for example the citation of [1978] 2 W.L.R. 2002 stands for:

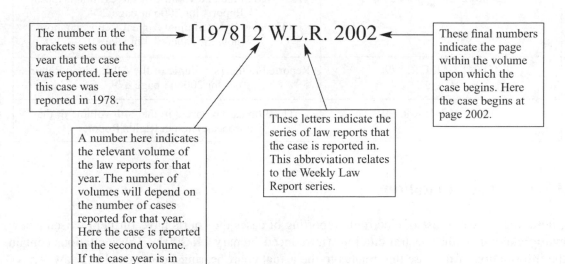

The number in the brackets sets out the year that the case was reported. Here this case was reported in 1978.

A number here indicates the relevant volume of the law reports for that year. The number of volumes will depend on the number of cases reported for that year. Here the case is reported in the second volume. If the case year is in round brackets ( ) then the volume is the most important number.

These letters indicate the series of law reports that the case is reported in. This abbreviation relates to the Weekly Law Report series.

These final numbers indicate the page within the volume upon which the case begins. Here the case begins at page 2002.

Below is listed a number of examples of the most commonly found case citations and law series abbreviations, coupled with an explanation of what these citations mean:

Citation	Meaning
[2003] A.C. 556	Reported in the Appeal Cases for 2003 at page 556
[2001] 3 W.L.R. 93	Reported in the 3rd volume of the Weekly Law Reports for 2001 at page 93
[1997] 1 Q.B. 1039	Reported in the 1st volume of the Queen's Bench Reports for 1997 at page 1039
[2008] F.L.R. 56	Reported in the Family Law Reports for 2008 at page 56
(1978) 67 Cr. App. R. 14	Reported in the 67th volume of the Criminal Appeal Reports at page 14. The Criminal Appeal reports were identified by the volume number until post the 99th volume. After the completion of the 99th volume this series of case reports subsumed the more traditional way of reporting cases with the focus on the year as opposed to the volume number.
[2006] 2 Cr. App. R. 274	Reported in the 2nd volume of the Criminal Appeal Reports for 2006 at page 274 (The new style Criminal Appeal Report citation (note the square [ ] brackets))
[2004] 1 All E.R. 879	Reported in the 1st volume of the All England Reports for 2004 at page 879
(1997) 24 E.H.R.R. 39	The 39th case reported in the 24th volume of the European Human Rights Reports

3.2.6   Neutral citations

Due to the increased use of electronic reporting of cases the courts have further devised a new citation known as the 'neutral citation' (introduced January 11, 2001). These citations contain the information of the case that relates to the actual court hearing (as opposed to a law series). Neutral citations can be broken down into:

- the year the case was heard
- the court in which the case was heard
- the case number as heard by the court

So for example the neutral citation [2007] UKHL 13 stands for:

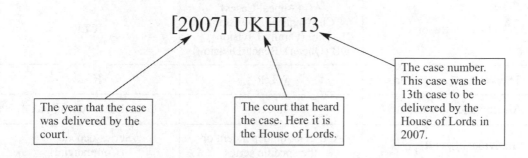

The common abbreviations of the neutral citations are as follows:

Abbreviation	Court
UKHL	United Kingdom House of Lords
UKPC	United Kingdom Privy Council
EWCA	England and Wales Court of Appeal (the abbreviation will normally be followed by either 'Crim' or 'Civ' so as to indicate whether it was heard under the Court of Appeals criminal or civil jurisdiction)
EWHC	England and Wales High Court

3.2.7   The case reporting hierarchy

Not every case that is heard within the justice system is reported; only those that are deemed to be of sufficient legal interest will make it into the case books. Those cases heard in the superior courts (so the House of Lords and Privy Council) will often be reported as they will set out some important rule of law or principle etc., that will be of use to future cases (by way of precedent). Often a single case can be found reported in a number of different law series and it is important to know which report of the case in which series is the most appropriate report to cite. There is a hierarchy of law reports, and both judges and lawyers alike adhere to the use of this hierarchy.

Series Title	Abbreviation	Publisher
The Law Reports	AC (Appeal Cases) Ch (Chancery Division) Fam (Family Division) QB (Queen's Bench Division)	ICLR
The Weekly Law Reports	W.L.R.	ICLR
All England Law Reports	All E.R.	Lexis Nexis (Commercial)
Individual Law Reports	Abbreviation dependent on the specific series	Series dependent (Commercial)

3.2.8   Incorporated Council of Law Reporting

The Incorporated Council of Law Reporting (ICLR) was established in 1865 with the object of:

> Preparation and publication, in a convenient form, at a moderate price, and under gratuitous Professional control, of [The Law] Reports of Judicial Decisions of the Superior and Appellate Courts in England
>
> (ICLR Memorandum and Articles of Association, 1870)

The ICLR is currently registered as a charity and it is a non-profit making organisation. It aims to report all cases that:

- introduce, or appear to introduce, a new principle or a new rule

- materially modify an existing principle or rule

- settle, or materially tend to settle, a question upon which the law is doubtful

- for any reason are peculiarly instructive

The guidelines for what should be contained in a case set out that a law report should be accurate, contain everything material and useful and be as concise as is consistent with these objectives. In particular the report should show the parties, the nature of the pleadings, the essential facts, the points contended by counsel and the grounds on which the judgment was based, as well as the judgment, decree, or order actually pronounced. The ICLR sets out that there is a universal view amongst judges that there are too many cases published per year and that therefore they are determined to only publish those cases that really matter and which create binding precedent.

Lord Woolf C.J., in the *Practice Direction (Judgments: Form and Citation) (Supreme Court)* [2001] 1 W.L.R. 194, stated in relation to the citation of judgments in court that:

For avoidance of doubt, it should be emphasised that both the High Court and the Court of Appeal require that where a case has been reported in the official Law Reports published by the Incorporated Council of Law Reporting for England and Wales it must be cited from that source. Other series may only be used when a case is not reported in the Law Reports.

Therefore the law reports published by the ICLR, and especially the Law Reports, are the preferable source to be cited wherever possible. The rationale behind this is that the judge and counsel in the case check the cases for their accuracy before they are published in the Law Reports. This ensures that the Law Reports provide accurate and accepted versions of the case. The Weekly Law Reports (or the 'Weeklies' as they are informally called) are also published by the ICLR but these are not double checked by the judge involved in the case before publication. This means that the Weeklies are often quicker to be published but that their accuracy cannot be guaranteed. Those cases published in the Weeklies will normally make it into the Law Reports after a while.

3.2.9 Commercial reports

The remainder of the law reports series are published for commercial purposes. The most commonly used commercially available law reporting series is the All England Law Reports, published by Lexis Nexis and these are readily found on the online legal databases, as well as in the law libraries up and down the country. The commercial law reports can be an excellent source to turn to, especially where the case under consideration is not on a principle of law that has found its way into the higher courts (so for cases which are reported in the Road Traffic Reports (R.T.R.), or a case that was heard in the Technology and Construction Court (TCC)) but is important nonetheless. Caution should be heeded when considering the commercial reports simply due to the possibility of issues of accuracy and if a case is reported both in Law Reports and a commercial report the Law Report should always be used as this will be viewed as the most authoritative source.

3.3 How to use the law (case analysis)

Once the student has found the law it is not always easy for them to then know what to do with it. A reported case will have some important element to it (decision and principle) as otherwise it would not have been reported. Being able to analyse a case so that the specific importance of an individual case can be identified is an essential skill to develop. To be able to assess whether a case is relevant and useful it is necessary to be able to extract three essential pieces of information from it (and what is meant by relevant and useful will wholly depend on the reasons for the case being referred to). These are the material facts, the legal issues and the *ratio decidendi*. The material facts of an individual case will not always be relevant to the matter in issue, as often it is simply the principle in the case that is pertinent and not how the principle arose. Below is an extract from the case of *R. v Cockburn* [2008] EWCA Crim 316 that will illustrate how to distil these key points from the case.

Regina v Cockburn

Case No: 2007/03792-C4

Court of Appeal (Criminal Division)

28 February 2008

[2008] EWCA Crim 316

2008 WL 546399

Before: The President of the Queen's Bench Division
Mr Justice Davis and Mr Justice David Clarke

Date: 28/02/2008, Hearing dates: 12th February 2008

On Appeal from the Crown Court at Maidstone Mr Recorder Wilson

Representation

- Mr M Magarian for the Appellant.
- Mr J. Higgs for the Crown.

Judgment

President of the Queen's Bench Division:

1   These are our reasons for dismissing the appeal by Nigel Cockburn against his conviction in the Crown Court at Maidstone. The statement of offence alleged setting a mantrap with intent, contrary to section 31 of the Offences against the Person Act 1861. The particulars were that between 1st January 2006 and 11th July 2006, the appellant set or placed, or caused to be set or placed, a mantrap or other engine calculated to destroy human life or inflict grievous bodily harm, with intent that the same or whereby the same may destroy or inflict grievous bodily harm on a trespasser or other person coming into contact therewith.

2   This offence is rarely charged. The question in this appeal was whether, having heard evidence from a defence expert, the Recorder was right to reject the submission that, as a matter of statutory construction, an undoubtedly dangerous contraption

---

positioned by the appellant on top of some farm equipment in a shed on his land was capable or not of falling within the ambit of section 31. The Recorder decided that it was so capable. He directed the jury accordingly. The jury concluded that the contraption was indeed an engine for the purposes of section 31 and that the necessary intent had been proved: hence this appeal.

3   Section 31 of the 1861 Act provides:

'Whosoever shall set or place, or cause to be set or placed, any spring-gun, man-trap, or other engine calculated to destroy human life or inflict grievous bodily harm, with intent that the same or whereby the same may destroy or inflict grievous bodily harm upon a trespasser or other person coming in contact therewith, shall be guilty . . . Provided that nothing in this section contained shall extend to make it illegal to set or place any gin or trap such as may have been or may be usually set or placed with the intent of destroying vermin: Provided also, that nothing in this section shall be deemed to make it unlawful to set or place, or cause to be set or placed, or to be continued set or placed, from sunset to sunrise, any spring-gun, man-trap, or other engine which shall be set or placed, or caused or continued to be set or placed in a dwelling house for the protection thereof.'

4   The contraption set by the appellant was neither a spring-gun nor a man-trap. The conviction could only have been sustained if it was an 'other engine calculated to destroy human life or inflict grievous bodily harm'. Briefly, it is a spiked metal object made from two pieces of heavy steel plate into which some 20 4-inch long nails, protruding at different angles, are welded. It was connected by a metal rod or wire to the roof frame of a shed on the appellant's land. Another wire connected it to the shed door. When the shed door was opened it was activated and the force of gravity caused it to swing downwards and catch the person entering through the door.

5   On 11 July 2006, in the course of a lawful investigation of the appellant's property, an army officer pushed open the shed door. As he did so, with good sense, he took the precaution of holding his arm across his face. The spiked object struck his forearm rather than his face. Two nails entered into his clothing, and a third punctured his forearm. His injuries could well have been very much more serious than they were.

5   It was submitted on behalf of the appellant that this object was not and could not be treated as an engine. The power needed to work it was applied exclusively by nature, gravity. No other form of stored energy or force was involved. This therefore was not a mechanical contrivance at all, and the decision of this court in *R v Munks* [1964] 1 Q.B. 304 provides clear authority for the proposition that if the object was not such a contrivance it could not be an 'other engine' for the purposes of section 31.

6   In *Munks* the appellant connected a wire from an electric light in the kitchen, through into the living room, and fastened it to the handle of the French window. He

fixed another wire leading from the kitchen so that it would hang down inside the window in such a way that anyone opening the window from the outside, and coming into contact with the hanging wire, would suffer a severe electric shock. The electric wires were deliberately arranged so as to create the risk of electric shock if an electric light switch happened to be switched on at the time. It was deliberately fixed by the appellant to prevent his wife getting into the house. The point at issue was whether the two wires fastened and draped at the window, bringing electricity to it when the kitchen switch was on, amounted to an 'engine' calculated to inflict grievous bodily harm. The appellant was convicted on the basis that it was, and he appealed arguing that the word 'engine' had two distinct meanings, one broader than the other. The court accepted the analysis that the broader meaning included a contrivance or device, and would extend to what was described as the electrical contrivance in the case. The narrower meaning however was equally recognised, and was limited to a mechanical contrivance or machine. By contrast with the broad approach taken by the court in *Allen v Thompson* [1970] L.R. 5 Q.B. 336, where section 3 of the Game Act 1831 was under consideration, the court adopted the narrower rather than the broader of the two possible meanings. In argument it was in effect conceded by the Crown that the word spring-gun and man-trap both referred to mechanical contrivances. Given that concession it was virtually inevitable that the court would conclude that the words 'or other engine' must mean 'other mechanical contrivance'. It was decided that although the arrangements of these wires amounted to an electrical contrivance, it did not constitute a mechanical contrivance, and was therefore not an 'other engine' for the purposes of section 31.

7   On the face of it any engine calculated to kill or inflict grievous bodily harm falls within the ambit of section 31. The Oxford English Dictionary, among other descriptions, describes an engine as a 'mechanical contrivance, machine, implement, tool'. Something of the breadth of its meaning at the time when the Act came into force is identified in the Dictionary itself where, among other references, we find a pair of scissors described as a 'little engine' in the *Rape of the Lock* (1712–1714) and a description of 'engines of restraint and pain' at the victim's feet in *Death Slavery* (1866). None of these references dilutes or could dilute the authority of *Munk*s, although they suggest that the Crown's argument in that case was more constrained than it perhaps should have been.

8   In these circumstances, there is no reason for giving (and every reason, given the evident purpose behind the legislation, for not giving) the words 'spring-gun' or 'man-trap' or 'other engine' an unduly narrow meaning. In *Munks*, it is true that a very wide definition of the word 'engine' was rejected, and in the context of the electrical device with which it was concerned the word 'engine' was said to connote a mechanical contrivance. However we reject the argument implicit in the submissions that *Munks* was intended to or could redefine the statutory language of section 31 by replacing the words 'other engine' with 'other mechanical contrivance'. The court cannot re-write

statutory language which has been unamended for nearly 200 years. In any event the words 'mechanical contrivance', as used in *Munks*, are not to be applied restrictively so as to lead to the exclusion of a contraption which falls within the ambit of the statute. On the rare occasions when this question arises for decision, the object itself as well as the manner, if any, in which it may be activated should be examined pragmatically to see whether, looked at overall, it falls within the statutory language. In *Munks*, the placing of cables on or by a door through which an electric current could pass was held not to be sufficient of a mechanical contrivance to be an 'engine'. In the present case, using ordinary language, the contraption was certainly a contrivance. It was mechanical, since as a mechanism, it was triggered into dangerous movement by inadvertent pressure on a wire or string. In short therefore it is properly described as a mechanical contrivance or machine, and it unquestionably is an 'other engine' for the purposes of section 31 of the 1861 Act. For these reasons the main ground of appeal failed.

3.3.1   The material facts

When analysing a case it is important to be able to identify which facts in the case are material (important) and which facts are immaterial. There are often set out in the judgment a number of facts that were important to the specific case (maybe even a few pages worth) but all of these facts will not necessarily be described as 'material facts'. Material facts are generally described as those facts that were vital to deciding the outcome of the case and they may include both matters of fact and matters of law. They link in directly with the issue and the *ratio* of the case and if they were omitted or changed then the outcome of the case (the *ratio*) or the legal issue would be different.

To illustrate what could be considered as material facts look at the list below. These facts have all been taken from the case of *Cockburn* but not all are material. Attempt to select those facts which could be viewed as 'material'.

3.3.1.1   Selecting the material facts

- The appellant was convicted at Maidstone Crown Court.

- The appellant's name was Nigel Cockburn.

- The appellant was convicted of an offence under s.31 of the Offences Against the Person Act 1861, which states: "Whosoever shall set or place, or cause to be set or placed, any spring-gun, man-trap, or other engine calculated to destroy human life or inflict grievous bodily harm, with intent that the same or whereby the same may destroy or inflict grievous bodily harm upon a trespasser or other person coming in contact therewith, shall be guilty [of an offence]".

- The offence is rarely charged.

- The appellant had set a contraption, which was neither a spring-gun nor a man-trap, which was calculated to destroy life or inflict grievous bodily harm.

- The contraption was a spiked metal object from which some nails protruded.

- The nails were four inches long.

- The contraption was connected by a metal rod or wire to the roof frame of a shed on the appellant's land.

- The contraption was connected to the door of a shed on the appellant's land.

- The contraption was set as such that when the shed door was open the contraption was activated and the contraption would swing down towards to the door, striking any person who was entering the shed at that time.

- The appellant submitted that this object was not and could not be treated as an engine. The power needed to work it was applied exclusively by nature, gravity.

- The victim was an army officer who had lawfully attended the appellant's property on the July 11, 2006.

- The victim had opened the shed door and had been hit by the contraption, but had managed to shield their body and face so that the injuries were only inflicted upon the victim's arm.

- Two nails entered into his clothing, and a third punctured his forearm. His injuries could well have been very much more serious than they were.

3.3.1.2 The material facts of *Cockburn*

The facts that are material to the case of *Cockburn* are as follows and the reasons as to why they are material will become clearer once the legal issue has been identified.

- The appellant was convicted of an offence under s.31 OAPA 1861 which states "Whosoever shall set or place, or cause to be set or placed, any spring-gun, man-trap, or other engine calculated to destroy human life or inflict grievous bodily harm, with intent that the same or whereby the same may destroy or inflict grievous bodily harm upon a trespasser or other person coming in contact therewith, shall be guilty [of an offence]".

- The appellant had set a contraption, which was neither a spring-gun nor a man-trap, which was calculated to destroy life or inflict grievous bodily harm.

- The contraption was made from a spiked metal object, from which nails protruded.

- The contraption was connected to the door of a shed on the appellant's land.

- The contraption was set as such that when the shed door was open the contraption was activated and the contraption would swing down towards to the door, striking any person who was entering the shed at that time.

- The victim had opened the shed door and had been hit by the contraption, but had managed to shield their body and face so that the injuries were only inflicted upon the victim's arm.

As can be seen many of the facts identified above (in the 'Selecting the material facts' heading at 3.3.1.1) are not material to the case decision. It does not matter whether the victim was an army officer or a local vet, his profession is not relevant to the legal issue. It is not important to identify whether the incident occurred on July 11, 2006, it could have easily have occurred on November 5, 2007, or December 24, 1988. The court are not concerned with the fact that the nails entered his clothing, or that his forearm was punctured, they are only concerned with the fact that he had been injured and that these injuries had the potential to be much worse. It would not change anything had the appellant been convicted at Leicester Crown Court instead of Maidstone Crown Court and the appellant's name is not relevant, as if he had been called Chris Cringle this would not have changed the outcome and principles of the case. As stated above the material facts are directly linked to the legal issue and the *ratio*. So what is a legal issue and what is the legal issue in the case of *Cockburn*?

3.3.2   The legal issue

A legal issue can be described as the question that the court have been asked to resolve. The legal issue will be termed as a question and it goes to the crux of the case. Often the legal issue is quite easy to identify as the court will make a statement such as 'The question in this appeal is . . . ', or 'We have been asked to consider whether . . . '. Frequently the court will set out the legal issue clearly in the terms of the 'certified question' (so they may state 'The certified question in this case is as to whether . . . '). A point to note here is that there can also be more than one legal issue in a case, there can often be found two or three legal issues that all need to be resolved by the courts, and although they may be interrelated they will have their own specific focus.

A good example of a legal issue being set out clearly and concisely (and quite helpfully) by the court can be found in the House of Lords case of *R. v Kennedy (No.2)* [2007] UKHL 38. In *Kennedy* the appellant had been convicted of manslaughter. The facts of the case are that he prepared a syringe of heroin and handed it to the victim, who immediately injected himself and returned the syringe to the appellant. The appellant then left the room. The victim died shortly thereafter as a result of the injection and the appellant was charged with supplying a class A drug and manslaughter. He was convicted on both counts. The appellant then appealed to the Court of Appeal on the manslaughter conviction but his appeal was dismissed as the court held that even though he had not physically injected the victim with the drug he had been acting jointly with the victim in the administering of the drug by preparing and supplying him with the syringe. The appellant then appealed to the House of Lords contending that the victim was an autonomous individual who had injected the heroin by his own free will and therefore the appellant had not caused the victim to administer the drug to himself and therefore should be acquitted. The legal issue in the case is found in the speech of Lord Bingham (at para.2) where he states:

> The question certified by the Court of Appeal (Criminal Division) for the opinion of the House neatly encapsulates the question raised by this appeal:

"When is it appropriate to find someone guilty of manslaughter where that person has been involved in the supply of a class A controlled drug, which is then freely and voluntarily self-administered by the person to whom it was supplied, and the administration of the drug then causes his death?"

The issue to be determined is easy to identify, it is the question that needs to be decided so that the overall decision as to whether the appellants appeal will succeed or fail. The legal issue also provides a good pointer for when considering whether a decision in a case is binding upon a future case or not. If the issue concerns the same matters then it may well have to be taken into account in later cases on that point.

Not every court will set out the legal issue so concisely and succinctly and this often means that the legal issue in the case has to be determined by a process of elimination and deduction. For example if we return now the case study of *Cockburn* it can be seen that there is no specific part of the judgment that clearly sets out the legal issue. This means that an educated guess must be taken as to what the legal issue in the case was.

From looking at the judgment we can deduce that the case is not about what constitutes grievous bodily harm. Although the case is based on the Offences against the Person Act 1861 it does not consider whether the injuries suffered by the victim amount to grievous bodily harm (this is why the fact that the victim's clothes and forearm were punctured was not a material one). Further it can be assumed upon reading the case that the issue was not as to whether a person is allowed to set up a booby trap to protect his land from trespassers. If that were the issue then more would have been made about the fact that the victim had attended the appellant's property to lawfully search the premises.

The issue in the case revolves around the statutory provision that the appellant was convicted under, namely s.31. Section 31 sets out that:

Whosoever shall set or place, or cause to be set or placed, any spring-gun, man-trap, or other engine calculated to destroy human life or inflict grievous bodily harm, with intent that the same or whereby the same may destroy or inflict grievous bodily harm upon a trespasser or other person coming in contact therewith, shall be guilty [of an offence].

The court concluded that the contraption set by the appellant was not a spring-gun or a man-trap. The only other factor that could therefore be under consideration by the court was as to whether the contraption was an 'engine' as defined under the Act. If consideration is given to para.5 of the case it can be seen that the appellant in the case submitted that the contraption could not be an engine as it was not a mechanical contrivance and worked purely by the forces of gravity. The submission was based upon the authority of the case of *Munks* [1964] 1 Q.B. 304, which provided for the proposition that if the object was not such a contrivance it could not be an 'other engine' for the purposes of s.31.

Therefore the logical conclusion to come to after analysing the case would be that the legal issue in the case was:

Whether an 'engine' under s.31 OAPA 1861 had to be a mechanical contrivance.

It is not an easy issue to initially identify but with a little perseverance and the use of logical and considered deduction it is possible to conclude as to what the question was that the court were trying to resolve. If the issue is not immediately apparent (as in the case of *Cockburn*) it is worth considering the questions of 'what is the case concerned with?' and 'what are the court trying to decide?' so as to try and pinpoint what the specific legal issue is.

After determining the legal issue it is always prudent to go back and check the material facts identified so as to ensure that they are actually material to the legal issue. For example, in the case of *Cockburn* if the fact that the nails were four inches long had originally been selected as a material fact then it is at this point that it would hopefully become apparent that this fact is actually not a material one as the legal issue is concerned with whether the contraption had to be mechanical or not, not how lethal it was.

3.3.3 Identifying the *ratio decidendi*

What is meant by the term *ratio decidendi* has been discussed in detail in Chapter 2. What will now be considered is how a *ratio* can be identified. A common misconception is that the *ratio* is considered to be the overall decision in the case, so whether the appeal was allowed or dismissed or whether the conviction was quashed or upheld, and although the overall decision is certainly important (especially to the parties involved) it does not form part of the precedent created by the case. The *ratio* is essentially the court's reasoning behind their decision (why they came to the conclusion that they did) and their answer to the question (the legal issue) before them.

Unfortunately there is no clear part in the case where the judge sets out the *ratio*, there is no heading of '*Ratio*' found within a case, nor will the judge show consideration to the those who will later read his speech and try to distil the principles from within it by saying 'and the *ratio* of this case is . . . '. Finding the *ratio* can often feel like trying to find a needle in a haystack, especially when new to the law, but it does become easier over time with practice and experience. The *ratio* is really the opinion of the judge as to the answer to the legal issue. If there is more than one judge handing down their decision then there may well be more than one *ratio* in the case (each judge may have their own different opinion as to the reasoning to the overall conclusion); in fact even a decision from a single judge can provide for more than one *ratio* (often confusingly). Take for example the question of whether a school is good or not. One parent whose child goes to the school may say that the school is good because their child is happy there, another parent may say that the school is good because the teachers are all engaged in with the pupils. A person who has no connection with the school may determine that the school is good because they perform well in the league tables or a pupil who attends the school may conclude that the school is good because they study subjects that they like and because all their friends go there. The overall collective answer to the question (is the school good?) is that, yes the school is good, but each person asked has their own individual opinion(s) as to what actually makes the school good (they each provide their own *ratio*).

If we return to the decision of the House of Lords in *Kennedy* the court answered the legal issue by stating:

The answer to the certified question is: 'In the case of a fully-informed and responsible adult, never.' The appeal must be allowed and the appellant's conviction for manslaughter quashed.

In *Kennedy* the House of Lords held that to establish the crime of unlawful act manslaughter, it had to be shown that the defendant had committed an unlawful act, which was criminal in nature, and that it was a significant cause of the death (the elements of the offence). The court concluded that the criminal law generally assumed the existence of free will and that informed adults of sound mind were to be treated as autonomous beings, able to make their own decisions on how to act. Therefore a defendant could not to be treated as having caused the victim to act in a certain way if the victim made a voluntary and informed decision to act in that manner. In *Kennedy* the court concluded that the victim had freely and voluntarily administered the injection to himself and that the appellant had not helped in the administration of the injection, nor had the appellant and the victim acted together as the heroin had been self-administered by the victim. The overall decision of the case was that the appeal should be allowed but the reasoning behind why it should (the *ratio*) is far more complex than just a simple yes or no answer.

Returning now to the case study of *Cockburn*, here the *ratio* of the case (in the author's opinion) is as follows:

> That an 'engine' under the s.31 OAPA did not have to be a mechanical contrivance as, if this is had been what Parliament intended then they would have stated so in the legislation. (This is the answer to the general question together with the reasoning for the answer.)

> However, the contraption in the instant cases did amount to a mechanical contrivance as the mechanism was triggered by the opening of the shed door, upon which gravity then took over, and therefore it fell firmly within the meaning of 'engine' under the statute. (This is a more case specific *ratio,* which relates directly to the material facts of the case.)

A way in which the accuracy of the *ratio* can be determined is to consider it alongside the legal issue to see if they match. Does the *ratio* answer the legal issue? Does it set out the reasons for the answer? If the answer is yes, then it is likely that the *ratio* has been correctly identified; if the answer is no then it is time to return to the case, check the material facts and the legal issue, and then reconsider the case to see how the question raised was ultimately answered.

3.4   Finding and using legislation

All legislation passed by Parliament is catalogued by the Office of Public Sector Information (OPSI) and copies of the legislation are freely available online through Her Majesty's Stationary Office (HMSO), which is now part of the OPSI.

Statute law (or Acts of Parliament) can also be found in hard copy in the library. There are many texts that are solely concerned with providing the relevant statutory provisions for a specific area of law. For example, Blackstones (published by OUP) publish an entire series of Statute Books which comprehensively covers all topics from Criminal Law and Family Law through to Medical and Public Law. Each statute book will contain all the pertinent and necessary statutes for that area of law (so in a Family Law statute book there will be reproduced the relevant statutory provisions on divorce, financial matters, child care law and adoption etc.). As well as the individual statute books there is also the *Halsbury's* series, which sets out all the laws of England and Wales within one book.

Online sources will generally hold all the relevant statutory provisions in their database and this is where the online sources come into their own (although do not forget the comments made above about the usefulness of the hard copy sources) as it is possible to search for the exact section and/or subsection that is required without having to trawl through pages and pages of irrelevant sections.

To illustrate how to find a specific statutory provision online we will once again return to the Westlaw UK database. The focus of the search will be on the statutory defence of provocation for murder.

To search specifically for Legislation it is advisable to go to the link entitled Legislation (the arrow with the dotted line on the screen below), although simply un-ticking all of the boxes on the left hand side of the screen except for 'Legislation', will allow you to perform a general search by way of the search box on the Westlaw UK main home page (below).

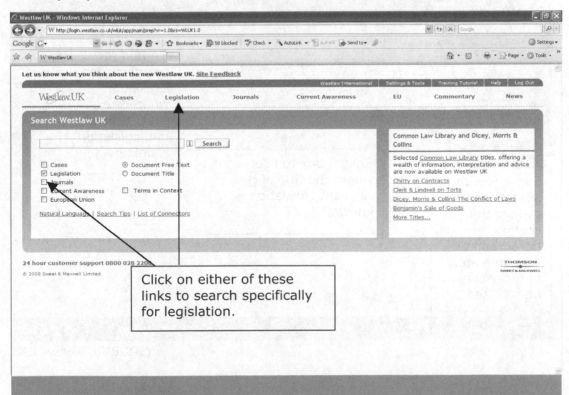

(SOURCE: Westlaw UK)

If the exact title of the Legislation is not known then the 'Free Text' box can be used to input related words so that a general search is performed. For example if the required legislation concerned the defence of provocation for murder then the term 'provocation' could be typed in here. This would then bring up a list of related provisions and each would have to be searched through manually to find the specific section required. For example with the term 'provocation' 16 results are returned and each one would have to be looked at individually so as to identify the relevant provision.

If the exact title of the Legislation were known then this could be typed into the 'Act/SI Title' box (for example here the Homicide Act 1957). If the search were conducted with the term the 'Homicide Act 1957' then only that specific Act would be returned by the search engine. The box below shows an example of the different methods that can be used to search for one particular source.

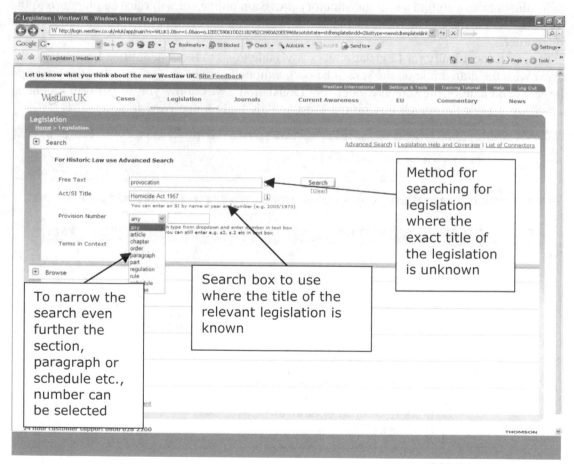

(SOURCE: Westlaw UK)

Clicking on the link entitled 'Arrangement of Act' (see box below for an illustration) will then allow access to what is effectively the contents page of the Act. The different sections will be set out in a list (s.1, s.2, s.3 etc.), each with a link that can be clicked upon to access that specific individual section.

Westlaw UK is a relatively helpful online database, as if a certain section has been repealed (removed from the statute books) or if there are amendments pending to a certain section or sections then these will be highlighted on the contents page (Arrangement of Act), which will provide an indication as to the legislation's status. A red 'R' means that the section has been repealed and an '!' means that amendments are pending. This helps to ensure that only up to date legislation is used.

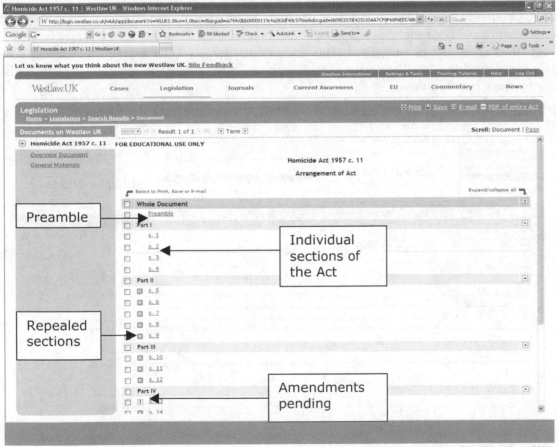

(SOURCE: Westlaw UK)

3.4.1 Referring to legislation

There are a number of different ways that legislation can be referred to. The usual way of referring to an Act is by what is known as its 'short title'. The short title of the Act currently under discussion is the 'Homicide Act 1957'. However, an Act can also be referred to by its 'Long title' or 'Preamble', as well as its 'Chapter number'. The Long title or Preamble sets out the purpose of the Act (in the case of the Homicide Act 1957 this was to make amendments to the law relating to homicide). Long titles used to be far more complex and informative, some running to a number of paragraphs, whereas now the method of referencing to the Long title has been reduced dramatically and, as a result, although they are still used they no longer contain such a large amount of information.

The 'Chapter number' is an interesting historical remnant as to how the law was traditionally referred to. Originally Acts of Parliament were bound into a single book for each year; so all the laws passed in a specific year (say 1957) would be bound together to create one large volume containing all the law for that year. Each Act added to the book over the course of the year would be assigned a Chapter number and this related to the order in which the laws were made during that year. So the Homicide Act 1957 would have been the 11th statute passed in 1957. Originally Acts of Parliament were generally referred to by their chapter number only and so it would have been said that a defendant had contravened s.1 of the 11th Chapter for 1957, rather than s.1 of the Homicide Act. This tradition has largely fallen by the wayside and now only the short title is really referred to (although in America they still continue to refer to the law by the Chapter number).

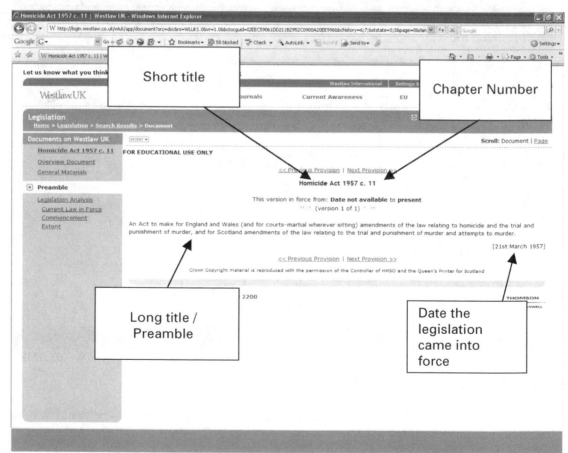

(SOURCE: Westlaw UK)

Returning now to the Arrangement of the Act (or the contents page) it can be seen that each individual section of the Act has its own hyperlink, which if clicked upon will take the reader to that specific section of the Act. As we have been considering the defence of provocation it would be useful to follow this to its logical conclusion and look at the actual law (within the statute) governing this defence. The defence of provocation is found within s.3 of the Homicide Act 1957 and clinking on s.3 would bring up the current in force law on provocation as a defence to murder (see screen below). As can be seen here there is only one section (with no further subsections) which sets out the elements (the current law) required to argue provocation as a defence to murder.

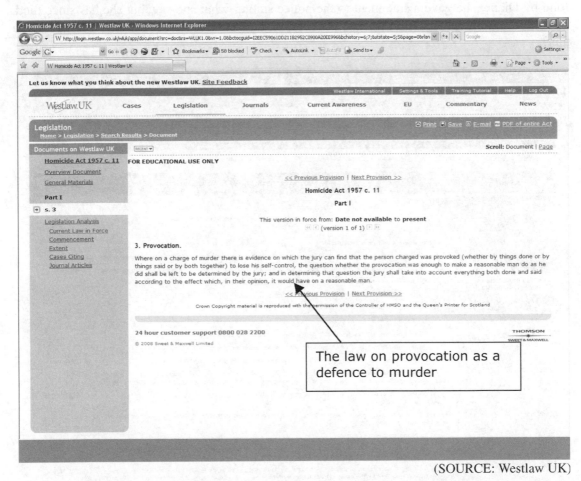

The law on provocation as a defence to murder

(SOURCE: Westlaw UK)

3.4.2 Reading a statute

It is relatively easy to read a statutory provision that only has one section (e.g. s.3 Homicide Act 1957 above) but matters become more complex where a single section then has a number of subsections, each dealing with different matters and situations. When a statutory provision has a number of subsections it is crucial to ensure that the correct section and subsection are cited when referring to them. It may be that one subsection is not applicable to the circumstances whilst another is highly relevant; citing the incorrect section and subsection in court could have dramatic consequences (although it is more likely that the judge or another lawyer would point out the mistake so it may only result in embarrassment, which is still bad enough). Take for example the provisions found within s.116 of the Criminal Justice Act 2003 (CJA 2003) (shown in the box below). The CJA 2003, as a complete statute, is notorious for its bad drafting and its sections can at times seem convoluted and difficult to understand as they tend to include a lot of detail. Section 116 concerns the admissibility (allowing) of evidence into a criminal court when the witness (whose evidence it is) is not available. E.g. Brenda witnessed the murder of John by Diane, she gave a statement to the police stating what she saw but she has since died. At John's trial the prosecution want to adduce Brenda's statement. What does s.116 say about this?

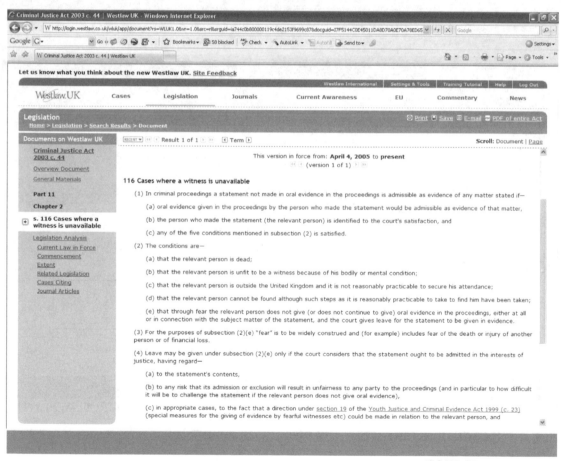

(SOURCE: Westlaw UK)

Section 116(1) sets out that such a statement as described above can be admitted as evidence so long as the person could have given the evidence personally in court (subject to the usual rules of evidence), that they have been identified to the court's satisfaction (subsection (b)) and that one of the conditions in subsection (2) have been satisfied. Brenda has died and so the relevant condition can be found under s.116(2)(a). If this specific subsection is cited then there should be no issue with respect to allowing the evidence into court, but if by accident s.116(2)(c) was cited instead (the relevant person is outside of the UK and they cannot attend court) then there would be questions raised as to why she could not attend; this could be slightly awkward and sensitive considering the fact that Brenda is dead. The exact provision relied upon has to be identified. Also simply stating that the evidence could be admitted under s.116 would not be sufficient, as this would not satisfactorily identify the reason behind why Brenda is not able to give evidence in person. When considering statutory provisions, exactness is the key.

3.4.3 Explanatory notes

To accompany the enactment of new legislation Parliament now produce explanatory notes to help explain the new provisions and the intentions of Parliament behind its creation. These explanatory notes help to set the scene as to why the legislation as a whole has been created, as well as explaining the details and rationale behind the provision within the Act. For example the summary of the explanatory notes for the Criminal Justice Act 2003 states that:

In July 2002 the Government published a White Paper outlining its plans for the criminal justice system, from crime prevention through to the punishment and rehabilitation of offenders. *Justice for All* (Cm 5563) focused particularly on reforms to court procedure and sentencing, to make trials faster and to deliver clear, consistent and appropriate sentencing. On these issues the White Paper built on the proposals in two consultation documents: *Review of the Criminal Courts of England and Wales by Sir Robin Auld* (2001) and *Making Punishment Work: report of a review of the sentencing framework of England and Wales (2001)* by John Halliday.

This Act is intended to introduce reforms in these two areas. With regard to court procedure, the Act aims to improve the management of cases through the courts by involving the Crown Prosecution Service in charging decisions, by reforming the system for allocating cases to court, and by increasing magistrates' sentencing powers so that fewer cases have to go to the Crown Court. It will enable action to be taken to reduce breaches of bail by introducing a new presumption against bail in certain circumstances.

The Act is designed to ensure that criminal trials are run more efficiently and to reduce the scope for abuse of the system. It will reform the rules on advance disclosure of evidence and will allow for judge-alone trial in cases involving threats and intimidation of juries, and paves the way for judge-alone trial in exceptionally long, complex serious fraud cases. It will ensure the wider involvement of the community as a whole by reforming rules on jury service. Rules on evidence will be changed to allow the use of previous convictions where relevant, and to allow the use of reported (hearsay) evidence where there is good reason why the original source cannot be present, or where the judge otherwise considers it would be appropriate. It will enable any witness to give evidence using live links. A right of appeal for the prosecution against judicial decisions to direct or order an acquittal before the jury has been asked to consider the evidence will be introduced to balance the defendant's right of appeal against both conviction and sentence. The Act will also make it possible in certain very serious cases for a retrial to take place despite an earlier acquittal if there is new and compelling evidence of an accused's guilt.

The notes here help to give a clear indication as to the driving force behind the Act and they can be invaluable to those attempting to understand and interpret it. When considering the detail provided regarding the admissibility of absent witnesses (which are applicable to the example concerning Brenda above) the notes state that:

> The provisions in [...] are intended, so far as necessary, to codify the law relating to the admissibility of out of court statements in criminal proceedings. They aim to simplify the law and to provide greater certainty as to the circumstances when such evidence will be admitted. The main provisions [...] remove the old common law rule against the admission of [such] evidence and provide that such evidence will be admissible (on behalf of the prosecution and defence) provided certain safeguards are met.

Explanatory notes can be an extremely useful tool, and they are relied upon increasingly by the judiciary in their efforts to interpret legislation. In fact it is not uncommon to come across a case where the judge has turned to the explanatory notes to a statute as an aid to statutory interpretation (see 2.8.3).

3.5   Summary

(a)   The law (statutes, cases and other sources) can be found both online and in the library. Most educational institutions will have a well-stocked law library and will subscribe to a number of online legal databases, such as Westlaw UK and Lexis Nexis.

(b)   Students are advised to make the most of the online databases but it is stressed that the hard copies found within the libraries should not be forgotten about and should be used on a regular basis so that valuable research skills can be developed.

(c)   The case names are helpful to identify the type of proceedings, the parties in the case and their respective roles.

(d)   Citations indicate where a reported case can be found. The citations set out the year, volume, law reports series and page number where the case is reported. Neutral citations are used to identify the case by their court hearing. There is a hierarchy of law report series, with the Law Reports (published by the ICLR) being the most authoritative, going down to the commercial individual law reports.

(e)   The material facts of a case are those facts that are vital to the outcome and the reasoning behind the case. Details such as party names and dates are not generally material and the material facts often need to be identified by a process of elimination, which can involve taking into consideration the legal issues and *ratio decidendi* of the case.

(f) The legal issue is the question posed to the court that they are required to resolve. This can often be identified by the use of the phrase 'the certified question', or by the fact that it is set out clearly as a specific question. However, there are many cases where the legal issue is not readily identifiable and the case will require careful scrutiny to deduce it.

(g) The *ratio decidendi* is the legal reasoning behind the decision in a case. There may be more than one *ratio* per case and even per judge. The *ratio* is really the judge's opinion as to why they have come to the conclusion that they have. The *ratio* should match up with both the legal issue and the material facts.

(h) Legislation can be referred to by a number of different methods, such as the short title (the most common reference), the long title/preamble and the chapter number. When using a statute it is important to be very specific when referencing it.

(i) Many statutes are supplemented by explanatory notes that are published by Parliament to aid the understanding and interpretation of a statute. Reference to explanatory notes is becoming more common place in respect of statutory interpretation by the judiciary.

3.6   Self-test questions

1. Authoritative case law can be found:

   (a) online
   (b) in the library
   (c) in a journal
   (d) all of the above

2. The case name *Charleston v DPP* means that:

   (a) Charleston is appealing and the DPP is the defendant
   (b) the DPP is appealing and Charleston is the defendant
   (c) Charleston is being prosecuted by the DPP
   (d) the Attorney-General is clarifying a point of law upon Charleston's conviction

3. The citation [2000] 5 Q.B. 202 means:

   (a) the case was the 5th case reported for the Queen's Bench Division for 2000
   (b) the case was the 202nd case reported for the Queen's Bench Division for 2005
   (c) the case was reported in the 5th volume of the Queen's Bench Reports for 2000 at page 202

(d) the case was the 202nd case reported in the 5th volume of the Queen's Bench Reports for 2000

4. The All E.R. reports are:

(a) the most authoritative law reporting series
(b) the least authoritative law reporting series
(c) published by the ICLR
(d) commercially published

5. The most commonly used reference title for legislation is the:

(a) chapter number
(b) short title
(c) long title
(d) preamble

3.7 Further reading

J. Holland and J. Webb (2003) *Learning Legal Rules,* 5th edn, Oxford University Press.

R. Huxley-Binns, L. Riley and C. Turner (2005) *Unlocking Legal Learning*, Hodder Arnold Chapters 4 and 5.

4 The legal profession

The landscape in respect of the legal profession is undergoing a monumental change at present. It is doing so quietly and quite unassumingly, but the change will have an impact upon every aspect of the profession and may eventually change the face of the profession from as we know it today. The change began to occur over twenty years ago, but it has, on the whole, slipped by unnoticed by the public and many legal professionals alike. The changes may begin to affect the way that legal education is provided and it will certainly affect the professional life of those who are now beginning to think about pursuing a career in the law.

This chapter will discuss the state of the legal profession as it is today, consideration will be given to the legal personnel who work within the system, the changes that have occurred so far to date and the way that the future of the profession is being shaped.

4.1 Legal personnel

There are approximately 400,000 people who work within the criminal justice system in England and Wales. A large number of these people work within an administrative capacity (i.e. court clerks and listing officers) or within one of the peripheral agencies involved in the maintaining of justice (i.e. the Probation Service and the Prison Service). However a large number of people included in this figure are those who are known colloquially as the 'legal professionals'. This rather large title encompasses those who are viewed as the traditional 'lawyers' of the profession (solicitors and barristers), as well as those individuals who work within the system, such as paralegals and legal executives, who are present in high numbers, but are less well known by lay people outside of the legal world.

4.1.1 Paralegals

Within the hundreds and thousands of law firms up and down the country there will be regularly found employees who hold the title of a 'paralegal'. A paralegal is person who carries out a lot of the basic work for a law firm. They generally undertake the type of work that does not require a highly paid (and therefore expensive) solicitor to do. Paralegals may or may not be legally qualified, as there is no specific requirement that they have to be so qualified. Quite often undergraduate law degree students will work as a paralegal either during their study vacations whilst undertaking their degree or, on a more full time basis after they have completed their degree and are considering what their next career step will be.

The exact nature of the work they undertake will depend entirely on the focus of the firm that they are employed by. If the firm is a criminal defence solicitors then a paralegal may find themselves regularly visiting prisons to take statements from a client, or they may often be found sitting behind a barrister in court taking down notes for the case file. If the firm deals with matters of personal injury then a paralegal may be responsible for meeting clients and taking down details of their claim, they may be required to fill out the necessary forms required for a Conditional Fee Arrangement (CFA) (see 11.3 for further detail on CFA's) or they may be charged with instructing counsel or expert witnesses. If conveyancing (buying and selling houses) is the main staple of the firm's work then a paralegal may be responsible for taking instructions from the clients, conducting the relevant searches on the property and making an application for the title deeds etc. As can be seen the work covered by a paralegal is not particularly complex and as the issues are generally straightforward it is more appropriate that it is carried out by them rather than a highly paid fee-earner.

4.1.2 Legal executives

Another type of employee that is regularly found within law firms is a Legal Executive. Legal Executives are Fellows and Members of the Institution of Legal Executives, which is otherwise known as 'ILEX'. ILEX was established in 1963, with the support of the Law Society, and it describes itself as being recognised as 'the third branch of the legal profession'. They provide training and regulation for non-solicitor staff employed in fee earning work so that these staff can be recognised for their skills and knowledge and so that the standards within the profession can be improved.

ILEX currently has over 22,000 members (Legal Executives) and a Legal Executive is a qualified lawyer (although they are not a solicitor or a barrister) who specialises in a particular area of law. To become a Member of ILEX an individual must undergo the two-stage academic training process. To be eligible to start qualifying as a Legal Executive an individual must have passed at least 4 GCSE's at grade C or above. The academic qualification provided by ILEX then takes a person through A-level standard (Level 3 ILEX Professional Diploma in Law) and then degree standard education (Level 6 ILEX Higher Professional Diploma in Law) to the point where they are competent to work within their specialist area of law as a fee-earner. ILEX requires their Fellows to have successfully completed the ILEX Professional Qualifications in Law and to have worked under the supervision of a qualified solicitor in legal practice, a company or a government department for a period of no less than five years, including a minimum of two years after passing all their qualifications. Once the individual has successfully completed these educational and vocational requirements they will become a Fellow of ILEX and they will be issued with an annual practising certificate. After becoming either a Member or Fellow of ILEX there is then a further option to continue on and take the one-year-long Common Professional Examination (a postgraduate law course often called a Graduate Diploma in Law) to eventually become a fully qualified solicitor.

Essentially becoming a Legal Executive is simply a different route that can be taken to become a solicitor from that of a traditional law degree. To become a Member of ILEX takes approximately four years to complete and this is done by a combination of studying and working in practice. The advantages of becoming qualified via ILEX are that a student can work and earn a wage as the same time as studying, thereby reducing the potential for accruing debt whilst also gaining valuable work experience. Also if a person has become a full Fellow of

ILEX then they do not have to undergo a training contract (see 4.1.3.2) on completion of their Common Professional Examination, as they will have already satisfied the work placement requirement when becoming a Fellow of ILEX.

Qualifying as a legal professional by way of ILEX is not to be considered as a second rate option. Members and Fellows of ILEX are often responsible for the mainstay of a solicitors' firms work, and the Law Society, who supported its initial establishment, recognises the quality of the training provided by ILEX and describes the process as 'lengthy, demanding and challenging'.

Figure 4.1 ILEX career routes

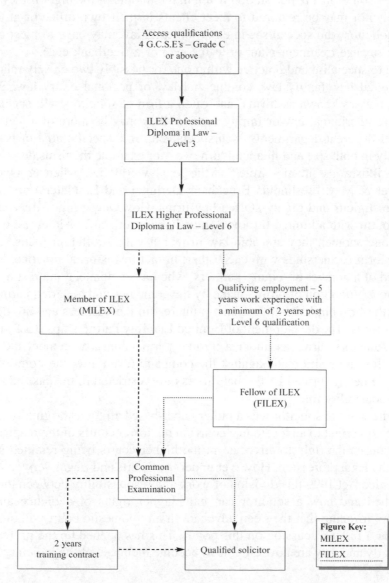

4.1.3 Solicitors

Solicitors are often perceived to be the front line of the legal profession by members of the public. This is generally because solicitors are the first port of call for anyone considering undertaking any form of legal action or who are being prosecuted or being litigated against. The public can directly access solicitors and as such the majority of their work involves face-to-face contact with their clients or contact via the telephone or by way of email and fax. The nature and place of the client contact will generally be dependent upon the focus of the work undertaken by the particular solicitor. For example a criminal solicitor may be required to see their clients at a prison or in a police station (even in the middle of the night if they are on call), a commercial solicitor may be required to meet clients in their own office or at the company premises and a solicitor who specialises in environmental law may have to meet clients out in the field (so at a sewage treatment plant or at the side of a riverbank etc.).

Solicitors tend to specialise and practice within one (or possibly two closely related) areas of law such as criminal law, family law, commercial law or personal injury law. Solicitors are employed by businesses known as 'firms' and often a firm of solicitors will specialise in only one area of law (e.g. criminal law or family law), or they may be more of a general firm and have a number of different departments each specialising in a specific area of law. Firms can vary tremendously in both size and financial turn over, for example the firms described as being members of the illustrious 'magic-circle' of the legal world (i.e. Allen & Overy, Clifford Chance, Slaughter & May, Freshfields Bruckhaus Deringer and Linklaters) are multi-million pound, highly-prestigious and highly-staffed law firms. However, a high street law firm may only be a small outfit with a limited turnover and a handful of staff. Neither are more superior or inferior than one another, they are both law firms but with a different focus.

Solicitors can form partnerships with each other; in fact this is usual practice, as most firms will be comprised of a number of 'equity partners' who have a financial interest in the business and are entitled to a proportion of profits made by the company, and 'salaried partners' who are paid a salary by the firm but have no ownership interest in the business and are not eligible to any share of the profits. The development of Limited Liability Partnerships (LLP) is also on the increase within solicitors' firms as under a normal partnership arrangement the partners are personally liable for any claim made against the company (even after the point of retirement) however, under the newly formed LLP's liability is only restricted to the cases that the partner had personal responsibility for.

Traditionally the work of solicitor was a rather paper-based affair, as originally they only had rights of audience (the right to advocate in a court) in the lower courts of the magistrates' courts and the county courts; the right to advocate in the higher courts being retained solely by the barrister side of the legal profession. However under the Courts and Legal Service Act 1990 and the Access to Justice Act 1999 this division of work and responsibility between the professions has been abolished and now a solicitor can gain higher rights of audience and become a solicitor-advocate, meaning that they can advocate in any domestic court within England and Wales (see 4.3 for a fuller discussion on this point). This has opened up the professional remit of a solicitor greatly and they are now eligible to become members of the judiciary and Queen's Counsel (see 4.1.4.2).

4.1.3.1 Composition

According to the Law Society's *Annual Statistical Report 2007* there were 134,978 solicitors on the Roll as at July 31, 2007, which was an increase of 2.3 per cent on the previous year's figures. Out of this figure 108,407 held practising certificates (a certificate is required by any person holding themselves out to provide legal work under s.1A of the Solicitors Act 1974 and in 2007 they cost £950 per year) and 82,577 (76.2 per cent) of these worked within the 10,114 private practice firms throughout the country, the remainder working mainly in commerce and industry or the public sector.

Table 4.1 Growth in the number of solicitors with practising certificates 1950–2007

Source: Law Society's REGIS database.

The profession is quite equally split in terms of gender with 43.4 per cent of all solicitors holding practising certificates being female and since 1997 the number of women holding a practising certificate has increased by an incredible 100.6 per cent.

Table 4.2 Solicitors on the Roll with and without practising certificates by gender as at July 31, 2007

Source: Law Society's REGIS database.

		No.	%
With practising certificates			
	Male	61,337	56.6
	Female	47,070	43.4
	Sub-total	108,407	100.0
Without practising certificates			
	Male	13,454	51.8
	Female	12,517	48.2
	Sub-total	25,971	100.0
Total solicitors on the Roll			
	Male	74,791	55.7
	Female	59,587	44.3
	Total	134,378	100.0

Solicitors from ethnic minorities accounted for 10.1 per cent of all solicitors on the Roll, 9.5 per cent of all solicitors holding a practising certificate and 9.1 per cent of all solicitors in private practice.

Table 4.3 Minority ethnic group solicitors on the Roll and with practising certificates as at July 31, 2007

Source: Law Society's REGIS database.

	Minority ethnic group solicitors		
	1	2	3
Ethnic origin	On the Roll	With practising certificate	Participation rate (2 as a % of 1)
African-Caribbean	868	741	85.4
Asian	6,782	5,829	85.9
Chinese	2,612	983	37.6
African	1,188	1,027	86.4
Other ethnic origin	2,086	1,726	82.7
All minority ethnic group solicitors	13,537	10,306	76.1
White European	102,546	84,572	82.5
Unknown	18,296	13,529	73.9
Total	134,378	108,407	80.7
Minority ethnic group solicitors as a % of all solicitors	10.1	9.5	
Minority ethnic group solicitors as a % of solicitors with known ethnicity	11.7	10.9	

4.1.3.2 Qualifying as a solicitor

Qualifying as a solicitor has traditionally been viewed as the less competitive route of entry into the legal profession (as compared to that of a barrister) but over recent years the allure of becoming a legal practioner has become an increasingly attractive prospect, with a higher number of students undertaking a relevant undergraduate and/or postgraduate course so as to enter the profession. As a result of these increased numbers of students vying to become a solicitor the competition for entry into the profession has dramatically increased as well. The decision to become a solicitor may not involve quite the high levels of risk that the decision to become a barrister does (see 4.1.4.4) but it is certainly not far behind.

The Law Society set out that there are seven potential routes to becoming a solicitor and these are as a:

- law graduate
- non-law graduate
- overseas lawyer (transfer)
- barrister (transfer) (see below at 4.1.4)
- Scots/Northern Irish lawyers (transfer)
- Fellow of the Institute of Legal Executives (FILEX) (see above at 4.1.2)
- justices' clerk (see 5.8)

This text will consider the two most usual routes taken to become a solicitor; by way of a law degree and a non-law degree.

The initial starting point is for a potential solicitor to undertake an undergraduate degree and achieve at least a 2:2 (lower second class degree), the degree does not have to be a law degree (LL.B (Hons)) and can be in any discipline that the student finds interesting. The main requirement is that reasonable grades are achieved in all assessments from the very start of the degree (even in the first year) as individual assessment grades will be considered by firms when deciding whether or not to offer work experience and/or a training contract.

If a student undertakes a degree in a non-law discipline then they will be required to complete a further year of study known as the Common Professional Examination (or Graduate Diploma in Law). This qualification allows the student to gain the legal knowledge known as the 'seven foundations of law', and which includes contract law, torts law, land law, European Union law, crime, public law and trusts, as required by the Law Society (or the Bar Council if the individual wishes to become a barrister (see below)).

Table 4.4 Number of students graduating in law from universities in England and Wales 2001, 2005 and 2006[1]

Source: Law Society's *Annual Statistical Report 2007*.

Year of graduation	University Graduates in Law		
	Male	Female	Total
2001	3,512	5,736	9,248
2005	4,392	7,692	12,084
2006	4,633	8,225	12,858
% change 2006/2005	5.5	6.9	6.9
% change 2006/2001	31.9	43.4	39.0

1. Figures relate to single honours law degrees and do not include modular or joint honour degrees which may also allow graduates to proceed directly to study the Legal Practice Course (para. 7.6).

Sources of data: 1995 and onwards, Higher Educational Statistical Agency.

Out of the 12,858 students that completed a law degree in 2006 over half of them (55.4 per cent) achieved a 2:1 (upper second class degree) or higher, which sets the standard at a high level from the start and requires students to have something about them (work experience etc.) that makes them stand out from the other candidates who are all applying for places on the Legal Practice Course (LPC) and training contracts.

Upon successful completion of this undergraduate study the student must then obtain a place on the LPC. This is a year-long post-graduate course that covers the theoretical aspect of being a solicitor. On the LPC a student will learn the necessary skills, such as conveyancing, litigation, accounts, ethics and professional conduct, and there will be the further option to take further electives in the area of law that an individual student is interested in (i.e. family law, criminal law or corporate law etc.). Securing a place on the LPC is becoming an increasingly difficult task in itself as there are only a limited number of institutions that offer the course nationwide and these providers are restricted as to the number of places that they can offer. Potential solicitors who have secured a place on the LPC may be able to gain sponsorship for the course if they are able to secure a training contract with a firm who is willing to pay the fees (the LPC fees cost approximately £10,000 for the year) in return for a number of years guaranteed employment upon qualification, although securing a training contract at an early stage has become very difficult due to the sheer volume of students. In the academic year 2006–2007 a total of students 9,850 enrolled on to the LPC, with 60.1 per cent of them passing the course and with 22.2 per cent gaining a Diploma with Distinction, and for the academic year 2007–2008 the number of available places on the LPC was increased by 3.4 per cent (to 10,675).

Prior to beginning the LPC a student must enrol with the Law Society as a student solicitor. The Law Society is the organisation responsible for representing the profession of solicitors within England and Wales and they maintain the records of every person who has enrolled to become a solicitor. In the year ending the July 31, 2007 a total of 11,351 students enrolled with the Law Society, of these 62.7 per cent (7,121) were women and 30.7 per cent (3,482) were from an ethnic minority. These figures show that the profession of being a solicitor is increasingly beginning to buck the traditional composition trend as found in other legal careers (barristers and the judiciary) as the majority of those coming into the career are female and there is a high number of people from ethnic minorities, meaning that the profession is becoming more reflective of the society of which it serves.

Following successful completion of the academic stage of the training to become a solicitor a graduate is then required to secure a two-year training contract before they are allowed to obtain a practising certificate. A training contract is effectively a two year-long apprenticeship where the individual will sit in a least four different 'seats' (areas of law) and gain sufficient experience of the law in practice to then become a competent solicitor themselves. As alluded to above the competition to gain a training contract is becoming increasingly fierce and in 2007 there were 6,012 new traineeships registered with the Law Society. This figure is an increase on the number of training contracts offered in previous years but it still does not sufficiently meet the demand for training contracts due to the high number of students completing the LPC with good grades. Trainees do receive a wage for the two-year period and the figures recommended by the Law Society for the minimum wage were £17,660 for trainees in London and £15,820 for trainees outside of London.

Upon successful completion of the training contract period the trainee is normally employed by the firm that they undertook their traineeship with and they are then required to undertake at least 16 hours worth per year of continuing professional education throughout the duration of their career.

Figure 4.2 Route to becoming a solicitor

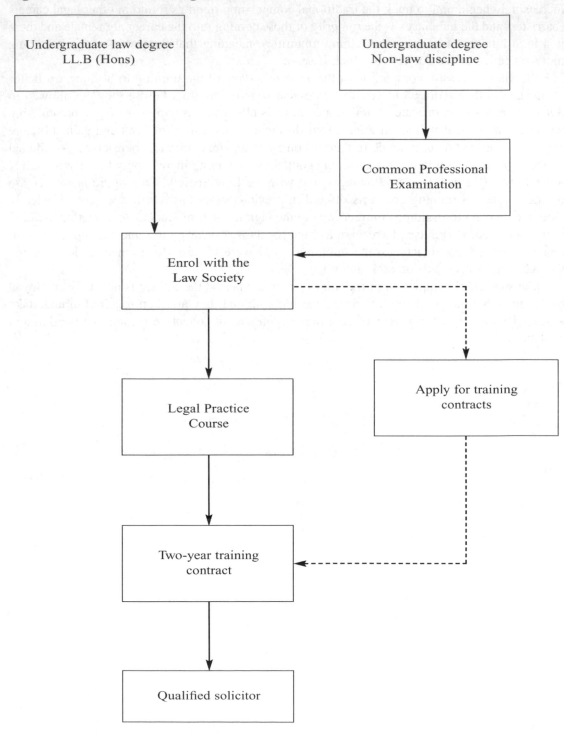

4.1.3.3 Regulation of the profession

The regulation of the profession has been the focus of unreserved criticism over recent years with the result that the bodies providing regulation have undergone numerous changes, although often these changes only amounted to what was essentially a change of a name as opposed to any direct action to address the criticisms raised. To discover how the profession is now regulated it is necessary to consider the historical development and functions of the bodies involved.

4.1.3.3.1 The Law Society

The Law Society was founded on June 2, 1825, although originally its title was that of 'The Society of Attorneys, Solicitors, Proctors and others not being Barristers, practising in the Courts of Law and Equity of the United Kingdom', by 1903 the Society had reduced this title to that of simply 'The Law Society'. The Law Society were originally the only organisation charged with both representing solicitors' rights and regulating their behaviour and it was as early as 1834 when the Society first brought proceedings against practitioners who were acting dishonestly. Criticisms were then voiced about the fact that the Society tended to side with the solicitors when any allegation was made against them (obviously a Society that had both the function of representation and regulation of the same professionals was faced with a rather large conflict of interest) and in 1983 the Solicitors Complaints Bureau was established as an independent limb of the Law Society in an effort to tackle these criticisms. The Bureau was not the success that it was hoped it would be as it was not truly independent of the Law Society and it could only work under the powers delegated to it by the Society. The Bureau could only impose the maximum compensation payable by a solicitor at a meagre £1,000 and it was viewed to be inefficient to the point of almost incompetence when dealing with the claims made. To address these new criticisms levied at the Law Society the Bureau was changed to the Office for Supervision of Solicitors in 1996, but the issues were still not directly addressed and the problems identified with the original Bureau remained. As a final effort to tackle the concerns the Office for Supervision of Solicitors became the Consumer Complaints Service in 2004, although this again appeared to be more of a name change than an effective addressing of any of the problems identified. In 2007 wide spread change occurred in respect of the organisations charged with regulating the profession and dealing with consumer complaints. These responsibilities were removed entirely from the Law Society by the establishment of the Solicitors Regulation Authority and the Legal Complaints Service (both discussed below). The Law Society is now only charged with the representation of solicitors by way of negotiating with and lobbying the newly created regulatory bodies and government, and providing training, advice and support to all solicitors within its jurisdiction.

4.1.3.3.2 Solicitors Regulation Authority

The Solicitors Regulation Authority (SRA) was established in January 2007 (although it had previously existed under the guise of the Law Society Regulation Board). The SRA is the independent regulatory body of the Law Society and it sets out its aim as being:

To set, promote and secure in the public interest standards of behaviour and professional performance necessary to ensure that clients receive a good service and that the rule of law is upheld.

The organisation's key objectives are to set the standards for the profession, provide support and monitoring to the profession in respect of compliance with the required standards set, ensure that consumers are protected, to ensure that any disciplinary action taken and enforcement of such are appropriate for the circumstances, and to help provide access to justice and consumer information and ensure transparency across the profession. The SRA produces the Code of Conduct that members of the profession must abide by and they are charged with the responsibility of issuing practising certificates to all practising solicitors.

4.1.3.3.3 Legal Complaints Service

This is a further organisation established in 2007 with the primary purpose of being an independent complaints handling body. Effectively the Legal Complaints Service (LSC) is the old Consumer Complaints Service. The LSC is part of the Law Society but it operates independently of them as the Law Society has delegated the handling of complaints to it and has charged it with the powers to handle any complaints made in a manner that is found to be in the public interest. The LSC is comprised of a board of 14 members who are an equal split of lawyers and non-lawyers and they can deal with issues concerning the poor service of a solicitor and complaints about a solicitor's bill (although these matters are dealt with under separate procedures). In three years time the responsibility of handling complaints will be passed from the LSC to the Office of Legal Complaints as established under the Legal Services Act 2007 (see 4.3).

4.1.3.3.4 The Solicitors Disciplinary Tribunal

The Solicitors Disciplinary Tribunal (SDT) is a statutory tribunal enacted under s.46 of the Solicitors' Act 1974. The SDT adjudicates upon alleged breaches of the rules of professional conduct that are designed to maintain the reputation of the solicitors' profession in respect of honesty, probity, trustworthiness, independence and integrity. The SDT has the power to strike off a solicitor from the Roll, suspend them from practice, or fine or reprimand them. Any fines imposed are payable to HM Treasury and the tribunal can award costs but not compensation. The SDT is currently comprised of 30 members, all of whom are appointed by the Master of the Rolls (see 6.1.2.2), two thirds of the tribunal are solicitors and one third are lay-people. The Annual Report for 2007 shows that the SDT struck off 67 solicitors, suspended 20 solicitors indefinitely from practice, imposed 86 fines totalling £441,800 and reprimanded 20 solicitors during 2007.

4.1.4 Barristers

When most people think of a barrister the image of an individual embodying the spirit of Rumpole of the Bailey or Kavanagh Q.C. tends to spring to mind (or for the slightly younger readers the characters from *This Life* or *North Square*), meaning that the general view of a barrister is a person who wears a wig and gown and is responsible for presenting a case in the courtroom (and in respect of *This Life* and *North Square*—also having a great social life). This general image is not incorrect (even regarding the social life when they get time) but it is not a complete picture of the work that a barrister undertakes professionally. Barristers do present cases (advocate) in the courtroom but they also undertake a lot of research to be able to do so (they do not have assistants to help them with this but must do all the work themselves), they draft opinions, they give advice, act as negotiators and mediators and a whole lot more. In fact barristers who specialise in certain areas of the law, such as banking and maritime law for example, may spend very little time advocating in court and the majority of their time negotiating on behalf of and advising their clients instead. The Bar Council (see 4.1.4.5.1 for further information on this organisation) describes barristers as:

> [s]pecialist legal advisers and court room advocates. They are independent and objective and trained to advise clients on the strengths as well as the weaknesses of their case. They have specialist knowledge and experience in and out of court which can make a substantial difference to the outcome of a case.

The main difference between solicitors and barristers is that a barrister is refrained from 'conducting litigation' on behalf of their client and they can only act upon the client's instructions, whereas a solicitor can act in place of their client and conduct the litigation for them (so write letters, make applications to the court and even sign documents in place of the client).

Barristers are generally self-employed professionals, they cannot form partnerships with other barristers, but they do usually work out of (become tenants of) shared offices known as 'chambers'. Chambers can vary in size from those where there are only a handful of barristers; to ones known informally as 'super-chambers', where there can be well over 100 barristers working from within the premises. A set of chambers may be specialised and only focus on one specific area of the law, for example criminal law or family law and all the barristers who work out of that set will only practise in that area of law, or it may be a common law set and offer a range of different areas of law (e.g. civil law, personal injury, criminal and family law) and the law that it covers will depend on the specialisms of the individual barristers who work from the chambers. The unique structure of chambers allows a number of barristers to pool together and share facilities (such as office space, office equipment and administrative support etc.) and the costs that these resources incur, as normally each barrister is required to pay rent or fees towards the upkeep and day-to-day running of the chambers. Administrative support for the barristers is provided by an employee of the chambers (or employees depending on the size of the chambers) known as a 'clerk(s)'. A barrister's clerk is responsible for allocating the work that comes into chambers from solicitors to the individual barristers, they keep the barrister's diaries, chase outstanding bills and ensure that all the work is adequately covered by an appropriately experienced practioner (for example at a common law set they would ensure that a criminal case is allocated to a barrister who has relevant criminal law experience and not a barrister who practises solely in medical negligence law).

Not every barrister is self-employed though and many work in an employed capacity within industry and commerce, government departments and as members of in-house legal teams. The benefits to being an employed barrister is that there is the security of a regular wage, holiday entitlements, sick pay and pension etc., whereas a self-employed barrister who is responsible for and only accountable to themselves do not benefit from the perks and allowances that are gained from an employed status; if a self-employed barrister does not work then they simply do not earn. According to the statistics compiled by the Bar Council there were 15,030 practising barristers in England and Wales as at December 2007 and 2,972 of these were working in an employed capacity.

4.1.4.1 Inns of Court

Barristers have existed since about the 13th Century and as a result the modern day profession is steeped in tradition. For a barrister to be able to practise he must first be 'called to the Bar'. This does not mean that he or she has been invited down to the pub by their friends or fellow barristers, but rather that they have been inaugurated into the profession by becoming an accepted member of one of the four Inns of Court. The Inns of Court are almost as old as the profession itself and they have played an integral role in the development and regulation of the profession since about the 17th Century. The four Inns of Court are:

- Lincoln's Inn
- Inner Temple
- Middle Temple
- Gray's Inn

Lincoln's Inn appears to be the oldest Inn of Court, with records detailing its activities dating back to 1422 in the Black Books, and it currently has the highest number of members of any Inn of Court. Each Inn is equal in its status and is individual in its own history and traditions. The Inns of Court seem to have originated as the living quarters for apprentices at law during the 14th and 15th Centuries, and the word 'Inn' seems to be derived from the term 'hospitium' meaning a town house or mansion that was used to house students. The Inns used to provide (and still do to a large degree) everything that was then required by the students of law, they provided the students with a place to sleep, a hall to eat and drink in, a chapel to pray in and a library to conduct their research and learning within. By the 17th Century it was a requirement for any person who wished to advocate in the courts to be a member of one of the Inns.

The Inns of Court still play a vital role in the development of an individual's career as a Barrister-at-law and they are heavily involved in the provision of educational activities, bursaries and scholarships and dining facilities, as well as calling members to the Bar and disciplining barristers. As barristers are no longer all based within the confines of London and there are many who now work in the provinces (outside of London) the Inns do not offer the level of accommodation that they once did but they still provide all of the other functions (the chapel, library and dining facilities) that have been available to its members since their establishment over 500 years ago.

It does not matter which Inn of Court a budding barrister decides to join, it is simply a matter of personal choice. Some will join Lincoln's Inn because of the grandeur of the buildings, others because of the educational activities it offers, others will prefer to join Gray's Inn or one of the two Temples because of the smaller and more exclusive feel that these Inn's offer or because of their previous famous members and associations. The author Bram Stoker (*Dracula*) was a member of Inner Temple and the Inn is reputed to have links with Geoffrey Chaucer (the *Canterbury Tales*); Middle Temple had members such as Sir Walter Raleigh and Charles Dickens, and Gray's Inn is where William Shakespeare's play '*A Comedy of Errors*' was first performed in 1594. Lincoln's Inn boasts Lord Denning as a past member and its alumni include many previous Prime Ministers such as Baroness Thatcher and Tony Blair. The decision to apply for membership to a particular Inn is an individual decision but once an Inn of Court has been decided upon and admittance has been granted the individual barrister will belong to that Inn for life (unless they are later disbarred).

A prospective student barrister is required to choose and join an Inn of Court before the commencement of their vocational studies on the Bar Vocational Course (discussed below). Upon being accepted into the chosen Inn as a student barrister (or 'inner' barrister if the traditional terminology is to be used, a barrister becomes an 'outer' barrister upon call) the student is then required to undertake a tradition known as 'keeping terms' before they can be formerly called to the Bar as a Barrister-at-law. Keeping terms means that a student is required to attend 12 qualifying sessions at the Inn before they can be called and admitted fully into the Inn. These qualifying sessions are normally achieved by the individual dining at their Inn of Court (each dining session counts as one qualifying unit). Dining takes place during one of the four dining terms (each term lasts for between nine and 14 days) spread over the year, the dining periods are split into Hilary, Easter, Trinity and Michaelmas. Originally the idea of keeping terms revolved around the fact that the student barristers all resided in or near their Inn of Court and the requirement for them to keep terms meant that they were heavily involved in the day-to-day life of their chosen Inn (students were originally expected to complete 48 qualifying sessions). Nowadays the number of sessions required to be completed has been reduced down to 12 due to the fact that many students do not live and work in London (the Bar Vocational Course can be studied at institutes up and down the country and there are now barrister's chambers found in nearly every major town and city) and therefore the requirement to dine 48 times would be too onerous. By requiring potential barristers to still satisfy the keeping terms requirement the Inns are helping to ensure that the traditions of the Inns are continued and that the student barristers who do live and work at the other end of the country are afforded the opportunity to become and feel part of the very fabric of the Inn. Often individual Inns will now provide an educational day or weekend where students can gain more that one qualifying unit in a short space of time.

The highest rank of membership that an individual can achieve in an Inn is that of a Master of the Bench (informally known as a Bencher). The Benchers of an Inn preside over the Inn and form its governing body, and they are responsible for student admissions to the Inn, call to the Bar and member (especially student member) discipline. On average each Inn of Court has approximately 200 Benchers and they are generally selected from those members of the Inn who hold judicial office or have been appointed as Queen's Counsel (see below), although Honorary Benchers may also be appointed (often from the Royal family) and they do not need to be a member of the Inn or even be a lawyer (although they are not permitted to vote or hold office within the Inn).

4.1.4.2 Queen's Counsel

The title of Queen's Counsel (post-nominal Q.C.) is bestowed on those barristers (although now solicitors can also become Q.C.'s due to the introduction of higher rights of audience (see 4.3)) who have been called for at least ten years and are deemed to be professionally excellent and successful in their chosen field of law. When a lawyer becomes a Q.C. they are permitted to wear a gown made of silk to identify their status as opposed to the traditional heavier cloth gown worn by the other members of the Bar. As a result of wearing this silk gown Q.C.'s are informally referred to as 'silks', other barristers who have not achieved this status are called 'junior barristers' (regardless of their age or time at the Bar). The title of Q.C. is a mark of distinction against the individual lawyer's name and it is often viewed as a 'kite mark' or 'gold star' depicting the individual's high legal ability, intellect and competence.

When a Q.C. is involved in a case they will sit on the very front bench of the courtroom directly in front of the judge and they will be the first to speak on behalf of the client. They are also permitted to take into court a lectern upon which to rest their notes if they so wish (junior barristers are not permitted this luxury). Q.C.'s will be called to undertake the most complex and lengthy cases and those that are of a high public profile, and they are often accompanied in a case by a junior barrister who will assist them by undertaking a lot of the less complex work (assisting a Q.C. in such a way has been said to be the making of more than one junior barrister's career).

The selection of Q.C.'s from the ranks of the junior Bar (solicitors were originally unable to become Q.C.'s until the introduction of higher rights of audience) used to be conducted by way of a secret sounding in the same way that judges were selected (see 6.3.1 for a detailed explanation of this process) and in 2003 the process of selecting Q.C.'s by this method was suspended for consultation and it was at this point believed by most of the legal profession that the post of Q.C. would ultimately be abolished. The consultation process then uncovered a large amount of support for the position of Q.C.'s, in that the title allowed the excellence of those individuals who had gained it to be recognised by persons outside of the immediate legal circle. The idea of abolishment was replaced by one of reform and the reform was to focus on the appointments method as opposed to the actual position of Q.C.'s.

The reform that followed involved the establishment of an independent Selection Panel that has the aim of providing a fair and transparent means of identifying excellence in advocacy in the higher courts. The Panel is charged with being rigorous and objective in its selection, whilst promoting diversity, equality and fairness. The Panel is comprised of nine individuals who are a mix of retired members of the judiciary, senior barristers and solicitors and lay members, and the Panel is chaired by a lay member (currently Sir Duncan Nichol CBE). To determine whether a candidate should be appointed as a Q.C. the Panel assess the applications against a Competency Framework, which includes criteria such as:

- Understanding and Using of the Law
- Oral and Written Advocacy

- Working with Others
- Diversity
- Integrity

Interviews of those applicants shortlisted are then conducted and references taken, as is the normal process for a job or promotion, with appointments then being formally made by the Secretary of State. In 2006 the first round of open competition included the appointment 175 Q.C.'s, of which 33 were women, 10 were of an ethnic origin other than white and four solicitor-advocates were successful. A competition for appointment in 2008 closed on April 3, 2008 and the figures released so far by the Selection Panel show that 247 candidates have applied, of which 215 (87 per cent) are male and 29 (12 per cent) are female (1 per cent declined to identify their gender). Out of all the applicants 230 (93 per cent) are white in origin, two currently work at the employed Bar and four of the applications were made by solicitors. How many will actually be appointed as Q.C.'s will not be known until after the publication of this text.

It appears upon consideration of the above figures that the issues of equality and diversity in the selection process has been addressed by the establishment of the Selection Panel but that the composition of the candidates actually applying to become Q.C.'s is still at this moment rather reflective of the stereotypical view of the Bar (that it is dominated by white middle class males). This fact may be a left over remnant from the days of secret soundings or it could simply be a reflection of the composition of the Bar as at present. Whether the new selection process helps to address the imbalance in the composition of the higher ranks of the legal profession (as is its intention) remains to be seen.

4.1.4.3 Access to barristers

Traditionally barristers were only allowed to take instructions from 'professional clients', in other words from solicitors, and as a result members of the public could not gain direct access to a barrister. This resulted in barristers being seen as unapproachable and set above the other members of the legal profession. In 1999 the Bar Council set up a pilot study, known as BarDIRECT, to assess the effects of certain professionals and organisations, such as the police force and trade unions etc., being allowed to have direct access to a barrister without the need to instruct a solicitor; effectively cutting out the middle man. The pilot study was heralded to be a success, despite the reservations of the Law Society who were of the opinion that allowing direct access to barristers was a further erosion of the profession remit of a solicitor, and in 2004 the Bar Council rolled out the ability for an individual to access a barrister direct by way of the Public Access Rules.

There are now three ways in which a barrister can be instructed, these are:

- Professional Client Access
- Public Access
- Licensed Access

Professional Client Access is the traditional method of instructing a barrister and this can be done either via a solicitor, designated legal advice centres, other authorised litigators and employed barristers etc. A barrister can be instructed by this method to act in any matter and in relation to all types of work and the majority of work undertaken by barristers results from them being instructed in this manner.

Public Access (by way of the 2004 Public Access Rules) allows members of the public and commercial and non-commercial organisations to instruct barristers directly. For a barrister to undertake Public Access work they must have been qualified post pupillage (see below) for a period of at least three years, they must have undertaken a one-day training course and registered their intentions to accept work in this way. Public Access is permitted for most civil work but a barrister cannot accept any work involving criminal law, family law or immigration law, and if the proposed work involves any of these prohibited areas then the client must be referred back to a solicitor or other approved professional organisation. A barrister must also be careful not to undertake any work that amounts to conducting litigation (issuing proceedings, instructing experts or paying court fees etc.) as this is also prohibited under the Public Access Rules. In such a case the barrister would again be obliged to refer the client to an appropriate professional body. The Bar Council website (*http://www.barcouncil.org.uk*) provides a searchable database for barristers who participate in the Public Access scheme.

Licensed Access is the modern interpretation of the old BarDIRECT (or Direct Professional Access scheme). This method of access involves certain organisations becoming licensed by the Bar Council to instruct barristers directly, although responsibility for licensing has been passed to the Bar Standards Board since January 1, 2008. An organisation will be deemed to be suitable to receive such a license if it is felt that they have sufficient experience in a particular area of law. Examples of those organisations currently licensed include the Institute of Chartered Accountants, the Royal Institute of British Architects, the Asylum Support Appeals Project, the Devon Fire Authority, the British Transport Police and the Kennel Club.

Despite the concerns of the Law Society that the work of solicitors would be further diminished due to the increased accessibility of barristers it appears that the main recourse of the individual client to a barrister is still conducted in the traditional method by way of a solicitor and that the new Licensed Access scheme has not impacted too detrimentally on the quantity of work available to either profession.

4.1.4.4 Qualifying as a barrister

Becoming a barrister is not an easy task and is certainly not one that should be approached lightly as the profession is highly competitive and difficult to get a foothold in, as such it is a career that involves considerable determination, dedication, a large financial investment and very thick skin. The initial starting point is for a potential barrister to undertake an undergraduate degree and achieve at least a 2:1 (upper second class degree), the degree does not have to be a law degree (LL.B (Hons)) and can be in any discipline that the student finds interesting. The main requirement is that a high grade is achieved in all assessments from the very start of the degree (even in the first year) as individual assessment grades will be considered by chambers when deciding whether to offer work experience and/or pupillage. Overall at least a 2:1 must be attained, as there are many potential candidates out there who an individual will be competing against, and as such an individual must attain a mark and other achievements (such as mooting, debating, work experience and a placement year) that will set them apart from these other candidates. There are barristers in practise who only attained a third or 2:2 at degree level and who have carved themselves out a very successful career, but due to the sheer volume of students who now wish to pursue a career at the Bar this level of academic achievement is simply no longer acceptable by the majority of the modern Bar; there is anecdotal evidence that chambers, when considering potential pupils, will simply bin without further consideration all applications from applicants achieving anything less than a 2:1.

If a student undertakes a non-law discipline then they will be required to complete a further year of study known as the Common Professional Examination (or Graduate Diploma in Law). This qualification allows the student to gain the legal knowledge of the seven foundations of law (see 4.1.3.2) as required by the Bar Council (or the Law Society if the individual wishes to become a solicitor). Upon successful completion of this undergraduate study the student must then obtain a place on the Bar Vocational Course (BVC), which is a year-long post-graduate course that covers the theoretical aspect of being a barrister. On the BVC a student will learn the necessary skills so as to enable them to become an effective advocate, be able to draft complex legal documents and opinions, undertake negotiation, prepare cases and develop conference skills (such as interviewing a client). The core modules that are taught include civil litigation and remedies, criminal litigation and sentencing, professional ethics and evidence. A student will also be given the choice to undertake a number of elective modules, such as advanced criminal litigation or immigration, depending on where their individual interests lie. Securing a place on the BVC is a difficult task in itself as there are only a limited number of institutions that offer the course nationwide and these providers are restricted as to the number of places that they can offer. Invariably there are more applicants than there are places and each year a large number of hopeful barristers are disappointed when their applications to undertake the BVC are rejected. If an individual is successful on gaining a place on a BVC course then it is important that they achieve a good mark at the end of it. There is again further anecdotal evidence that applications for pupillage made by individuals who have not attained either a Very Competent or Outstanding on the BVC are filed into the bin without further consideration.

Upon completion of the BVC then, providing that the student has kept the requisite number of terms as prescribed by the Inns of Court (see above), they will be called to the Bar as a Barrister-at-law. However the bestowing of this title does not allow a newly called barrister to begin practising as a barrister. All barristers must undergo a year-long period of work experience known as 'pupillage' to be able to gain a practising certificate. This is where the competition really begins to hot up, as there are simply not enough pupillages available to accommodate the yearly supply of BVC graduates (often over 250 applications will be received for just one pupillage). Pupillages must be undertaken in chambers under the supervision of a recognised pupil master or mistress. These supervisors are barristers of at least seven years call who are willing to undertake the supervision of a pupil for the length of the pupillage. A pupil barrister must now be paid a wage by the chambers that is training them (the minimum that must be paid is £10,000 per annum although the larger sets of chambers can often pay considerably more than this). The requirement that chambers pay a pupil a minimum wage is a relatively new one stipulated by the Bar Council and it arose as a method to address the severe financial difficulties that many pupil barristers were faced with. However the imposition of a minimum wage has had the effect of curtailing the number of pupillages on offer as the wage must be paid directly by chambers and as each barrister in chambers is self-employed this has meant that the number of pupillages offered by an individual chambers has been reduced, and in the cases of the smaller chambers they are often not able to offer any pupillages at all. According to the Bar Council's statistics for 2007 there were 1,776 individuals called to the Bar, but that there were only 527 pupillages undertaken in this time. This means that essentially only a third of those people called to the Bar were successful in obtaining a pupillage. There are currently only 334 chambers that are able to offer pupillages nationwide and therefore competition to attain a pupillage is intensely fierce with the rejection rate (even to get an interview let alone a pupillage) being extremely high. When the fact that a similar number are called to the Bar each year is coupled with the fact that the number of pupillages on offer very rarely increases (in fact the number decreased in 2007 from 552 in 2006) then the extreme competitiveness can be appreciated as those who did not attain a pupillage the previous year will still be applying for one the following year along with the newly graduated BVC cohort for that year.

If an individual perseveres until they obtain a pupillage (or if they are simply gifted or lucky and get one almost immediately) then the year-long pupillage is split down into two parts. The 'first six' (essentially the first six months) will be spent following their pupil master or mistress to and from court and conferences and helping them to conduct research and draft documents etc., during this first six months the pupil is prevented from undertaking any paid work (except some agency work) and they are simply learning from watching. The 'second six' then involves the pupil being allowed to take on their own case load and conduct these cases under the watchful eye of their supervisor. Throughout the pupillage a pupil is required to undergo further training on advocacy and other practical skills as organised by the Bar Council or the Inns of Court so as to further their professional development. Upon completion of a pupillage it is then necessary for the pupil barrister to find a permanent tenancy in a set of chambers. This can often be quite a difficult task to achieve in itself (which seems very unfair considering how close they are to becoming a fully fledged barrister), as many chambers do not have the space or the work to accommodate another tenant (remember all barristers are self-employed and are effectively in competition with one another for work). Many chambers will not take on a pupil if they do not have the ability to offer them tenancy at the end of the year, however there are a number of more unscrupulous chambers out there who will offer pupillage to a number of pupils but will then only have the space for one (or even no) tenants at the end of it. Those pupils who are not able to secure tenancy are often allowed to 'squat' within chambers for a number of months (often called a 'third six') until they manage to secure a tenancy at another set of chambers.

It is after all this that an individual will eventually become a practising barrister who can then begin to build up their own client base and start their professional career, although they are still required to undertake continuing profession development (CPD) so that they remain competent and up-to-date practitioners. Successfully becoming a barrister is a very trying affair and at the end of it all an individual can be left with debts that on average exceed £50,000 to pay back.

Figure 4.3 Route to becoming a barrister

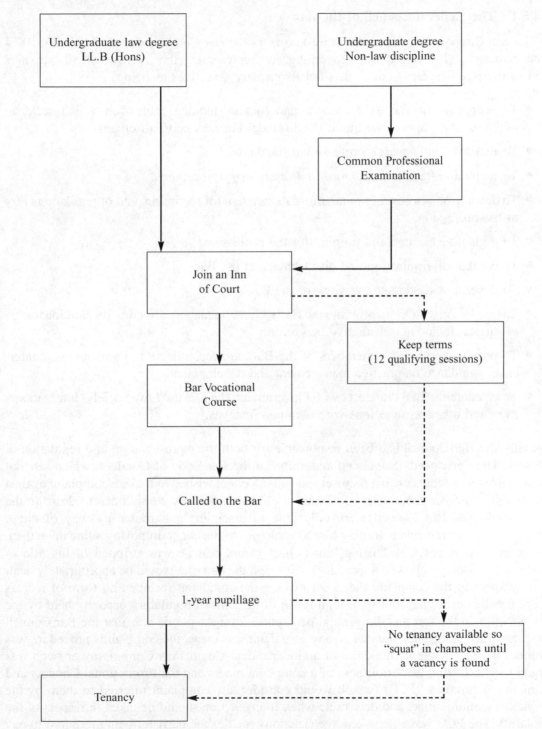

4.1.4.5 Regulation of the profession

4.1.4.5.1 The General Council of the Bar

The General Council of the Bar, otherwise known as the Bar Council, was established in 1894 as the primary body charged with governing and representing the interests of all barristers called to the Bar. The Bar Council sets out its primary objectives as being:

- To represent the Bar as a modern and forward-looking profession which seeks to maintain and improve the quality and standard of service to all clients.

- To maintain and enhance professional standards.

- To maintain effective complaints and disciplinary procedures.

- To develop an effective, fair and affordable system for recruiting, and of regulating entry to the profession.

- To regulate education and training for the profession.

- To combat discrimination and disadvantage at the Bar.

- To develop and promote the work of the Bar.

- To conduct research and promote the Bar's views on matters affecting the administration of justice, including substantive law reform.

- To provide services for members of the Bar, e.g. fee collection, publications, conferences, guidance on practice management and development.

- To promote the Bar's interests with Government, the EC, the Law Society, International Bars and other organisations with common interests.

Originally the Bar Council had been responsible for both the representation and regulation of barristers. They produced, maintained and enforced the Bar Code of Conduct, which sets out how all barristers should conduct themselves, and if a client wished to make a complaint against an individual barrister about their behaviour or conduct then they would have to do so to the Bar Council. The Bar Council were only able to discipline a barrister by way of either suspending him from practice, forcing him to apologise to the client, imposing a fine upon them or, in very serious cases, disbarring him (which meant that he was stripped of his title as barrister and no longer allowed to practice). Although the barrister would be appropriately dealt with in respect of the complaint the client making the complaint received no form of redress (except for the occasional apology). As a result of the limited regulatory capacity held by the Bar Council, and the fact that the general perception from the public was that the Bar Council closed ranks around its barristers when any complaint was made, the complaints procedure was reformed in 1997 by the introduction of an independent Complaints Commissioner (who was charged with assessing the seriousness of a complaint made) and the Professional Conduct and Complaints Committee (PCC) (which would consider any complaint referred to them by the Complaints Commissioner and determine what, if any, action should be taken in respect of the complaint). The PCC was able to enforce sanctions such as the barrister being required to pay the complainant up to £5,000 in compensation and they were able to suspend, fine or disbar a barrister, as originally could the Bar Council.

The Complaints Commissioner was an individual who was not a lawyer and who was independent of the Bar Council. The PCC however, although composed of both lawyers and non-lawyers, was still a Committee of the Bar Council. Essentially the one organisation was still performing both representative and regulatory functions, which involved competing interests.

4.1.4.5.2 The Bar Standards Board

To combat this duel role of both representation and regulation the Bar Standards Board (BSB) was established in January 2006 by the Bar Council so as to act as an independent regulatory body for barristers. The BSB sets out its functions as:

- Setting the education and training requirements for becoming a barrister.

- Setting continuing training requirements to ensure that barristers' skills are maintained throughout their careers.

- Setting standards of conduct for barristers.

- Monitoring the service provided by barristers to assure quality.

- Handling complaints against barristers and taking disciplinary or other action where appropriate.

As a result the BSB now deal with any complaints made against a barrister. The Complaints Commissioner (currently Robert Behrens, who is not a lawyer but whose career background was as a civil servant dealing with the standards of conduct in public life) moved over to the BSB from the Bar Council and he is still responsible for initially assessing the merits of any complaint made against a barrister. The BSB can deal with complaints that concern matters of professional misconduct (such as misleading the court, not adhering to rules of client confidentiality or acting against a client's instructions), or matters of inadequate professional service (such as poor or inadequate work on a case or being rude to a client), but they are limited in their powers to deal with professional negligence and they will not enter into a complaint which focuses on a barristers conduct in their personal life. All complaints must be made within six months of the event that is being complained about occurring. Upon receipt of a complaint the Commissioner will assess the validity of the complaint and dismiss the matter if it does not contain any evidence of professional misconduct or inadequate professional service (or if it is received out of time). If the complaint shows valid grounds then the Commissioner will investigate the matter further and upon conclusion of the investigation he may either dismiss the complaint (if there is found to be insufficient evidence) or refer the complaint to the Complaints Committee.

The Complaints Committee (essentially the old PCC) will consider the evidence gathered and determine whether disciplinary action should be taken against the barrister in question. The Committee consists of a number of people who come from law and non-law backgrounds and it endeavours to be reflective of the society that it serves. If the Committee decide that disciplinary action is appropriate then it will refer the matter to one of three panels, these panels are:

- **The Adjudication Panel**. This panel considers allegations of inadequate professional service only and can require the barrister to apologise, reduce fees or pay up to £5,000 in compensation. The average compensation award in 2006 was £1,100. However, compensation is not always ordered, even where the barrister is found to have provided an inadequate professional service.

- **The Summary Procedure Panel.** This panel deals with relatively simple cases, where the facts are not in dispute and would not be likely to lead to the disbarment of a barrister.

- **The Disciplinary Tribunal**. This panel deals with the most serious cases, or cases where the facts are in dispute. Tribunals can impose fines, suspend the barrister from practice for a limited period and exceptionally, disbar the barrister.

If the client is unhappy with the manner in which their complaint was dealt with by the BSB then they may still refer the matter to the Legal Services Ombudsman who oversees the complaints system of the legal profession (see 4.2 for more detail on this body).

4.1.4.5.3 Professional negligence

The BSB only considers complaints that involve matters of professional misconduct or matters of inadequate professional service and they only have very limited powers when the issue being complained about involves professional negligence. The reason for this is that traditionally barristers were immune to complaints and actions brought against them in respect of claims for professional negligence, as set out in the case of *Rondel v Worsley* [1969] 1 A.C. 191. In *Rondel v Worsley* the House of Lords held that a barrister was to be immune from being sued and that this decision was based on matters of public policy due to the facts that the administration of justice required that a barrister should be able to carry out his duty to the court fearlessly and independently, that the actions for negligence against barristers would make the retrying of the original actions inevitable and so prolong litigation contrary to the public interest, and that a barrister was obliged to accept any client, however difficult, who sought his services and so consequently it would be unjust if the barrister could then be sued by a client simply because they were not satisfied with the result obtained.

This immunity was then abolished by the House of Lords in the landmark case of *Arthur J S Hall v Simons* [2002] 1 A.C. 615. *Arthur J S Hall v Simons* was a case that involved three cases of negligence brought against solicitors. The solicitors relied on the immunity of advocates from negligence suits and at first instance this argument succeeded and the claims were struck out as being unsustainable. On appeal the Court of Appeal then reversed this decision finding that the cases had been wrongly struck out and there were no public policy reason for allowing immunity on the grounds that there was no longer any valid justifications for the exemption as it deprived a client injured by the professional negligence of his legal representatives of an appropriate remedy. On appeal to the House of Lords, the House, on dismissing the appeal, held that the Court of Appeal was correct in its conclusion that the public policy arguments in favour of exemption were no longer appropriate. It concluded that the effect of the wasted costs jurisdiction (a method of sanctioning advocates for improper case conduct) was empirical evidence that the standards of advocacy had not declined with such a liability being imposed and as the courts were able to judge between errors of judgment, which were inevitable in the art of advocacy, against true negligence then the floodgates would not be opened to negligence claims. Lord Hope, Lord Hutton and Lord Hobhouse dissented by holding that immunity was still required in criminal proceedings but the majority determined that, although there was a different and broader remit for reinvestigation in criminal proceedings, the immunity should be removed in both spheres of legal work.

The courts have since interpreted this principle quiet narrowly, as can been seen in the later case of *Moy v Pettman Smith* [2005] UKHL 7. Here the House declined to impose liability on a barrister in a claim for negligence, holding that the purpose of the removal of immunity was not to stifle an advocate's independence of mind and that the advice given by the barrister in question fell within the range of that to be expected of reasonably competent counsel of the barrister's seniority and purported experience. This approach to the application of the principle and the reluctance to find liability against members of the legal profession differs to the approach taken by other professions (i.e. the medical profession) where the competence of an individual is to be judged alone by the standards of a reasonably competent practioner (regardless of the individual's seniority or purported experience).

4.1.4.6 Professional ethics

As stated above the profession is regulated by the Bar Code of Conduct (8th edition, October 31, 2004). This Code contains the rules and regulations on how the individual members of the profession should conduct themselves professionally. There are a couple of interesting and important rules that should be taken note of at this point. Part III of the Code sets out the Fundamental Principles that are applicable to all barristers and para.301 sets out that:

> 301. A barrister [. . .] must not:
>
> (a) engage in conduct whether in pursuit of his profession or otherwise which is:
>
> > (i) dishonest or otherwise discreditable to a barrister;
> > (ii) prejudicial to the administration of justice; or
> > (iii) likely to diminish public confidence in the legal profession or the administration of justice or otherwise bring the legal profession into disrepute;
>
> (b) engage directly or indirectly in any occupation if his association with that occupation may adversely affect the reputation of the Bar or in the case of a practising barrister prejudice his ability to attend properly to his practice.

This applies to all barristers whether they are self-employed, employed or even non-practising. This principle applies to not only a barrister in their professional life but it also crosses over into their private life and it would mean that any barrister who acted in a manner contrary to these principles (e.g. was moonlighting as a loan shark, or a lap-dancer) could face disciplinary actions for their behaviour.

Paragraph 302 sets out that:

> 302. A barrister has an overriding duty to the Court to act with independence in the interests of justice: he must assist the Court in the administration of justice and must not deceive or knowingly or recklessly mislead the Court.

This rule applies to all practising barristers and it is of the utmost importance that this rule is strictly adhered to. For example if a client in a criminal case told their barrister that they had committed the offence that they were being tried for then the barrister could not continue representing the client to the court as an innocent person, to do so would be to deceive the court and would breach their overriding duty to the Court. In such a case the barrister could only put the prosecution evidence to proof (try and show that the prosecution evidence was weak and that they could not prove the case against the defendant to the required standard of proof (see 10.3.2)) or they could withdraw from the case due to being professionally embarrassed. This is a difficult situation for a barrister to find themselves in as para.303(a) states that they must promote and protect fearlessly and by all proper and lawful means the lay client's best interests and do so without regard to his own interests or to any consequences to himself or to any other person, but this cannot be done at the expense of their duty to the Court.

The Code of Conduct is a lengthy document that provides guidance and regulation on almost every facet of a barristers professional (and personal) conduct and it is not intended to recount in detail every provision set out by the Code, this is something that is studied in great detail on the BVC. However attention will be drawn to one final part of the Code and that is the provision found in para.602, which is known as the 'cab-rank rule'.

Paragraph 602 provides that:

> [A barrister] must in any field in which he professes to practise in relation to work appropriate to his experience and seniority and irrespective of whether his client is paying privately or is publicly funded:
>
> (a) accept any brief to appear before a Court in which he professes to practise;
> (b) accept any instructions;
> (c) act for any person on whose behalf he is instructed;
>
> and do so irrespective of (i) the party on whose behalf he is instructed (ii) the nature of the case and (iii) any belief or opinion which he may have formed as to the character reputation cause conduct guilt or innocence of that person.

The cab-rank rule essentially requires a barrister to accept any case presented to him regardless of the identity of client, the facts of the case or the barrister's own opinion as to the salubriousness of the client. The rule takes its name from the principle employed at taxi ranks. If a person goes to catch a taxi at a taxi rank then he cannot pick and choose which taxi he will take, he must take the first taxi in the queue at the rank and cannot opt for the fifth one along just because the driver looks nicer or the vehicle looks safer. The same principle applies to a barrister's acceptance of work, he could not refuse a case simply because the client was a drug-dealer and he had strong views against drug pushers, or he could not refuse to defend a client even if they were a paedophile or a child murderer or a serial killer; no matter how unpleasant or personally offensive a barrister finds a case or a client he is obliged to accept it so long as he has the expertise to conduct the case, and upon acceptance of the case the barrister is obliged to promote and protect fearlessly the client's interests as set out under para.303(a) of the Bar Code of Conduct.

4.2 Legal Services Ombudsman

Discussed above are the methods that an individual can take to make a complaint against a solicitor or a barrister. If however after completing the procedures provided by the relevant agencies (the LSC or the BSB) the complainant is still not satisfied with the outcome of their complaint then they have the further option of complaining to the Legal Services Ombudsman (LSO).

The Courts and Legal Services Act 1990 created the office of LSO and the current Ombudsman is Zahida Manzoor CBE. She is a non-lawyer and is independent of the legal profession. The LSO is not there to investigate the facts from which the original complaint was derived or to review the actions of individual lawyers but rather her role is to ensure that the professional body that dealt with the original complaint did so in a correct and appropriate manner. Upon investigation the LSO has the powers to:

- recommend that the professional body in question re-investigates some, or all, aspects of the complaint

- formally criticise the professional body

- award compensation for any distress or inconvenience the professional body may have caused

The 2007 Annual Report for the LSO sets out that in during that year it received 1,738 new cases and that 1,680 of the complaints it dealt with during the year (including those carried over from the previous year) concerned the Law Society and 166 concerned the Bar Council. As a method to tackle the dissatisfaction created by the Law Society's inability to deal with complaints in an effective manner the government has further created the role of Legal Services Complaints Commissioner (LSCC) to oversee and supervise the CCS. The LSO, Zahida Manzoor, has also been appointed to this role and in 2006 she invoked her powers in this capacity and fined the Law Society complaints arm £250,000 for failing to provide her with an adequate plan detailing its complaints handling processes. The duel role held by Zahida Manzoor does raise questions over the compatibility of these two roles as with one hand she is setting the standard and then with the other assessing whether the meeting of these standards have been achieved, and in doing so she wields a lot of power over the Law Society.

4.3 The merging professions

Only 25 years ago the demarcation between the two main limbs of the legal profession (solicitors and barristers) was clear, with each profession having clearly defined roles and responsibilities, but over the recent years these two professions have begun to merge and the line between them has begun to blur to the point of there being little distinction and the feeling of there being really now only one profession, that of a 'lawyer'.

Originally solicitors rarely undertook advocacy work outside the realms of the magistrates' court and the county courts, as these higher rights of advocacy was the privilege of the barristers. Solicitors were prevented by way of the professional codes of conduct from advertising their services and they had the monopoly on the provision of conveyancing services. The change in the services provided by the professions, and in effect the beginning of the merging of the professions, really started with the 1979 report on the legal profession conducted by the Royal Commission on Legal Services (otherwise known as the Benson Commission). The Benson Commission was charged with considering the exclusivity that existed between the two professions and the assessment of whether such a state of affairs provided a fair and workable system, as at that time an individual who wished or needed to bring litigation was forced to employ two lawyers whereas it was considered that there was the possibility that only one was actually needed. The Commission also considered the issue of reserved work, which was work that could only be carried out by a body as specified by statute. Overall the Commission reported that the legal profession was functioning as well as could be expected and it did not recommend any immediate or radical changes to the provision of legal services.

The Law Society were not satisfied with the findings of the report and began to mount a challenge to the fact that solicitors were prevented from being able to advocate in the higher courts. It was felt that often it was inappropriate and unnecessary for a case to be handed over to the care of a barrister for presentation in court especially as there were many solicitors who were capable and willing to advocate in court if given the opportunity.

The Administration of Justice Act 1985 was the legislation that brought about the first significant change to the work conducted by solicitors and marked the beginning of the dissolution between legal professions. The monopoly enjoyed by solicitors in the previously reserved area of conveyancing was removed by the 1985 Act, as is provided for a system of licensed conveyancers who could also provide this service. The Act set out that the service of conveyancing could be conducted by any person who was suitably qualified (although this did not mean that a qualification as a solicitor was required), as long as they were insured and accountable for the work undertaken. The enactment of this change appears to have stemmed from the fact that a large number of solicitors had to an extent been abusing their hold over this area of the market. Criticisms had been levied against the fact that the fees charged for the work were astronomical and the level of service and quality of work received was often inadequate. Other bodies such as estate agents and banks had voiced a strong opinion that they should be allowed to provide conveyancing services and that this would in effect be more beneficial for the customers who required these services as they would only have to access one professional as opposed to two or three (e.g. the Halifax now encompasses an estate agents, a mortgage advisory department and conveyancing services). The Administration of Justice Act 1985 allowed this extended provision of services to occur, despite the lamenting of the Law Society as to the encroachment upon the work of solicitors.

The enactment of the Courts and Legal Services Act 1990 (CLSA 1990) five years later had the next major impact upon the provisions of legal services, this time however the change was more favourably weighted in respect of the solicitor's branch of the profession. The CLSA 1990 provided for what the Law Society had been campaigning for; higher rights of audience for solicitors. Under the provisions of the Act the provision of advocacy was to be determined by assessment of an individuals qualifications and membership of a regulated profession. Section 27 allows the Law Society to be able to grant a Certificate of Advocacy upon a solicitor who has undergone the requisite training. These solicitors who have been successful in achieving the higher rights of advocacy are called 'solicitor-advocates' and as a result of these higher rights they are now eligible to be selected as a Q.C. and a member of the judiciary. The Bar Council were not overly enthused with the prospect of solicitors being allowed the right to advocate in the courts as there were originally concerns over the fact that advocacy was traditionally a skill of a trained barrister and so there was the possibility that the quality of the advocacy in the courts would be diminished as a result of the introduction of solicitor-advocates. The Bar was also concerned over the fact that such rights would lead to unfavourable competition in respect of the amount of work available at the Bar. These concerns have not really become apparent as so far only just over 2,000 solicitors have taken the step to become a solicitor-advocate, the quality of advocacy provided is viewed as being on the whole equal to that as provided by barristers and, in respect of the availability of work the Legal Services Commission were forced to ask solicitor-advocates to undertake work refused by the members of the Bar when they were recently on strike over issues of pay, so this has not transpired as an issue.

The movement towards a greater merging of the professions was again discussed in the 2001 report published by the Office of Fair Trading (*Competition in the Professions*). The Report was focused on considering the future of the professions and the effect that the distinct division between the two limbs was having on the provision of legal services to the public. The conclusions of the report were that the restrictions upon direct access to barristers constrained healthy competition between the two professions, that such competition was essential for the development and continuation of the high standards of both of the professions and that the role of Q.C.'s should be abolished (the result of this recommendation has already been discussed above). The Bar Council acted to a degree upon these recommendations of direct access to barristers by the pilot and then widespread introduction of the BarDIRECT and Public Access schemes (see 4.1.4.3).

In 2003 the government conducted a further review into the regulation and provision of legal services (*Review of the regulatory framework for legal services in England and Wales* (2003)), which was headed by Sir David Clementi. The review had two main terms of reference, these being:

- to consider what regulatory framework would be best to promote competition, innovation and the public and consumer interest in the legal sector
- to recommend a framework which will be independent in representing the public and consumer interest

129

In essence the Clementi report recommended the reduction in self-governance by the professions, that a new Office of Legal Complaints be established in respect of the providers of legal services and that a new Legal Services Board should be set up in respect of overseeing the regulating of the profession. The report and its recommendations were in the whole warmly accepted by the Government, the result being the enactment of the Legal Services Act 2007, which received Royal Assent on October 31, 2007 and which provides for a number of key changes to the profession.

The new measures provided for by the Legal Services Act 2007 are for:

- A single and fully independent Office for Legal Complaints (OLC) to remove complaints handling from the legal professions and restore consumer confidence.

- Alternative Business Structures (ABS) that will enable consumers to obtain services from one business entity that brings together lawyers and non-lawyers, increasing competitiveness and improving services. The Act will also allow legal services firms to have up to 25 per cent non-lawyer partners in the near future, before the full ABS regulatory structure is implemented, and will allow different kinds of lawyers to form firms together in the near future.

- A new Legal Services Board (LSB) to act as a single, independent and publicly accountable regulator with the power to enforce high standards in the legal sector, replacing the maze of regulators with overlapping powers. The chair of the Board will be a lay-person and recruitment for members of the Legal Services Board has already begun. David Edmonds, a previous senior civil servant, was recruited as the Chair of the LSB on April 23, 2008.

- A clear set of regulatory objectives for the regulation of legal services which all parts of the system will need to work together to deliver, including promoting and maintaining adherence to professional principles.

The ethos behind the Legal Services Act 2007 is to provide a legal profession that works together as opposed to against each other and is more accessible and user-friendly for the consumer. This will inevitably have far reaching consequences for those now entering the legal profession as it may be that the Bar as we currently know it is significantly reduced in its functions and that the solicitors and barristers of the future are more likely to be all round lawyers as opposed to belonging exclusively to one camp or the other of the 'old style' legal profession.

4.4   Summary

(a) Paralegals are individuals who are either not legally qualified or who are legally qualified but who are working in a non-fee earning capacity within a legal firm. They are essential to the running of a firm as they undertake a large majority of the work that it would be un-cost effective to require a fee-paid member of staff to do.

(b) Legal Executives are described as the third limb to the legal profession. They are qualified under and regulated by the Institute of Legal Executives, and they work in a fee-paid capacity. Becoming a Legal Executive can provide an individual with a non-traditional route to becoming a qualified lawyer.

(c) Solicitors are at the front line of the legal profession, dealing with their clients on a face-to-face basis. They are allowed to conduct litigation on behalf of their clients and the majority of their work is paper based, although they are now also able to achieve higher rights of audience and advocate in the higher courts.

(d) To qualify as a solicitor an individual must first undertake a law degree or a non-law discipline degree followed then by the Common Profession Examination. Upon successful completion of this they must then register with the Law Society as a student solicitor before commencing on to take the one-year Legal Practice Course (LPC). Finally upon completion of the LPC the individual must secure a two-year training contract before being fully qualified to practice as a solicitor in his or her own right.

(e) The Law Society provides representation for all solicitors within England and Wales, whereas the Solicitors Regulation Authority acts in a regulatory capacity over the profession. The Legal Complaints Service investigates complaints made against members of the profession, and the Solicitors Disciplinary Tribunal is a statutory body that disciplines solicitors who are found to have breached the rules of professional conduct.

(f) Barristers traditionally act as advocates within the courtroom. They are prevented from conducting litigation on behalf of their client and can only act upon the instructions of the client. They are generally self-employed and work out of shared facilities with other barristers known as chambers.

(g) A barrister must belong to one of the four Inns of Court, which are the bodies responsible for the calling of barristers to the Bar (inaugurating them into the profession).

(h) Upon ten years call, barristers (and now solicitor-advocates) are eligible to become Queen's Counsel (Q.C.'s). Q.C.'s are those advocates who are viewed as being professionally excellent and successful in their chosen field of law.

(i) Originally access to barristers could only be obtained through a solicitor but now a barrister can be instructed by one of three ways. These being, Professional Client Access (so a solicitor or other authorised litigator), Public Access in respect of civil matters, and Licensed Access through a licensed body.

(j) To qualify as a barrister an individual must undertake either a law degree or a non-law discipline followed by the Common Professional Examination. This is then followed by the completion of the Bar Vocational Course (BVC), and then the individual must try and secure a one-year work placement known as pupillage. Pupillage can be very

131

difficult to achieve due to the high number of BVC graduates and the limited number of pupillages available.

(k) The Bar Council is the representative body for the barrister's profession, whereas the Bar Standards Board deals with any complaints made against a member of the profession. Barristers can now also be personally sued for professional negligence.

(l) Barristers are governed by the Bar Code of Conduct which sets out that their primary duty lies to the court and that they are bound by the 'cab-rank' rule which sets out that they cannot refuse a case based on their personal opinions and prejudices.

(m) The Legal Services Ombudsman (LSO) is an independent body that reviews and investigates complaints made where an individual is not satisfied with the conduct of the complaints procedure employed by the professions.

(n) The individual professions of solicitors and barristers have begun to merge together over the last quarter of a century and their individual roles are no longer clearly defined. The enactment of the Legal Services Act 2007 is expected to almost completely erode any distinction between the two limbs of the legal profession due to the introduction of Alternative Business Structures.

4.5 Self-test questions

1. The body that represents solicitors in England and Wales is the:

   (a) Legal Services Commission
   (b) Law Society
   (c) Solicitors Regulation Authority
   (d) Legal Complaints Service

2. Barristers are called to the:

   (a) Bar
   (b) Bench
   (c) Cloth
   (d) Inn

3. Queen's Counsel are otherwise known as:

   (a) satins
   (b) velvets
   (c) silks
   (d) God

4. Barristers can refuse to take a case because:

   (a) they do not like the client

    (b) they are disgusted by the nature of the case

    (c) they suspect the defendant to be guilty

    (d) they are inexperienced in the area of law involved

5. The higher rights of audience for solicitors were introduced by the:

    (a) Administration of Justice Act 1985

    (b) Courts and Legal Services Act 1990

    (c) Access to Justice Act 1999

    (d) Legal Services Act 2007

4.6 Further reading

D. Hunt, "Reforms could ruin profession" [2006] 8(29) Legal Week 19.

G. Leggatt, "A vexed question?" (2006) Counsel Nov, 10–11.

J. Peysner and Mary Seneviratne, "The legal profession: fusion or diffusion?" [2000] 9(2) Nott. L.J. v–vi.

R. Ramage, "What Clementi forgot to mention" [2006] 156 (7224) N.L.J. 784–785.

J. Robins, "A step up the ladder" [2007] 104(4) L.S.G. 22–24.

M. Seneviratne, "Legal Profession: Negligence The rise and fall of advocates' immunity" [2001] 21(4) L.S. 644.

P. Shaw, "Celebrating difference in an evolving legal market" [2006] 168 Legal Bus. 44–45.

Lord Steyn, "The Role of the Bar, the Judge and the Jury: Winds of Change" [1999] UKPL 51.

M. Stobbs, "An end to conflict" [2006] 103(3) L.S.G. 11.

K. Underwood, "The Legal Services Bill—death by regulation?" [2007] 26 C.J.Q. 124–133.

G. Vos, "Raising the bar" [2007] 104(3) L.S.G. 18–19.

5 Magistrates

5.1 Introduction

The magistrates' court is one of the busiest courts within the justice system. They are found in every major town and city, as well as in a number of the smaller market towns throughout the country. The magistrates' court is a court with (primarily) criminal jurisdiction, but it also has some jurisdiction in relation to a number of civil matters, such as liquor licensing appeals and gaming issues, as well as having a limited family law jurisdiction.

The magistrates' courts are a part of Her Majesty's Courts Service (HMCS), which is in turn an executive agency of the government department now known as the Ministry of Justice. HMCS sets out its mission goal as being:

> All citizens according to their differing needs are entitled to access to justice, whether as victims of crime, defendants accused of crimes, consumers in debt, children in need of care, or business people in commercial disputes. Our aim is to ensure that access is provided as quickly as possible and at the lowest cost consistent with open justice and that citizens have greater confidence in, and respect for, the system of justice.

Every criminal case will pass through the doors of the magistrates' court at some point in time, even if this is very briefly on their way to being sent to the Crown Court. In fact the volume of work considered in the magistrates' court can be illustrated by the fact that the court deals with over 95 per cent of all criminal cases from start to finish. To aid the working of such a busy court there are approximately 29,000 magistrates (who are more formally known as Justices of the Peace) employed by the court, as well as 419 District Judges (see 6.1.4.3 for further details on District Judges). When the magistrates hear a case they will sit in a panel of three, known as the 'Bench', and they will be divided into two 'wingers' and one 'chair'. The chair will announce the decision of the magistrates to the court and deliver their reasoning for the decision, whilst the two wingers will remain silent when in the courtroom. All three magistrates, however, take the decision in the case equally and this can be done by way of a majority vote (two to one), hence the need for a panel of three so as to avoid any stalemate positions.

5.2 History

The first mention of a magistrate dates back well into the 12th Century, as in 1195 the then King, Richard I, appointed a number of his knights to be charged with the position of keeping law and order. These knights became known as the 'Keepers of the Peace' and were effectively the first magistrates of the land, although at this point they did not have an overly judicial role and were probably more akin to an early police force.

In 1361 the title of the 'Keepers of the Peace' changed to its modern day name of 'Justices of the Peace' by way of the enactment of the Justices of the Peace Act 1361. This Act is quite unusual in the fact that it only contains one section (statutory provision), and this one section states that:

> Who shall be Justices of the Peace. First, That in every County of England shall be assigned for the keeping of the Peace, one Lord, and with him three or four of the most worthy in the County, with some learned in the Law, and they shall have Power to restrain the Offenders, Rioters, and all other Barators, and to pursue, arrest, take, and chastise them according to their Trespass or Offence; and to cause them to be imprisoned and duly punished according to the Law and Customs of the Realm, and according to that which to them shall seem best to do by their Discretions and good Advisement; [. . .]; and to take and arrest all those that they may find by Indictment, or by Suspicion, and to put them in Prison; and to take of all them that be [not] of good Fame, where they shall be found, sufficient Surety and Mainprise of their good Behaviour towards the King and his People, and the other duly to punish; to the Intent that the People be not by such Rioters or Rebels troubled nor endamaged, nor the Peace blemished, nor Merchants nor other passing by the Highways of the Realm disturbed, nor put in the Peril which may happen of such Offenders.

Following the enactment of this statute the Justices of the Peace now had the ability and powers to be able to arrest alleged offenders, investigate the offences and punish the offender appropriately. At around the same time as the enactment of the Justices of the Peace Act 1361, Parliament also passed a statute that required the Justices of the Peace to meet four times a year so as to conduct matters of local business; these session became known as the 'Quarter Sessions'.

The magistrates' role continued to expand over the years and they were responsible for not only conducting criminal matters, but they also began to develop a large administrative role. In the 14th Century they became responsible for the regulation of wages; in 1576 they were required to provide 'houses of correction' (early prisons) where those who had committed criminal acts could be detained; in 1597 they assumed responsibility over the Poor Laws and in 1652 they were granted the powers to be able to conduct marriages. The remit of the work of the magistrates became massive, almost to an unworkable point and, consequently, from about 1829 onwards the magistrates began to be relieved of the large share of their administrative duties and, by the latter end of the 19th Century, the local councils had assumed the large majority of these functions, leaving the magistrates to deal with mainly criminal matters and the occasional administrative role in relation to issues such as liquor licensing laws.

The criminal side of the magistrates' work also expanded rapidly over the years, so much so that the Quarter Sessions were quickly found not to provide a sufficient amount of time in which to deal with large volume of cases appropriately. Consequently in 1605 the Privy Council set out that the magistrates should meet at more regular intervals than four times a year (many of the local magistrates had been meeting on an informal basis in between the Quarter Sessions by this point anyway). These more frequent meetings became known as the 'Petty Sessions' and around the same time the 'Court of Assizes' was also developed, with its function being to deal with the more serious criminal cases where a jury was required. The Petty Sessions and the Court of Assizes continued for 600 years until, under the Courts Act 1971, the Petty Sessions became formally known as the magistrates' court, and the Court of Assizes became the Crown Court.

Figure 5.1 Historical development of the magistracy

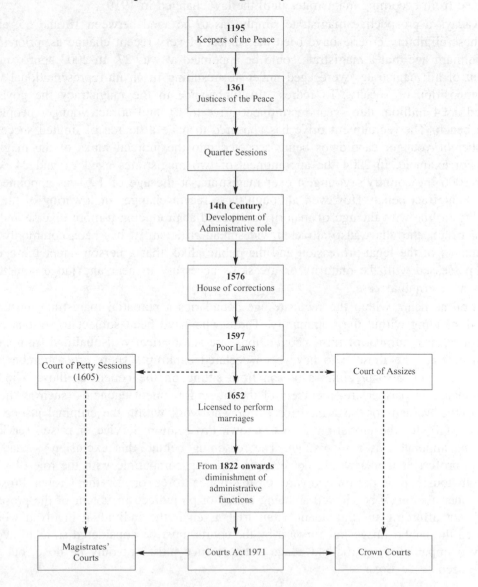

5.3   Eligibility

The first point to note in respect of magistrates is that they are not required to have any legal or professional qualifications; they need know no law and they must simply be interested in and dedicated to serving the community in which they live. In fact the eligibility criteria are generally quite wide and therefore this leaves the possibility of becoming a magistrate open to a broad sector of society. This has not always been the case though, as prior to 1906 there was a property qualification restriction upon becoming a magistrate, meaning that any person who wished to stand as a magistrate had to own their own land. Women were also originally prevented from becoming magistrates until the law changed in 1919.

Nowadays a prospective magistrate simply has to be aged between 18 and 65, although even these eligibility criteria have been the subject of very recent change as, prior to 2004, the minimum age that a magistrate could be appointed at was 27. In 2003 approximately 4 per cent of all magistrates were aged under 40, resulting in an un-representational view of the composition of society. To redress this imbalance in the magistracy the government initiated a £4 million, three-year recruitment drive to try and attract younger people to sit on the bench. The recruitment drive has appeared to have a degree of limited success with a number of younger candidates being accepted into the judicial ranks of the magistrates' court. For example, in 2004 the appointment of two magistrates aged 21 and 24 occurred and in 2006 the country's youngest ever magistrate, at the age of 19, was appointed to sit on the Pontefract bench. However, although these recent changes of lowering of the age of eligibility in line with the age of majority are aimed at producing a more diverse and varied judicial bench, they have also attracted widespread criticism. It has been commonly opined by members of the legal profession and the public alike, that a person under the age of 27 is not possessed with the maturity or life skills necessary to hear and judge something so serious as a criminal case.

As well as being within the requisite age boundaries a potential magistrate must also be of good standing within the community. Those who have been subject to serious criminal convictions, or a number of minor convictions, are automatically disqualified from sitting as a magistrate, as are those who have been declared bankrupt. There are a number of professions that will also preclude a person from sitting on the bench, as those who are, or whose spouse or partner are, members of the law enforcement agencies (such as the police force, traffic wardens or the armed forces) or who work within the criminal justice system (as court staff, for the probation service, Crown Prosecution Service or prison service etc.) cannot be appointed as a magistrate. The reasoning behind this exclusion is that such a person's professional role would not be seen as being compatible with the role of a magistrate. Obviously if a person worked for the police force or for the Crown Prosecution Service then they may be viewed as being biased or prejudiced in favour of the prosecution, thereby not affording the defendant a fair trial. Even if the individual involved would not be biased the public image put forward by the courts must be considered so as to avoid any perceived impartiality; as the old adage states 'justice must not only be done, but it must also be seen to be done'.

5.4   The role of a magistrate

Sitting as a magistrate is not a financially rewarding occupation as all magistrates sit as unpaid volunteers. They are individuals who are willing to give up their spare time and help to deliver justice within their own community. Becoming a magistrate is certainly not a way for a person to make their fame and fortune, but it is a method for allowing individuals to give something back to society, and a desire to sit as a magistrate can often be said to come from an individual having a strong sense of civic duty and responsibility. Although magistrates are unpaid, they are allowed to claim back any expenses that they have incurred in the course of carrying out their judicial functions. This means that they can recoup any monies spent on travel or subsistence but these losses must have actually been incurred and they must also be reasonable; putting in a claim for a £200 lunch would certainly be viewed as excessive.

The level of dedication and commitment required to become a magistrate can also be viewed as quite an onerous task, as the minimum that they must agree to sit is a least 26 half-days per year. A half-day is classed as either between the hours of 10 am to 2 pm, or 2 pm to 5 pm, with arrival to be half an hour prior to the commencement of court so that the magistrates can prepare in advance of sitting. Some magistrates' courts are organised on a full-day basis and in such situations the magistrates must be able to sit for full days as and when required by the court. Even though the minimum required time to sit is 26 half-days per year it is hoped and envisaged that a magistrate will regularly sit more frequently than this, and the average sitting time is set at between 35 and 45 half-days per year. If a magistrate sits more regularly than this then there becomes the danger that the bench will not be representative of the local community. The Magistrates' Courts Association sets out that a magistrate should not spend more than 70 half-days sitting per year, unless the sittings are spread out within different courts (youth courts, family courts etc), and the absolute maximum that a magistrate is permitted to sit is 100 half-days per year.

Arrangements for sittings are worked out well in advance on a rota basis and it is usually possible to make changes in an emergency. Obviously sitting as a magistrate requires a great deal of considered commitment, as the requirements can have an impact on both the magistrates' work and home life. It is preferred that individual magistrates' sittings are scheduled at regular intervals thorough out the year so that they can maintain the necessary level of competence required for court, but it is also accepted that certain individuals may need to have their sitting times scheduled during periods such as term-time, for example if they have school age children, or during school holidays if they are a school teacher. Employers are legally obliged to allow their employees time off to undertake lay magistracy duties.

As well as the regular required sitting days, magistrates are also expected to attend extra-curricular meetings and training sessions. This is to ensure that they are kept up to date with any new developments in the law, as well as to ensure that they receive continuous professional development so that they remain competent in their roles. These extra sessions are generally held outside of normal working hours (often at weekends) so that all magistrates should be able to attend these additional commitments. If a magistrate has more time to spare, then they may volunteer, when sufficiently experienced, for extra sittings or train to join the Family or Youth

Panels, the Betting and Gaming or Licensing Appeals (see below for further details on the work of these courts).

As stated above the majority of a magistrate's work will involve them sitting in the magistrates' court. The Ministry of Justice (http://www.direct.gov.uk) sets out that a magistrate's role includes, amongst other things:

- determining whether a defendant is guilty or not and passing the appropriate sentence
- deciding on requests for remand in custody
- deciding on applications for bail
- committing more serious cases to the Crown Court

Deciding to sit as a magistrate is a decision that carries with it a large amount of responsibility as the role involves deliberating upon a person's guilt and innocence, and ultimately determining issues concerning their welfare and liberty. They consider the evidence in each case and reach a verdict. If a defendant is found guilty, or pleads guilty, they decide on the most appropriate sentence. Magistrates deal with the less serious criminal cases, such as minor theft, criminal damage, public disorder and motoring offences.

Furthermore, magistrates do not just appear in the adult criminal courts, and after receiving appropriate training, an individual magistrate may decide to undertake further judicial functions in the other courts where they have jurisdiction.

5.4.1   The Family Court

Magistrates can undertake a large degree of family court work. Magistrates who sit in the family courts are specially selected and trained magistrates and they will deal with issues such as those relating to the breakdown of a marriage, child contact and residence orders under the Children Act 1989, adoption orders, protection orders in relation to cases of domestic violence and public law matters relating to the care and control of children.

5.4.2   The Youth Court

As young persons under the age of 18 cannot normally be tried in the adult criminal courts (the magistrates' or the Crown Court) then there is a court system in place so that they can be tried effectively and fairly. The Youth Court will hear cases involving offenders aged between 10 and 17 years. The magistrates who sit in the youth court are again specially trained and they sit on what is known as a 'youth panel'. Youth courts are courts that are heard *in camera*; this means that they are not open to the public and only those involved in the case will attend the hearing. The court hearings are far more informal than the traditional adult courts and there is more interaction between the defendant, their family and the court than is usually found in other courts. Magistrates in the Youth Court have extended sentencing powers as they can sentence for up to 24 months (as opposed to the usual six months in the adult courts).

5.4.3 Civil courts

Despite losing the vast majority of their administrative powers over the years magistrates still sit within the civil justice system and deal with matters such as appeals relating to the refusal to grant a liquor licence (local authorities are responsible initially for deciding whether or not to grant such a licence) and issues relating to betting and gaming. They also hear cases involving debt recovery on behalf of utility companies and local authorities (i.e. non-payment of council tax etc).

5.4.4 Crown Court

Magistrates may also occasionally appear in the Crown Court when hearing appeals from the magistrates' court (see Chapter 13 on Appeals for further details).

5.5 Appointment

According to government statistics (Eighth Judicial Appointments Report—October 1, 2005 to March 1, 2006) there were 2,212 magistrates appointed for the year 2005 to 2006; this figure was a slight increase on prior years as previously the recruitment figures of new magistrates was between approximately 1,400 and 1,700. The Lord Chancellor under s.10 of the Courts Act 2003 will officially appoint a new magistrate and this will be done in Her Majesty's name. Prior to the enactment of the Courts Act 2003 the areas of Lancashire, Greater Manchester and Merseyside were unique in the appointment of magistrates, insomuch as a magistrate would not be appointed by the Lord Chancellor, but rather by the Chancellor of the Duchy of Lancaster. The reasons for the difference in the person appointing them is one that was steeped in history but now, due to the introduction of s.10, this rather quaint British tradition has been eroded and the appointment of magistrates is now a unified system countrywide. The Lord Chancellor's decision as to which individuals are to be suitable for appointment to the magistracy is guided by the involvement of the Advisory Committees, as they will assess the potential candidates and make recommendations to him.

5.5.1 The Advisory Committees

There are a number of Advisory Committees over the length and breadth of the country, forming a network of Committees, each one of which serves their local geographical area. Their role is to determine the number of magistrates that should be appointed per year for their local area and they will consider the individual applications made by any potential magistrates. The

Committees are also responsible for monitoring and ensuring that appointed magistrates are fulfilling their allotted sitting duties and they may be called to investigate and advise if any issues regarding the competency of a magistrate is raised. The Committees are responsible directly to the Lord Chancellor.

The Committees are composed of a number of people who live within the local area. At least one third of the Committee must be comprised of persons who do not hold a judicial role (so not be magistrates themselves), whereas the remaining two thirds of the Committee will consist of serving magistrates. The purpose of having lay-people involved in the appointment of magistrates is that it is hoped that such people will bring a different perspective to the table on the needs and requirements of the local area, thereby ensuring that a representative bench is maintained.

5.5.2 Personal qualities of magistrates

To determine whether a candidate will make a suitable magistrate the Advisory Committee will initially consider the application in line with reference to the six key personal qualities set out by the Lord Chancellor. These six key qualities are:

- good character
- understanding and communication
- social awareness
- maturity and sound temperament
- sound judgement
- commitment and reliability

Theses qualities go towards assessing the candidate's judicial qualities; whether they will make a good magistrate or not. Firstly a magistrate must be of good character, as they must command the confidence, respect and trust of the public and have personal integrity. If they possessed a number of criminal convictions or were bankrupt themselves there would be a concern over whether they would be able to make unbiased decisions as to the culpability of the defendant in a case; they may not be able to view the case objectively and therefore this could result in unfair and unjust decisions being taken. The necessity for a magistrate to possess understanding and the ability to communicate effective is of high importance for what really are obvious reasons. If a magistrate had poor language skills or a very limited level of intelligence then they would not be able to effectively assess the evidence presented to them in a case, this lack of understanding could have severely detrimental consequences upon the fairness of a case and could result in perverse decisions being made. The same reasoning can be applied to the necessity for a magistrate to be able to communicate effectively. Magistrates must work together in their deliberations and, if one member of the bench could not put forward their views on the case in a comprehensible manner, then this may also result in an unjust decision being made. Magistrates also need to possess the ability to convey their reasoning and decision to the court in an understandable manner and this would be severely impeded if the magistrate in question lacked competent communication skills.

Social awareness is also a required quality of a magistrate; this awareness is to include an appreciation of and acceptance of the rule of law, as well of the ability to respect people from different ethnic, cultural or social backgrounds. By being socially aware the magistrate will be able to assess the evidence and the manner of the case being presented to them and they will be able to use such inherent information to assist them in the making of the appropriate decision. One of the principles behind the role of a magistrate is that they are aware of the social issues that directly affect the local area in which they sit, as well as the wider societal values and issues. For example, if a local area has a large drug and gun crime problem then the magistrates' social awareness may allow them to consider imposing a heavier sentence so as to act as a deterrent to others continuing in the area. What is a social issue in one geographical area may not be in another and as such the magistrates will need to possess such information so as to be able to serve their community effectively.

Maturity and sound judgment and temperament are all a prerequisite of being appointed into a judicial position. Such skills are to encompass the willingness to listen, to be decisive, and to be firm but fair where necessary, but always with a high degree of courtesy and humanity. If a magistrate does not hold these qualities then there will be the possibility that there will be no consistency or logic in their decision making process. The requirement of these judicial qualities, especially in relation to maturity, has been raised as a concern in relation to the appointment of young magistrates. As stated above, it can be argued that a person who is only 19 or 20 years old has not 'lived enough' to gain sufficient life experience to then enable them to make rationalised and sound decisions on the future fate of another human being. They must also possess the ability to think logically, to be able to weigh up both sides of the argument and balance them to be able to reach a considered conclusion, and in doing so they must also work with an open and objective mind, nor should they be influenced by any prejudices of any kind.

Finally there is a direct need for a potential magistrate to be able to commit to the role and be reliable in their judicial functions. These qualities will be assessed by the Committee when considering whether the candidate will be able to meet the minimum sitting days quota set down by the Lord Chancellor (see 5.4 above). If candidates' personal circumstances allude to the fact that they will not be able to fully dedicate themselves to the requirements of the role (maybe due to work or family commitments) then the Committee may find themselves coming to the conclusion that the candidate does not satisfy this element of the six key qualities. The Committee will look to see if the candidate has the help and support of their family, friends and employer as all of these could have a bearing on their level of reliability. They must also be of good health. The court system would become inefficient and slow if magistrates did not turn up to court when required as cases would be delayed, and the longer there is a delay in a criminal case then the higher the chance the defendant will not be afforded a fair trial.

Overall aspiring magistrates need to be well-rounded and balanced people. They must be able to assimilate factual information as they will be presented with a wealth of evidence to work their way through, they must be able to make reasoned decisions with care, thought and impartiality, they must also be able to work together as a team and take account of the reasoning and views of others.

5.5.3 The selection process

Appointments to the magistracy are not conducted by way of a set competition where an advert for vacancies is published with a closing date for applications to be made, but rather the application process is rather an open one where an interested candidate can make an application at any time during the year. The application is made, by way of a set application form, to the local magistrates Advisory Committee who will then review and sift the applications in preparation of calling those potential candidates who appear to possess the necessary skills and criteria on paper to interview.

The interview stage of selection is normally a two-stage process whereby the potential candidates will be asked to attend a first interview, which will be concerned with assessing whether they do in fact possess the personal qualities and attributes necessary to become a magistrate. This initial interview will be conducted by either a Sub-Committee of the Advisory Committee or a specially convened interview panel comprising of members of the Advisory Committee. The panel will normally interview a number of potential magistrates on the same day and the interview will take the form of a standard job interview, with the candidate being asked general questions about themselves.

If, after the initial interview, the panel are convinced that the individual in question does possess the necessary qualities required to become a magistrate then they may, depending on the local Advisory Committee policy, be requested to return at a later date for a second interview. This second interview will predominately focus on determining the candidate's judicial aptitude and ability to cope with such a role. To assess these skills the candidates will be given a number of case studies to consider. These case studies will involve common scenarios that occur regularly within the magistrates' court, and the candidates will be questioned about them so that the panel can ascertain their views on issues such as crime and punishment. The candidates may be asked to identify the relevant issues in a case, or to suggest an appropriate sentence and they may also be asked about their response to certain ethical and moral issues. The case studies and the candidates' reactions to them will then allow the panel to judge whether they would be a suitable person to become a magistrate. Obviously a person who indicates that they would acquit all defendants who come before them due to their high level of empathy and sympathy would not be an appropriate person to sit as a magistrate. Conversely, nor would a person be thought to be suitable if they were insistent on handing out six-month sentences for all offenders, regardless of the offence or its circumstances.

Once the Advisory Committee have identified those candidates who they believe are suitable for selection as magistrates then they will notify the Lord Chancellor (by way of his office) so that he may then appoint them officially. The process to be selected and appointed as a magistrate is a rather long one that can, on average, take somewhere between six and 12 months to achieve.

5.5.4 A reflective bench

As the bench in the magistrates' court effectively replaces the role of the jury in the Crown Court, the Advisory Committee must try to ensure that the bench is reflective of the community which it serves. To ensure that a defendant has a fair trial the composition of the bench that hears the case should be a diverse one; the Committee should only seek to recommend those persons for appointment who will ensure that the bench is broadly reflective in terms of this diversity. The Magistrates' Association (http://www.magistrates-association.org.uk) sets out the guidelines as to what factors should be considered in achievement of this. There should be a balance of:

- gender
- ethnic origin
- geographical location
- occupation
- age
- social background
- political affiliation

For example the guidelines state that the gender split between male and female should be roughly equal. This is so that there are sufficient numbers of both sexes who are eligible to sit on the bench in the courts. This is particularly important in respect of the family and youth courts as there it is necessary to have at least one man and one woman sit on the bench of three, unless it is completely impractical to do so. The statistical figures available (Eighth Judicial Appointments Report—October 1, 2005 to March 1, 2006) in relation to the number of magistrates appointed between 1998 and 2006 show that this roughly equal split is being achieved, with the average being that fractionally more males than females are appointed to the bench; in the year 2005 to 2006 there were 1,132 men and 1,080 women appointed.

The ethnic origins and diversity of the bench must also be considered, and this should be assessed in relation to the general ethnic composition of local area of the specific magistrates' court. The number of persons from ethnic minorities is a more telling figure as to the true diversity of the bench as in 2005–2006 only 10.17 per cent of all magistrates were from a BME group, although this figure is a slight rise from previous years where it has been between six and nine per cent.

The geographical location of the candidates will also have a bearing on the recommendation of appointment. Prior to the enactment of the Courts Act 2003 it was a necessary requirement for a magistrate to live within 15 miles of their local court where they were to serve. This requirement has now been made obsolete and the Committee will now simply check to ensure that a number of candidates do not live very close to each other, i.e. on the same street, or within a close geographical area. Magistrates do generally still need to live near the community that they serve though, so as to ensure that they have an understanding of the social issues relevant to that area.

The occupation of a candidate is another determining factor, as the Magistrates' Association sets out that no more than 15 per cent of the magistrates on a bench should be from the same occupational group. Magistrates are also required to reveal if they are members of certain clubs and organisations, such as the Freemasons, and their political affliations will be taken into consideration.

These guidance factors and the drive to achieve a diverse and full reflective magistracy does have the possible effect that a potentially suitable candidate may not be appointed if there was the possibility that their appointment would increase or cause an imbalance in one of these key areas. If a local bench of 100 magistrates already has 15 people who were classed as being in the 'professional category' (as classified by the Office for National Statistics), but only three people from the 'sales or customer services category' then the Advisory Committee would be prevented from appointing any other person from the 'professional category' until such a time that the occupation balance had been equalled out slightly. This would be the case no matter how suitable and appropriate the candidate was; in these circumstances such a candidate would have to wait until a later time when their appointment would not unbalance the composition of the bench.

An example of the typical composition of the magistrates' court bench can be seen in the below figures, which have been taken from the Department of Constitutional Affairs Judicial Appointments Annual Report for 2003–2004.

Figure 5.2 Composition of the magistrates' court bench

Commission Area	Total	Age				Gender		Political affiliation						Ethnic background				
		Under 40	40–49	50–59	60–69	M	F	Con	Lab	Lib Dem	Pl Cy	Other	Un	W	B	A	O	NK
Avon and Somerset	837	35	114	385	303	405	432	269	170	141	0	2	255	803	19	10	5	0
Cambridgeshire	350	14	50	175	111	171	179	134	79	41	0	21	75	336	4	9	1	0
Cheshire	446	20	77	208	141	228	218	145	120	54	0	53	74	435	2	8	1	0
Cleveland	472	20	77	214	161	260	212	165	146	34	0	35	92	452	2	15	3	0
Derbyshire	399	16	41	195	147	205	194	141	112	48	0	19	79	382	4	10	2	1
Devon and Cornwall	721	18	87	352	264	355	366	255	108	132	0	65	161	713	0	3	5	0
Durham	287	12	42	143	90	153	134	56	98	20	0	19	94	281	3	3	0	0
Dyfed Powys	352	6	42	187	117	197	155	89	76	49	43	29	66	350	0	2	0	0
Essex	605	6	75	317	207	305	300	233	111	94	0	48	119	590	7	7	1	0
City of London	120	5	29	52	34	53	67	49	21	12	0	6	32	101	12	4	3	0
Gloucestershire	249	3	28	105	113	134	115	121	39	38	0	21	30	239	4	5	1	0
Humberside	437	14	52	210	161	225	212	166	106	47	0	27	91	429	0	7	1	0
Kent	798	22	102	412	262	416	382	323	146	111	0	44	174	765	7	20	6	0
Leicestershire	511	21	67	243	180	261	250	163	120	62	0	14	152	465	12	26	8	0
Lincolnshire	375	13	51	180	131	187	188	149	70	50	0	42	64	368	0	6	1	0
Norfolk	426	12	43	219	152	213	213	141	88	56	0	22	119	417	1	5	3	0

Con = Conservative, Lab = Labour, Lib Dem = Liberal Democrats, Pl Cy = Plaid Cymru, Oth = Other, Un = Uncommitted/not known/other
W = White, B =Black, A = Asian, O = Other, NK = Not known
Source: Department of Constitutional Affairs Judicial Appointments Annual Report for 2003–2004. Reproduced with kind permission of the Ministry of Justice.

5.6   Recruitment

Despite the clear appointment guidelines the government found that the magistracy was still over-represented in some social groups (white, middle-aged and middle-class professionals) and under-represented in other social groups (ethnic minorities, young persons and those from disadvantaged backgrounds) and in 2003, under the guidance of the then Secretary of State and Lord Chancellor, Lord Falconer, the National Strategy for the Recruitment of Lay Magistrates was launched. In his foreword to the National Recruitment Strategy 2003 Lord Falconer set out that it would:

> [e]xamine not only how to raise the profile of the magistracy generally, but also to develop a framework to target the recruitment and retention of magistrates from under-represented groups, whilst continuing to draw on the support of those who have traditionally provided the backbone of local recruitment.
>
> The strategy will aim to highlight the importance of the work of magistrates, particularly to employers, who must be persuaded that, by allowing staff who are magistrates time off to carry out their duties, they are contributing enormously to the maintenance of local justice and the values of good citizenship. This approach will also be designed to encourage the self-employed that they, too, have a role to play in serving their community by directing their individual talents towards furthering the cause of justice in the community.

The idea behind the Strategy was for it to combine best practice and ensure that recruitment was carried out in a targeted, professional and co-coordinated manner. The three main strategic objectives were:

- to recruit and retain magistrates from a diverse spectrum of the population
- to raise the profile of the magistracy and dispel generally held misconceptions about its make up and the entry requirements
- to support the appointments process

In relation to the recruitment and retaining of magistrates the Strategy highlighted two areas of high importance; the first was in relation to targeting and encouraging employers to release staff so that they could fulfil their magistrates' duties, and the second related to the revision of existing methods of recruitment with the consideration of alternative methods. The proposed action for tackling the first high priority issue was to develop a campaign specifically directed towards employers so that they became aware of the benefits that can be gained from having an employee who also sits as a magistrate. The Strategy sets out that these benefits could include the employee gaining a number of marketable skills that are transferable to the workplace at no added cost to the employer. The examples given in the Strategy of the types of transferable skills acquired were, the moral authority to make difficult decisions, self-confidence, teamwork, appraisal, mentoring and communication skills. As a result of the action taken to tackle this part of the Strategy, the employers of potential magistrates are now provided with an information pack on the role and the functions of the magistracy and how it may benefit them.

The proposed action for the second high priority point was for a well-directed recruitment campaign to be conducted through a variety of media outlets, such as the local newspapers and radio, as well as specialist publications that targeted specific groups, i.e. Asian community newsletters, local community groups and community centres etc. A large part of the recruitment problem appeared to stem from the fact that people were simply not aware that they could apply to become magistrates without any formal qualifications or experience. Adverts now go out across a range of media outlets which reach a far wider and more diverse sector of society than ever occurred previously.

The Strategy also highlighted the need, amongst other things, to:

- provide an online application system
- develop a simple leaflet setting out the role, responsibility and duties of a magistrate and the training that will be provided so that candidates can achieve the necessary competencies
- research into the possible barriers that existed to stop people coming forward, such as age or self-employment, and take appropriate steps to break down those barriers
- create networks to support and encourage magistrates from ethnic minorities and those with disabilities
- build in more flexibility in relation to court sitting requirements

The objectives highlighted by the Recruitment Strategy were to ensure that there was a continued improvement in the recruitment of magistrates from a socially wide and diverse background so that the bench could move towards fully reflecting the society which it serves. However, there will always be issues with achieving such a reflective composition of the magistracy due to everyday practicalities of life. Those who put themselves forward to sit as a magistrate are generally those who have the time, resources and inclination to do so. This invariably means that they are people who have already established their careers and they do not need to impress their employers with complete job commitment, or they have developed the confidence in themselves to approach their manager to request the time off to fulfil their duties. It would be very unusual to find a person in their early twenties who would feel comfortable enough to approach their employer to discuss such matters. As a result the magistracy consists of a larger number of middle-aged persons than younger ones (although do note the earlier comments on this point). Additionally the occupation or the class of an individual can have an effect on their abilities and desires to become a magistrate. Many magistrates are people who hold middle management and professional roles, where the idea of serving a civic duty is quite readily accepted, or they are semi-retired individuals who are looking for something to occupy their time. People from every walk of life (bar the exceptions mentioned above) can apply to sit as a magistrate, but again it is difficult to envisage a single mum of four children having any spare time, or being willing to give up any spare time that they do have, to be able to sit as a magistrate. Due to circumstances of life, and despite the recruitment drive initiated by the government, the magistracy is still heavily weighted in favour of middle-aged, middle-class white people, which unfortunately falls short of being a truly reflective representation of our society as it is today.

5.6.1   The oath

Upon appointment all new magistrates must swear the judicial oath in a confirmation that they will carry out their judicial duties in an appropriate and responsible manner. The judicial oath is:

> I,.., swear that I will well and truly serve our Sovereign Lady Queen Elizabeth the Second, in the office of Justice of the Peace and I will do right to all manner of people after the laws and usages of the Realm without fear or favour, affection or ill will.

By pledging their allegiance to the Crown it is envisaged that magistrates will uphold the oath and commit to carrying out their duties and functions in an appropriate manner.

5.7   Training

As magistrates generally have little knowledge of the law and the court system it is important that they are sufficiently trained so that they can carry out their role effectively. This does not mean that they need to be taught the laws of the country in detail, as they have a legal adviser in the courtroom to aid and assist them with such intricacies (see 5.8 below), but they do need to be aware of issues such as the relevant court procedures and their powers of sentencing etc. The training of magistrates is supervised by the Magistrates' Committee of the Judicial Studies Board, as directed by the Lord Chancellor; however the majority of the training is actually undertaken and delivered by the local legal advisers. The training is mandatory for all new magistrates, and even once initially trained all magistrates are expected to continue on with their professional development and attend further training so that they can maintain their competences within the courtroom. Details of the training are found in the framework laid down by the Magistrates' National Training Initiative (MNTI 2), which, in 2004, refined the first Initiative (MNTI 1),which was introduced in 1998. The MNTI 2 sets out that the three basic competencies required to be demonstrated by a magistrate are:

1. managing yourself
2. working as a member of the team
3. making judicial decisions

Each competency involves a number of different skills that a magistrate is required to master, but every competency (and skill) is equally as important as the others. Examples of the skills required under the first competency of 'Managing yourself' would include obtaining and reading the relevant paperwork, ensuring that each person is aware of their role in court that day, being aware of the documentation that may provide guidance whilst in court and checking to identify any potential conflicts of interest. The second competency of 'Working as a member of the team' includes skills such as being able to express views clearly and concisely, being able to listen to and give consideration to colleagues' contributions and being able to challenge discriminatory comments made by colleagues. The final competency of 'Making judicial decisions' sets out skills such as having a knowledge of the legal framework and principles that apply to the magistrates' court, being able to identify, analyse and assess the relevant information and evidence and having an understanding of the court system and the doctrine of precedent.

All magistrates should receive their own copy of the competence framework, as well as details as to the level and sequence of training that they need to undertake. The Annual Agreement on the National Minimum Training Provision for Magistrates 2008/09, as provided by the Judicial Studies Board, sets out the details of the training that must be taken by a newly appointed magistrate before they are allowed to sit in the court and so that the magistrates can achieve the three competencies detailed above.

The first training that a new magistrate will receive is known as 'Initial Introductory Training' and this is where the new magistrates will be introduced to the magistracy and the life of the bench. This initial training period will be for at least a three hour period, and no less. After the new magistrates have completed the initial training they will then go on to undertake what is known as the 'Initial Core Training'. The training requirements of this Core Training are set out in the Justices of the Peace (Training and Development Committee) Rules 2007, which came into force on July 13, 2007. The training involves the completion of 12 separate modules, and each one must be completed before the magistrate may sit in the court. The 12 separate modules follow the syllabus set by the Judicial Studies Board and they cover:

- a magistrate's training and development

- judicial decision making

- the jurisdiction of magistrates

- case management and preliminary decisions

- plea before venue and mode of trial

- summary trial, evidence and determining guilt or innocence

- sentencing

- road traffic cases, disqualification and endorsement

- enforcement of court orders

- out-of-court business, applications and other hearings

- magistrates in context

- review and planning for ongoing training and development

This core training will take place over an absolute minimum of three days (18 hours), although this feasibly may take longer due to individual magistrates' commitments. The training will also be supplemented by a number of activities so that the magistrate gains a well-rounded view of the role of the magistrate. These activities will include a number of court observations, visits to other institutions (i.e. prisons), and there will also be a degree of mentoring provided by an experienced magistrate. After the magistrate has successfully completed the Initial Training they will be ready to sit in court. At first this will be by way of mentored sittings, and then they will eventually progress on to sitting as a (winger) magistrate in their own right on the bench.

Approximately 12 months after being to sit as a magistrate a newly appointed magistrate is required to undergo 12 hours of Consolidation Training (existing magistrates are not compelled to undertake this training, although it is advised), so as to consolidate and examine all that they have learnt so far. After a magistrate has sat for approximately two years they will then be appraised so as to check that they are meeting the required competencies and it is at this point that any issues can be identified and addressed as necessary. If a magistrate is found to not be meeting the competencies then the appraiser will recommend that they receive further training so that they are able to improve and meet the necessary criteria. If, after further training and appraisals, the magistrate is unable to evidence that they can satisfy the competencies then the matter will be referred to the Bench Training and Development Committee, who upon review may decide to recommend to the Lord Chancellor that the magistrate is relieved of their position.

Even after a magistrate has undertaken the Consolidation Training and their appraisal they are still expected to attend further training so as to continue on with their professional and personal development. The further training consists of six hours' worth of 'First Continuation Training', which prepares the magistrate for their second appraisal and introduces the idea and possibility of becoming a chair of the bench and then after this point they will undergo 'Winger Continuation Training'. This continuation training is scheduled to take place every three years before their next appraisal and it has the purpose of providing the magistrates with an opportunity to review their current practices and competencies.

If a magistrate decides that they want to become a chair, or that they wish to work within the family or youth courts, then they must undergo the relevant training for that role as each one carries with it its own competencies and framework that must be achieved.

The structure and training of magistrates has become far more focused over the past ten years due to Lord Justice Auld's comments in his 2001 review of the Criminal Courts. Lord Auld identified that the then MNTI 1 was overly complicated and in parts unachievable (for example it had 104 core competencies) and that there was a lack of consistency and standard of training provided by different magistracy areas. The government and those involved in the administration of the magistracy listened to those criticisms and took them onboard, resulting in a generally well-trained and fit for purpose training programme, although this training is still continuously under review by the Judicial Studies Board so that the level currently being attained is at least sustained, if not bettered.

Figure 5.3 The training process for magistrates

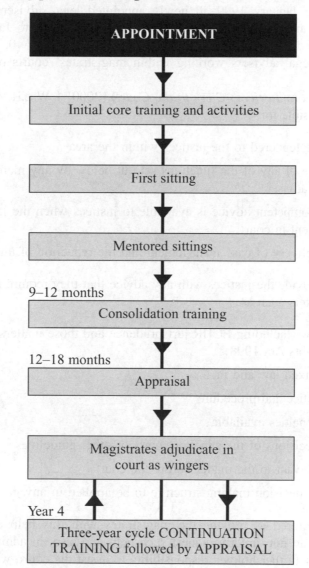

Source: An Introduction to MNTI 2 for New Magistrates by the Judicial Studies Board (www.jsbtutors.co.uk).

5.8   Legal advisers

As magistrates are not legally qualified it is imperative that they are advised by someone who is well versed in the law so that they can make the right decision in the circumstances. So that the magistrates can be advised appropriately and carry out their judicial functions there is, in every magistrates' court, a person who is known as a 'legal adviser' (formerly known as a Justices' Clerk). Since January 1999 all newly appointed legal advisers must be either a qualified solicitor or barrister, and those who were appointed prior to January 1999 had to become legally qualified within ten years unless they were aged over 40. There are currently approximately 1,800 legal advisers working within magistrates' courts over the length and breadth of the country.

The *Practice Direction (Justices: Clerk to the Court)* [2000] 1 W.L.R. 1886 sets out that a legal adviser is responsible for:

- the legal advice tendered to the justices within the area
- the performance of any of the functions set out below by any member of his/her staff acting as legal adviser
- ensuring that competent advice is available to justices when the justice's clerk is not personally present in court
- the effective delivery of case management and the reduction of unnecessary delay

And that they must provide the justices with any advice that they require to properly perform their functions on matters such as:

- questions of law (including ECHR jurisprudence and those matters set out in s.2(1) of the Human Rights Act 1998)
- questions of mixed law and fact
- matters of practice and procedure
- the range of penalties available
- any relevant decisions of the superior courts or other guidelines
- other issues relevant to the matter before the court
- the appropriate decision making structure to be applied in any given case

A legal adviser is required to provide the magistrates with this help and advice even in situations where they do not directly request such help and also, in addition to advising the court, the legal adviser further holds a responsibility to assist the court, where appropriate, as to the formulation of reasons and the recording of those reasons. The *Practice Direction* further places an onus on the magistrates to refer to the legal adviser at any point where they feel it necessary, as it states:

> At any time, justices are entitled to receive advice to assist them in discharging their responsibilities. If they are in any doubt as to the evidence which has been given, they should seek the aid of their legal adviser.

There are a number of procedural issues that must be taken into account when considering the role of a legal adviser within the magistrates' court, especially in relation to ensuring that the defendant receives a fair trial. The main one of these is that the magistrates, and not the legal adviser, are to be the triers of fact in the courtroom and it is of vital importance that the legal adviser does not exert any undue pressure or influence upon the magistrates in their decision making processes; there is an inherent danger that this could occur simply due to the legal adviser's knowledge and the magistrates' reliance upon them for guidance. To ensure that the defendant's rights are not breached the Practice Direction sets out that any advice sought from or received from the legal adviser should be done in open court so that all parties to the proceedings are privy to the advice. The magistrates can request that the legal adviser joins them in the retiring room whilst they are deliberating, but this must only be for a reasonable length of time for the purposes of delivering the requested advice. In the case of *R. v Eccles Justice Ex p. Fitzpatrick* (1989) 89 Cr. App. R. 324 it was held that it was not acceptable for a legal adviser to retire with the justices for 25 minutes out of the 30 minutes that it took for the justices to make their decision. To decide otherwise would have been to have allowed ostensible bias, and even if there were no actual bias, then the appearance of such bias would have been overwhelming to the point of denying the defendant a fair trial.

If the magistrates wish their legal adviser to join them in the retiring room then this request must be made in open court and in the presence of all parties. If the legal adviser does provide them with legal advice whilst they are retired from the court then the legal adviser must repeat this to all parties when the court reconvenes, and upon this occurring all parties will then be permitted to make representations on this advice if they so wish.

5.9 Sentencing powers

As the magistrates' court deals with summary and less serious either-way offences they only have limited sentencing powers. Currently the maximum custodial sentence that a magistrates' court can impose for an offence is six months imprisonment. This can be increased to 12 months where there are two or more offences and the sentences are to run consecutively (one after the other). Where there is more than one offence the magistrates' decision to run the sentences consecutively or concurrently (at the same time as one another) will be dependent on the seriousness of the offence and the appropriate totality of the sentence imposed.

As well as being able to impose custodial sentences the magistrates can also impose a variety of non-custodial sentences (see 12.9 for further details on available sentences), and they can also impose a fine of up to the value of £5,000.

There has been an element of impending reform in recent years in relation to the sentencing powers of the magistrates' court. So as to enlarge the potential number of cases that could be heard by the magistrates' court the government felt that it would be best to increase the magistrates' maximum sentencing powers to 12 months (24 months with consecutive sentences) and that the level of fine that they could impose should be increased to £15,000. The idea of increasing the fine quickly fell by the wayside, but the magistrates' court sentencing powers were increased by way of statute to a maximum of 12 months under the provisions found in s.154 of the Criminal Justice Act 2003 (CJA 2003). Magistrates around the country received comprehensive training on the extent of their new powers in anticipation of them coming into force, but to date, this section is not in force and it looks unlikely that it will be implemented into the court system anytime in the near future.

Figure 5.4 Magistrates' court sentencing powers

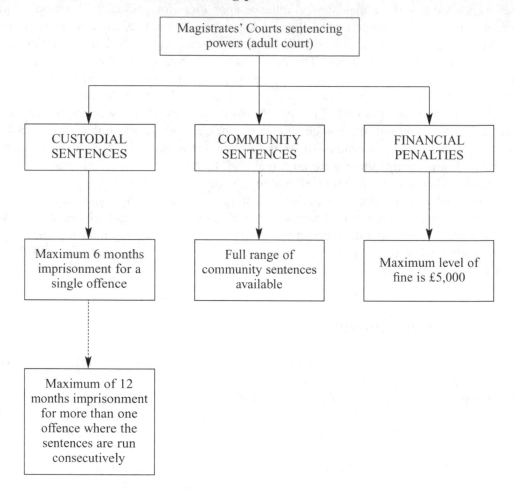

5.10 Resignation and removal

The resignation or removal of a magistrate is governed by s.11 of the Courts Act 2003 (CA 2003). Section 11 states that:

(1) A lay justice may resign his office at any time.

(2) The Lord Chancellor may, with the concurrence of the Lord Chief Justice, remove a lay justice from his office by an instrument on behalf and in the name of Her Majesty—

(a) on the ground of incapacity or misbehaviour,

(b) on the ground of a persistent failure to meet such standards of competence as are prescribed by a direction given by the Lord Chancellor, or

(c) if he is satisfied that the lay justice is declining or neglecting to take a proper part in the exercise of his functions as a justice of the peace.

Section 11(1) sets out that a magistrate can resign at any time from the bench, but it is hoped that once appointed a magistrate will continue to serve for at least five years before deciding to resign from their duties. If a magistrate decides to serve for as long as they are allowed then they will be retired from service when they reach the age of 70. Upon retirement or resignation a magistrate is allowed to keep their official title of 'Justice of the Peace' as a sign of recognition for their services to the court and their community.

Every year there is a very small number of magistrates who do not wish to leave the bench when it is thought appropriate for them to do so, and as a result the Lord Chancellor has been granted the powers to remove such persons under s.11(2). Under subs.(2)(a) the Lord Chancellor can require a person to be removed from the list of magistrates if it is felt that they are incapable of continuing on with and conducting their responsibilities. A magistrate will generally be removed under this process where they are too ill to be able to sit in court but they have not resigned from their post.

The alleged misbehaviour of the magistrate is another ground for removal under subs.(1)(a), and the reasons for such a removal will generally be where a magistrate has been convicted of a criminal offence. However, a criminal conviction is not always a necessary prerequisite for a removal from post, as can be shown by a number of recent incidents. In 2007 a magistrate walked out of the courtroom where evidence was being given by a woman wearing the full veil (or niqab); the case is still under investigation but there is a possibility that the magistrate in question will be removed from office upon its conclusion. Earlier in 2008 a magistrate was barred from sitting in court following his dismissal from his employed work due to allegations of gross misconduct. The magistrate is currently appealing against his employer's decision to dismiss him, but if he is unsuccessful in his action then again it is likely that he will be removed from his position as a magistrate; he is suspended from sitting until the matter has been determined.

Where there is a persistent failure by a magistrate to meet the standards of competence then the Lord Chancellor has the power to remove such a magistrate under s.11(2)(b). This power of removal is there to help reinforce the training initiative (MNTI 2) and to ensure that all magistrates comply fully with the training requirements.

The final reason for removal is found under s.11(2)(c), and this can be employed by the Lord Chancellor where a magistrate refuses to, or neglects to, fulfil their judicial obligations. Examples of when this power may be used are where a magistrate continuously fails to sit for the required minimum number of sittings, or if they keep failing to turn up for court when they are obliged to do so. A magistrate can also be removed under this provision if they refuse to operate a law enacted by Government. In 2007 a magistrate refused to hear cases in the family court on the basis of religious grounds. The lay justice in question stated that they could not deliberate on cases which involved issues of gay adoption as such matters offended their religious beliefs. The magistrate formally resigned from his post, but had he not done so then the Lord Chancellor could have requested his removal from post due to his refusal to implement the law.

Advantages	Disadvantages
Lay participation The average cost of employing lay magistrates is £52.10 per hour. If all the lay magistrates were removed from the system and replaced with professional judges then the cost would increase by several million pounds.	**Low acquittal rate** There is an approximately 90% conviction rate in the magistrates' court. Concerns have been raised as to whether there is an element of prosecution bias as the magistrates will often see the same prosecutor, which may possibly affect their judgement.
Gender balance Approximately 49% of magistrates are women. In comparison only 10% of the judiciary (fee paid and legally qualified persons) are female.	**Inconsistent** Differing sentences for very similar offences. For example, in 2001 for the offence of burglary in Teeside only 20% of offenders received immediate custody, whilst in Birmingham 41% received custody for the same offence.
Reflective of society Ethnic minorities are well represented at approximately 10%, as opposed to 1% in the judiciary. Magistrates can come from all sectors of society so they can be (for example) dinner ladies, bus drivers, plumbers, accountants, teachers, housewives and doctors.	**Not truly diverse** The composition of the magistrates' bench is perceived as being middle-class and middle-aged. Despite recruitment drives and initiatives there is still only a minority of magistrates who are under the age of 40.
Local knowledge They have to live within the locality of the court in which they serve and so should have an idea of the social and political factors that affect the local area.	**Inefficient** Magistrates do not have the legal skills and knowledge that a full-time member of the judiciary possesses and as a result hearing may take much longer due to the magistrates becoming weighed down with irrelevant and immaterial matters.
Legal Adviser Magistrates have access to a qualified legal person who can assist and advise them whenever necessary and so there are few instances where an error of law is made.	**Reliance on the legal adviser** Legal advisers are not able to assist with matters such as sentencing, which consequently results in geographical inconsistencies in the severity of the sentences handed down.
Low appeal rate There are relatively few appeals from the magistrates' court and those that do occur are mainly against sentence as opposed to conviction.	**Limited sitting requirements** Due to the fact that they are voluntary, magistrates are not required to sit very often and therefore they may not be as up to date with matters as a professional judge will be.

5.11 Summary

(a) There are approximately 29,000 lay magistrates working in the courts across England and Wales. They deal with over 95 per cent of all the criminal cases brought to court and also have limited jurisdiction in other courts, such as the family, youth and civil courts.

(b) The bench in the magistrates' court will usually consist of three lay magistrates (a chair and two wingers) or a single district judge. Where there are three lay magistrates on the bench then the decision will be made by way of majority. Magistrates do not have to be legally or professionally qualified to sit in such a capacity.

(c) The role of a magistrate has existed since about the 12th Century. Originally magistrates were appointed as keepers of the peace, and could almost be described as an early police force. The powers and responsibilities have developed and changed dramatically over the years to arrive at their current role.

(d) To be eligible to sit as a magistrate a person must be between the ages of 18 and 70, although a person over 65 years old would not normally be selected to sit as a magistrate. The person must not be disqualified from sitting or work within the criminal justice system or associated agencies.

(e) A lay magistrate sits in a voluntary capacity and only receives payment of any reasonable expenses incurred. They must be able to commit to sitting for at least 26 half-days per year.

(f) Applications to become a magistrate are reviewed by the Advisory Committee for the local area and they will consider the applicant in line with the six key qualities. These are: good character, understanding and communication, social awareness, maturity and sound temperament, sound judgement and commitment and reliability

(g) The Advisory Committee will select candidates who meet the six key qualities and who will ensure that the local bench is one reflective of the society in which it is based. To achieve a balanced representation on the local magistracy factors such as a candidate's gender, age, occupation, geographical location, ethnic origin, social background and political affiliation will be taken into account. Even if a candidate is viewed as being highly suitable for appointment they may still not be so selected as a magistrate if their appointment would unbalance the bench in one of the above key areas.

(h) Magistrates undergo a structured training process upon appointment so that they are able to become fully competent in the skills that they require to sit on the bench. Training and appraisal continues throughout their time as a magistrate, and magistrates are required to be able to evidence the three key competencies, which are, managing yourself, working as a member of the team and making judicial decisions.

(i) Magistrates, as lay people, are aided and advised on the law by a Legal Adviser. The Adviser is there to direct them on the appropriate law but is not permitted to direct the magistrates as to what their decision should be. Any advice given by a Legal Adviser should be done in open court, and if the Adviser does give the magistrates any advice out of court then they must explain the advice given to the court once the court reconvenes.

(j) Magistrates have the powers to impose a maximum custodial sentence of six months (rising to 12 months for more than one offence with consecutive sentences), community sentences or a fine of up to £5,000.

(k) A magistrate is required to retire at the age of 70, but they may resign at any point prior to this. The Lord Chancellor has the powers to remove a magistrate from office when they are either incapable of carrying out their judicial functions, they have misbehaved, they are deemed to be incompetent or they are neglecting or refusing to carry out their responsibilities.

5.12   Self-test questions

1. The maximum length of time that a magistrates' court can impose a custodial sentence for an offence is:

   (a) 6 months
   (b) 12 months
   (c) 24 months
   (d) they cannot impose custodial sentences

2. Magistrates can sit in the:

   (a) Youth Court
   (b) Family Court
   (c) Crown Court
   (d) all of the above

3. Magistrates are appointed on their:

   (a) political views
   (b) sentencing policies
   (c) personal qualities
   (d) physical appearance

4. Once trained, magistrates are appraised:

   (a) annually
   (b) every three years

(c) every five years

(d) never

5. Magistrates are expected to sit in court for a minimum of:

(a) 10 days per year

(b) 26 half-days per year

(c) 52 half-days per year

(d) 100 days per year

5.13   Further reading

C. Barnett, "Justices' clerks" [2006] 62(5) Magistrate 135.

I. Dennis, "Judging magistrates" [2001] Crim. L.R. Feb, 71–72.

A. Mimmack, "The Auld Review: what does it mean for us?" Part 1 [2002] 4(6) P.S.P. 8–10.

A. Mimmack, "The Courts Act 2003" [2005] M.C.P. 9(3) 2–3.

A. Mimmack, "The legal adviser and the retiring room—where is the boundary?" [2007] Magistrate 63(3) 91.

St John Pilkington, "Putting justice first" Counsel 2007, June, 27–28.

G. Robson, "A long farewell" [2006] J.P. 170(29) 548–551.

G. Robson, "Thinking the unthinkable: judging the judges" [2004] 168(27) J.P. 512–515.

P. Veits, "The role of the justices' clerk" Magistrate [2007] 63(7) 196–197.

P. J. Veits, "Justices' Clerks' Society and the future" [2007] 171(38) J.P. 668–669.

6 The judiciary

The judiciary are a fundamental element of the English legal system. They help to ensure that the rule of law (see 1.3.2.2) is upheld and that all of those people who come to the law are dealt with fairly and justly. In an everyday capacity the judges sit within the courts of England and Wales and hear the disputes between the different parties. As a collective they cover every individual area of law that can be brought before the courts, from criminal cases to family matters through to civil claims and more. Their role within the court is to make decisions and deliver judgment on the matters before them, or in the case of a criminal trial with a jury they are required to explain the law to the jury and direct them on how to apply it to the facts. Judges are the primary triers and deciders of fact and in being so they are required to carry out this function in an impartial and objective manner (otherwise known as the rule of law). They must keep all of their personal views and prejudices away from the courtroom and must only apply the laws of the country as they are at that time.

The judiciary, as one of the limbs of the state's administrative system, is also charged with ensuring that the other limbs (the executive and the legislature (see 1.3.2.1)) do not become too powerful or abuse their positions in anyway. The introduction of the Human Rights Act 1998 (HRA 1998) has provided the judiciary with more scope to be able to undertake this function and the case of *A & X v Secretary of State for the Home Department* [2004] UKHL 56 (as discussed at 1.3.2.2) is an example of how the judiciary can use their powers in this way. The decision by the House of Lords in the case of *A & X v Secretary of State for the Home Department* resulted in the legislation under which the appellants were detained (the Anti-Terrorism, Crime and Security Act 2001) being declared unlawful and so consequently Parliament were forced to repeal the legislation. The judiciary had challenged the extent of Parliament's law-making abilities and won.

6.1 The judicial hierarchy

Just as the court system is based on a hierarchy so too is the judiciary. There are superior (or senior) judges who sit within the superior courts and there are inferior judges who sit within inferior courts. The use of the terms 'inferior' and 'superior' should not be allowed to cloud the perception of the equal importance of all the judges within the legal system, as an individual magistrate could be argued to be just as important as a Law Lord, because if magistrates were taken out of the judicial system then the whole legal system would be liable to collapse. The inferior judges keep the legal system ticking over on an everyday basis whereas the superior judges are there to deliberate and decide upon certain principles of law that then have far-reaching implications on the law and everyone who lives under it.

6.1.1   The Lord Chief Justice

Following the introduction of the Constitutional Reform Act 2005 (CRA 2005), which came into force on April 3, 2006, the Lord Chief Justice became the head of the judiciary of England and Wales and the President of the Courts of England and Wales. These roles were traditionally the responsibility of the Lord Chancellor until the implementation of the CRA 2005 (see 6.2 below), which removed the judicial functions from the post of the Lord Chancellor. Before the introduction of the Act the Lord Chief Justice was historically the second highest judge in the English legal system.

At present Lord Phillips of Worth Matravers (who was appointed to the position in October 2005) holds the position of Lord Chief Justice. He has over 400 statutory duties but his key responsibilities are:

- representing the views of the judiciary of England and Wales to Parliament and government

- the welfare, training and guidance of the judiciary in England and Wales within resources made available by the Lord Chancellor. The Lord Chief Justice discusses with government the provision of resources for the judiciary

- the deployment of judges and allocation of work in courts in England and Wales

He is also involved in sitting on the most important criminal, civil and family cases, giving judgments and laying down practice directions in many of the most important appeal cases. He shares responsibility with the Lord Chancellor for the Office for Judicial Complaints (the body which investigates complaints made against judicial office holders) and he also chairs the Sentencing Guidelines Council (a public body designed to support sentencers in their decision-making, and encourage consistency in sentencing throughout the court system). Further, he is the President of the Courts of England and Wales and he may sit and hear cases in any English or Welsh court, including the magistrates' courts.

The Lord Chief Justice is selected by a specially appointed panel from within the Judicial Appointment Commission (JAC) (see below for further details on the JAC) and the Lord Chief Justice is normally appointed from within the ranks of the Appeal Court Judges (the Lord and Lady Justices). However, the JAC are not prevented from selecting the Lord Chief Justice from within the ranks of the Law Lords who form the Judicial Committee of the House of Lords if they wish to do so.

It was announced on July 8, 2008 that Lord Justice Judge will become the Lord Chief Justice when Lord Phillips becomes a Senior Law Lord later this year.

6.1.2   Heads of Division

As the scope of the courts of England and Wales is so vast there are also the Heads of Division who work underneath the Lord Chief Justice to ensure that the courts run smoothly. At present there are five Heads of Division, each with a different area of responsibility. These Heads are:

6.1.2.1 The Lord Chief Justice

Although the Lord Chief Justice is the head of the judiciary, part of that role is to also preside over the Court of Appeal (Criminal Division) as the head of that division. However, as he is already the President of the Courts and therefore in a position of substantial authority he is entitled to appoint another Court of Appeal Judge to sit in this position in his place.

6.1.2.2 The Master of the Rolls

The Master of the Rolls (M.R.) is the head of the Court of Appeal (Civil Division). Traditionally he was charged with the safekeeping of charters, patents and records of important court judgments written on parchment rolls. He still has responsibility for documents of national importance, and is the person responsible for authorising the practice of solicitors (professional rules and regulations), although his main work is involved with the organisation of the civil justice system.

The role of M.R. is viewed as being the second most important judicial role (under that of the Lord Chief Justice) and he is responsible for the deployment and organisation of the work of the judges of the division, as well as presiding over the court (he will often hear the most difficult and sensitive cases).

The M.R. is appointed by the Queen on the recommendation of the Prime Minister, who is advised by the Lord Chancellor after consultation with senior members of the judiciary and again, like the Lord Chief Justice, the M.R. is normally appointed from among the ranks of the Appeal Court Judges.

6.1.2.3 The President of the Family Division

The President of the Family Division and Head of Family Justice presides over panels hearing family law matters in the Court of Appeal, and is also the administrative head of the Family Division of the High Court. The current President of the Family Division and Head of Family Justice is Sir Mark Potter.

The President of the Family Division is appointed by the Queen on the recommendation of the Prime Minister, who receives advice from the Lord Chancellor after he has consulted with the senior members of the judiciary. The Head of this Division is normally selected from within the Appeal Court Judges.

6.1.2.4 The Chancellor of the High Court

The Chancellor of the High Court (previously known as the Vice-Chancellor prior to the CRA 2005) is the vice-president of the Chancery Division of the Supreme Court (the Lord Chancellor is the president). The role of Vice-Chancellor was created in 1813 and the Vice-Chancellor's duties were to help the Lord Chancellor in the administration of justice. The role disappeared in 1873 but was then re-instated in 1970. The modern-day role of the Vice-Chancellor is to organise and manage business of the Chancery Division on a day-to-day basis. The Vice-

Chancellor is appointed by the Lord Chancellor from among the High Court Chancery Division judges.

6.1.2.5 The President of the Queen's Bench Division

The President of the Queen's Bench Division is a brand-new appointment created by way of the CRA 2005. He is responsible for the everyday work of the Queen's Bench and at present the President is Sir Igor Judge.

The President of the Queen's Bench Division is appointed by the Queen on the recommendation of the Prime Minister who receives advice from the Lord Chancellor after he has consulted with the senior members of the judiciary. The Head of this Division is normally selected from within the Appeal Court Judges.

6.1.3   The superior judges

6.1.3.1   Lord of Appeal in Ordinary

The Lords of Appeal in Ordinary (or the Law Lords as they are more commonly referred to) are the twelve most senior judges within the jurisdiction of England and Wales. They sit within the House of Lords, which is the highest court in the land and is the supreme court of appeal, as well as the Privy Council. Since the enactment of the Appellate Jurisdiction Act 1876 the judicial work of the House of Lords can only be undertaken by the Law Lords. The 'in Ordinary' part of their title means that they are employed on a full-time basis in respect of their judicial roles.

Law Lords are members of the House of Lords and on appointment they become life peers and may speak and vote on nearly all matters heard within the House, the only limitation being that whilst they are a serving member of the judiciary they are precluded from engaging in matters involving any element of party political controversy. If they were to become involved in such matters then they would be prevented from sitting in their judicial capacity if the matter later came before the judicial section of the House, as they would not be perceived as being impartial. They also occasionally chair major public inquiries such as the one conducted into the death of the Ministry of Defence scientist Dr David Kelly.

On average the House of Lords hears between 80 and 90 appeals per year and the Law Lords sit from Monday to Thursday throughout the law terms (the time of the year when the court sits). The composition of the Appellate Committee (which is the name given to the court when the Law Lords are sitting) is normally five Law Lords, although this may increase to a panel of seven or nine depending on the nature and interest of the case. A hearing by the Appellate Committee is rather an informal affair as the Law Lords sit around a horseshoe table and do not wear robes. The hearing is almost conversational in style with the counsel for the parties presenting their cases but with the Law Lords frequently asking questions and challenging them on points. The length of an average hearing with the House of Lords is two and a half days. Judgment in the case is then delivered at 9:45 am on a Wednesday a few weeks following the hearing. The judgment is delivered in the House of Lords and any member of the House may attend to hear its delivery. Their judgment is known as an 'opinion' and they do not read them out in full when delivering judgment but rather give a brief summary setting out details of how they are to dispose of the appeal. A full written copy of their prepared speech is then posted on the Parliamentary judicial pages immediately after the judgment is pronounced.

Law Lords are appointed by the Queen on the advice of the Prime Minister, usually from the ranks of the senior appeal court judges in each part of the UK—the Court of Appeal for England and Wales, the Court of Session in Scotland and the Court of Appeal for Northern Ireland. However this process of selection by invitation only is likely to change in the near future and it is anticipated that Law Lords will be appointed by the Queen following the recommendation of the JAC, as is the position now for the appointments of inferior judges.

The role of the Law Lords will soon change (October 2009), as under the CRA 2005 the judicial element of the House of Lords will be abolished and this is to be replaced by a Supreme Court which will separate the judiciary from the legislature entirely. The Law Lords will transfer over to the jurisdiction of the Supreme Court and will become known as the first Justices of the Supreme Court.

The Law Lords who sit in the House of Lords (in order of seniority) as of October 2007 are:

- Bingham of Cornhill, L. (Senior Lord of Appeal in Ordinary)
- Hoffmann, L. (Second Senior Lord of Appeal in Ordinary)
- Hope of Craighead, L.
- Saville of Newdigate, L.
- Scott of Foscote, L.
- Rodger of Earlsferry, L.
- Walker of Gestingthorpe, L.
- Hale of Richmond, B. (the first female Law Lord (appointed 2004))
- Carswell, L.
- Brown of Eaton-under-Heywood, L.
- Mance, L.
- Neuberger of Abbotsbury, L.

The chart below gives an indication of the volume of work that the House of Lords deals with, where its work comes from, and the number and types of decisions handed down. In 2005 there were 87 appeals presented to the House of Lords, of which 59 were from the Civil Division of the Court of Appeal and five from the Criminal Division, nine overall from the High Court and 14 from outside the direct jurisdiction of England and Wales. In total 102 appeals received judgment from the House.

House of Lords: Appeals presented and disposed of, showing the courts appealed from and results, 2005					
				Appeals disposed of	
				Judgement	
Courts from which appeals were brought	Number of petitions presented	Without a judgment	Allowed	Dismissed	Total
England and Wales:					
Court of Appeal					
Civil	59	7	40	28	75
Criminal	5	–	8	4	12
High Court					
Civil	2	1	–	–	1
Criminal	7	2	–	5	7
Scotland:					
Court of Session	11	2	2	–	4
Northern Ireland:					
Court of Appeal					
Civil	3	1	1	–	2
Criminal	–	–	–	1	1
High Court					
Civil	–	–	–	–	–
Criminal	–	–	–	–	–
Other:					
Courts Martial Appeal Court	–	–	–	–	–
Attorney General's reference	–	–	–	–	–
Total	87	13	51	38	102

© Crown copyright. Source: Judicial Statistics Annual Reports 2005 (revised), p.14

6.1.3.2   Lord Justice of Appeal

There are currently 37 Lord Justices of Appeal who preside over the Court of Appeal (though originally under the Supreme Court of Judicature Act 1881 the number of Lord Justices was fixed at only five). Lord Justices of Appeal are normally selected from the ranks of the High Court judges and they will be appointed by the Queen on the recommendation of the Prime Minister, who receives advice from the Lord Chancellor after he has consulted with the senior members of the judiciary (the statutory requirements for becoming a Lord Justice of Appeal are set out in s.10 of the Supreme Court Act 1981 (as amended by s.71 of the Courts and Legal Services Act 1990)).

Originally a judge appointed to sit in the Court of Appeal was required to be called 'Lord', regardless of their gender, as it was not envisaged that a female would ever hold such a position. Elizabeth Butler-Sloss, who was the first woman to be appointed to the position of a Lord Justice of Appeal in 1988, was called Lord until the law was changed under the Courts Act 2003. Section 63 of the Act now permits a female Court of Appeal judge to be called 'Lady Justice of Appeal'. Upon appointment men are knighted and women are made a Dame.

To illustrate the scope of the volume of work that the Court of Appeal (Criminal Division) deals with (as opposed to the House of Lords) consider the chart below and then compare it to that above.

Court of Appeal (Criminal Division): Results of appeal heard by Full Court, 1995-2005[1]											
	1995	1996	1997	1998	1999	2000	2001	2002	2003	2004	2005
Conviction:											
Allowed	253	250	236	290	171	150	135	166	178	240	228
Dismissed	521	469	367	403	380	333	313	319	364	384	386
Sentence:											
Allowed	1,222	1,379	1,468	1,589	1,564	1,284	1,101	1,302	1,685	1,348	1,534
Dismissed	538	603	602	609	614	522	561	500	679	589	619
Number of retrials ordered	52	53	33	73	70	72	58	50	45	66	

[1] From 1997, figures relate to applications rather than appellants

© Crown copyright. Source: Judicial Statistics Annual Reports 2005 (revised), p.18

6.1.3.3   Justices of Her Majesty's High Court of Justice

As at January 1, 2006 there were 108 Justices of Her Majesty's High Court of Justice or High Court judges (otherwise known as 'puisne' judges (pronounced as 'puny')) working within the jurisdiction of England and Wales. They can theoretically sit anywhere within the High Court, although in practice they are generally assigned to one of its three divisions (Queen's Bench, Chancery and Family). Their work consists of trying the most serious criminal cases in the Crown Court, hearing important civil cases and assisting the Lord Justices of Appeal to hear criminal appeals.

High Court judges are appointed by the Queen, on the recommendation of the Lord Chancellor after an open competition administered by the JAC. This means that the vacancy will be advertised in the national press and applications are made in the same way as with any other type of job, although there is no job interview but rather a system of consultation. To be suitably qualified for selection as a High Court judge an individual must have had a right of audience (the right of a lawyer to appear and speak as an advocate in a court case) for all proceedings in the High Court for at least ten years, or have been a circuit judge for at least two years. High Court judges are generally selected from the ranks of Queen's Counsel (see Chapter 4) and although solicitor-advocates are eligible to be appointed as a High Court judge only two have been appointed so far from this background.

The High Court is found in the Royal Courts of Justice on The Strand in London and this is where the High Court judges are based, however they do work throughout the country in the major trial centres (such as in Birmingham, Manchester etc.)

The number of days sat by each particular type of judge in the Court of Appeal in 2005 is shown in the chart below. This serves as a good indicator of the fact that the High Court judges spend a significant period of time in the Court of Appeal as well as the High Court.

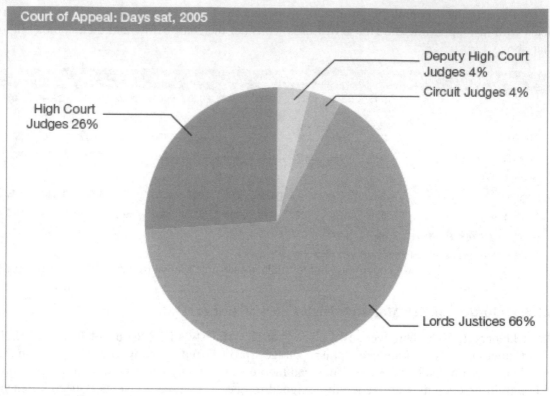

Court of Appeal: Days sat, 2005

Deputy High Court Judges 4%

Circuit Judges 4%

High Court Judges 26%

Lords Justices 66%

© Crown copyright. Source: Judicial Statistics Annual Reports 2005 (revised), p.134

6.1.4   Inferior judges

6.1.4.1   Circuit Judges

A Circuit Judge is at the top of the hierarchy of inferior judges. They carry out the majority of the Crown Court work and in 2004 they accounted for just over 74 per cent of all sitting days in this court. There are 619 Circuit Judges currently working within the jurisdiction. As well as sitting in the Crown Court, Circuit Judges have the jurisdiction to sit in the Court of Appeal Criminal Division when requested to do so and in 2005 they accounted for four per cent of the total days sat.

Circuit Judges take their name from the fact that they are assigned to a particular legal area (circuit) in the country. There are six legal circuits throughout England and Wales and each circuit has at least two presiding High Court Judges who are responsible for the judicial business within that area. The six circuits of England and Wales are:

- Midlands and Oxford circuit
- North Eastern circuit
- Northern circuit

- South Eastern circuit

- Western circuit

- Wales and Chester circuit

Circuit Judges are appointed by the Queen on the recommendation of the Lord Chancellor after an open competition as administered by the JAC. The statutory qualifications required are the same as for a High Court Judge, or the individual in question must have already been a Recorder (see below) or have held another full-time judicial office for at least three years previously. Vacancies are advertised through the national press and interested candidates must make an application to the JAC for consideration.

6.1.4.2 Recorders

A Recorder is essentially a part-time judge who has mainly criminal jurisdiction but can sit in the County Courts as and when required. Serving as a Recorder is sometimes seen as being like an apprenticeship for becoming a Circuit Judge. As a Recorder is quite often new to a judicial role they will receive training as regards their duties and responsibilities. There are currently 1,394 Recorders in England and Wales.

Recorders are appointed by the Queen on the recommendation of the Lord Chancellor after an open competition as administered by the JAC. They are appointed on a five-year basis that can be automatically renewed.

6.1.4.3 District Judges

District Judges are at the bottom of the judicial hierarchy in terms of employed judges (as opposed to magistrates). They can appear in the criminal and civil magistrates' courts (although the vast majority of District Judges sit within the civil jurisdiction). To become a District Judge most will have ready served as a Deputy (part-time) District Judge for at least a two-year period. They are again appointed by the Queen on the recommendation of the Lord Chancellor after an open competition as administered by the JAC.

Originally criminal jurisdiction District Judges were called 'Stipendaries', and civil jurisdiction District Judges were known as 'Registrars', and there are 419 District Judges currently in post.

To illustrate the different volume of work undertaken by the various different judges within the English legal system consider the graph below. It can be seen that the majority of the work in the legal system is undertaken by Circuit Judges, closely followed by District Judges.

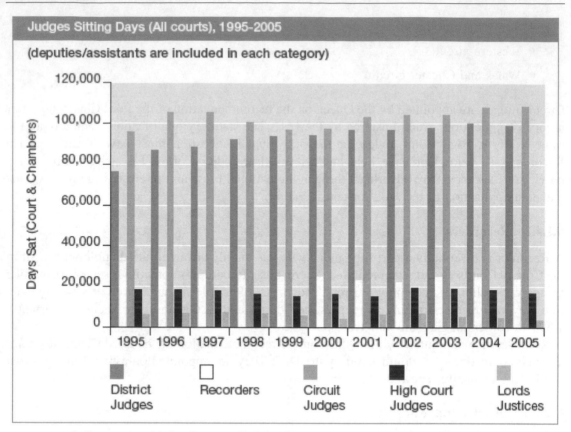

© Crown copyright. Source: Judicial Statistics Annual Reports 2005 (revised), p.130

6.2   The Lord Chancellor

The role of the Lord Chancellor has existed since at least the 14th Century, although it has been mooted that the role has actually existed in some form or other since as far back as 605 AD. Historically the role has been the highest judicial office that could be held within England and Wales, and it is a role that has been central to the development of the English legal system. The Lord Chancellor originally wielded a great deal of power over each of the different arms of the state, and his (there has not to date been a female Lord Chancellor) more modern-day role during the last century has included him being a both Cabinet Minister, a Speaker in the House of Lords and the Head of the Judiciary and the Lord Chancellor's Department. As a result of the Lord Chancellor's wide remit the position came under a great deal of criticism due to the fact that it spanned across all three limbs of state administration, which went directly against the separation of powers doctrine as propounded by Montesquieu (1.3.2.1). By being involved in every limb there were the concerns raised regarding the independence of the judiciary. It was argued that this was being compromised, and that full transparency could not be achieved due to the fact that the legal system was presided over by a politician.

In June 2003 the Prime Minister undertook a Cabinet reshuffle and Lord Irvine, who was the then Lord Chancellor, was removed from his role (this was easily achievable as the Lord Chancellor is appointed by the Prime Minister and so can be removed from office as simply as any other Cabinet Minister). The announcement was made that the role of the Lord Chancellor was to be abolished, and the Lord Chancellor's department was disbanded and replaced with the Department for Constitutional Affairs. The intention of the reshuffle was to transfer the Lord Chancellor's ministerial powers to a newly created position of 'Secretary of State for Constitutional Affairs', and to transfer the judicial powers held by the Lord Chancellor to the newly created position of 'Lord Chief Justice'. Lord Falconer was then duly appointed under the title of 'The Secretary of State for Constitutional Affairs and the Lord Chancellor'. Under the first half of his title he was given the responsibility of abolishing the second half. However this change in roles means that Lord Falconer has no right to sit as a member of the judiciary or be heavily involved in the appointment process of new judges (as could the old Lord Chancellor), nor can he be a Speaker in the House of Lords. The legislation that was the driving force behind this monumental change was to be found in the Constitutional Reform Bill 2004.

Upon these changes being implemented by the government there was a widespread outcry against them. There was much criticism levied against the fact that the changes had been carried out in great haste, that the Bill had passed through Parliament too quickly, and little consideration had been given to its implications. The judiciary were concerned that the removal of the role of the Lord Chancellor would actually impede their independence as opposed to expand it, and Lord Woolf (who had been appointed into the role of Lord Chief Justice) stated in 'The rule of law and a change in the constitution' ([2004] C.L.J. 63(2), 317–330) that the announcement made as to the abolition of the role of the Lord Chancellor "clearly indicated an extraordinary lack of appreciation of the significance of what was being proposed". So as to address the concerns that were voiced from the highest reaches of the judiciary and the fact that the House of Lords were opposing the Bill, the government drafted a consultation paper (Department for Constitutional Affairs, *Constitutional Reforms: Reforming the Office of the Lord Chancellor* (2003) CP 13/03) and the result of this was that the judiciary and the government were able to reach a consensus under what is now known as the 'Concordat' (Department for Constitutional Affairs, *The Lord Chancellor's Judiciary-Related Functions: Proposals* (2004)), which was made by way of an oral statement to the House of Lords on January 26, 2004, and which focused on the future role of the Lord Chancellor. The Concordat set out that:

- The Lord Chief Justice, as head of the Judiciary of England and Wales, would take on a new role in relation to judicial appointments, judicial well being, and complaints and discipline.

- The Lord Chancellor would no longer be a judge but would be responsible for the administration of the courts and ensuring that the judiciary was able to fulfil its role.

- A new administrative support office for the Lord Chief Justice and senior judiciary would be set up in April 2006. This new office would reaffirm the policy separation between the judiciary and the executive, ensuring that the Lord Chief Justice and senior judiciary would be able to discharge all their statutory functions in relation to the judiciary, magistrates and the delivery of justice effectively and efficiently.

- A Judicial Complaints Office would also be launched in April 2006, and would improve the service provided to court users. It would be jointly responsible to both the Lord Chief Justice and the Lord Chancellor for the operation of the judicial complaints and discipline system.

- The roles and responsibilities of the Lord Chancellor and Lord Chief Justice in relation to the Judicial Appointments Commission and the appointed of judges were also set out in the Concordat (and the Constitutional Reform Act).

The Constitutional Reform Bill was duly amended so as to not abolish the role of the Lord Chancellor but rather to modify the role as set out under the Concordat. The Bill was then passed by the House of Lords and become the Constitutional Reform Act 2005 (CRA 2005). As a result of this process the Lord Chancellor now no longer sits as a member of the judiciary, he is no longer the head of the judiciary, nor does he have any significant powers over the judicial appointments process, further he is also no longer a Speaker in the House of Lords. He does however remain the head of the government department called the Ministry for Justice (formerly called the Ministry for Constitutional Affairs). Jack Straw was appointed as the Secretary for State and Lord Chancellor on June 28, 2007, and the Ministry of Justice sets out his responsibilities as including:

- overall strategy

- resourcing

- judicial appointments

- judicial diversity

- Lords reform

- party funding

- constitutional renewal

The focus of the Lord Chancellor is now far more political than legislative or judicial, and there has been a degree of separation of powers achieved as per the original aim. However whether the separation has gone too far or not far enough remains to be seen. One other change to come from the CRA 2005 is that the Lord Chancellor no longer needs to be legally qualified (obviously if he no longer heads the judiciary or sits as a judge then legal qualifications are not a necessity) and now, by way of s.2 of the CRA 2005, the only qualification requirement is for the person appointed to be qualified by 'experience'. Consequently this opens up the doors for a government minister, an MP or even a university law lecturer to become Lord Chancellor in the future.

6.3 Judicial appointments

6.3.1 Old style appointments

The method by which judges were appointed prior to 2006 received much condemnation as it was seen as a secretive and discriminatory process that was dominated by politicians. Originally the pool of potential judicial candidates was quite limited as only those with higher rights of audience (so essentially barristers) could be appointed. In 1990 this limited source of candidates was extended due to solicitors being permitted to gain higher rights under the Courts and Legal Service Act 1990 (CLSA 1990) (see 4.3).

As can probably be gathered from the discussion above the Lord Chancellor used to play a major role in the selection and appointment of the judiciary. Judges were to be appointed by the Queen who was advised by the Lord Chancellor, and in the case of the Law Lords and Lord Justices of Appeal, the Lord Chancellor would advise the Prime Minister who would then go on to advise the Queen. The normal way of applying for a job is that an advertisement is placed, interested candidates put in their applications and then those who make it through the short-listing process are called for interview. However senior judicial positions (from the High Court and upwards) were never advertised in this open and transparent way, but rather it was done more by way of a tap on the shoulder, or a whisper in the ear in the robing room. This meant that the individuals put forward for High Court judicial appointments were not really repre-sentative of the judiciary as a whole as they were essentially handpicked on the back of the personal opinion of the Lord Chancellor and senior members of the judiciary.

Once an individual had expressed their interest in a judicial vacancy then their suitability for the position would then be determined by way of an informal inquiry known as a 'secret sounding'. Here the Department of Constitutional Affairs, under its Legal and Judicial Services group, would gather information about the potential candidate that would then be scrutinised before a decision as to whether or not to appoint them would be made. The information gathered on the potential candidate varied widely in quality and relevance as to the individual's abilities to become a judge. Leading barristers and judges would be approached to offer their views on the individual and so much personal opinion as to the candidate's character was included. This could be both positive or highly negative depending on whether the person offering their opinion liked the candidate or not, and there is anecdotal evidence that informa-tion, such as what the candidate got up to socially and who they were friends with, was taken into account.

As a result of the criticisms voiced in respect of this method of recruitment the government set up an inquiry into the judicial appointments process. The inquiry was carried out by Sir Leonard Peach, and his finding were published in *The Independent Scrutiny of the Appointment Process of Judges and Queen's Counsel* in December 1999 (this report is commonly known as the Peachy Report). The findings of the Peachy Report were that the judicial appointments process was mainly satisfactory, but there were three main criticisms, these being that the process was secretive, discriminatory and dominated by politicians (as stated above).

In respect of the first criticism of it being secretive, it was found that the judicial appoint-ments system often favoured those with a good network of contacts over those who had the potential to become an excellent judge. It seemed that the odd adage 'it's not what you know but who you know' was very much in effect. The Law Society mounted a campaign against the process of secret soundings by refusing to take part in any recruitment conducted by that method. They equated it to that of the 'old boys' network', stating that it did not allow fair competition as it was controlled by barristers looking to appoint other barristers into the higher ranks of the judiciary, and consequently that solicitors were therefore never considered. They also argued that it did not allow those who had been put forward for a judicial vacancy to know what was being said about them, and therefore they were unable to bring any defence or make countenances to any allegations made against them. The Association of Personal Injury Lawyers and the Equal Opportunities Commission, amongst other bodies, also expressed their support for the Law Society and their disappointment in the way that the judiciary were selected.

The second criticism focused on the fact that the appointments process could be seen as discriminatory. Research undertaken by the Association of Women Barristers showed that most judges recommended barristers from within their own set of chambers and that approximately 50 per cent of all judicial appointments came from within only seven sets of chambers. This research emphasised the fact that there was a monopoly on the market held by a small niche of the legal world and that this had the effect of ethnic minorities and women being bypassed in relation to becoming members of the higher judiciary. The secretiveness of the secret sounding process allowed for discrimination to take place, as those who were proposing the candidates would look to those who they were close to and respected by. It was mainly therefore white middle-class males putting forward other white middle-class males.

The fact that the process was overseen by the Lord Chancellor and the Prime Minister was the main focus of the final criticism; that the selection process was dominated by politicians. The Lord Chancellor, in his then role, was a member of both the judiciary, legislature and the executive, and as such there was the possibility that his position within the executive could be seen to potentially have an effect on the candidates he chose for judicial office (even if in practice it did not). Also the fact that the Prime Minister had to approve any appointments into the higher judicial offices could also to be taken as an interference with the independence of the judiciary (i.e. Lady Thatcher once selected the Lord Chancellor's second choice of candidate over the first). The enactment of the Human Rights Act 1998 also helped to force this issue as under it the government are obliged to ensure that everyone has the right to be tried by a fair and impartial tribunal (art.6) and the fact that the executive was involved in the appointments process could be argued as undermining this obligation.

Although the Peachy Report did not recommend any radical changes to the appointments process (including the secret soundings), it did recommend that a Commissioner for Judicial Appointments be appointed to oversee the recruitment process. The government accepted this proposal and the first Commissioner was appointed into post in 2001. However the main flaw with the newly created role of the Commissioner was that they had no power over the appointments process, they were simply there to supervise and audit. After being in post for two years and reviewing the appointments process the Commissioner undertook a full scale audit of the High Court judge appointment process and concluded that it was in urgent need of reform and that no further appointments of High Court judges should take place under the system, as it lacked both accountability and transparency. In response the government drafted a consultation paper (DCA, *Constitutional Reform; A New Way of Appointing Judges*, July 2003), which set out in its foreword that:

> In a modern democratic society it is no longer acceptable for judicial appointments to be entirely in the hands of a Government Minister. For example the judiciary is often involved in adjudicating on the lawfulness of actions of the Executive. And so the appointments system must be, and must be seen to be, independent of Government. It must be transparent. It must be accountable. And it must inspire public confidence.
>
> There is a second point. As the existing Commission for Judicial Appointments pointed out in its first annual report, the current judiciary is overwhelmingly white, male, and from a narrow social and educational background. To an extent, this reflects the pool of qualified candidates from which judicial appointments are made: intake to the legal professions has, until recently, been dominated by precisely these social groups.
>
> Of course the fundamental principle in appointing judges is and must remain selection on merit. However the Government is committed to opening up the system of appointments, to attract suitably qualified candidates both from a wider range of social backgrounds and from a wider range of legal practice. To do so, and, to create a system which commands the confidence of professionals and the public, and is seen as affording equal opportunities to all suitably qualified applicants, will require fresh approaches and a major re-engineering of the processes for appointment. Those processes must be resourced with the appropriate professional skills and expertise and underpinned by modern human resource best practice.

This reflected many of the criticisms raised earlier by the Peachy Report and so as to combat that these criticisms and to ensure that the appointments process was fair and transparent it was announced that:

> [t]he Government intends to establish an independent Judicial Appointments Commission to recommend candidates for appointment as judges on a more transparent basis. There is already such an independent commission in place for selecting judges in Scotland and one forms part of the agreed settlement in Northern Ireland. There will now be one for England and Wales.

The proposals to create an independent body who were to be charged with overseeing the appointments process was greeted with much enthusiasm and under the CRA 2005 the Judicial Appointments Commission (JAC) was established.

6.3.2 New style appointments

The JAC took over the recruitment process of the lower ranks of the judiciary (up to and including High Court judges) on April 3, 2006. They set out that they:

[s]elect candidates for judicial office. We do so on merit, through fair and open competition, from the widest range of eligible candidates.

Their statutory responsibilities under the CRA 2005 are:

- to select candidates solely on merit

- to select only people of good character

- to have regard to the need to encourage applications from a wider range of candidates

The Commission is comprised of 15 commissioners who are drawn from the judiciary, the legal profession, the tribunals, the lay magistracy and the lay public. The Chairman of the Commission must be a lay-person and the composition of the remaining 14 members must be five judicial members, two professional members (one barrister and one solicitor), five lay members, one tribunal member and one lay justice member.

The appointments process under the JAC now begins with a request from Her Majesty's Court Service or the Tribunal Service to appoint a new judge. The position is then widely advertised in the national press, in legal publications and online. On receipt of the applications the JAC will check the candidates' eligibility for the post and make a good character assessment of the applicants; references may also be taken at this point. The applications will then be short listed by way of either a qualifying test or by way of paper sifting. Those candidates that are then short listed are invited to attend a selection day where they may be asked to partake in role play and a formal interview. Following the selection day the Commission will prepare a report on their findings as to the candidates' suitability, and these reports will then be passed to the Lord Chief Justice and another suitably qualified person for statutory consultation as required under ss.88(3) and 94(3) CRA 2005. Finally any outstanding good character checks on the proposed candidates will be performed by way of consulting with the police, Her Majesty's Revenue and Customs and any other relevant professional bodies before their final recommendations are made to the Lord Chancellor. The JAC will only recommend one candidate per vacancy to the Lord Chancellor and the Lord Chancellor can reject that recommendation but only if he provides reasoning for doing so, and he cannot select another candidate as a replacement (this is to prevent any personal preferences coming into the process).

In making their selection the JAC will consider the five core qualities and abilities, which are required to hold judicial office. These are cited as:

1. **Intellectual capacity** (a high level of expertise in their chosen area or profession, the ability quickly to absorb and analyse information, an appropriate knowledge of the law and its underlying principles, or the ability to acquire this knowledge where necessary).

2. **Personal qualities** (to include integrity and independence of mind, sound judgement, decisiveness, objectivity and an ability and willingness to learn and develop professionally).

3. **An ability to understand and deal fairly** (an ability to treat everyone with respect and sensitivity whatever their background, a willingness to listen with patience and courtesy).

4. **Authority and communication skills** (an ability to explain the procedure and any decisions reached clearly and succinctly to all those involved, an ability to inspire respect and confidence and an ability to maintain authority when challenged).

5. **Efficiency** (the ability to work at speed and under pressure, the ability to organise time effectively and produce clear reasoned judgments expeditiously and the ability to work constructively with others (including leadership and managerial skills where appropriate)).

The Legal Service Act 2007 (LSA 2007) has also had an impact on the people who can apply to be a judge. Prior to the 2007 Act those eligible to be appointed into the judiciary had to have held a lower court right of audience (essentially barristers and solicitors) for at least seven years, but the Act has relaxed the qualification requirements from the number of the years that rights of audience have been held, to that of post-qualification experience (now reduced to only five years). The aim behind this relaxation is to widen the diversity of the judicial bench and to make the position of a judge accessible to a wider number of people. This means that in some point in the very near future, individuals with legal qualifications, such as through ILEX, will become eligible to apply to sit as a judge.

Figure 6.1 The judicial selection process

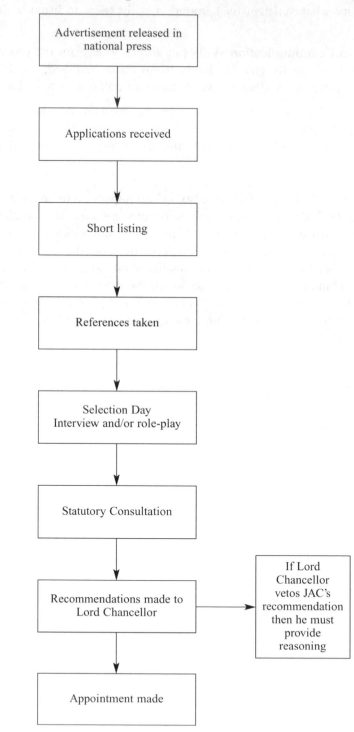

6.4 Training

Even though members of the judiciary are generally viewed as being among some of the finest brains in the country they are still required to undergo periodic training so as to ensure that they are up to date with the new law and developments in society. Judicial training is predominately undertake by the Judicial Studies Board (JSB), although occasionally outside agencies, such as social workers or doctors, may be involved in imparting certain specialist knowledge to the judiciary.

The JSB was set up in 1979 to provide training for full- and part-time judges in England and Wales, and for overseeing the training of lay magistrates and chairmen, as well as members of Tribunals. The JSB Strategy 2007—11 sets out that its purpose is to ensure that high quality training is delivered to enable those who discharge judicial functions to carry out their duties effectively, in a way which preserves judicial independence and supports public confidence in the justice system. An essential element of the philosophy behind the JSB is that the training of judges and magistrates is under judicial control and directions. The JSB's ethos is set out as being:

> To convey in a condensed form the lessons which experienced judges have acquired from their experience . . .

The JSB sets out that its five key objectives are:

- To provide high quality training to full- and part-time judges in the exercise of their jurisdiction in Civil, Criminal and Family Law.

- To advise the Lord Chancellor on the policy for and content of training for lay magistrates, and on the efficiency and effectiveness with which Magistrates' Courts Committees deliver such training.

- To advise the Lord Chancellor and Government Departments on the appropriate standards for, and content of, training for judicial officers in Tribunals.

- To advise the Government on the training requirement of judges, magistrates, and judicial officers in Tribunals if proposed changes to the law, procedure and court organisation are to be effective, and to provide, and advise on the content of, such training.

- To promote closer international co-operation over judicial training.

The JSB is proactive in providing suitable training for the judiciary so that the high standards of the profession are maintained, and they often offer refresher and intensive weekend courses to all members of the judiciary. However this was not always the case, and prior to the creation of the JSB, and also whilst it was still in its infancy, there was little training available in relation to the undertaking of judicial duties. Thankfully though the situation has changed for the better and the JSB now offer excellent training, which they then further supplement with the production of useful guidance books for judges. There is now no reason for a judge to be uninformed as to the developments in the law or as to any topics of current social importance.

6.5   Judicial robes

The judiciary began to wear robes in medieval times and then from around 1400 a colour coding system began to emerge, with violet robes being worn during the winter, green robes in the summer and red robes for full dress occasions. In 1635 Westminster produced the 'Judge's Rules' which set out the definitive guide to what robes should be worn by the judiciary on what occasion. A judge's status could be identified due to the gown that they wore, so for example High Court judges were often called the 'red judges' due to the fact that their robes were predominately red in colour. Then in the 17th Century, under the reign of Charles II, the judiciary began to wear the horsehair wigs that have now become synonymous with the position of a judge. The tradition of the judiciary wearing wigs and gowns stems from the concept of what was thought to be decent attire for a person holding such office, and it has also been thought that the wearing of such garments would help to protect the judge's anonymity from the criminals with whom they were dealing.

Very recently there has been a break in tradition in respect of the judiciary and legal counsel wearing wigs and these garments are no longer required to be worn in family cases or civil courts (although their use remains for the moment in the criminal court room). The traditional gowns that were worn by the judiciary are also undergoing a radical change as the fashion designer Betty Jackson has recently designed a whole range of more modern judicial robes to replace the traditional wig, wing collar and bands, and black gowns. Now the gowns will be made in a dark navy fabric with a velvet trim on the cuffs. As a nod to tradition and to denote the seniority of the judge the gowns will be trimmed with coloured bands. These will be gold for the Court of Appeal judges and the heads of the High Court divisions, red for High Court judges, lilac for circuit judges when they sit as deputy High Court judge, and blue for district judges. The Law Lords sit in lounge suits and therefore do not wear traditional robes and so are not included in the new revamp of the judicial fashion. Currently there are 800 new robes in production and these will be distributed to all of the civil judges in the near future at the cost of £450,000. Once the judges have their new robes they must ensure that they take care of them, as a spokesman for Lord Phillips stated:

> They will be replaced after ten years. At present they get one set of robes and they have to keep them for life—like a RSPCA dog—however flea-ridden.

> (*Model judge and his funky new gown*, *The Times*, Tuesday May 13, 2008)

6.6   Termination of appointment

6.6.1   Retirement

Under the Judicial Pensions and Retirement Act 1993 all judges must retire on their 70th birthday.

6.6.2   Dismissal

Generally judges are safeguarded from dismissal under the principle of 'security of tenure during good behaviour' as set out under the Supreme Court Act 1981 (formerly this principle was provided for by the Act of Settlement 1701). This means that they will only be removed from office if they misbehave badly. It provides security in their position and ensures their independence, as government cannot simply remove them if they make a ruling that the establishment does not agree with. It would be a sorry state of affairs if a judge refused to make a ruling on the basis that they were worried that they would get the sack because of it. The principle of security of tenure follows on from the doctrine of the separation of powers in respect of the different limbs of the state administration (as discussed at 1.3.2.1).

Heads of divisions, Law Lords, Justices of Appeal and High Court Judges are extremely well protected in their tenure as they can only be removed formally by the Queen, after the removal has received approval by way of an affirmative vote on the resolution in both Houses of Parliament. No judge in either the 20th Century, or so far in the 21st Century, has ever been removed from office by this method.

The Lord Chancellor can, under the Courts Act 1971, dismiss inferior judges on the grounds of incapacity or misbehaviour. This power has only been invoked once in modern times and that was on December 5, 1983 in relation to Judge Bruce Campbell, who was dismissed after being caught smuggling 125 litres of whisky and 9,000 cigarettes into Britain on his private yacht. He had pleaded guilty to the offence of evading duty. He was given the option to resign by the Lord Chancellor (as is normally the case, and this is the likely reason as to why there is only one reported precedent of a judge being dismissed in such a manner) but he refused to accept it and opted for dismissal instead because due to a small quirk in the law it meant that he was still able to keep his judicial pension.

The option to dismiss a judge on the grounds of their incapacity also exists but it is rarely exercised. There is anecdotal evidence (*The Telegraph*, 'His honour is gone. His honour must go' October 1, 2006) that the inability of even a senior judge to perform his duties fully will be given the blind eye.

> Even judges who have developed Alzheimer's disease while still on the job have not been forced out. In 1979, when Lord Widgery was Lord Chief Justice, he was, according to more than one observer, "visibly and distressingly half-senile". But his fellow judges covered up for him and wrote his judgments. He was not dismissed: he continued to fall asleep on the bench for another nine months before he retired.

Even though a senior judge such as Lord Widgery mentioned in the extract above would have to have been removed by Parliament, the rumours continue that this culture still pervades within the lower judiciary and a judge will only be removed if there is no other option available.

6.6.3 Discipline

Judges can be disciplined in relation to their actions to a certain degree. A judge may be suspended from sitting in a judicial capacity if they are the subject of ongoing criminal enquiries or if it is felt by the Lord Chancellor to be a necessary precaution to take in the face of preserving public confidence. The higher courts can also have a sanctioning effect on a judge by giving them a dressing down in the courtroom and the media can have a far reaching and quite dramatic effect in respect of publicly humiliating a judge whose decision or behaviour they do not agree with. An example of this can be seen by the media reaction to the case of Judge Khan in 2006. Judge Khan was an immigration judge who allegedly employed an illegal immigrant as a cleaner and was involved in blackmail and drugs with another immigration judge. He was investigated as to his behaviour, suspended from his judicial duties but still received full pay whilst the investigation was ongoing. The media, especially the tabloids, had a field day with this and certainly provided some impromptu discipline in respect of shattering his reputation.

6.7 The Supreme Court

The higher court system is due to undergo a dramatic change come October 2009. One of the changes to be made by the CRA 2005 is that the Appellate Committee of the House is to be abolished and replaced with a Supreme Court of England and Wales. The Ministry of Justice, who are the government department responsible for undertaking the change, state that:

> The introduction of a Supreme Court for the United Kingdom will provide greater clarity in our constitutional arrangements by further separating the judiciary from the legislature and the executive. It will assume the jurisdiction of the current Appellate Committee of the House of Lords and the devolution jurisdiction of the Judicial Committee of the Privy Council.

The jurisdiction of the Supreme Court will be to:

- hear appeals on arguable points of law of general public importance
- act as the final court of appeal in England, Wales and Northern Ireland
- hear appeals from civil cases in England, Wales, Northern Ireland and Scotland
- hear appeals from criminal cases in England, Wales and Northern Ireland

- assume the devolution jurisdiction of the Judicial Committee of the Privy Council, while the Commonwealth jurisdiction of the Council will remain unchanged

However the powers of the Supreme Court of England and Wales will not go as far as its counterparts in other jurisdictions which have a similar court system. For example in America the Supreme Court can strike down legislation, whereas that power in the UK will still be reserved for Parliament only.

The introduction of a new higher court of England and Wales will obviously impact upon the judges who sit in the higher courts, and it is proposed that the current Law Lords will be transferred to the Supreme Court to become the first Justices of the new court. The court will also continue to operate the procedure of *stare decisis* so that all judgments made by the previous House of Lords will still stand as good precedent for the new court. As the idea behind the creation of the new court is to ensure greater separation of powers between the judiciary, legislature and the executive, the CRA 2005 provides that any new judge appointed to sit as a Justice of the Supreme Court will not receive automatic peerage (as has previously been the tradition), however the current Law Lords will retain this power.

New appointments to the court will be considered by a specially convened selection commission that will be composed of the President and Deputy President of the Supreme Court, as well as other members of the appointment bodies for England, Wales, Scotland and Northern Ireland.

Originally the proposals (under the Constitutional Reform Bill) to create such a Supreme Court were rejected by the House of Lords, and to add further to the problems, a suitable site to house the court within London could not be found. The Bill has since been passed through the House and they have accepted the creation of the new court, and a site for the new court has now also been settled upon. The Supreme Court is to be based in Middlesex Guildhall on Parliament Square, opposite the Houses of Parliament. Middlesex Guildhall is a Grade II listed building, which was a working Crown Court until March 30, 2007. The rejuvenation of the building so that it can become the Supreme Court will involve an extensive restoration and improvement process, the cost of which has been estimated as being approximately £32 million pounds!

6.8   Criticism of the composition of the judiciary

The main criticism that can be levied at the composition of the judiciary is that is it is still dominated by white, middle-class, middle-aged men. The introduction of the JAC is one method of trying to resolve this lack of diversity on the bench, but this resolution can only happen slowly as current members of the judiciary resign or retire and new vacancies are created. The figures provided by the Judiciary of England and Wales in the Annual Diversity Statistics (as at April 1, 2007) show that the judiciary is still heavily weighted in favour of the stereotypical judge (white and male). The statistics show that female judges make up less than 30 per cent of all judges in the lower courts and that this percentage is reduced as the seniority of the judge (and court) increases. The number of judges sitting who are from an ethnic minority is also less than representative of society as this does not reach over five per cent of the total judiciary in any court and in the higher courts there is not a single judge who is from an ethnic minority.

Figure 6.2 The composition of the judiciary

Post	Total	Female No.	Female %	Of Ethnic Minority Origin No.	Of Ethnic Minority Origin %
Lords of Appeal in Ordinary	12	1	8.3	0	0.0
Heads of Division (excl. LC)	4	0	0.0	0	0.0
Lord Justices of Appeal	37	3	8.1	0	0.0
High Court Judges	108	10	9.3	1	0.9
Circuit Judges (incl. TCC)	639	73	11.4	9	1.4
Recorders	1206	182	15.1	53	4.4
District Judges (incl. Family Division)	450	101	22.4	14	3.1
Deputy District Judges (incl. Family Division)	780	219	28.1	30	3.85
District Judges (MC)	139	33	23.7	7	5.1
Deputy District Judges (MC)	169	42	24.85	9	5.3
Total	3544	664	18.7	123	3.5

Source: Annual Statistics as at April 1, 2007, Judiciary of England and Wales.

6.9 Summary

(a) There is a judicial hierarchy, just as there is for the court system. The judiciary can be split into two groups, the superior (or senior) judges and the inferior judges. The category of superior judges includes High Court Judges, Lord Justices of Appeal and the Law Lords and the Head of Divisions. The category of inferior judges includes Circuit Judges, Recorders and District Judges.

(b) The Lord Chancellor originally was a member of the executive, legislature and judiciary as he was the Head of the Judiciary, Head of the Lord Chancellor's Office, a Speaker in the House of Lords and a Cabinet Minister. To try to achieve a clearer separation of powers it was declared in 2003 that the role of the Lord Chancellor was to be abolished. This received a strong negative reaction and so the Constitutional Reform Act 2005 created a modified role of Lord Chancellor. The Lord Chancellor is now mainly a Cabinet Minister and his judicial responsibilities have been passed to the newly created post of Lord Chief Justice.

(c) Traditionally judges were appointed into post by way of secret sounding. This involved the Lord Chancellor gathering information about the candidate from a variety of sources and then making a personal judgment on the candidate's suitability. The process was criticised as being dominated by politicians, secretive and discriminatory.

(d) The Judicial Appointments Commission was establish in April 2006 to appoint all judges up to and including High Court judges. They now consider the merits and judicial qualities and potential of the individual. The Commission consists of a panel of 15 people who are a mix of the judiciary, legal profession and lay people etc., and after the recruitment process they recommend a candidate to the Lord Chancellor for appointment. The Lord Chancellor can reject the Commission's selection but he must give reasons and not appoint anyone else in that place.

(e) The judiciary undergo continuous training via the Judicial Studies Board and other relevant agencies.

(f) The tradition of wearing horsehair wigs and different coloured robes has almost come to an end now. Wigs are to only be worn now in the Crown Court and the traditional robes are to soon be replaced with ones that are of a more modern design.

(g) All judges must retire at age 70. They can resign before this date if they so wish. The judiciary work under the principle of security of tenure, meaning that they cannot be easily removed from post if they make a decision that the government does not agree with. The use of this principle is to help maintain the separation of powers.

(h) Judges who are High Court judges or above can only be removed from office by the Queen upon a resolution being approved by both Houses of Parliament. This has not been done in living memory.

(i) Inferior judges can be removed due to either misbehaviour or incapacity and only one judge has been removed from office in this way in recent years.

(j) The Supreme Court will open its doors in October 2009. It will replace the jurisdiction of the House of Lords and the Privy Council. The current Law Lords will become the first Justices of the Supreme Court.

(k) The composition of the judiciary can still be criticised as it is currently dominated by white, middle-class, middle-aged men although the Legal Services Act 2007 has opened up the eligibility criteria so it is hoped that in the future the judiciary will be more reflective of society.

6.10   Self-test questions

1. The most superior type of judge in England and Wales is the:

   (a) Lord Chancellor
   (b) Circuit Judge
   (c) Lord Justice of Appeal
   (d) Lord of Appeal in Ordinary

2. The Lord Chancellor is now:

   (a) the Head of the judiciary
   (b) the Head of the Ministry for Justice
   (c) a Speaker in the House of Lords
   (d) a member of the judiciary

3. Judges used to be appointed by way of:

   (a) secret soundings
   (b) secret ballots
   (c) open competition
   (d) automatic promotion

4. Judges are now appointed by:

   (a) the Commissioner for Judicial Appointments
   (b) the Judicial Appointments Commission
   (c) an election process
   (d) the Judicial Appointments Committee

5. The Supreme Court will incorporate the:

   (a) Court of Appeal and House of Lords
   (b) Court of Appeal and Privy Council
   (c) House of Lords and Privy Council
   (d) House of Lords

6.11   Further reading

R. Cornes, "The UK Supreme Court" [2003] N.L.J. 153(7087) 1018–1019.

P. Darbyshire, "Where do English and Welsh judges come from?" [2007] C.L.J. 66(2), 365–388.

B. Hale, "Equality and the judiciary: why should we want more women judges?" [2001] P.L. Aut, 489–504.

D. McLean, "Judicial reform in the United Kingdom" [2005] 16(1) Com. Jud. J. 25–27.

Lord Steyn, "Democracy, the rule of law and the role of judges" [2006] 3 E.H.R.L.R. 243–253.

R. Walker, "The new Supreme Court and the changes in the justice system" [2006] L.I.M. 6(4) 292–296.

Lord Windlesham, "The Constitutional Reform Act 2005: ministers, judges and constitutional change: Part 1" [2005] P.L. Win. 806–823.

Lord Windlesham, "The Constitutional Reform Act 2005: the politics of constitutional reform: Part 2" [2006] P.L. Spr, 35–57.

D. Woodhouse, "The office of Lord Chancellor" [1998] P.L. Win, 617–632.

D. Woodhouse, "The Constitutional Reform Act 2005—defending judicial independence the English way" [2007] I.J.C.L. 5(1), 153–165.

Lord Woolf, "The rule of law and a change in the constitution" [2004] 63(2) C.L.J. 317–330.

D. Wurtzel, "Women on the bench", Link AWS 2006, 21, 16–18.

7 Juries

"The jury is often described as 'the jewel in the Crown' or 'the corner-stone' of the British criminal justice system. It is a hallowed institution, which, because of its ancient origin and involvement of 12 randomly selected lay people in the criminal process, commands much public confidence. In the van of such confidence are the judges and legal practitioners who, when asked, invariably say that, in general, juries 'get it right'. For most it is also an important incident of citizenship; De Tocqueville memorably described it as 'a peerless teacher of citizenship'. However, support for it is not universal, not least among those who have been jurors. And there are many, in particular leading academic lawyers, who express reservations because we do not, and are not permitted by law to, know how individual juries reach their verdicts. It is also well to keep in mind how rarely juries are used in the criminal trial process given the enormous importance with which they are invested by the public, politicians and legal professions. Only about 1 per cent of criminal cases in England and Wales culminate in trial by jury." (*per* Lord Justice Auld, *Criminal Courts Review* (2001) at Ch.5, para.1).

7.1   History

The English jury system, as we know it now, originally appears to have its roots steeped in the Norman Conquest, during which a very early concept of it was brought to Britain. In 1166 King Henry II then began to develop the idea of a more evidentiary form of settling disputes by the issuing of the Assize of Clarendon (an Act of the King). This Assize was to replace the earlier case settlement methods of 'trial by battle' (where the parties duelled to determine the successful party) or 'trial by ordeal' where an accused person would have to undergo a rather gruesome and painful task on the premises that if they completed it without injury, or if their injuries healed quickly, they would then be taken to be innocent of whatever charge lay against them. When first introduced though, this system was nothing like the modern day 'jury' as originally the jurors were mainly used for providing local knowledge, acting as witnesses and gathering information, rather than making decisions. In 1215 the concept of an accused person's right to be 'tried by their peers' was then formalised further by being set out in the Magna Carta. The role of the jury continued to change over hundreds of years and by about the 15th Century they had began to assume the role of the independent assessors of fact in a case, and it is from this that their modern day role has developed.

   The modern day fundamental principle behind a jury is that an alleged offender is provided with the opportunity to be tried by 12 of their peers in an effort to ensure that justice is done. A jury should be free from judicial and other pressures and their final decision in the case as to the defendant's guilt or innocence cannot be challenged (except under the allowed routes of appeal). This principle was established in the case known as *Bushell's Case* (1670) Vaugh 135. Prior to this case the judge would wield a lot of power over a jury's decision and could effectively coerce them into making the decision that he felt was appropriate in the circumstances, regardless of whether this was the verdict that the jury wanted to return or not. In *Bushell's Case* the defendants were Quakers who had been charged with unlawful assembly. At the end of the trial it became apparent that a number of the jurors were refusing to convict the defendants and the jury returned a not guilty verdict. The trial judge refused to accept this verdict as he was of the opinion that the defendants were guilty and therefore should be convicted as such. In an effort to persuade the jury to officially return a guilty verdict the judge ordered that they be detained to reconsider their verdict, but without any food or water. The jury again refused to reach a guilty verdict, at which point the judge then fined each of the jurors and committed them to prison until they could pay their fines. The jurors appealed the judge's decision and the Court of Common Pleas (the then appeal court) ordered that the jurors be immediately released holding that jurors cannot be punished for their verdicts. Following this case it has been widely accepted that jurors are independent of the judge, they are charged with the role of deliberating and deciding upon the defendant's guilt or innocence and as such they are the sole arbitrators of fact. The judge is there to simply direct on the law but cannot intervene in the jury's decision no matter how much he disagrees with it. If a judge (or other party) attempts to place unacceptable pressure upon the jury to reach a decision then the conviction will be quashed.

Bushell's Case is obviously a very old case (over 300 years) but this principle is still as applicable to the modern day jury system, if not more so, as can be demonstrated by the more recent case of *R. v McKenna* [1960] 1 Q.B. 411. In this case the defendants were convicted of charges arising out of the theft of a van containing radio sets. After the jury had retired for more than two hours the judge told them that if they did not reach a verdict within ten minutes they would be kept all night. The jury then returned verdicts of guilty after a further six minutes. On allowing the appeal against conviction the court held that:

> It is a cardinal principle of our criminal law that in considering their verdict, concerning, as it does, the liberty of the subject, a jury shall deliberate in complete freedom, uninfluenced by any promise, unintimidated by any threat. They will stand between the Crown and the subject, and they are still one of the main defences of personal liberty.

By allowing the appeal, the court confirmed that, as binding authority indicated, a judge had no power to pre-empt the jury's verdict by directing it to convict and that there was no good reason to depart from that authority.

The fact that a judge in a case cannot interfere with the jury's decision making does, however, mean that the jury can acquit a person even if they are technically guilty under the law, as was confirmed by the House of Lords in the case of *R. v Wang* [2005] UKHL 9. In *Wang* the appellant had been waiting for a train when his bag was stolen. A search was made and the bag found in the possession of a thief who tried to deter the appellant from calling the police by suggesting that the bag contained items the appellant should not be carrying. From the bag the appellant produced a curved martial arts sword, in its sheath. The police were called and on a further search of the bag a small Gurkha style knife was found. The appellant was then charged and tried for the possession of the weapons. At trial the appellant testified that he was a Buddhist and practised Shaolin, a traditional martial art. He gave evidence that he had the articles in question, a sword and a knife, with him because he had not liked to leave them in his place of residence and because he liked to stop at remote and uninhabited places to practise Shaolin. At the end of the defence case, the trial judge directed the jury to return guilty verdicts on the ground that W had failed to advance a lawful defence. The appellant then appealed contending that there were no circumstances in which a judge was entitled to direct a jury to return a verdict of guilty. The House of Lords, allowing the appeal and quashing the convictions, stated that the decision of all the factual questions in a case, including the application of the law, was a matter for the jury alone and it was for them to decide whether the defendant was guilty or not.

7.2   The role of the jury

The jury system is mainly used within the Crown Court, although juries do regularly sit in the Coroner's Court and on the very rare occasion in the High Court and the county court. They are an extremely important part of the criminal justice system in ensuring that justice is done, and although they are not failsafe, they are one of the most effective and fair methods of trying those accused of the more serious crimes.

The jury's role in a criminal case is to listen to the evidence presented in court and then decide upon whether they believe it or not in coming to a conclusion about the defendant's guilt. The judge in the case will direct the jury as to what the law is; it is then for the jury to apply the law to the facts of the case. The jury should have no prior knowledge of the case prior to entering the court (although if the case has been of high profile in the media this is difficult to control) so that they can hear the evidence in an unbiased way. The jury will return the verdict of guilt or innocence in the case, and if the verdict is one of guilty the judge will then pass sentence upon the defendant. Once a case has begun the defendant is placed in the charge of the jury and only the jury can discharge them. If the defendant changes his plea to one of guilty after the start of the trial then the jury must still officially return a formal verdict of guilty (this will be done on the court's directions, which are allowed in these instances) before the court can deal with them.

7.3   Eligibility

Prior to 1972 there was a property qualification required for a person to be able to sit as a juror. This meant that a prospective juror had to either own a property or be a tenant (rent) a property. This automatically disqualified a large number of people from being able to do jury service. In the 1950s and 60s, and earlier, it was extremely unusual for a woman to own her own house as property was generally viewed as a right to be had by the males in society. Where a woman did live in a property with her husband or her partner, then only his name would be on the title deeds to the house, or if rented, then on the tenancy agreement, thereby she was not eligible to sit on a jury. The other sector of society that was automatically discounted from sitting on the jury by the property qualification were young people who were over the age of 18, but who were unable or unwilling to move from the family home to a property of their own. Remember that in these times a woman would rarely leave the family home until they were married and moving on to the matrimonial home; thankfully times have changed dramatically since then.

The Morris Committee in 1975 undertook a review of the jury service system and concluded that, as the law stood then, over 95 per cent of women were ineligible for jury service. They concluded that this state of affairs was unfair on both the defendants in a case and to those precluded from jury service due to the property qualification. Juries were supposed to be representative of the society in which they served and as the vast majority of women, and young persons, were prevented from sitting upon a jury then this could not be a fair representation of society. As a result of the Morris Committee report the law was completely overhauled in 1974 by the enactment of the Juries Act 1974 (JA 1974), which became the governing statute in respect of jury composition.

Section 1 of the JA 1974 (as amended by the Criminal Justice Act 2003) sets out the qualifications required for a person to be eligible to sit as a juror. Under s.1 every person shall be qualified to be a juror if:

- they are aged between 18 and 70;
- they are registered on the electoral roll;
- they have lived in the UK for at least five years;
- they are not disqualified or a mentally disordered person.

Schedule 1 of the JA 1974 states that a person will be classified as mentally disordered if they suffer or have suffered from a mental illness, psychopathic disorder, mental handicap and are a resident in a hospital or similar institution, or they regularly attend for treatment by a medical practitioner. Unfortunately the schedule does not seem to distinguish between those who suffer from psychotic behaviour (whom it is assumed the schedule is intending to prevent from sitting as a juror) and those people who suffer from a mild depressive illness and attend their local GP's practice occasionally. If a person is deemed to have a mental disorder under the Act then they are not just disqualified from sitting as a juror but rather they become ineligible to sit as a juror (as does any one who is under 18 or over 70, or who has lived abroad for the past 15 years etc).

The term 'disqualification' is also used within the Act and for the purposes of the Act an individual can also be disqualified from jury service following the imposition of a criminal conviction. If a proposed juror has been sentenced to life imprisonment, detention at Her Majesty's pleasure, a period of imprisonment for public protection, or been imprisoned for five years or more then the individual in question will be disqualified for life from serving as a juror. If they have served a prison term in the last ten years, or received a suspended sentence or a community order then they will be disqualified from sitting as a juror for a period of ten years. These are now the only ways by which a person will be disqualified from jury service. If a person who is disqualified attends for jury service and they fail to declare the fact that they are disqualified, then, if this disqualification is subsequently discovered they can then be faced with a fine of up to £5,000. This imposition of a fine as a sanction for failing to declare their inability to sit as a juror has been put in place as a deterrent. If a person has been subject to a criminal conviction, as detailed above, then it is thought that they will not be able to undertake their jury responsibilities in an impartial and unbiased way. If a person has spent a number of years within the prison system it is unlikely that they will wish to send another person into the system, no matter how damning the evidence is. This could then have the result of perverting the justice system and resulting in unfair acquittals. Further, if it came to light at a later date that a defendant had been convicted by an unconstitutional jury then the appeal process would be open for them, which could result in an acquittal and/or a re-trial. This would then take up further time and resources of the criminal justice system, which is already overstretched, and could result in the public losing confidence of the workings of the justice system.

7.3.1   The impact of the Criminal Justice Act 2003

The initial revision of the jury eligibility criteria, under the JA 1974, went a long way to remedying the potential for having an unrepresentational jury. However, prior to 2004 there were still a few categories of people who were still viewed as being automatically ineligible for jury service (these were persons who were involved in the administration of justice, so judges, lawyers or the police, or who were member of the clergy), and some who held a right to be excused from jury service upon request (doctors, armed forces, and those aged between 65 and 70). The rationale behind these excusals was so as to ensure that those who worked within the system did not influence a jury, and to ensure that the requirements for a jury service did not impact negatively on society in general.

In June and July of 1999 a Home Office research project (*Jury Excusal and Deferral, Research Findings No.102*, Home Office Research Development and Statistics Directorate) was undertaken to consider the composition of the jury and the numbers of people excused from jury service under the law at that time. The key points of the review were that:

- About 50,000 of those summoned were included in the sample—one-third was available for jury service, half of whom were given deferral to a later date.

- Of the remaining two-thirds, 13 per cent were ineligible, disqualified or excused as of right, 15 per cent either failed to attend on the day or had their summonses returned as 'undelivered' and 38 per cent were excused.

- The most common reasons for granting excusal were medical (40 per cent of all excusals) and care of young children or the elderly (20 per cent of all excusals).

- Three-quarters of all deferrals were given for either work (39 per cent) or holidays (35 per cent).

From the quarter of a million people summoned for jury service every year the research project set out that only a third of them were actually available to undertake jury service. So the representational jury that was envisaged by the increasing of the potential pool of jurors under the JA 1974 still did not seem to have come to fruition.

Lord Justice Auld, commenting on the Home Office research in his *Review of the Criminal Courts* (2001), considered the composition of the jury and concluded that:

The variety of mechanisms and broad scope for avoidance of jury service illustrated by these figures suggest that public perception of it as a civic duty is far from universal. And it is unfair to those who do their jury service, not least because, as a result of others' avoidance of it, they may be required to serve more frequently and for longer than would otherwise be necessary. Most of the exclusions or scope for excusal from jury service deprive juries of the experience and skills of a wide range of professional and otherwise successful and busy people. They create the impression, voiced by many contributors to the Review, that jury service is only for those not important or clever enough to get out of it.

In my view, no-one should be automatically ineligible or excusable from jury service simply because he or she is a member of a certain profession or holds a particular office or job. Where the demands of the office or job are such as to make jury service difficult for him over the period covered by the jury summons, he should be subject to the same regime as the self-employed or ordinary wage earners or others for whom jury service is also costly and burdensome, that is, discretionary excusal or deferral.

The result of the recommendations by Lord Justice Auld, that all persons should be eligible for jury service with the exception of the mentally disordered, caused a lot of controversy, but the recommendations were accepted by the government and enacted by way of the CJA 2003 (amending s.1 of the JA 1974). This now means that every person, as long as they are not mentally disordered and they satisfy the criteria set out in s.1, will be eligible for jury service.

When the first judge, Dyson L.J., was summoned in June 2004 for jury service under the new rules, the Lord Chief Justice issued observations, by way of a letter dated June 15, 2004, for judges who were called for jury service. His guidance to the judiciary set out that:

- When a judge serves on a jury he does so as part of his duty as a private citizen.

- If judges are called for jury service they should undertake this duty, unless they can demonstrate 'good reason' as to why they should not serve as summoned.

- A judge should make an application for deferral where he has significant judicial commitments which would make it particularly inconvenient for him to do jury service at the time he was called to do so. Judicial commitments should only be a reason for deferral where, if there was no deferral, there could be a significant interference with the administration of justice.

- Where a judge attends a court for jury service and finds that he is a member of a jury panel where he is familiar with the judge presiding, a legal representative, the defendant or a potential witness he should raise the matter with the judge presiding.

- It is a matter of discretion for an individual judge sitting on a jury whether he should disclose the fact of his judicial office to fellow members of the jury.

- Judges should avoid the temptation to correct guidance they perceive to be inaccurate as this is outside the scope of their role as jurors.

Since the recent amendments to the JA 1974 numerous barristers, solicitors, Q.C.s and judges have sat on juries without consequence, although there have been a few reported cases where the lawyer in question has not been able to sit on the jury due to knowing somebody involved in the case. It is submitted that this will occasionally continue to occur as the legal world is a small one and jurors are selected to sit on the jury in the area where they reside, and this is generally the area in which they also work.

The right for a person involved in the administration of justice to sit on a jury was challenged in the case of *R. v Abdroikov* [2007] UKHL 37. The appeal was a conjoined appeal of three appellants, each of whom had been convicted by a jury that contained either a police officer or a member of the Crown Prosecution Service. The grounds of appeal were that whilst individuals concerned with the administration of justice were now eligible for jury service, the presence of the police officer or the prosecuting solicitor on the jury had deprived them of a fair trial, contrary to the common law and art.6 of the Convention for the Protection of Human Rights and Fundamental Freedoms. The Court of Appeal dismissed all three appeals holding that a fair minded and informed observer would not conclude that there was a real possibility that a juror was biased merely because he was involved in some capacity in the administration of justice. The appeal was then taken to the House of Lords, who allowed the appeals in part due to the fact that although lawyers and serving police officers were no longer ineligible for jury service, the common law rule that justice should not only be done, but should manifestly be seen to be done, still applied. They held that there was no difference between the common law test and the requirement under art.6 that a person should be tried by an independent and impartial tribunal and that justice was not seen to be done if, on the particular facts of a case, a fair minded and informed observer would conclude that there was a real possibility of jury bias, whether conscious or unconscious. The House of Lords were not saying that a CPS solicitor or a police officer could never sit on a jury, just that it had to be considered whether there would be an element of bias present, due to the individual facts of the case, if they were to sit on the jury.

Figure 7.1 Who can sit as a juror?

Eligible	Ineligible	Disqualified
Aged between 18 and 70; *and*	Mentally disordered (as defined under Sch.1, JA 1974)	PERMANENTLY Imprisonment for life, at HM's pleasure, for public protection, or for more than 5 years
Registered on the electoral roll; *and*		FOR 10 YEARS Served a term of imprisonment, had a suspended sentence or a community sentence
Have lived in the UK for the past 5 years		

7.3.2   Excusal from jury service

Just because most people are now eligible to sit on a jury does not mean that they will be forced to serve under any circumstances. The court still has available to it a discretion to excuse a person from jury service where it seems appropriate to do so. For instance, it would be ridiculous to make the mother of a new born baby serve on a jury as this would be detrimental to both the mother and the child, as well as the defendant in the case; the mother would probably be thinking so much about her child that she would not be giving the evidence in the case her full attention and therefore the defendant could be said to be deprived of a fair trial. Other situations where the court may feel it is appropriate to excuse a person from jury service is where they have a pre-arranged holiday or business meeting, or they are a student who has scheduled exams to take in that period or they are ill at that time. The court will only excuse someone who has a genuine reason that prevents them from attending court at that time, and the person will normally only be granted a deferral from jury service (meaning that they will still have to attend jury service at a more convenient time in the future).

The court guidance (*Jury Summoning Guidance: Guidance for summoning officers when considering deferral and excusal applications*, HMCS, April 2004) as to excusal and deferral clearly sets out the court's view regarding excusal, as it states:

> The normal expectation is that everyone summoned for jury service will serve at the time for which they are summoned. It is recognised that there will be occasions where it is not reasonable for a person summoned to serve at the time for which they are summoned. In such circumstances the summoning officer should use his/her discretion to defer the individual to a time more appropriate. Only in extreme circumstances should a person be excused from jury service.

If, however, a person simply refuses to attend jury service and they are without a reasonable excuse for doing so then they will commit an offence under s.20 of the JA 1974. This means that they will be punished by way of a fine of up to £1,000.

7.4   Selection

Jurors are initially requested to attend court by way of a jury summons; a computer at the Central Summoning Bureau determines exactly who receives a jury summons. Generally twenty jurors are summoned for each courtroom so as to ensure that there will be twelve suitable jurors to hear the case. If the court in question is a large centre (has a high number of courtrooms) then there may be sent out well over 100 jury summons per fortnight. A juror is normally expected to attend the court for a two-week period, although this may be extended depending on the length of the trial—some criminal cases have been known to run into months. Once the twenty jurors are at court each of their names will be put on to a card and the court clerk will then randomly select twelve of the cards, so as to decide who will be empanelled (formally sworn into court) as the jurors in the case.

Even once a juror has been summoned and they are eligible to sit as a juror they may still be discharged due to 'lack of capacity' (s.10 JA 1974). A juror will be viewed as having a lack as capacity if, for some reason, they are unable to cope with the demands of the trial, such as not understanding English, being deaf or blind. Having a disability will not automatically exclude a person from sitting as a juror (s.9B(2) JA 1974), but if they are not able to understand what is being said, or they are unable to see or hear the evidence then they will not be deemed capable of judging the trial and carrying out their functions as a juror fully. This principle, that a judge has a residual discretion to discharge a particular juror who ought not to be serving on the jury, has existed at common law for many years and it is considered part of the judge's duty to ensure that there is a fair trial. The origins of this principle can be traced back to the case of *R. v Mansell* (1857) 8 E. & B. 54, where Lord Campbell C.J. stated that a judge had the discretion and duty to discharge such juror in order to "prevent scandal and the perversion of justice". However this discretion should never be used to discharge a competent juror in an attempt to secure a jury drawn from particular sections of the community, or otherwise to influence the overall composition of the jury.

7.4.1   Jury vetting

Once the panel of jurors have made it through this process they can still be vetted by the lawyers for both the prosecution and the defence. This vetting means that lawyers are allowed to check the jurors for suitability to ensure that they are appropriate members of society to hear and try the case. There are two forms that jury vetting can take; a routine check or an authorised jury check.

A routine check involves either a random criminal records office check (Home Office Circular 43/1988) or a specific check (Annex to the Attorney-General's Guidelines on Jury Checks *Juries: Right to Stand By: Jury Checks* (1989) 88 Cr. App. R. 123 at 125). In respect of the random check, at regular intervals throughout the year the Crown Court officials submit to their local police, for a CRO check, a pre-determined number of names from those called for jury service in each Crown Court centre. This system of checks is really to keep an eye on those who are sitting for jury service and to make sure that people who are disqualified are not regularly sitting, or attempting to sit, on juries. A specific jury check involves either a Chief Constable or the Director of Public Prosecutions (DPP) running a CRO check on the names of potential jurors in a case. Such a specific check will be undertaken where the Chief Constable or the DPP considers that it would be in the interests of justice so to do. If it is discovered by either of these procedures that a person is disqualified from jury service but has presented themselves as being capable of serving on a jury then the police will consider whether an offence has been has been committed under s.20(5)(c) of the Juries Act 1974, and will seek advice from the CPS where appropriate.

The second type of check that may be made for the purposes of jury vetting is an 'authorised jury check'. This is a far more in-depth check on an individual juror and it may involve a CRO check, a Special Branch records check and sometimes a Security Services check. An 'author-ised jury check' can only be authorised by the Attorney-General in accordance with the Attorney-General's Guidelines on Jury Checks. The Attorney-General's justifications for this in-depth check on a specific individual are set out in the Guidelines:

> There are, however, certain exceptional types of case of public importance for which the provisions as to majority verdicts and the disqualification of jurors may not be sufficient to ensure the proper administration of justice. In such cases it is in the interests of both justice and the public that there should be further safeguards against the possibility of bias and in such cases checks which go beyond the investigation of criminal records may be necessary. The particular aspects of these cases which may make it desirable to seek extra precautions are (a) in security cases a danger that a juror, either voluntarily or under pressure, may make an improper use of evidence which, because of its sensitivity, has been given *in camera*, (b) in both security and terrorist cases the danger that a juror's political beliefs are so biased as to go beyond normally reflecting the broad spectrum of views and interests in the community to reflect the extreme views of a sectarian interest or pressure group to a degree which might interfere with his fair assessment of the facts of the case or lead him to exert improper pressure on his fellow jurors.

Therefore this type of vetting should only be used in a limited instance of cases which involve either:

(a)   cases in which national security is involved and part of the evidence is likely to be heard *in camera*: or

(b)   terrorist cases.

The issue of vetting has been a rather controversial one over the years. The practice first came into the public knowledge during the course of the 'ABC' trial in 1978. The trial involved allegations of the Official Secrets Act being breached and it was discovered during the course of the trial that the jury had been vetted for their suitability and their 'loyalty'. This lead to the trial being stopped, the jury being discharged, and a fresh trial with a new jury being ordered. There was public outcry upon the discovery of this practice of jury, as it called into question the extent to which a jury was actually randomly selected. The resulting media and public attention from the trial forced the Attorney-General to become more transparent with regard to this practice and this resulted in the general publication of his guidelines on jury vetting which, it was acknowledged, had gone on behind the scenes for many years beforehand.

The in-depth jury checks under the second method can only be authorised by the Attorney-General upon the advice of the DPP, and they can only be carried out in extreme cases (as listed above). However, under the present day state of modern society, especially post the September 11th terrorist attacks in America and the subsequent successful and attempted terror attacks around Britain, it must be considered whether these extended jury checks will become a more regular feature of the jury selection process, and if they do whether they will result in an element of a hand picked jury who will ultimately do the bidding of the government in response to the political climate at that time.

The legality of jury vetting has been challenged on a number of occasions in the courts. In the case of *R. v Sheffield Crown Court Ex p. Brownlow* [1980] 2 W.L.R. 892 the Court of Appeal were required to consider this very issue. Two police officers had been charged with assault occasioning actual bodily harm. Prior to the hearing of the trial the officers applied to the judge for the criminal history of all the potential jurors to be supplied to the defence solicitors, so that they could be vetted. The judge in the case ordered that the Chief Constable should supply both the defence and prosecution solicitors with this information requested, from which the Chief Constable then appealed. The Court of Appeal, dismissing the appeal, held that although they had no power to intervene in the decision they felt that the practice of jury vetting was in principle wrong. Lord Denning M.R. gave a damning condemnation of the practice stating (at 542):

> To my mind it is unconstitutional for the police authorities to engage in 'jury vetting.' So long as a person is eligible for jury service, and is not disqualified, I cannot think it right that, behind his back, the police should go through his record so as to enable him to be asked to 'stand by for the Crown,' or to be challenged by the defence. If this sort of thing is to be allowed, what comes of a man's right of privacy? He is bound to serve on a jury when summoned. Is he thereby liable to have his past record raked up against him—and presented on a plate to prosecuting and defending lawyers—who may use it to keep him out of the jury—and, who knows, it may become known to his neighbours and those about him? Furthermore, as a matter of practical politics, even if jury vetting were allowed, the chances are 1,000 to one against any juror being found unsuitable: and, if he should be, the chances of him being on any particular jury of 12—so as to influence the result—are minimal—especially in these days of majority verdicts.

However, there has not been consistency in the condemning of the practice of jury vetting between the courts. In the same year as hearing *Brownlow* a differently constituted Court of Appeal heard the same issue be once raised again in the case of *R. v Mason* [1980] 3 W.L.R. 617. Here, before the trial, the police had checked the local criminal records and had supplied the prosecution with the names of those called for jury service who had been convicted of criminal offences. Consequently four members of the jury were asked to step down as three of them had criminal convictions, although at least one of them was not disqualified by the conviction. The applicant was convicted of two offences of burglary and two offences of handling stolen goods and, upon conviction, he applied for leave to appeal. The Court of Appeal then approved of the jury vetting (even though it was unauthorised) with Lawton L.J. setting out that both the Crown and the defence had a right to challenge a member of the jury panel and the random selection of jurors had always been subject to the qualification that the judge and the parties were to decide which members of the jury panel were suitable to serve on a jury in a particular case. The rationale of the court appears to be that the checking of the potential jurors' criminal records is a method of preventing a crime being committed as it will stop a disqualified juror sitting when they ought not to. The case of *Mason* has since been overruled on another point of law but on this principle it still remains good law.

7.5   Challenging the jury

Once the 12 jurors have been selected, but before they are empanelled by way of taking the oath, the prosecution and defence have the opportunity to challenge the composition of the jury. There are two forms of challenge that can be made towards a juror and these are known as:

- a challenge to the array
- a challenge for cause

A challenge for cause involves the challenging of an individual juror on the basis that the defendant or a witness knows the juror, or knows that the juror is disqualified from undertaking jury service.

7.5.1   A challenge to the array

The right to challenge the array is provided for under s.5 of the JA 1974 and the challenge is made towards the entire jury on the basis that it is un-representational of society or is biased in some way. Although a challenge to the array is not often made, a classic example of such a challenge can be found in the case of *R. v Danvers* [1982] Crim. L.R. 680. The defendant, who was charged with the offences of rape and indecent assault, was of an ethnic minority but the jury who were empanelled to hear his case consisted entirely of jurors who were Caucasian in origin. The defendant challenged the entire composition of the jury (challenged the array), stating that the jury panel did not reflect the ethnic composition of the community, and on the further ground that an all-white jury could not understand the mental and emotional atmosphere in which black families live, so that a black defendant could not have unreserved confidence in an all-white jury. Essential this argument was that the jury did not provide a full representation of a cross-section of society and therefore he could not be afforded a fair trial. The court held, dismissing his appeal, that there was no requirement in law that there should be a black member of a jury or of a jury panel.

As the jury was selected randomly it was taken by the court to be the best representation of society that could be achieved by the current method of jury selection; just because the defendant was from an ethnic minority did not mean that at least one member of the jury should be from that origin as well. Imagine if there was the requirement that the jury must always be composed of at least one person who shared the same ethnic origin as the defendant; if the defendant came from Mongolia or was Innuit by origin then it could become extremely difficult to always find a juror from the same ethnic background. If this was a requirement, or even a right by the defendant to request this, then selecting a jury for a trial could become nigh on impossible; the law would move towards a positive selection system for jury selection, as opposed to a random one, which would bring with it its own inherent problems and possible allegations of bias or positive discrimination. Couple this fact with the points considered above regarding the problems that can be faced with even compiling a full jury for a case under the current system, even with the amendments under the CJA 2003 to extend the pool of potential candidates, and it would seem that the court has made the correct decision on the basis that the selection system, even if slightly flawed at times, is the best method that we have available to us at present. The court further confirmed this point in the case of *R. v Ford* [1989] 3 W.L.R. 762 where Lord Lane C.J. stated that:

> The racial composition of a particular panel or part panel would not be grounds for challenge to the array. A challenge to the array is a challenge to the whole panel on the ground of some irregularity in their summoning by the officer responsible. [. . .] [i]n the absence of evidence of specific bias, ethnic origins could not found a valid ground for challenge to an individual juror. The alleged discretion of the judge to intervene in the selection of the jury does not therefore fall within any acknowledged category of judicial power or discretion. [. . .] The conclusion is that, however well-intentioned the judge's motive might be, the judge has no power to influence the composition of the jury, and that it is wrong for him to attempt to do so. If it should ever become desirable that the principle of random selection should be altered, that will have to be done by way of statute and cannot be done by any judicial decision.

7.5.2 A challenge for cause

A challenge for cause is a more specific challenge to an individual's right to sit on the jury. Such a challenge is likely to arise where the defendant, or witness, knows or is related to a juror, or knows that a juror is disqualified from jury service.

In the case of *R. v Wilson, The Times,* February 24, 1995 the wife of a prison officer was called to attend jury service. She asked to be excused from service on the fact that her husband worked within the criminal justice system (as could be allowed prior to 2004). Her request was refused and she was required to serve on the jury. The two defendants in the case had been charged with and were subsequently convicted of robbery. It later transpired that both of the defendants had been on remand in the same prison in which the juror's husband worked. An appeal was brought on this basis, and the Court of Appeal stated that although there appeared to be no actual bias in this case the justice system required that not only must justice be done but that it also must be seen to be done. The presence of the prison officer's wife on the jury prevented this from occurring and therefore the defendants' convictions were quashed and their appeal allowed. This concept of justice being seen to be done, as well as actually being done, is a fundamental principle of the English legal system as it helps to instill public confidence in the whole process. It is not only the lower courts who must adhere to this principle, as even the highest court in the land, the House of Lords, has been found to be subject to it as evidenced by the case of *R. v Bow Street Metropolitan Stipendiary Magistrate Ex p. Pinochet Ugarte (No.2)* [2000] 1 A.C. 119.

In both challenges the party making the challenge must give valid reasons as to why the juror(s) should not be allowed to sit on the jury in the case in question.

7.5.3 Stand by

The prosecution only also have the right to request that an individual is made to stand by. This means that the individual juror selected to stand by will be put to the bottom of the list of potential jurors and only used to try the case if no other suitable jurors are available. If the prosecution wish to request that a certain juror is made to stand by they are not required to provide any reasoning for their decision. This method of challenging a juror is not the same as the American system, where the prosecution and defence are allowed to question the jury prior to the trial to determine whether (in their eyes) they would make a good or bad juror in the case.

The issue of questioning the jury to discover whether there was any potential bias was raised in the case of *R. v Andrews (Tracey)* [1999] Crim. L.R. 156. The appellant in the case had been convicted of murdering her boyfriend by stabbing him but her defence throughout the case was that another motorist had killed him in a fit of 'road rage'. The case received a lot of media coverage and the defence were concerned with whether an unbiased jury could be composed due to the amount of publicity surrounding the case. The defence made a submission to the court that all potential jurors should answer a questionnaire, but this was rejected by the judge. The appellant appealed but the appeal was dismissed on the ground that only in exceptional circumstances should jurors be questioned as it was against the principle of random selection. The prosecution therefore, when wanting to use stand by, only have the information available to them by way of jury vetting (if this has taken place) and their instincts.

It may seem a little unfair that only the prosecution have the right of stand by, but until fairly recently (1988) the defence also had a right to challenge individual jurors without particular cause; this was known as a peremptory challenge. Under a peremptory challenge the defence could select up to three jurors who they would stand by. This meant that the defence could effectively attempt to try and tailor the jury to one that they felt would be more likely to acquit. For example, in rape trials it is a commonly known fact that men are more likely to acquit a defendant than women, so being able to use a peremptory challenge to remove three women from the jury meant that the defence could try and balance the jury so that it was more male orientated, and therefore more likely to acquit. This right of challenge was removed from the defence after Lord Roskill's 1986 Fraud Trial's Committee highlighted the potential for abuse by the defence, and recommended its abolishment.

Shortly after the abolition of this right of peremptory challenge a number of defendants, in the case of *R. v Thomas* (1989) 88 Cr. App. R. 370, made an invitation to the court for the judge to stand by some jurors on their behalf. The defendants in the case were four black men who were charged with murder. The jury empanelled in the case consisted entirely of 12 white jurors. Worried about the potential for bias in the case the defendants made the invitation to the court in an attempt to ensure some level of black representation on the jury (they could not challenge the array for the reasons described above). The court, whilst acknowledging that the court did have its own power to stand by a juror and that it could use this power to secure a proportion of black representation upon the jury, held that the power should only be used sparingly and in very exceptional circumstances. They dismissed the appeal stating that in the case before them there were no apparent racist undertones, and therefore there was no risk that the defendants would not get a fair trial from an all-white jury.

A question could be raised over how well the removal of the defendant's right to challenge a juror without cause, whilst the prosecution retain their right, is compatible with art.6 of the ECHR. Surely this difference in power goes firmly against the defendant's right to a fair trial and the doctrine of equality of arms (where both sides should be on a level playing field, and neither one be more disadvantaged than the other). If the prosecution can pick and choose those who it accepts onto the jury then why should the defence also not be able to do so? This argument is briefly addressed by Gillespe (2006 at p.354) but he concludes that the practice may be acceptable by way of the right to derogation from art.6 on issues of national security. It cannot be envisaged though, that issues of national security will be overly dominant in the normal daily life of the Crown Court where this practice regularly occurs, and surely if the rationale behind it was that of being able to protect the interests of the state then simply providing the judiciary with the power of stand down (which they already possess) would be sufficient to deal with such a situation upon the application of the prosecution; there is no real need for the prosecution to have this 'right' as a right.

Figure 7.2 The trials and tribulations of becoming a juror

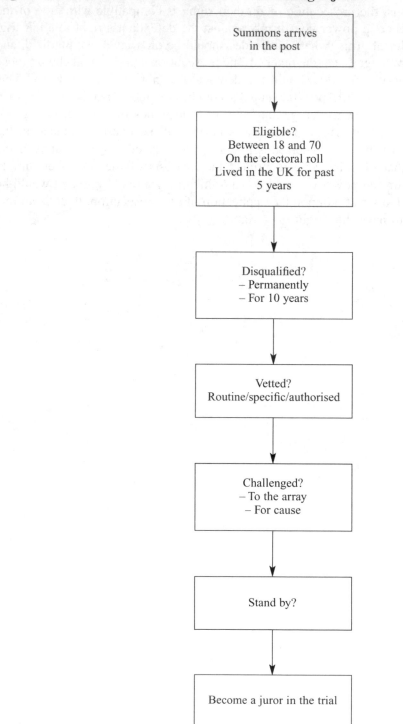

7.6   Jury room secrecy

One of the very distinct and special things about the jury is that nobody outside of the jury room will ever (or at least should never) know the reasons for the jury's verdict or how they reached that decision. This principle of jury room secrecy is one that is held very dear to the justice system and, to ensure that it is complied with, it has been legislated for under s.8 of the Contempt of Court Act 1981 (CCA 1981) so as to make it a criminal offence. Section 8 sets out that:

(1) Subject to subsection (2) below, it is a contempt of court to obtain, disclose or solicit any particulars of statements made, opinions expressed, arguments advanced or votes cast by members of a jury in the course of their deliberations in any legal proceedings.

(2) This section does not apply to any disclosure of any particulars—

(a)   in the proceedings in question for the purpose of enabling the jury to arrive at their verdict, or in connection with the delivery of that verdict, or
(b)   in evidence in any subsequent proceedings for an offence alleged to have been committed in relation to the jury in the first mentioned proceedings,

or to the publication of any particulars so disclosed.

Essentially s.8 sets out that any deliberations that take place in the jury room are to be kept secret and no enquiry as to how the jury reached their decision in a case may be made. There are a number of reasons as to why jury room deliberations should remain secret. By making the divulgence of jury room deliberations a criminal offence it is hoped that jurors will be thoroughly dissuaded from selling their stories to the media after the conclusion of the trial; the ban on discussing the conversations within the jury room will also help to protect an individual juror from any potential recriminations following an unpopular verdict, as if no one person can speak out and say who was for or against the conviction or acquittal then no single juror can be targeted in the case of any reprisals.

To stop the publication of jury deliberations the case of *Attorney-General Respondent v Associated Newspapers Ltd* [1994] 2 W.L.R. 277 held that the scope of s.8 was wide enough to catch not just the jurors who divulge the jury rooms deliberations, but also any person who then publicises the contents of the deliberations after being told them by the juror. In *Associate Newspapers Ltd* an article was published in *The Mail on Sunday* revealing the deliberations of a jury in the course of reaching their verdict in a criminal trial. The article referred to how three jurors in the case had allegedly reached their decisions. The journalist who wrote the article had been passed the information by way of a third party who had been in direct contact with the jury members. On publication of the article the Attorney-General applied for the journalist and the newspaper's editor and publisher to be held in contempt of court under s.8(1) of the Contempt of Court Act 1981. The judge held that s.8(1) did extend to include the newspaper's publisher, editor and journalist and they were subsequently held in contempt of court. On dismissing the appeal, the House of Lords held that the wording in s.8(1) did include the publication by the journalist as it amounted to a disclosure, as opposed to a recounting of known facts and that s.8

207

had been enacted by Parliament as a remedy against the publication of jury deliberations as well as their disclosure by individual jurors.

The courts are also extremely reluctant to investigate any allegations surrounding jury room deliberations, even where there are allegations relating to irregularities as to the way in which the jury reached their decision. In the case of *R. v Thompson* (1962) 46. Cr. App. R. 72 the Court of Appeal refused to hear evidence pertaining to the fact that the jurors had been shown a list of the defendant's previous convictions before returning a guilty verdict, even though it was alleged that the majority of the jury had come to the conclusion, prior to being aware of the defendant's criminal history, that the defendant was innocent of the offence alleged. The Court of Criminal Appeal held that the court had no power to inquire, by taking evidence from jurymen, about what had occurred either in the jury box or in the jury room.

If, however, the discrepancy occurs outside of the realm of the jury room the court will be more minded to intervene and investigate any allegations of irregularity, even if this investigation may affect the process of the jury deliberations, as was shown in the case of *R. v Young* [1995] 2 Cr. App. R. 379. In the case of *Young* the jury had retired to a hotel overnight and the allegations related to the ways in which a number of the jury had conducted themselves during this period. The case was one involving an alleged murder and on retirement to the hotel four members of the jury met up and attempted to contact the deceased by way of a ouija (a ouija board is used at a séance to seek messages from the spirits of absent or deceased persons). They apparently achieved contact with the victim and they asked questions which went directly to the heart of the case, such as who had committed the murder, and the board then allegedly spelt out the defendant's name in response. On return to court the following day the jury returned a unanimous verdict of guilty. Later one of the jurors approached the solicitor in the case and provided them with a written statement of what occurred at the hotel, upon the basis of which the appellant lodged an appeal. The Court of Appeal allowed the appeal and held that the instances at the hotel were conducted during a hiatus in the jury sessions and therefore investigation of the jury's actions within this time was not to be viewed as a breach of s.8. The court also held that the investigations could only focus on this specific period of time and could not continue on to the point at which the jury officially reconvened the following morning.

The fact that there is a common law rule against the investigation of jury misconduct has lead to a number of cases challenging the validity and lawfulness of this rule under the art.6 right to a fair trial provisions. The leading authority in this matter is, at present, found within the conjoined appeals of *R. v Mirza; R. v Connor* [2004] 2 Cr. App. R. 8. In *Mirza*, after the defendant's conviction a juror had written to his counsel suggesting that there had been a racial element in the jury's verdict. In *Connor*, there had been a letter from a juror raising concerns about the deliberations of the jury and alleging that the defendants had been found guilty in order to teach them a lesson. Both of the defendants appealed against conviction. The issues before the court were whether evidence which revealed a lack of impartiality about the deliberations of a jury was always inadmissible under the common law secrecy rule, and whether s.8 of the CCA 1981, if prohibiting the admission of such a statement, was incompatible with art.6.

The court held that art.6 was not infringed by the common law rule of secrecy. The role of the jury was that of a collective decision maker, and during the decision making process the jurors were to be free from outside interference. The common law rule worked by ensuring that the jurors, following their decision, were protected from external ridicule, criticism and harassment, and it was this that gave the system its strength. The court recognised that the risk of perversity could not be entirely eliminated but that the balance of advantage lay firmly in favour of preserving the common law rule as a proportionate response to the needs of the jury system. The role of the secrecy rule was recognised in the European jurisprudence as essential to the operation of the jury system so that the rule was compatible, without modification, with a defendant's right to a fair trial under art.6(1).

Following the case of *Mirza; Connor* the House of Lords issued the Practice Direction *Crown Court: Guidance to Juror, The Times*, February 27, 2004, which states that:

> Trial judges should ensure that the jury is alerted to the need to bring any concerns about fellow jurors to the attention of the judge at the time and not wait until the case is concluded. At the same time, it is undesirable to encourage inappropriate criticism of fellow jurors, or to threaten jurors with contempt of court.

A year after the issuing of this Practice Direction the House of Lords were again faced with the issue of a juror divulging details of the jury deliberations in the case of *Attorney-General v Scotcher* [2005] UKHL 36. Following a trial in which the defendants had been convicted by a majority vote of 10 to 1, the dissenting juror had written to the defendants' mother to urge her to consider an appeal. He had deliberately disclosed statements, opinions, arguments and votes of the members of the jury in the course of their deliberations, and had done so with the intention of proving that there had been a miscarriage of justice. The juror based his defence on the submission that his art.10 rights (freedom of expression) would be breached if he were to be held in contempt of court for disclosing the deliberations, when his main aim and purpose had been to prevent a miscarriage of justice.

The House, on dismissal of the appeal, held that it was not disputed that the juror in question genuinely believed that there had been a miscarriage of justice. Had he written to the Crown Court or to the Court of Appeal with his disclosures then he would not have been in contempt of court. However, by writing to the defendants' mother, he had made disclosures to a third party who had no authority to receive disclosures on behalf of the court. He had created all the risks to the confidentiality of the jurors' deliberations, which s.8 was designed to prevent, and he was in contempt of court. Further the court held that s.8 of the Act was not incompatible with the right to freedom of expression enshrined in art.10 of the Convention since a juror could draw his concerns to the attention of the trial judge before the jury returned its verdict.

Therefore both the timing of the alleged irregularities and the party to whom the allegations are made are critical to the question as to whether they can be investigated by the court or not. If the irregularities occur outside of the jury room (as in *Young*) then they can be investigated by the court, as can irregularities that occur during the course of the trial, or irregularities raised *directly* with the court as opposed to a third party.

The problems that this rule of secrecy carries with it is the fact that there is never any certainty as to how and why a jury has reached a certain decision (was it by way of careful consideration of all the evidence, or by the toss of a coin?), nor can comprehensive research be carried out into how juries reach their decisions. Over recent years studies into how juries deliberate have been carried out by the use of mock juries; this is where a second jury will sit alongside a real jury in a case but their deliberations will be free for the researchers to film and scrutinise as they will not be the determining jury in the trial. The practice of using a mock jury as a method of research and study has even made it into the mainstream media in the past few years by way of programmes such as 'Consent' (Channel 4, January 21, 2007) and 'The Verdict' (BBC 2, February 11–15, 2007). But, as compelling as these programmes were, and as access-all-areas as the research is, it is doubted that these 'mock' juries will ever truly replicate the deliberations that go on behind the closed jury room door. The jurors in the mock trials know that they are being watched, they may even see the cameras filming them, and it is questioned whether a person under these circumstances will act in the same way if they were in a real jury situation, where no one can be held publicly to account for their comments or decisions.

The Government published a consultation paper in 2005 (*Jury research and impropriety* (2005)) where it considered the appropriateness of extending the ability to research into the jury decision-making process. The consultation paper received 41 responses from a wide range of people such as judges, lawyers, academics, the police and the CPS. Overall the respondents were in favour of allowing some degree of research into the jury decision-making process. The main reason given for this was that 'research would permit a better understanding of how juries operate and would allow trial procedures to be improved, thereby assisting jurors in the performance of their duties'. However there were also a lot of reservations apparent about the research becoming too invasive, and consequently the general consensus and recommendations were that any research conducted should be carried out in line with s.8; effectively meaning that the continuation of research into jury decisions should, for the time being, continue to be conducted by way of mock juries.

Figure 7.3 Summary of arguments for and against jury room secrecy

Arguments for jury room secrecy	Arguments against jury room secrecy
Helps to maintain public confidence in the jury system	Research into how jurors reach their decisions could be undertaken
Helps to preserve the finality of the verdict	Miscarriages of justice could be avoided
Helps to ensure the jury can speak frankly	It would ensure that the jurors are accountable for their decisions
Helps to protect jurors from threats and intimidation	Would enable the public to become more educated in the ways of the justice system
Protects the privacy of jurors	It would remove the possibility of bias

7.7   Verdicts

After all the evidence has been heard in the case and the judge has summed up the evidence for the jury and directed them on the relevant law the jury will retire to consider their verdict (their decision as to whether the defendant is innocent or guilty of the offence they have been charged with). Initially it is hoped that a jury will return a unanimous verdict (a verdict upon which all the members of the jury agree). If, however, after at least two hours of deliberation it appears to the court that the jury are not able to agree unanimously then they may direct the jury to return a majority verdict instead. The courts are given the power to make such a direction under s.17 of the JA 1974. Section 17(1) states that:

(1) [T]he verdict of a jury in proceedings in the Crown Court or the High Court need not be unanimous if—

(a) in a case where there are not less than eleven jurors, ten of them agree on the verdict; and

(b) in a case where there are ten jurors, nine of them agree on the verdict.

The court can make such a direction if it appears to the court that the jury have had a reasonable period of time for deliberation when having regard to the nature and complexity of the case. Majority verdicts were originally introduced in 1967 to try and reduce the number of cases where there was the possibility of 'jury nobbling' as, when only a unanimous verdict was acceptable, there would be instances where a jury member would be bribed or intimidated (or 'nobbled') into giving a certain verdict (generally not guilty). As the court required unanimity then a situation of a stalemate would arise and, if the stalemate continued unbroken then the court would be forced to discharge the jury and order a retrial. The introduction of the majority verdict was a way of avoiding this stalemate as, even if one juror had been 'nobbled' into finding the defendant not guilty, it would not matter as the court could accept a guilty verdict from the other 11 members of the jury. The problem of jury nobbling escalated during the 1980s in relation to a number of IRA terrorist trials that were occurring at the time and in 1991 it became an offence, under s.51 of the Criminal Justice and Public Order Act 1991 (CJPOA 1991), to threaten or intimidate any person involved in a criminal trial. More recently s.54 of the Criminal Procedure and Investigations Act 1996 (CPIA 1996) allows for an acquitted person to be retried if subsequently a person is convicted of intimidating or threatening anyone involved in the trial (witnesses or juror). This is a major step forward by the law to ensure that juries are unbiased by outside influences as it goes against the principle of finality (that once a person is acquitted of a crime that is the end of the matter).

Where a jury do give a majority verdict it is vitally important that the foreman of the jury (the person who stands up in court and pronounces the jury's verdict) provides details of the majority that the decision was made by, so either 11 to 1, or 10 to 2. This is to ensure that a lawful majority verdict has been given. If the foreman only had to say that the defendant was guilty by majority then all those involved in the case would be left forever wondering if they were found guilty by 11 to 1, or 7 to 5. It is acceptable by the court (under *R. v Pigg* [1983] 1 All E.R. 56) for the foreman to simply state how many members of the jury agreed with the verdict.

If for any reason the jury has diminished in size since the start of the trial, so perhaps a juror has become ill or has died, then there must only be one person who dissents from the majority verdict for it to be lawful. Where the jury number has dropped to nine then the decision must be unanimous, and if for some reason the jury number has fallen below nine then the trial must be stopped and a new trial begun with a fresh jury.

If a defendant is acquitted by way of a majority verdict then it is not necessary for the court to be informed about the jury split on who voted one way or the other; in these instances the simple fact that a majority has decided that the defendant is innocent is sufficient enough detail for the court.

7.8   Advantages and disadvantages of the jury

The English jury system is held in high esteem by a large part of the westernised world, but it is not without its foibles and problems. As Penny Darbyshire stated in her article 'The lamp that shows that freedom lives—is it worth the candle?' ([1991] Crim. L.R. Oct. 740–752):

> Too often, eulogies are heaped upon the jury by its defenders who blindly follow their predecessors' mistakes (on Magna Carta) or atheoretical assertions (on jury trial as a constitutional right). They confuse randomness with representativeness and justify the jury as a democractic guardian of civil liberties re-writing the law on our behalf.
>
> In heaping unquestioning praise on the jury, the commentators deceive themselves and the public into thinking jury trial is the 'centrepiece' of the criminal justice system. A mass of research on pre-trial decision-making and plea-bargaining has taught us that this is simply not the case. As Ashworth reminded us in 1988: "There are few who would now propound the view that the centrepiece of the English criminal process is the trial," but the jury defenders are still doing just this.

Below is set out a table incorporating into it the main advantages and disadvantages of the jury trial. The points included do not identify every plus or minus to the jury system but they set out the main headings, that of course can be expanded upon.

Figure 7.4 Advantages and disadvantages of the jury

Advantages	Disadvantages
Public confidence The right to be tried by one's peers is a fundamental right under the English legal system. It is a system that is seen as an effective one and, as famously quoted by Lord Devlin, juries are viewed as "the lamp that shows that freedom lives".	**Lack of competence** The jury are not legally trained or experienced in any way and they are required to deal with complex matters of law, upon their understanding of which often depends a person's liberty. The average randomly selected jury is often not intelligent enough to cope with complicated legal matters.
Public participation This links into public confidence. The public become involved in the legal system and consequently the courtroom is not viewed as a closed world wholly dominated by lawyers.	**Attendance** Despite the recent reforms in the law it is difficult to find people willing to undertake jury service and many will make excuses and request a deferral. Those people who can attend are often of the same social and economic background, which does not result in a representative jury.
Jury equity Juries are not bound by precedent and can make decisions on the facts of each individual case, nor are they required to give reasoning for their decisions. This means that the jury can make their decisions based on "fairness" as opposed to the law.	**Perverse verdicts** The jury will occasionally come to a decision (normally an acquittal) which is difficult to reconcile with the evidence and the law—this is known as a perverse verdict. However, due to the rule on finality the appeal courts will not generally interfere with such a verdict.
A representative panel As there are 12 people on a jury, all of whom have been randomly selected, the jury should represent a cross-section of society. Due to the number of people on a jury it is envisaged they will be able to make decisions without bias.	**Bias/racial composition** The jury may be biased for a number of reasons (media influence, personal views) and this bias may affect the verdict. There is no requirement for the jury to reflect the ethnic origin of the defendant, and this has been held in a number of cases not to breach a defendant's art.6 rights.
Certainty The jury's verdict provides finality of answer in that the case is finished upon the verdict and is not open to dispute. The verdict cannot be misinterpreted in any way.	**Nobbling** A juror/jurors may be intimidated or threatened into returning a verdict, which they would otherwise not have done. The jury system is not impenetrable from outside influences.

7.9 Alternatives to jury trial

The final point to note in relation to juries is that, although they are predominately the main way in which an indictable offence will be tried in the Crown, they are not the only way as, over recent years, other systems which are alternatives to jury trial have been developed.

7.9.1 Trial by judge alone

The total abolishment of juries in all criminal cases has been considered by the Government on a number of occasions, although this consideration has not been taken forwards as of yet. The arguments for the abandonment of the jury are that it would remove the possibilities of jury bias, perverse verdicts and jury nobbling and the 'Diplock courts' in Northern Ireland are viewed as a prime example of how well trial by judge alone can work. The Diplock courts were set up in 1972, on the recommendations of Lord Diplock, to hear cases involving serious terrorist threats where a fair hearing by a jury (due to instances of jury nobbling) could not be expected. Lord Justice Auld in his *Review of the Criminal Courts* (2001) also supported the notion of trial by judge alone stating that:

> In short, trial by judge alone, if defendants wish it, has a potential for providing a simpler, more efficient, fairer and more open form of procedure than is now available in many jury trials, with the added advantage of a fully reasoned judgment.

There are also many arguments against the abandonment of the jury trial, these mainly being that the judge will often not be of the same social class as the defendant and therefore will not have the social awareness that is brought by the jury, that the judge will be biased in favour of the prosecution and they will be case hardened which will be projected onto the defendant.

The government have recently provided for trial by judge alone in certain specified cases, namely fraud trials, under s.43 of the Criminal Justice Act 2003 (CJA 2003) (although this is not yet in force), and for cases where they may be a danger of jury tampering (s.44 CJA 2003).

7.9.2 Trial by a number of judges

Although trial by a panel of judges may remove the possibility that a single judge is biased towards the defendant in some way, it would require a complete restructuring of the criminal justice system that could simply not be afforded. To have a panel of three or five judges sat in each case triable on indictment would push the criminal justice bill up massively (by hundreds of thousands of pounds). The reason that magistrates are employed in the majority of criminal cases is to avoid such cost implications.

7.9.3 Trial by judge and lay-people

This method would be effectively a consolidation of the two systems that we have at present (the magistrates and the Crown Court judges). Here a judge would sit alongside two lay-people (most likely magistrates but they could also be randomly selected members of the public) to decide the case. This system does seem to have a lot of advantages in that there would be reduced potential for bias and there would be a certain element of cross-society representation. However, one of the drawbacks could be that the lay-people acquiesce to the judge in their decisions due to his standing in the court.

7.10 Summary

(a) Juries have existed in one form or another since their introduction into the English legal system by King Henry II in the 1100s. The modern day role of the jury is to be the triers of fact responsible for determining the guilt or innocence of the defendant who stands before them as the accused.

(b) Jury independence is a sacred principle of the jury system and so a jury should be free from judicial and other pressures and their final decision in the case as to the defendant's guilt or innocence cannot be challenged. Neither a judge, nor any other party, is allowed to intervene or interfere with the jury's decision-making process.

(c) To be eligible to be selected as a juror an individual must be between the ages of 18 and 70, be registered on the electoral roll, have lived in the UK for at least five years and not be either disqualified or mentally disordered. A person will be classed as disqualified for life if they have been sentenced to life imprisonment, detained at Her Majesty's pleasure, been imprisoned for public protection or for a period of five years or more. Disqualification from jury service for ten years will occur where a person has served a prison term in the last ten years, or received a community sentence or a suspended sentence.

(d) The Criminal Justice Act 2003 opened up the potential number of jury candidates by removing the restrictions on persons such as judges, lawyers and those employed within the criminal justice system from sitting on a jury.

(e) An individual may be excused from jury service where there are exceptional circum-stances that would make it inappropriate for the potential juror to sit on a jury at that time. Most persons excused from jury service receive a deferral and therefore must sit as a juror at some point in the near future.

(f) A jury will consist of twelve individuals who have been randomly selected by a computer at the Central Summoning Bureau to serve on the jury. There will, on average, be twenty people summoned to sit on each jury so as to ensure that there are at least twelve appropriate individuals who can hear the case.

(g) Even once selected it is not definite that any individual will be on the final jury panel as jurors may be dismissed due to lack of capacity, or because they have been deemed unsuitable following jury vetting checks. Jury vetting checks are investigations into the potential jurors' criminal records, or in certain cases, the jurors' wider background.

(h) The whole jury can be challenged (under a challenge to the array) where it is submitted that the jury is not representational. If this challenge is successful then a fresh jury will be empanelled into the case. The right of an individual to sit on the jury can also be challenged (by way of a challenge for cause) where the defendant knows a juror, or it is known that the juror is disqualified or ineligible for jury service. The prosecution also have the right to request a juror to 'stand by'.

(i) The discussions that occur within the confines of the jury room are privileged and, after the verdict, they cannot be discussed or investigated by any person. If a person does divulge the deliberations that occurred within the jury room then they will commit an offence under s.8 of the Contempt of Court Act 1981.

(j) Initially the jury should attempt to reach a consensus and return a unanimous verdict. If they are unable to agree then they are permitted to return a majority verdict after a period of at least two hours' discussion and on the direction of the judge.

7.11   Self-test questions

1. To be eligible to sit as a juror a person must be:

(a) registered on the electoral roll
(b) between the ages of 18 and 65
(c) have lived in the UK for at least three years
(d) own their own property

2. A person is disqualified from serving as a juror for ten years if they have:

(a) been cautioned by the police
(b) received a speeding ticket
(c) received a community sentence
(d) been declared bankrupt

3. Routine jury vetting involves checking a juror's:

(a) credit score
(b) employment history
(c) professional qualifications
(d) criminal record

4. An individual's right to sit on a jury can be challenged on the grounds that:

    (a) they look like they will convict the defendant
    (b) a witness in the case knows them
    (c) the defendant lives in the same town as them
    (d) the jury is unrepresentative

5. Section 8 of the Contempt of Court Act applies to:

    (a) the court
    (b) the defendant
    (c) the prosecutor
    (d) any person who discloses details of the jury room deliberations

7.12 Further reading

W.R. Cornish, "Report of the Departmental Committee on Jury Service" [1965] 28(5) M.L.R. 577–583.

G. Daly and R. Pattenden, "Racial bias and the English criminal trial" [2005] 64(3) C.L.J. 678–710.

P. Darbyshire, "The lamp that shows that freedom lives—is it worth the candle?" [1991] Crim. L.R. 740–752.

P. Darbyshire, "What can we learn from published jury research? Findings for the Criminal Courts Review" [2001] Crim. L.R. Dec. 970–979.

P. R. Ferguson, "The criminal jury in England and Scotland: the confidentiality principle and the investigation of impropriety" [2006] 10(3) E. & P. 180–211.

N. Haralambous, "Protecting the secrecy laws surrounding jury deliberations: the ongoing saga" [2008] 172(7) J.P. 97–98.

J. Hostettler, "Diminishing the power of trial by jury" [2004] L. Ex. Jul, 4–7.

R. F. Julian, "Judicial perspectives on the conduct of serious fraud trials" [2007] Crim. L.R. Oct. 751–768.

D. Kirk, "A tale of two juries" [2008] 72(1) J. Crim. L. 1–3.

S. Lloyd-Bostock, "The Jubilee Line Jurors: does their experience strengthen the argument for judge-only trial in long and complex fraud cases?" [2007] Crim. L.R. Apr. 255–273.

K. Quinn, "Jury bias and the European Convention on Human Rights: a well-kept secret?" [2004] Crim. L.R. Dec. 998–1014.

J.R. Spencer, "Did the jury misbehave? Don't ask because we do not want to know" [2002] 61(2) C.L.J. 291–293.

N. Taylor, "Juries: bias—presence of police officer or employee of Crown Prosecution Service on jury" [2008] Crim. L.R. 134–138.

P. Thornton, "Trial by jury: 50 years of change" [2004] Crim. L.R. Sep. 683–701, [2004] Crim. L.R. Supp (50th Anniversary Edition), 119–137.

8 The civil justice system

8.1 Introduction

The civil law silently regulates everyone's lives although most individuals do not become aware of its existence until a certain matter dictates that they need to become involved with a specific aspect of it. Civil law as a whole governs the issues between private individuals (as opposed to criminal law which is the State regulating society's behaviour). It deals with matters concerning rights, obligations and duties, and it encompasses areas such as the regulating of the terms of a contact and any subsequent breach of those terms. It covers a variety of different aspects such as personal injury claims, matters of family law, the buying and selling of houses and employment law, through to wills, trusts and issues of inheritance. For example, if a person has a slip, trip or fall at work (remember those adverts?!), or if they have a car crash from which they sustain an injury, then they will turn to the civil law to try and achieve a remedy for their injuries; they will sue for compensation. Or if an individual employs a builder to build an extension on their house and the builder refuses to complete the work as agreed then the aggrieved party can bring a claim, in civil law, against the builder for a breach of contract. The civil law therefore can be involved in many aspects of a person's life and it would be virtually impossible for an individual to go through life without encountering at least one limb of the civil law at some point in time, as the reach of the civil law extends as far as everyday mundane matters such as getting on a train or a bus or buying an item from a shop.

8.2 The parties to a claim

The parties to a civil claim will be given a certain title depending on what their involvement in a case is and what the action is concerned with. The party bringing the claim is known as the 'claimant' and the person whom the claim is being brought against is known as the 'defendant'. Prior to the coming into force of the Civil Procedure Rules in April 1999 (see 8.4.1 below) the now 'claimant' was then known as the 'plaintiff'. This change in title was born out of the principle that the civil system needed to be simplified and changed so that it was understandable in the most part by a layperson coming to the proceedings. The term 'plaintiff' was thought to be an antiquated term, whose meaning could not easily be identified on first sight, whereas the term 'claimant' is more understandable in its meaning and application. As this change in UK terminology (plaintiff to claimant) is still relatively new, the title of 'plaintiff' can still be found amongst the older law reports.

Different jurisdictions use different terminology for the person bringing the cause of action and it is worth being aware of these so as to avoid confusion. In Scotland the term 'pursuer' is used to describe the party bringing a claim, whereas Hong Kong and America still refer to the party bringing the claim as the 'plaintiff'. The term 'defendant' has remained consistent throughout the changes and most jurisdictions also describe the person whom the claim is being brought against as the defendant, although in Scotland the word is changed slightly to 'defender'.

Although these party titles (claimant and defendant) are the most commonly used ones within civil law, a party may be known by a different title depending on the type of action being brought. If an application (such as an interim application for an injunction) is being made to the court then the party making the application will be known as the 'applicant' and the person responding to the application will be known as the 'respondent'. Likewise if the proceedings involve a petition to the court then the person bringing the petition will be called the 'petitioner' and the party responding to the petition will be known as the 'respondent'. If the proceedings involve the enforcement of a money order then the party issuing the proceedings will be the 'judgment creditor' and the opposing party the 'judgment debtor', and finally if the matter is one involving an appeal then the party appealing will be known as the 'appellant' and the party who the appeal is against will be the 'respondent'.

8.3   Standard of proof

As the civil law deals with disputes between individuals and as the remedies are often monetary in nature (as opposed to loss of liberty as in criminal matters) the standard of proof that needs to be shown by a party bringing the claim is of a lesser standard than of that in criminal law. To prove a claim within the criminal law system the party bringing the case (prosecuting) needs to prove their case beyond reasonable doubt (see 10.3.1), whereas in the civil justice system the party bringing a claim need only prove their case 'on the balance of probability' to be successful. The term 'on the balance of probabilities' basically means that they have shown that there is more than a 50/50 chance that the facts of the case are as they assert. The burden of satisfying the standard of proof rests on the party bringing their claim.

8.4   History of the civil justice system

The civil justice system has developed slowly and quite sporadically over the years. To begin with there were two distinct systems of law—these being common law and civilian law (civilian law is still used by many European countries such as France and the Netherlands). The use of these different systems caused a great deal of confusion which then resulted in delay and inefficiency. As time moved on the English system moved away from the concept of civilian law and the common law and equity elements were developed and transformed into the systems found within the modern day English courts.

Another factor that limited the effectiveness and usefulness of the earlier court system was that the majority of the civil courts were only found in London. This meant that a vast number of people who would have benefited from accessing the court system to resolve their disputes were precluded. Litigation in the courts was highly complex, overly convoluted by the lawyers and the judges and, as a result, very expensive. The system was neither accessible nor user-friendly (only the very rich could really access and benefit from it) and it was essentially not fit for purpose. To readdress the balance and to open up the possibility of litigation to the masses, a restructuring and expansion of the civil courts began to occur in the mid-1800s. County courts were introduced across the country so that people were not geographically barred from using the court system and this initiative was swiftly followed by the introduction of the Supreme Court (consisting of the Court of Appeal, High Court and Crown Court) and then slightly later the High Court was split into the three separate divisions (Family, Chancery and Queen's Bench) that still exist today.

Despite the reform and expansion of the civil court jurisdiction the whole civil system was still under-performing and struggling under the antiquated and elaborate procedures that were in place. Delay in the hearing of cases was rife, with the average waiting time for a case to be heard being at least two years for the county court, and up to five years for the High Court, and the costs that could be accrued where often astronomical. The system was obviously unsatisfactory and in need of urgent reform.

In 1953 one of the first of many reviews of the civil justice system was carried out by the Evershed Committee; this review was swiftly followed by the Winn Committee (1968) and the Cantley Committee (1979). Each of these individual reviews recognised that the main problems with the civil justice system, as it was then (see below for further discussion), were that the delay experienced and the costs accrued were disproportionate with the majority of the claims being brought. However despite highlighting the failings of the system, they did in fact do little by way of suggestions to remedy the situation. As a result, the first major review that had any impact on the culture of the system was the Civil Justice Review of 1988.

The Civil Justice Review 1988 undertook a full examination of the system and concluded that the delay experienced by litigants was a fundamental issue of the justice system that needed redressing. The review appreciated that delay had a negative impact on all those involved in litigation (the defendant, the claimant and any witnesses etc), that a lengthy delay could have the effect of valuable evidence being less reliable or even being unavailable, and that such problems would, and did, inevitably result in the erosion of public confidence in the whole civil justice system. To address the issues identified by the Review, it recommended that the county court's jurisdiction be widened so that it could cope with more complex and demanding cases; thereby relieving some of the burden from the High Court (this recommendation was later enacted by the Courts and Legal Services Act 1990). However, the extension of the county courts' powers did not directly deal with the issue of delay, as simply shifting the bulk of work from the High Court to the county court did not miraculously reduce the delay in waiting for a case to be heard, but rather simply shifted the emphasis away from the High Court towards the county court, who was already facing delays in excess of two years in the backlog of work waiting to be heard.

The Civil Justice Review 1988 was then followed by the Helibron-Hodge Committee in 1993. This Committee was set up by the Law Society in conjunction with the Bar Council and in their review of the system they concluded that the courts should be charged with taking over the management of the cases and that the majority of potential litigants were discouraged from commencing court proceedings due to the complexity and cost involved. These finding were not ground-breaking in their discovery as they mainly echoed the conclusions from the prior reports. Though again little was actioned from the report and the unsatisfactory status quo was maintained until the conclusion of the Woolf Report in 1995.

8.4.1   The Woolf reforms

In 1995 Lord Woolf undertook an in-depth and all encompassing review of the civil justice system as it was then. This review was called *Access to Justice* and it was charged with exploring all of the aspects of the civil justice system. Lord Woolf commented in his interim report (before the publication of the final report) that the need to undertake such a review stemmed from the fact that:

> "Throughout the common law world there is acute concern over the many problems which exist in the resolution of disputes by the civil courts. The problems are basically the same. They concern the processes leading to the decisions made by the courts, rather than the decisions themselves. The process is too expensive, too slow and too complex. It places many litigants at a considerable disadvantage when compared to their opponents. The result is inadequate access to justice and an inefficient and ineffective system."

While researching into the area of civil litigation in England and Wales, Lord Woolf identified a number of specific problems with the procedure. These problems included the facts that:

- the environment in which litigation is conducted was an adversarial one
- litigation was so expensive and unaffordable
- the costs incurred were disproportionate to the cases brought
- there was no certainty as to the cost in a case
- the costs incurred were not competitive
- the time taken to progress a case from the initial claim to a final hearing
- the time taken to reach settlement
- delay in obtaining a hearing date
- the time taken by the hearing itself
- the complexity of the procedures in place
- the unavailability of legal assistance and advice and
- the low priority status that civil justice carried

This is a rather a long list of flaws and problems in the civil justice system; obviously not a satisfactory state of affairs. So as to make the main issues clear Lord Woolf succinctly (and helpfully) summarised this long list down into three main problem areas; these being cost, delay and complexity (these areas being all interrelated and stemming from the uncontrolled nature of the litigation process). One of the main flaws that Lord Woolf voiced in relation to the civil justice system was that there was no clear judicial responsibility for managing individual cases or for the overall administration of the civil courts, which in turn resulted in the excessive cost implications, the long delays and the needless complexity of the cases as identified above.

To combat these problems Lord Woolf's review involved making numerous suggestions and recommendations on how to improve the civil justice system. The main drive behind the recommendations was for the legal system to accept that there was no alternative but to undertake a fundamental shift in the responsibility for the management of civil litigation. This shift was to involve the responsibility, which lay on litigants and their legal advisers, moving away from the individual and being assumed by the courts. It was acknowledged by Lord Woolf that such a shift in emphasis would require a radical change of culture for all. It would place a greater responsibility on the judges and the courts, for the way in which a case proceeded through the system to a final hearing, and also for the form that the final hearing would take. The system and the procedures therefore needed to be dramatically changed to provide a framework that would allow judicial control to be exercised effectively.

Following this in-depth review the Civil Procedure Rules 1998 (CPR) were enacted and brought into force on April 26, 1999. Since this date all civil litigation has been conducted under the provisions found within the CPR. The CPR is a vast document and so to be accessible to legal representative and lay people alike it is split down into 78 separate Parts, each Part dealing with a different aspect of civil procedure. Each Part is then split down further into a number of individual Rules and to provide further detail on how each rule and Part should be interpreted the Parts are then supplemented by a Practice Direction (PD), which provides the necessary information regarding the practical application of the Rules. Essentially the Rules set out the substance, and the Practice Directions add the detail.

The CPR provides guidance and rules for all the different situations that may occur during a civil claim, so for example Pt 1 sets out the Overriding Objective of the CPR, Pt 3 contains the rules on Case Management Powers, Pt 6 deals with the Service of Documents, Pt 7 provides details on How to Start Proceedings and Pt 32 lists how Evidence should be dealt with in civil cases.

8.4.2   The overriding objective

As indicated above, Pt 1 of the CPR sets out the overriding objective of the whole procedural code. Part 1 provides:

(1) These Rules are a new procedural code with the overriding objective of enabling the court to deal with cases justly.

(2) Dealing with a case justly includes, so far as is practicable—

(a) ensuring that the parties are on an equal footing;

(b) saving expense;

(c) dealing with the case in ways which are proportionate—

(i) to the amount of money involved;
(ii) to the importance of the case;
(iii) to the complexity of the issues; and
(iv) to the financial position of each party;

(d) ensuring that it is dealt with expeditiously and fairly; and

(e) allotting to it an appropriate share of the court's resources, while taking into account the need to allot resources to other cases.

The main purpose of the CPR is to enable the court to deal with cases justly. So as to achieve this aim the application of the overriding objective is not an optional or discretionary one, but one that must be applied rigorously and properly in any case that requires the court to exercise any power given to it by the rules or when it interprets the rules in any way.

The duty to abide by the overriding objective is not just imposed upon the courts but is also imposed upon all parties to the litigation. One of the reasons for this imposition on the individual parties to a case is so as to stop parties employing underhand tactics in an attempt to avoid adverse decisions in a case. For example, if one party to litigation (for illustrative purposes let us say the defendant) can afford the most expensive lawyers in the country, but their opponent (the claimant) has very limited means, then the requirement to abide by the overriding objective should prevent the financial difference between the two parties impacting negatively on the case. The wealthier of the two parties, the defendant, would be banned from running up large costs as a tactic to deter the less wealthy party, the claimant, from continuing with their case.

Part 1 of the CPR also sets out the court's duty to manage cases actively so as to further the overriding objective—this is done by the provision of a very clear and concise list of case management duties. Rule 1.4 states that:

Active case management includes—

(a) encouraging the parties to co-operate with each other in the conduct of the proceedings;

(b) identifying the issues at an early stage;

(c) deciding promptly which issues need full investigation and trial and accordingly disposing summarily of the others;

(d) deciding the order in which issues are to be resolved;

(e) encouraging the parties to use an alternative dispute resolution procedure if the court considers that appropriate and facilitating the use of such procedure;

(f) helping the parties to settle the whole or part of the case;

(g) fixing timetables or otherwise controlling the progress of the case;

(h) considering whether the likely benefits of taking a particular step justify the cost of taking it;

(i) dealing with as many aspects of the case as it can on the same occasion;

(j) dealing with the case without the parties needing to attend at court;

(k) making use of technology; and

(l) giving directions to ensure that the trial of a case proceeds quickly and efficiently.

Many of the factors are simple common sense, such as encouraging the parties to co-operate with each other; obviously if the parties can co-operate with each other then many issues will be resolved quickly. By doing so the case will therefore be dealt with expeditiously, thereby saving expense and ultimately fulfilling the aim of the overriding objective. In the same manner, the courts are required to make use of technology in relation to their case management duties. By using modern technology, such as computers, the court will again satisfy the overriding objective; for example by requiring the parties to use computers it will mean that information can be passed quickly between them (instantaneously via email compared with approximately three days by way of the traditional postal system) and so the case will be dealt with expeditiously. Also by demanding that the parties use resources such as standard word-processed forms this will help to avoid potential problems with the court documents (such as illegible handwriting) and will decrease the need for precious court resources to be spent on an individual case.

8.4.3   Case management powers

So as to enable the court to ensure that the overriding objective is achieved in all cases, and to give effect to Lord Woolf's recommendations, the courts have been granted extensive case management powers under Pt 3 of the CPR. This Part now requires the courts to take on the main responsibilities as to the management and progression of an individual case, and in doing so it alleviates the litigants and their legal advisors of a high level of responsibility that they once bore.

Rule 3.1 at (2) sets out a long list of the ways in which a court can actively manage a case under the CPR. Each of these individual powers relates back to the courts duty under r.1.4 and ultimately to the overriding objective. For instance, one of the case management powers found at r.3.1(2)(b) is that the court has the power to adjourn or bring forward a hearing; this power links into the duty found at r.1.4(2)(g) of the court to fix an appropriate timetable for the case and to control the overall progression of the case, thereby furthering the overriding objective to deal with cases expeditiously and justly. The court has all these options available to it to use but of course it will only use those powers that are appropriate in each individual case so as to achieve the overriding objective.

The court, under r.3.3, does not have to wait for a party to a case to raise a specific issue before making an order, but can make such an order on its own initiative. To illustrate how and why this power may be invoked, consider the following example:

> Jim is currently suing Bob for damages for personal injury following a car accident. Their trial is due to begin on Friday. On the Wednesday morning before the case is due to start the judge in the case decides to review the case file to check that all procedures have been complied with so far. The judge notices that the expert report commissioned by Jim as to

his injuries was only received by the defendant the day before (Tuesday) instead of three weeks before the trial date, as required by the case timetable. This report has the potential to impact greatly upon the outcome of the case and the defendant will need sufficient time to assimilate the information from the report.

In such a case the judge may be of the opinion that the defence will request an adjournment at the start of the trial so that they can deal properly with the contents of the report. Instead of waiting until the day of the trial for an adjournment application to be made the judge, by way of their case management powers, can order an adjournment immediately. This will then allow the defendant to be able to prepare fully for trial (so that both parties are on an equal footing and so that the case is dealt with justly) and will avoid wasting court resources and increasing the case costs as none of the parties, nor their legal teams, will need to attend court on the original day of the trial.

The court will always be mindful of their case management powers and duties whilst a case progresses, and there are various specific points over the course of a case where the court will generally conduct a formal review of the case progression and assess the needs of the case with regards to their powers. The formal introduction of case management powers to the court does appear anecdotally to have helped alleviate a number of the problems in the civil justice system as identified by Lord Woolf in his interim report.

8.4.4　Interpretation of the CPR

When the CPR was drafted it was decided that the style of language used for the rules should be plain, ordinary English, and that complicated legalese should be left behind in the past. The reasoning behind the decision to abandon the complicated and often antiquated legal terminology normally associated with the English legal system was that the use of such language alienated the lay person coming to the law; as the predominate users of the legal system were (and still are) people without legal education or experience it was thought that many persons were put off commencing and/or continuing with a claim due to the fact that they simply could not understand a lot of the procedures involved in their case due to the complicated terminology used. Lord Woolf, in his *Final Report*, commented on the rationale of introducing simpler and clearer language by stating that:

> "I said in the interim report that one of my aims was to modernise terminology. I have not approached this dogmatically but on the basis that terminology should be changed where it is useful to do so. I have sought to remove expressions which are meaningless or confusing to non-lawyers (such as 'relief' when used to mean a remedy) or where a different expression would more adequately convey what is involved (such as 'disclosure' of documents instead of the archaic 'discovery'). The various terms for methods of starting a case, such as writ, summons, originating application, will all be replaced by a 'claim'. The word 'plaintiff' will be replaced by 'claimant'.
>
> I have suggested that the word 'pleading' should be replaced by 'statement of case'. Although it is a very familiar expression to lawyers and in some respects a convenient one,

the word has become too much identified with a process which the legal profession itself readily acknowledges has to change. This is an instance where a change of language will, I believe, help to underpin a change of attitude and a real change of practice to a more open and straightforward method of stating a claim or defence.

I recognise that changes of terminology are discomforting and temporarily inconvenient for those who are very familiar with the existing expressions. But, as I made clear in the interim report, the system of civil justice and the rules which govern it must be broadly comprehensible not only to an inner circle of initiates but to non-professional advisers and, so far as possible, to ordinary people of average ability who are unlikely to have more than a single encounter with the system."

The Home Office, who was the department responsible for CPR at the time of its inception, was so committed to the use of plain English as a way to demystify the legal profession that they were awarded the gold level 'Crystal Mark' for the use of plain English by the Plain English Campaign; the CPR being one of the documents awarded the Crystal Mark.

Even though plain English is used throughout the CPR, problems as to the interpretation of a rule can and still do occur. It is commonly accepted that if there is an ambiguity or query over a word's meaning then initially the natural meaning of the word should be employed wherever possible (think back to the chapter on Statutory Interpretation and the use of the literal rule). Lord Woolf (again in his *Final Report*) anticipated that there would occasionally be problems and questions as to the meaning of some of the words used and suggested that where this did occur the court should look to the overriding objective as a compass to guide them on the right course. He stated that:

"Every word in the rules should have a purpose, but every word cannot sensibly be given a minutely exact meaning. Civil procedure involves more judgment and knowledge than the rules can directly express. In this respect, rules of court are not like an instruction manual for operating a piece of machinery. Ultimately their purpose is to guide the court and the litigants towards the just resolution of the case. Although the rules can offer detailed directions for the technical steps to be taken, the effectiveness of those steps depends upon the spirit in which they are carried out. That in turn depends on an understanding of the fundamental purpose of the rules and of the underlying system of procedure."

Over time the Court of Appeal has added further guidance as to the way in which the CPR should be interpreted and have set limits upon how the overriding objective should be used, holding that the courts should refer to the overriding objective whenever the rules are unclear as to their meaning but, when the rules are clear as to their meaning, then the courts should not resort to the overriding objective in an attempt to assist a deserving case when the plain meaning of the rules unfortunately prevents justice being done. This principle of interpretation is set out in the case of *Vinos v Marks & Spencer* [2001] C.P. Rep. 12 where Lord Justice Gibbson stated that:

"The construction of the Civil Procedure Rules, like the construction of any legislation, primary or delegated, requires the application of ordinary canons of construction, though the Civil Procedure Rules, unlike their predecessors, spell out in Part 1 the overriding objective of the new procedural code. The court must seek to give effect to that objective when it exercises any power given to it by the rules or interprets any rule. But the use in rule 1.1(2) of the word 'seek' acknowledges that the court can only do what is possible. The language of the rule to be interpreted may be so clear and jussive that the court may not be able to give effect to what it may otherwise consider to be the just way of dealing with the case, though in that context it should not be forgotten that the principal mischiefs which the Civil Procedure Rules were intended to counter were excessive costs and delays. Justice to the defendant and to the interests of other litigants may require that a claimant who ignores [procedures] prescribed by the rules forfeits the right to have his claim tried."

The Court of Appeal has effectively said that the overriding objective does not allow the court the luxury of discretion where the rules expressly permit this, even if the result is unjust and in essence goes against the spirit of the overriding objective.

The courts must also take into account the HRA 1998 when considering the interpretation of the CPR. Section 3(1) of the HRA 1998 requires the court to read primary and subordinate legislation in a way that is compatible with the Convention rights whenever it is possible to do so. Consequently problems may occur when the application of the plain meaning of a rule results in a decision that which is incompatible with Convention rights, as occurred in the case of *Goode v Martin* [2002] 1 W.L.R. 1828.

In *Goode v Martin* the appellant (who was the claimant in the original proceedings) applied to amend her statement of claim out of time due to reliance upon details raised by the defendant. The trial judge refused the application and the claimant appealed contending that the refusal amounted to a breach of her right to a fair trial under art.6. Her appeal was allowed and the court held that that both the requirement under CPR r.1.2(b) to give effect to the overriding objective of dealing with cases justly and the requirement in s.3(1) of the HRA 1998 to give effect to subordinate legislation in a way which was compatible with the Convention rights, enabled the court to interpret the language of a rule of court so as to produce a just result and avoid unjustifiable infringement of a litigant's right of access to the court. Not to allow the claimant to do so would prevent her from putting her amended claim before the court and would therefore restrict her access to the court in a way which could not be justified by any sound policy reason and that such a restriction could not be justified. In effect the court laid down the principle that the CPR must be interpreted in a way that is compatible with the HRA 1998 wherever possible, even if this interpretation goes directly against the plain meaning of the rule in question; effectively providing the court with a degree of discretion in certain circumstances.

Overall the introduction of the CPR has had a major and unprecedented impact upon the conduct of civil litigation and it can be described as a massive overhaul of this area of law. No matter how small or large a claim is, if it is based within the civil law system the CPR will be applicable to it. It appears, almost ten years on from its enactment, that the CPR is an unmitigated success; of course it has its problems and issues, as all areas of the law does, but on the whole Lord Woolf's vision of a streamlined civil justice system seem to have mainly come to fruition.

8.5   Jurisdiction

The civil justice system has its own separate court and judicial hierarchy to the criminal justice system, although there is a degree of overlap between them. In addition to the traditional court structure there are also a number of specialised tribunals (e.g. the employment tribunal and the immigration tribunal) that also are part of the collective civil justice system. It is at this point in the chapter that we will look at the traditional court hierarchy of the civil justice system and consider the types of cases each court is likely to hear, as well as the different judges that sit in each court.

8.5.1   The magistrates' courts

The first court, which is also generally considered to be the lowest court in the civil court hierarchy, is the magistrates' court. As considered in Ch.5 the magistrates' court is not just charged with considering criminal matters but its jurisdiction does extend to a certain amount into the civil realm of the law. When the magistrates' court hears civil cases the subject matter will normally be family law matters, regulatory law (such as liquor licensing appeals) or payment default matters (these are often local government matters and the claimant will be attempting to obtain missed payments for duties such as council tax from the defendant). The composition of the magistrates' court is the same as for the criminal justice system (see Ch.5).

8.5.2   The county court

The county court is one of the busiest courts in the civil justice system. There are currently 218 county courts spread over the country in different districts. The county court is governed by the County Courts Act 1984 and this statute provides the court with details of its jurisdiction, powers and types of cases it may hear. The types of cases that the county court will hear include:

- contract disputes (no upper financial limit)
- tortious matters (no upper financial limit)
- claims for personal injury damages (up to a limit of £50,000)
- claims for debt
- landlord and tenant matters
- family issues such as divorce or adoption

As the county court is allowed to hear contract and tort claims (except for personal injury claims) with any financial value this means that it shares jurisdiction with the High Court for a large number of cases. How cases are then allocated to either the county court or High Court is set out in s.1 of the Courts and Legal Services Act 1990 (CLSA 1990) and the High Court and County Court Jurisdiction Order 1991 (SI 1991/724) (HCCCJO 1991).

Generally the claimant in a matter will have the option to choose whichever court they feel would be most appropriate for their case and so they can decide which court in which to issue proceedings. There are only a few circumstances in which the claimant is confined to beginning his claim in the county court, such as when the total amount claimed is less than £5,000 or where the matter is one under the Consumer Credit Act 1974 and the total amount claimed is under £25,000. If the court is required to determine which is the most appropriate venue for the case to be heard then they will look to the criteria found in s.1(3) of the Courts and Legal Services Act 1990 (CLSA 1990), which focuses on the value of an action, the nature of the proceedings, the parties to the proceedings, the degree of complexity likely to be involved in any aspect of the proceedings, and the importance of any question likely to be raised by, or in the course of, the proceedings. The county court is essentially the forum in which all but the most complicated civil law proceedings are handled.

The different judges that may sit and hear cases in the county court are district judges, circuit judges and recorders (see Ch.6 for further detail on the judiciary). A district judge in the civil courts is very similar to a district judge in the criminal courts in respect of their qualifications and powers. In the County Court a district judge has the power to hear any undefended claim brought before them, to conduct trials in any case where the total claimed does not exceed £15,000 and to grant interim and final injunctions. The correct mode of address for a district judge in a county court is 'Sir/Madam'.

Circuit judges sitting in the county court will hear the multi-track cases (see explanation of this below) that a district judge is not permitted to preside over, as well as the more complex lower value cases. Recorders can often be found sitting in the county courts, and again their composition is the same as for the recorders found in the criminal courts. A recorder is a part time member of the judiciary, and is normally a practising lawyer as well; they possess the same powers as that of a circuit judge. The correct mode of address for a circuit judge or a recorder in the county court is 'Your Honour'.

An unusual and unique aspect of the county court is that it employs a specific individual to deal with the paper work (i.e. service of documents) and enforcement of judgments. This individual is called the Court Bailiff. The High Court has no such employee and is reliant upon the general enforcement officers if they need to enforce any judgment.

8.5.3 The High Court

The High Court is part of the Supreme Court of England and Wales (along with the Crown Court and the Court of Appeal), although this is due to become the Senior Court in the very near future. The High Court is split down into three separate divisions, and each division then specialises in different aspects of the civil law and has their own judiciary and administration. The three divisions of the High Court are the:

- Queen's Bench Division (QBD)
- Family Division
- Chancery Division

The Family Division deals with cases involving matters of family and matrimonial law and the Chancery Division deals with cases involving matters of trusts, probate, bankruptcy, intellectual property and land etc. The QBD has a far larger remit than the other two divisions in the subject matter of the cases it hears. It is made up of the Central Offices (based in the Royal Courts of Justice in London) and District Registries (which are spread throughout the country). The High Court generally shares jurisdiction with the County Court and therefore all the cases that do not fall into the Family or Chancery Division specialities will fall under the more general jurisdiction of the QBD. The QBD therefore deals with cases including:

- contract disputes
- tortious matters
- personal injury claims for over £50,000
- judicial review
- defamation cases (these matters must only be dealt with by the High Court)

As well as the three divisions in the High Court there are also a number of specialist courts within the divisions. These courts are the:

- Technology and Construction Court (QBD and Chancery Division)
  - This court hears cases which involve technical or scientific details—common parties will be architects, accountants, IT suppliers, engineers etc.
- Admiralty Court (QBD)
  - This court hears cases which involve shipping matters.
- Commercial Court (QBD)
  - This court hears cases which involve commercial matters.
- Company Court (Chancery Division)
  - This court deals with claims under a number of specialised company related statutes.
- Patents Court (Chancery Division)
  - This court hears cases involving patent and trademark issues.

Finally, just like the county courts, the High Court also has a number of different classifications of judges who sit within the three divisions; these are Masters of the QBD, District Judges and High Court Judges. Masters will only be found within the Central Offices of the QBD in

London, they have jurisdiction to deal with most matters that come before the court and there is only one function that they do not have the jurisdiction to perform; this being that they cannot grant injunctions in a case. The correct term of address for a Master is to call the judge 'Master'.

District Judges are the district registry equivalent of the London-based Master (London has a Master, whereas Nottingham or Sheffield will have a District Judge). Generally speaking the County Court district judge will be the same person as the High Court district judge (especially in small registry areas). A High Court district judge does not have the power to grant injunctions in the High Court, even though the same person may have the power to grant an injunction in the County Court. High Court judges hear the most complex and complicated cases in the High Court, as well as cases that involve a high financial value or are of public importance. High Court judges can grant injunction and also act in an appellant capacity for the High Court.

Beyond these courts lie the higher appeal courts of the Court of Appeal (Civil Division) and the House of Lords and for further discussion of these courts reference is directed to 9.4.

Figure 8.1 The civil court hierarchy

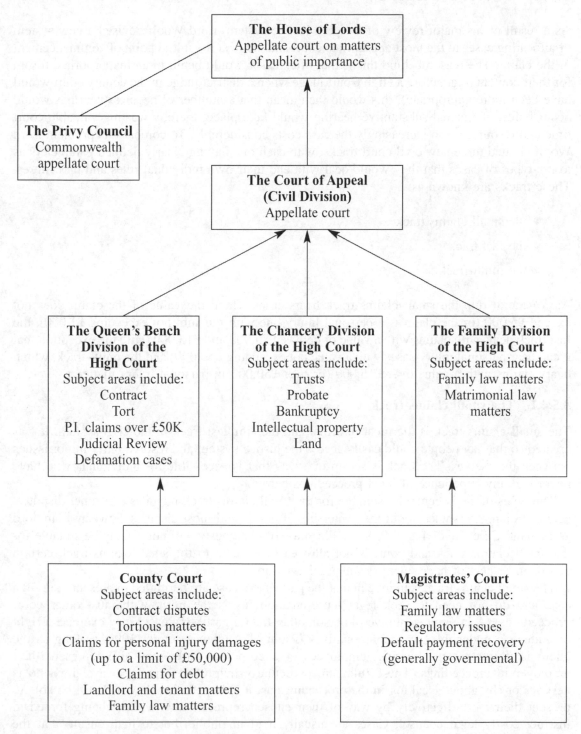

8.5.4   The court tracks

As a result of his major review of the civil justice system, Lord Woolf devised a new system of allocating cases to the most appropriate court and judge at the initial point of commencement of the claim. The reason behind this is that often cases would begin in an inappropriate forum for their content (e.g. before a High Court judge when a district judge in the county court would have been more appropriate), this would then mean that a number of needless hearings would occur before the actual substantive hearing would take place; thereby wasting valuable court time and resources, and increasingly the case costs considerably. To combat this problem Lord Woolf created three new civil court tracks, with each one having clearly defined parameters as to the types of cases that they would deal with and their own individual rules and procedures. These tracks are known as:

- the small claims track
- the fast track
- the multi-track

As a general rule the small claims track hears cases where the value of the claim does not exceed £5,000 (or the claim is a personal injury one with the sum not exceeding £1,000), the fast track deals with claims with a value of between £5,000 and £15,000 (with the exception that it can hear personal injury cases with a value not exceeding £50,000) and the multi-track, which hears claims with a value over £15,000 (or over £50,000 in personal injury matters).

8.5.4.1   The small claims track

The small claims track is the most informal and the simplest track in the civil system. It was created so that lay people could easily access the justice system and resolve fairly minor issues between themselves. The track is set up in a way that is accessible for individuals who have never had any experience of legal proceedings before.

The types of cases generally suitable for the small claims track includes consumer disputes, accident claims, disputes about the ownership of goods and most disputes between a landlord and tenant. Cases involving a disputed allegation of dishonesty will not usually be suitable for the small claims track and court is not allowed to allocate to the small claims track certain claims in respect of harassment or unlawful eviction.

The small claims track is unique in that the parties to a case are permitted to present their own case and do not need to seek legal representation (as is the norm with most other court proceedings). A lay representative (a person other than a party to a case) may exercise a right of audience, under the Lay Representatives (Right of Audience) Order 1999, as long as the client is present at the hearing; employees of a corporate party may also represent their employer in proceedings. These rules are particularly helpful to a party to a claim who is nervous or shy about speaking in the proceedings as, it is hoped, that they will still be able to present their case effectively by way of their chosen representative without being forced to instruct costly legal counsel. Cases are usually held in public, but to help ensure that the proceedings are not intimidating to any of the parties then this will generally be held within the confines of the judge's chambers. Judge's chambers are open to the public but they are normally very small rooms, with just enough seating for the parties and their representative and maybe one or two chairs for members of the public to sit on. Due to their small confines it is very unusual for members of the public who are not involved in the case to sit in on such proceedings.

As small claims cases are normally informal in their manner the usual rules on evidence and conduct are also more relaxed than is usual in legal proceedings and the court can adopt any method of proceeding that it believes is fair in the circumstances. The main aim of the court here is to ensure that just is done (remember the overriding objective) and to do this it is free to move away from the traditional procedural rules found in the courts. Lay persons bringing their claims are unlikely to be aware of the usual strict rules of evidence and so enforcing these strict rules would therefore result in delays and complications as the lay persons attempted to adhere to them. This would then go against the overriding objective of ensuring that the case is dealt with expeditiously and proportionally.

The other rules that differ in the small claims courts to those in other courts is that the parties are not required to give evidence on oath, cross-examination can be limited by the judge, the judge can question witnesses before any other person and the judge can change the order of the proceedings by requiring all the evidence in chief to be given before cross-examination is commenced. All of these changes are to ensure that the overriding objective is adhered to and ultimately achieved.

8.5.4.2   The fast track

The fast track was created to deal with cases where the financial value of the claim ranged between £5,000 and £15,000, or in the cases of a personal injury damages claim between £1,000 and £50,000. The normal trial length of a case on the fast track should be one day or less (this will generally equate to five hours or less of the court's time). There is a standard rule that cases which exceed the financial limits of the fast track, even by a few hundred pounds (so say £15,750) will be automatically allocated to the multi-track and will only be heard on the fast track if all parties to the case agree to the case being heard in this forum.

Once the court has decided that the fast track is the most appropriate track for a case the court will then begin the detailed court procedure required for such cases. The rules governing cases heard on the fast track are provided for in Pt 28 of the CPR. The first step that the court will take in relation to a fast track case is to set out the case timetable and either set the court date, or set a three-week window in which the case must be heard.

A typical timetable for a case that is to be heard on the fast track is as set out below at Figure 8.2.

Figure 8.2 A typical fast track timetable

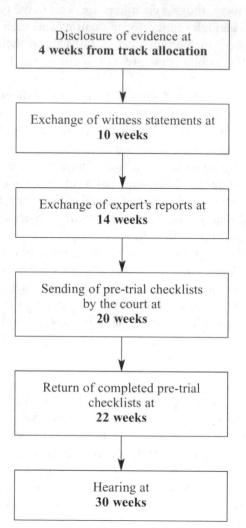

Disclosure of evidence at
4 weeks from track allocation

Exchange of witness statements at
10 weeks

Exchange of expert's reports at
14 weeks

Sending of pre-trial checklists
by the court at
20 weeks

Return of completed pre-trial
checklists at
22 weeks

Hearing at
30 weeks

This timetable may look daunting and even never ending as 30 weeks is basically seven months away, but when involved in litigation this time will pass very quickly and there are many things that need to be done during this time. Instructing experts and obtaining an experts report can take many months to achieve, there may be a number of witnesses to the incident that need interviewing and their evidence then assessing, plus it is never known what the other side will disclose until they actually disclose it and therefore it is difficult to prepare in advance. In fact many parties to litigation find that the 30 weeks passes too quickly and that they are not fully prepared (or prepared as much as they would like to be) when the trial date does eventually come round. The trial date will either be a specific date (if the court deems there to be satisfactory information provided so far to do this) or the case will be given a three-week window in which the case must be heard (so as to provide the parties with a date to work towards), and which will be refined to a specific date later in the proceedings.

To ensure that all parties are ready for trial when the trial date does come round, the court provides detailed directions in the form of the timetable above. The idea is that if the court can provide sufficient directions on any of the issues that might arise in the case then the case should be really for trial by the time of its allotted court date. Although the directions are standard ones the court will seek to tailor the directions it gives to the specific requirements of the case, taking into account any of the steps that the parties have already taken.

The first direction that parties to a case normally need to comply with is the disclosure of a statement of the documents on which they propose to rely. Disclosure will generally be required within 4 weeks of the track allocation. The court will set out a specific date and time that the documents need to be disclosed by (e.g. by 4pm on February 1, 2008). The next stage to occur is the exchange of witness statements; again this will be a requirement to provide to the other side the statements of all the witnesses upon which a party proposes to rely. This should be done within 10 weeks of the track allocation and the court will again set a specific date by which this direction needs to have been complied with.

By 14 weeks from the date of allocation the parties are required to have exchanged any expert reports being used within the case. The CPR limits one expert per party in relation to any expert field, and to expert evidence only being adduced in the maximum of two expert fields in any one case. The reasoning behind this is that cases on the fast track are expected to only last one working day and if more than two experts were called to give evidence (or even to just produce written reports) then there is a distinct possibility that the case will extend beyond the one day time limit and turn into a case that is in reality not suited to the fast track.

Once all the above direction dates have expired the court will send out to all parties a pre-trial checklist (otherwise known as a 'listing questionnaire'). All parties to the case are then required to complete and return the pre-trial checklist promptly (generally within 14 days). The idea of this checklist is for the parties to allow the parties to a case to set out the actions that they have taken so far in their preparation. It should highlight any issues or incidents of non-compliance with the directions that could jeopardise the trial going ahead at the expected time. The return of the checklist to the court is a mandatory requirement and if a party fails to comply with the direction then they face the possibility of their claim or defence being thrown out. If a party does not return the completed form on time then the court will issue them with an order stating that the above will happen without further notice unless they return a completed checklist within seven days.

Once the court receives the completed forms the trial date will be assessed for suitability. If no further issues have arisen the court will either confirm the court date (if a specific date had been already set) or, if a three-week window had been previously allocated, then the case will be listed for trial on a specific date.

The court should give directions as to the evidence, a trial timetable and a time estimate. The judge has the discretion here to set directions as to how long different stages of the trial should take, i.e. how long the claimant's case should take, how much time will be permitted for closing speeches etc. Directions will also be given as to the preparation of a trial bundle and a trial bundle must be prepared by and agreed by every party to a case, should contain all the documents relied upon in a case and be presented to the court in an indexed and paginated folder format. The claimant is tasked with the responsibility of preparing the trial bundle and they must supply the court, the other parties and all the witnesses to the case with a copy of the bundle at least seven days prior to the trial. The purpose of this bundle being agreed and provided to the judge in advance of the trial is so that the judge can become familiar with the case and the issues before the trial commences.

It is anticipated that the directions in any given case can be provided for in a written format so that the parties do not need to attend court prior to the trial date. However, if it becomes apparent during the course of the trial preparation that a pre-trial hearing will be advantageous, possibly so as to provide special directions or to explain the standard directions, the court can request that a Case Management Conference (CMC) is called so that the issues can be discussed in person. CMC's are dealt with in more detail in relation to the multi-track below.

8.5.4.3   The multi-track

The multi-track is the final track in the civil justice system and is the track that deals with all the cases that are not suitable for hearing on the small claims or fast track. The varieties of cases that may be heard on the multi-track are wide and therefore this is a track that needs to be flexible in its approach so that each case can be dealt with appropriately on its facts. Cases can range from a contract dispute where the sum involved amounts to just over the fast track threshold (remember that even if the financial value of a claim just exceeds £15,000, or £50,000 in personal injury cases, then the case will be automatically allocated to the multi-track unless all parties consent to it being heard on the fast track; even if it is apparent that the case is better suited to the fast track), to cases that are highly complex or involve multi-million pound claims.

The venue of a multi-track case will be dependent on where the claim originates. If the claim is issued in the London region then the case will normally be heard at the Royal Courts of Justice, unless the claim is for less than £50,000 where is can then be transferred to the county court. If the claim originates outside of the London district then it will normally be allocated to the nearest Civil Trial Centre (these being large trial centres in major cities across the country), however if the claim is not overly complex or does not involve a substantial sum of money then the claim may simply remain at the nearest district court.

Once a case has been assigned to the multi-track one of two options may occur. The first may be that the court already has sufficient information to be able to issue standard directions without the need for a preliminary court hearing. The court's primary concern will be to ensure that the issues between the parties are identified and that the necessary evidence is prepared and disclosed. If the court believes that it can set standard directions upon its own initiative then it will do so, but the parties to the case are encouraged to agree suitable directions between themselves wherever possible.

If the parties to a case can agree the directions then the court may well approve the suggested directions and give an order in those terms. To be able to achieve directions in this manner without the need for a formal hearing is certainly advantageous for the legal representatives involved in the case. Often the legal representatives will be aware of the majority of the issues in a case at this stage and therefore they should be able to suggest a timetable that can be realistically achieved. If the court is required to impose a timetable then they will not be so involved in the case and may set a shorter time period for preparation before trial than is realistically required. If this does happen and subsequently more time for preparation is required then the parties can return to the court to request that the timetable be varied, but this will increase the court costs and will effectively work against the overriding objective. It is always preferable to attempt to agree the directions and timetable without the need for court intervention. A point to note with multi-track cases, and it is one that separates it from fast track cases, is that there is no set timetable (i.e. the 30 week case progression timetable as for fast track cases) but the case will progress at an individual speed appropriate for the case in question.

When the court does not agree the proposed directions (which it is not obliged to do), or the parties cannot agree as to the directions then the court will call a Case Management Conference (CMC). A CMC will be organised for as soon as is practicable after the identification of its need, this is to ensure that there are no unnecessary delays in the progress of the case. The purpose of the CMC is to identify and deal with the issues that have arisen so far and those that may potentially arise in the near future. If a representative who is inexperienced with the case arrives at a CMC then it is unlikely that they will have sufficient understanding of the case, this may then lead to the CMC having to be adjourned so that the attendance of counsel competent with the case can be secured. If this occurs the offending party may be reprimanded by the court and face a wasted costs order.

The court will set a case timetable at the CMC and make any directions on the above points (or any other relevant point) that the court deems to be necessary for the progression of the case. The trial date will be set, or a three-week trial window will be allocated where ever possible, however due to the complex nature of a number of multi-track claims the provision of a potential trial date may not be immediately possible and this may need to be delayed until a point later in the trial preparation.

Figure 8.3 The court tracks

Track	Value of claim	Court
Small Claims	Claims up to value of £5,000 or personal injury claims up to £1,000	County Court
Fast track	Claims between £5,000 and £15,000 or personal injury claims between £1,000 and £50,000	County Court
Multi-track	Claims over £15,000, personal injury claims over £50,000 or highly complex cases	High Court or County Court

8.6   Pre-action protocols

One of the aims of the reformed civil justice system is to attempt to deal with cases without the need for recourse to a formal court hearing, or if it is determined that a formal court hearing is required then that that the matter is dealt with expeditiously, with all issues that can be resolved pre-trial being resolved at this time. One method of resolving disputes and issues at an early stage in proceedings is by way of 'pre-action protocols'.

Lord Woolf, in his review of the civil justice system, developed the concept of pre-action protocols as an aid to ensuring that the overriding objective was achieved. He stated in his *Final Report* that the introduction of pre-action protocols would help to:

> "Build on and increase the benefits of early but well-informed settlements which genuinely satisfy both parties to a dispute."

To date there have been nine pre-action protocols created, each dealing with a different cause of action:

- Personal Injury
- Clinical Negligence
- Construction and Engineering Disputes
- Defamation
- Professional Negligence
- Judicial Review
- Disease and Illness
- Housing Disrepair
- Possession Claims based on rent arrears

The objectives of the pre-action protocols are to encourage the exchange of early and full information about the prospective legal claim, to enable parties to avoid litigation by agreeing a settlement of the claim before the commencement of proceedings, and to support the efficient management of proceedings where litigation cannot be avoided.

The objectives of these pre-action protocols are set out in the accompanying practice direction and are:

- to achieve more pre-action contact between the parties
- to assist in the better and earlier exchange of information
- to better pre-action investigation by both sides
- to put the parties in a position where they may be able to settle cases fairly and early without litigation
- to enable proceedings to run to the court's timetable and efficiently, if litigation does become necessary
- to promote the provision of medical or rehabilitation treatment (not just in high value cases) to address the needs of the claimant

In essence the idea behind the protocols is to try and help the parties to negotiate and settle their claims without the need of recourse to the more formal claim procedures. By adhering to the protocols it is envisaged that the claimants will set out their case to the defendants and in doing so allow the defendants a proper chance to respond to the allegations before court proceedings are issued.

There are certain causes of action (e.g. breach of contract) that are not covered by the scope of the protocols but in these types of cases it is envisaged that the parties will follow a similar form of pre-action behaviour, such as considering negotiation pre-claim etc, so as to further the overriding objective and achieve a quick and fair resolution.

The protocols set out a sequence of events that should be undertaken prior to a claim. For example a claimant's initial step may be to send an informal letter to the defendant (and his insurer if known), which sets out their intention to initiate proceeds against and the brief facts of what the claim is. The purpose of this informal letter would be to open up the lines of communication between the potential parties and to offer the defendant an opportunity to make admissions and resolve the matter amicably before the more formal process is commenced. If the defendant denies the claim then this informal letter will at least alert him to the issue of pending litigation so that he can instruct a legal representative if necessary, and inform his insurers. The letter should contain a clear summary of the facts on which the claim is based and should include an indication of the nature of any injuries suffered, as well as any financial loss incurred and any documents that the claimant requires the defendant to disclose.

Once the defendant has received a pre-action protocol letter he should then reply within 21 calendar days of the date of posting of the letter. In his reply he should identify or confirm the identity of his insurer (if any) and, if necessary, identify any significant omissions from the letter of claim. If there has been no reply by the defendant or insurer within 21 days, the claimant will be entitled to issue proceedings without continuing with any further pre-action protocol requirements. Once the defendant has acknowledged the claim he will be allowed a maximum period of three months to investigate. After the expiry of this three-month period the defendant is required to reply to the claimant setting out whether they admit to the whole claim, part of the claim, or if they deny any liability. If they deny liability then they will need to supply their reasoning for doing so, as well as a their version of events. It is at this point that the defendant will need to disclose any relevant documents and set out whether they are arguing contributory negligence.

If a party fails to comply with the pre-action protocols a practice direction sets out the sanctions that may be imposed. If it is felt that the non-compliance has led to the commencement of proceedings which might otherwise not have needed to be commenced, or has led to costs being incurred in the proceedings that might otherwise not have been incurred, the court may make an order so as to put the innocent party in a no worse position than they would have been had the protocol been complied with.

8.7 Part 36 offers

The driving principle behind the civil courts is to ensure that cases are dealt with justly and expeditiously; this often means that the art of negotiation and compromise is viewed as the most preferable way in which to conclude a claim. In fact this principle is so strong that if the claim could have been concluded at an earlier point but the parties press on through the process of formal litigation, then they may find themselves being punished by the courts (normally by way of the division of the costs in the case). One of the methods open to the parties to a case to encourage and achieve early settlement can be found under Pt 36 of the CPR and is called an 'offer to settle', which is more commonly known as a 'Part 36 offer'.

Part 36 offers tend to come into play when informal negotiations have broken down and one of the parties to the claim (normally the defendant) wishes to try and conclude the claim on a more formal basis before the litigation reaches the courtroom. A Pt 36 offer will set out the amount that the party making the offer is willing to pay (or accept if the offer is made by the claimant) to settle the claim. Such an offer can be made by way of a simple letter to the other side stating the terms of the offer, so long as the letter complies with the regulations laid down by Pt 36 of the CPR.

Under r.36.2 a letter setting out a Pt 36 offer must:

(a) be in writing;

(b) state on its face that it is intended to have the consequences of Part 36;

(c) specify a period of not less than 21 days within which the defendant will be liable for the claimant's costs in accordance with rule 36.10 if the offer is accepted;

(d) state whether it relates to the whole of the claim or to part of it or to an issue that arises in it and if so to which part or issue; and

(e) state whether it takes into account any counterclaim.

Once a Pt 36 offer has been made then it may not be withdrawn or amended until the expiration of 21 days from the date that the offer is first made. Once the 21 days have expired the offeror can remove the offer from the table and either just proceed to trial or make a further, often less favourable offer, to the claimant.

An important point to note with the making of a Pt 36 offer is that such an offer is not an admission of liability by the defendant making the offer, nor does it necessarily indicate that the defendant believes that they have a weak defence, but rather it is a show of willingness by the defendant to deal with the claim and move on. Often a defendant to a claim would rather pay out a set sum at an early stage in the proceedings to conclude the claim rather than continue to a full hearing of the matter. The reasons for a defendant making such an offer can be numerous but normally it comes down to factors such as the defendant wishing to control the amount of money he ultimately pays to the claimant, or that the defendant wishes to avoid any bad publicity that may arise if the case were to progress to a full trial.

The clever thing about Pt 36 offers are that they are made in secret and if the case progresses to a full hearing then the judge in the case will not know the amount offered by the defendant under Pt 36 until after the case has finished, all issues of liability are decided and the judge has dealt with quantum (this being the amount of damages to be paid by the losing party to the winner). Only upon all of these matters being decided will the amount put forward in the Pt 36 offer be revealed to the judge and it is at this point that the amount set out in the offer may have an impact on one of the parties in the case. The effects of a Pt 36 offer are listed below.

(1) If the claimant is awarded by the court a sum greater than the amount put forward by the defendant in the offer then they have 'beaten' the offer. The consequence of this is that the claimant will have his costs in the case paid by the defendant, which is standard practice in a claim (see Costs below for further details).

(2) If the claimant is awarded by the court a sum equal to or less than the amount set out in the offer then the court will make what is known as a 'split order' to costs. What this means is that the defendant will pay the claimant's costs from date of the cause of action until the expiration of the 21 days after the making of the offer (as detailed in r.36.2 above). From this point on the claimant is then responsible for paying the defendant's costs until the date on which the trial has concluded. The claimant is effectively penalised for not being reasonable and accepting the original offer made by the defendant.

(3) If the defendant is successful at trial then the Part 36 offer is of no consequence as the claimant will be ordered to pay the defendant's full costs in the matter.

So for example: Jessica bought a homemade cake from her local bakery. She alleges that, after taking a few mouthfuls of the cake, she found half a cockroach. Jessica then decides to sue Louise (the owner of the bakery) for the mental anguish she has suffered from eating the cake. Louise has only recently opened the bakery and wants to avoid any bad publicity as she is worried that her business will fail if she has no customers. Louise offers, by way of a Pt 36 offer, to pay Jessica £2,000 in full and final settlement of the claim. Jessica decides to refuse the offer and press on to a full trial. At the trial the judge accepts Jessica's allegations and finds against Louise, but the judge only awards Jessica £1,500 in damages. The result of this is that Louise has to pay Jessica £1,500 in damages and Jessica's costs up until the expiration of the Pt 36 offer (the offer expires 21 days after it is put on the table). After this date Jessica is then liable to pay all of Louise's costs until the date of the conclusion of the trial. This may not sound such a bad deal, especially if the trial takes place in relative succession to the making of the offer, but, if the trial does not proceed for another five months then the costs accrued by Louise in this time may significantly exceed the £1,500 paid to Jessica in damages, which would have the effect of making her case completely pointless and disproportionately expensive.

Part 36 offers are useful tool for the party relying upon them. It could be argued that this style of offer actually forces or bullies the claimant into conceding to the offer made by the defendant due to the fear that if they do not 'beat the offer' at trial they will then be faced with a large bill for the defendant's costs. The main problem that a defendant considering making such an offer will have is what amount of money should their offer total? If the claim relates to a set figure (so X amount of pounds owed for goods supplied to the claimant) then the figure to put forward should be simple to calculate, but where the claim is for an unspecified amount (take for instance the cockroach scenario above) then the level of offer put forward will not be any more than an educated guess by the defendant. The defendant will always want to try and pay out the minimum amount possible and therefore it is likely that their Pt 36 offer will reflect this fact. A defendant in a case of unspecified damages needs to be wary though as their educated guess, even if advised by experienced counsel, will still only be a guess and this guess may have the possibility of backfiring if the claimant refuses to accept the offer and the amount later awarded in court exceeds that in the offer. The defendant also needs to calculate into their figure any interest that the court may award the claimant if they were to be successful at trial. It would be extremely bad luck for a defendant to beat the offer on the basic sum awarded (so they made a Pt 36 offer of £5,000 and the claimant was only awarded £4,500 at court) but then have this small victory stripped away from them when the court adds £750 of interest to the total; bringing the total to £5,250, meaning that the claimant has beaten the claim and the defendant is then liable to pay the claimant's full costs as well as their own costs in the case.

Part 36 offers are not just confined to use by a defendant in a case but can also be used as a tactical manoeuvre by the claimant to a claim. The claimant may put forward an offer that they are willing to accept in settlement of the claim in an effort to make the defendant accept the offer and therefore liability in the matter.

The final point to mention in respect of Pt 36 offers is that they do not just apply to monetary claims and they can be used to great effect in cases where the claimant is claiming another remedy, such as an injunction. If a claimant is claiming for a nuisance, take for example a smell produced from a process undertaken by a working factor, then the defendant may put forward an offer setting out that they will only undertake that process on two days of the week, as opposed to five days. If the claimant refuses the offer, the matter goes to court and the judge holds that the process can occur for three days a week, then the claimant will not have beaten the offer and will be liable for the defendant's costs as set out above.

8.8 Settling a claim

There are a number of ways in which a civil claim can be concluded and the most appropriate resolution will depend upon what has occurred so far in the case. The most obvious method is that the claimant is awarded their desired remedy by the judge at the conclusion of the trial, or that the claimant has not managed to satisfy the burden of proof and the claim is dismissed. However the other methods by which a claim can be concluded are detailed below.

8.8.1 Default judgment

One of the simplest ways in which a claim can be concluded is detailed under Pt 12 of the CPR, and is known as 'default judgment'. Default judgment can be utilised when the defendant to a claim fails to respond in any way to the claim made against them, either by not acknowledging service of the claim or not filing a defence to the claim in the prescribed time.

Rule 12.4 sets out the procedures for obtaining default judgment and the relevant procedure will differ depending on whether the claim is one for a specified amount of money, or if the claim is for any other type of remedy (e.g. an injunction). If the claim involves a specified amount, such as a defined debt, or for unspecified damages, for example as in a personal injury claim, then the procedure is a rather simple one. In such instances the claimant to the claim is required to fill out the prescribed form for requesting a judgment in default in the matter. If the claim is for a specified amount, e.g. A is alleged to owe B £3,000, then, if B fails to acknowledge service of the claim or file a defence in time, A can achieve default judgment in respect of the claim.

Where the claim is for an unspecified amount of damages (so A is suing B for personal injuries but these injuries have not yet been quantified by the courts) then the claimant will again fill in the relevant court form and the court, if satisfied with the request, will pass judgment on liability (so B is liable for the damages incurred by A) but will hold off deciding on the level of damages at this point. Once the judgment for liability is confirmed then the court will direct that a hearing be arranged so that an accurate assessment of the damages to be paid by B to A can be ascertained. This is a sensible method of dealing with such cases as if the defendant fails to respond to the claim they effectively accept liability and responsibility for the damages claimed, but the courts cannot simply pluck a number from the air in respect of what would be an appropriate level of damages. A later hearing in respect of the amount of damages is necessary so that the court can hear evidence on the damages and receive relevant evidence, such as an experts report etc, so that the appropriate figure can be determined.

Where the claim is for a remedy besides damages then the claimant is required to make a formal application for default judgment. This formal application is necessary so that the court has the opportunity to assess to the claim and make an appropriate judgment based on the claimant's claim. This formal hearing is necessary to ensure that claimants, such as vexatious ones, are not afforded the opportunity of sneakily succeeding in achieving remedies that would be deemed as inappropriate if the situation were fully explored. To determine whether the requested remedy is appropriate or not the court will consider the merits of the claim and the effect of the remedy claimed (e.g. does the injunction need to be permanent or would one lasting for six months suffice?).

The delivery of default judgment is a serious step for the courts to take; it basically imposes liability upon a party without the court having had the benefit of hearing directly from that party. It would be a very cruel and unfair justice system if a defendant who was faced with default judgment could not seek to remedy such matters. It may be the case that the defendant was unaware of the proceedings (even if service was correctly effected) or that they did not comprehend the meaning or seriousness of the proceedings until after the default judgment was delivered. In such circumstances the defendant is allowed the opportunity to apply for the default judgment to be set aside or varied. If the court decides that the judgment should be set aside or varied then this does not automatically mean that it is the end of the matter, rather it means that the claim is put back to the position where the defendant is able to enter a defence to the allegations made against them. The judgment is simply removed and the case will progress as if it had never been made in the first place.

8.8.2 Judgment on admission

The most satisfactory conclusion to a claim for the claimant is for the defendant to simply admit the truth of the whole claim and to accept liability for the matters set out in the claim form. This is a scenario that does not occur that frequently within the civil justices system, but it is not completely unheard of, and therefore the CPR makes provisions for such situations under Pt 14.

Part 14 sets out that a defendant to a claim can conclude that claim at any time by making an admission. This means that the defendant can aim to conclude matters quickly by making the admission before the commencement of the proceedings, or at a later point after the formal proceedings have commenced. The defendant is also not obliged always to admit to the whole of the claim against them, as they are provided with the ability to make admissions to certain parts of the claim and deny other elements of the claim that they still contest.

If the defendant makes a partial admission to the claim then it will be hoped, by the defendant, that the claimant will accept this partial admission as full and final settlement of the claim. A defendant may try and use this method of settlement as a way to avoid liability for the full amount allegedly owed, although this may still be viewed as acceptable by the claimant; for instance if the claimant alleges that the defendant owes them £700, but the defendant only admits to owing them £550, then, if the partial admission is accepted by the claimant, the defendant may get away without paying £150 of the alleged debt, whilst the claimant at least recoups a large portion, if not all of their money. The claimant does not have to accept the partial admission by the defendant if they feel that it is unreasonable, and they can still proceed against the defendant for the full amount claimed. If, however, the claimant does accept the partial admission then they are precluded from returning to the claim at a later date to try and achieve the remainder of the money allegedly owed to them (in the illustration above this would be the £150 difference between the amount claimed and the amount admitted).

8.8.3   Summary judgment

Summary judgment under Pt 24 of the CPR is an incredibly important and often used method of concluding a civil claim. Summary judgment can be used by *either* the claimant *or* the defendant and it will be allowed where either the claim is a spurious one and has no real prospect of success (here the defendant would be relying upon summary judgment), or the defence offers very little in the way of substance in that there is no real prospect of successfully defending the claim (here the claimant would be making an application for summary judgment). The parties to a case can make the application by their own volition, or the court can decide to make such a judgment by way of its own initiative after their consideration of the claim and/or defence.

The court, when determining whether summary judgment is appropriate, must also take into consideration whether there is any other compelling reason that the case should not be disposed of in such a manner. The courts' approach can be illustrated by the case of *Swain v Hillman* [2001] 2 All E.R. 91 where Lord Woolf M.R. stated:

> "The court now has a very salutary power, both to be exercised in a claimant's favour or, where appropriate, in a defendant's favour. It enables the court to dispose summarily of both claims or defences which have no real prospect of being successful. The words 'no real prospect of being successful or succeeding' do not need any ampflication, they speak

for themselves. The word 'real' distinguishes fanciful prospects of success or, [. . .] they direct the court to the need to see whether there is a 'realistic' as opposed to a 'fanciful' prospect of success."

It can be taken from the court's view of such proceedings that a summary judgment should only be used where appropriate. This is be taken as where the issues do not need to be fully investigated at trial, if there is the likelihood that the summary judgment hearing is likely to turn into a mini-trial of the issues then a summary judgment hearing will not be appropriate in the circumstances. However, the test is not so restrictive that there needs to be a substantial prospect of success, just simply a realistic one.

The idea of summary judgment is for the court to be able to deal effectively and expeditiously with unmeritorious and weak claims, and unsubstantiated and ill-fated defences. This method of case disposal goes towards furthering the overriding objective and helps to ensure that the court system is not overrun by worthless cases.

8.9 Enforcement of judgments

Civil cases differ dramatically to criminal cases in a number of ways. One of these differences occurs with respect to the enforcement of a decision. Under the criminal system, if a defendant fails to comply with the sanction imposed by the court (e.g. imprisonment or the service of a community order) then the defendant will often be found to have committed a further offence by way of their non-compliance. Ensuring that a party to a civil action complies with the decision of the court (or the agreement between the parties if formal proceedings were not commenced or concluded) is not quite as easy to achieve due to the fact that the matters are between two private individuals and there are not such persuasive sanctions available as in the criminal arena. Another problem with ensuring the enforcement of civil judgments is that the CPR does not directly govern the issue of enforcement, but the rules under the Rules of the Supreme Court (RSC) and the County Court Rules (CCR) are preserved under Sch.1 and 2 of the CPR, respectively.

The first point to note in relation to civil judgments is that the courts (be that the High court or the County court) do not automatically enforce the decisions of the court. Refusal to comply with a court order is contempt of court, but the party who wishes to enforce the order has to apply to the court for action to be taken against the party who is in contempt. The way in which an order can be enforced will mainly depend on what the focus of the order is (i.e. an order for payment of monies or an injunction etc), and the court which made the order will also have a bearing on the action that can be taken by the party wishing to enforce the order.

8.9.1 Writ/warrants of execution

It is not unusual for a judgment debtor (the party who has lost the case and owes the winning party money) to refuse to pay what they owe. To enable the creditor to be able to reclaim the money from the debtor a procedure, known as 'execution', has been developed by the civil law. Execution means that the goods of the debtor will be seized and then sold at auction to pay the monies owed to the winning party, as well as any legal costs and costs of enforcement etc incurred by the process. This method of enforcement is quite commonly known to the layperson as it involves the employment of bailiffs, who most people have at least heard of, even if they have not dealt with them personally.

If the High Court has issued the order then to execute the order the person who wishes to enforce it will have to obtain a High Court 'writ of execution' as prescribed under the RSC, Ord.45 and 46 as set out in the CPR, Sch.1. If the county court made the original judgment then the enforcement will be conducted under a 'warrant of execution' under the CCR, Ord.26 as set out in the CPR, Sch.2. Once the writ or warrant has been issued the enforcement (or execution) of it will be carried out by a relevant individual; this individual is not an employee of the court but rather a private person or company who hold themselves out as suitable for such work—and are otherwise known as enforcement officers or 'bailiffs'. The bailiffs are allowed, upon the receipt of such a writ to attend the debtor's premises and seize any goods owned by the debtor that can be sold at auction to satisfy the debt. The bailiffs cannot simply break into the debtor's property and they must gain lawful entrance to the property so as to be able to exercise their rights to seize the debtors' goods.

The civil law puts restrictions on the type of property that can be seized to satisfy a debt. As the dispute involves matters between private individuals, the law has to take into account the balancing of the different parties' interests in the case, as it would be unjust to make one person suffer exceptionally just so that the other party can prove a point. All decisions must be proportionate and reasonable to all the parties involved. Goods that cannot be seized include such tools, books, vehicles and other items of equipment as are necessary to the debtor for use personally by him in his employment, business or vocation, and such clothing, bedding, furniture, household equipment and provisions as are necessary for satisfying the basic domestic needs of the debtor and his family. The goods must also belong to the debtor and not be on hire purchase, or belong to another member of the debtor's family etc.

8.9.2 Third party debt orders

Another option available to a person owed money under a judgment is known as a 'third party debt order'. This method of enforcing judgment can be used where the debtor is owed monies from a third party and the person who is owed the money (and who is making the application) can intervene between the debtor and the third person, freeze the relevant assets and seize this owed money to satisfy their own debt owed to them by the debtor. Situations where such a method can be employed can be such as where the debtor is in business and is owed money by customers, or if the debtor simply has a bank balance in credit (as this is viewed as the bank owing a debt to the debtor). By using a third party debt order the person owed the money bypasses the debtor so as to realise the judgment by access to these assets.

8.9.3 Charging orders

Charging orders are a rather heavy-handed method of enforcing judgment that can result in serious consequences for the judgment debtor. A charging order itself is not actually a method of securing payment of the judgment but it allows the judgment creditor to secure the payment of the debt by placing a charge on the property of the judgment debtor. Thereby if the judgment debtor owns any land (normally this will be their residential house) then the creditor can have an interest in this property registered, which can be later realised so as to satisfy the debt owed. A charge of this nature can be placed upon the judgment debtor's property even if they own the property jointly with a person who is not involved in the proceedings.

A charge over a property is quite an easy order to achieve, especially since the recent changes in the way that the Land Registry stores its property details. As all the Land Registry details are now stored electronically it means that a judgment creditor can have virtually instant access to the Charges Register and Title Plan of any property for a nominal fee of £6. This means that it is very simple for an interested party to discover whether a judgment debtor has any beneficial interest in a property, and if they do, then they can provide substantive evidence of this to the court by the simple click of the mouse on a computer.

A party who obtains a charging order over the property is granted a pretty large axe to wield in respect of achieving payment of the debt. The court may, upon a claim by a person who has obtained a charging order over an interest in property, order the sale of the property to enforce the charging order. The property of the debtor can literally be sold out from under their feet so as to pay off the debt.

The court does have the discretion to refuse to make an order for an enforced sale and, in considering whether to make one or not, they will take into account the position of both the creditor and the debtor as they will try to avoid any disproportionate hardship being caused to either party. If an order of sale is granted then it is likely that the court will also order the judgment debtor and any other person living at the property to vacate the premises prior to the house being marketed for sale so that the sale can be achieved quickly and with the minimum of fuss.

8.9.4   Attachment of earnings

An attachment to the earnings of the judgment debtor can be a highly effective method of recouping monies owed to the creditor but such an order will only be made in very specific instances. Where the judgment debtor owes the creditor money and the debtor is in long-term gainful employment with no other substantial assets or any dependants then an attachment of earning order may be the most appropriate method to achieve enforcement.

The term 'earnings' does not just mean the judgment debtor's weekly or monthly take home pay but it can be expanded to encompass many forms of income including wages, salary, fees, bonus, commission, overtime pay, pensions (although not a State pension) and statutory sick pay. Forms of income that cannot be subject to an attachment of earnings order include sums paid by an authority outside the UK (including those from Northern Ireland, State benefits or allowances or self-employed income).

An attachment of earning order is obtained by a relatively straightforward procedure. The applicant makes an application to the court by way of the prescribed form, the judgment debtor is notified of the hearing date at least 21 days prior to the scheduled hearing and on notification of the hearing they are provided with a means questionnaire that they are required to complete.

249

Once the judgment debtor has completed and returned the means questionnaire to the court then an administrative office of the court will assess the information provided and make an order if they believe there to be sufficient information and that the order is appropriate. The only time that an attachment of earnings order will be reviewed by a judge is when a party to the proceedings disputes the application or the decision by the court officer. Upon the granting of such an order the court will notify the judgment debtor's employer, who will then deduct the required sum from the judgment debtor's earnings and pay this to the court so that it can be passed on to the judgment creditor.

8.9.5 Non-money judgments

In cases where the judgment relates to a non-money solution (i.e. an injunction) then the sanction for non-compliance is that the offending party is held to be in contempt of court so when a person refuses or neglects to do something set out in an order (a mandatory injunction) or restrains from doing whatever is set out in an order against them (a prohibitory injunction) then an application can be made for a committal order against that person. The order must contain the penal notice, which sets out that by refusing to obey the order they are placing themselves in contempt of court, and, if the individual continues to go against the order, then a hearing will be held to determine whether the individual needs to be remanded into custody as a sanction for their non-compliance.

An individual can be committed for up to two years for contempt of court under the Contempt of Court Act 1981. As the committal proceedings have originated from a civil action the courts are generally reluctant to imposed custody upon an individual and will only really turn to it as a last resort when the individual in question has flagrantly broken the order and there is no other alternative but to commit the offender into custody for a suitable amount of time.

8.10 Alternative dispute resolution

Bringing litigation to court may not always be the most appropriate or desirable course of action and as such there have developed alternative ways in which to resolve disputes. This method of alternative dispute resolution (ADR) has become quite formalised over recent years and there are now four recognised methods of ADR, these are:

- Negotiation

- Mediation

- Conciliation

- Arbitration

There are a number of different factors as to why parties to a dispute may wish to resolve the matter without recourse to the formal litigation process. These reasons may involve issues such as the cost of litigation, as once court costs and lawyers' fees are factored into the equation what seemed like a small and inexpensive claim to defend may become very expensive to the point of the costs being disproportionate to the amount of the claim. The uncertainty of the outcome may have a bearing on the decision to turn to ADR, as once the claim has entered the formal court process the parties to the dispute have no real power or influence over the decision of the court, by using ADR parties are able to steer matters to a degree so that they receive a more favourable outcome. The potential delay that may be incurred before the dispute is resolved may also be another factor that might be taken into account by those considering litigation as, even post the Woolf reforms, it may still take many months for a case to come to court, whereas ADR may help to have the situation resolved quickly. Litigation through the court process is a stressful procedure that can take its toll on those involved, the trauma of waiting for a case to reach court and the potential for massive legal bills can have an adverse effect on all the parties and their families, often the use of ADR instead will help alleviate some of this stress. Further, cases that go through the formal court process are often likely to attract some level of publicity. Depending on the parties in the case such publicity may be undesirable as if a party is, for example, a businessman then the bad publicity may have a negative effect on their livelihood. Using ADR as a method to resolve the dispute will help to avoid any media attention and will ensure that the reputations of those involved are preserved. Finally the fact that the atmosphere of a court is often intimidatory in nature may be off putting to a large number of potential litigants and the fact that ADR is a more informal and relaxed process may make it a more attractive one to undertake.

8.10.1　Negotiation

Negotiation between parties often occurs naturally at the beginning of any form of dispute and it is the quickest and easiest method to try and resolve the issues in an informal manner. Parties will try and attain an outcome that is mutually acceptable to all and it is often the case that parties will try and achieve a settlement by way of negotiation before moving on to more formal and structured forms of ADR. Negotiation can take place privately between the individuals of the claim, and it will involve them discussing the issues and putting forward a solution that they feel may be acceptable to all. It may be that one party will put forward an amount that they are prepared to settle the matter for and then the responding party will decide whether they are happy with the figure proposed, and if not then they will put forward a counter-offer of what they are prepared to pay so as to resolve the case. Negotiation can involve a lot of to-ing and fro-ing between the parties until a happy medium is realised.

If the parties to a claim cannot negotiate successfully between themselves then they may decide to appoint a trained negotiator to act in the matter. Solicitors often act as negotiators between the parties and they will endeavour to find a solution before the matter reaches the court doors. It is by way of the solicitors negotiating between themselves and the parties that out-of-court settlements are often achieved.

8.10.2   Mediation

With mediation an appointed person will act as a conduit through which the two disputing parties can communicate and negotiate in an attempt to resolve the problem. The individual who acts as a mediator is normally trained and experienced in such matters (although qualification is not a pre-requisite of acting as a mediator); they may be a lawyer who has undergone specialist training, or they may be an individual whose main work is mediation. The main aim of a mediator is to be an impartial facilitator in the resolution of the dispute.

Unlike negotiation where each party have their own representative, mediation will only involve the use of one mediator. The mediator's role is to discuss the issues with both parties so as to work out where the common ground lies and then to try and facilitate a satisfactory outcome between them all. Often a mediator will undertake an evaluative role in the proceedings by offering their opinion on the merits or disadvantages of a proposed solution, but they will not suggest what they believe to be the best way in which to conclude the matter, as that is for the parties only to decide. Her Majesty's Courts Service (http://www.hmcourts-service. gov.uk) sets out that mediation is based on the principles of:

- Collaborative problem solving between those in dispute, reaching a 'win/win' situation which is acceptable to all.

- A focus on the future, with emphasis on rebuilding relationships rather than apportioning blame for what has happened in the past.

- A belief that acknowledging feelings as well as facts allows participants to let go of their anger and upset and move forward.

Mediation will normally take place over the course of a single morning or afternoon, or possibly even a full day where the issues are particularly complex. The parties will attend a neutral venue (often the court) where each party will be provided with a private room. To begin with all the parties will take place in a joint meeting where the ground rules are agreed and the main issues are identified. After this each party will retire to their own room and the mediator will go between the parties, gathering information and building up a picture of the disagreement so that a solution can be explored. The mediator will build up and maintain the trust of the parties and will not disclose any information that was disclosed in confidence to them. It is hoped that by way of the mediation the parties are able to come to an amicable conclusion to the problem that will allow the matter to be resolved and for the parties to move on. If a consensus can be achieved then this will be drawn up into a binding agreement between the parties and ratified by the court. If the parties are unable to agree upon a course of action then the court will become involved and set future dates for a court hearing for the matter.

Mediation is often attempted where the dispute revolves around matters of the family, as the court system is not viewed as the best forum in which to attempt to resolve issues arising from divorce and the care of children. If the parties can come to a mutual, autonomous agreement over such matters then there is a higher chance that the decisions will be respected and stuck to, thereby causing less stress and trauma in the future.

8.10.3 Conciliation

Conciliation is very similar in nature to mediation in that there is a neutral third party involved in the discussion of a resolution, but whereas with mediation the mediator is mainly facilitative, with conciliation the third party is more interventionist and involved in the decision making process. With conciliation the third party will make suggestions as to the most suitable method for resolution (so more evaluative than facilitative) and try and move the parties forward towards settlement. A party to conciliation is not obliged to accept the proposals suggested by the third party and they can request that the case goes forward to a formal hearing if they do not find the proposals to be acceptable. Even where a dispute does go forward to a formal hearing following conciliation it does not mean that the conciliation was pointless as it will have helped to identify and narrow the issues in the case so that the matter can then be dealt with by the courts quickly and efficiently.

8.10.4 Arbitration

Arbitration could be described as a 'half-way' house between informal and formal dispute resolution. By agreeing to use arbitration as a method of resolution the parties agree to the matter being adjudicated upon by a third party (who is not a judge). The process of arbitration is governed by statute, namely the Arbitration Act 1996, and s.1 of the Act sets out that:

(a) the object of arbitration is to obtain the fair resolution of disputes by an impartial tribunal without unnecessary delay or expense;

(b) the parties should be free to agree how their disputes are resolved, subject only to such safeguards as are necessary in the public interest;

The agreement to undergo arbitration as opposed to more formal court procedures is one that is taken voluntarily by the parties involved in a dispute. The agreement to use arbitration is normally made well in advance of any dispute arising and is often written into the initial contract as a precautionary measure, but it can be selected as the most appropriate method of resolution upon a dispute occurring. Many trade associations, such as the Association of British Travel Agents (ABTA), automatically turn to arbitration as the primary method of resolution (for example dealing with customer complaints) and the decision to use arbitration will be set out in the paperwork that a customer signs when arranging their holiday etc.

Where the agreement to undertake arbitration is made in writing then the Arbitration Act 1996 will be applicable (however this Act does not apply to verbal agreements although the spirit of it should be followed where ever possible). The 1996 sets out (under s.33) the duty of the arbitrator, this being to act fairly and impartially between the parties, and to give each party a reasonable opportunity of putting his case and dealing with that of his opponent, but how this should be achieved is left to the discretion of the individual arbitrator.

Any person can be an arbitrator and there is no requirement that an arbitrator has to be specially trained in arbitration, although they will generally be an expert in the area under dispute. Quite often an arbitrator will be a legally qualified person who acts as an arbitrator alongside their professional capacity as a lawyer or they will be a person who is a member of the Chartered Institute of Arbitrators. The number of arbitrators appointed to resolve a dispute, and who the arbitrators are will be dependent upon the individual parties to a case. The contract may have set out that in the case of a dispute the parties will abide by the decision of a single arbitrator who is appointed by the Charted Institute of Arbitrators, or the contract may have not set out any more specifics than the fact that arbitration will be used. If it is the latter situation then the parties can decide between themselves as to who will be the arbitrator, or if they cannot do so then the court will appoint an arbitrator on their behalf.

So as to ensure that the general principles as detailed under s.1, above, are satisfied the arbitrator will schedule an oral hearing. Each party will be notified well in advance of the date so that they are given reasonable opportunity to prepare for, attend and present their case at the hearing. The objectives of avoiding deal and expense are kept firmly in mind when arbitration is undertaken and as such disproportionate, lengthy hearings are not accepted and if appropriate an arbitrator may attempt to resolve the dispute by only considering a paper-based case.

Upon an arbitrator making a finding in a case they are normally required to give an explanation of their reasons for their decision (unless the parties have specifically excluded this requirement in their agreement), and once made their decision becomes legally binding and therefore enforceable in the courts. The parties to the case may agree on the costs between themselves, however if they are not able to agree as to this then the issue of costs will rest on the arbitrator's discretion. If a party to the case disagrees with the final outcome of the arbitration then they are afforded the possibility of appealing to the High Court, but only where there is either a serious irregularity affecting the proceedings or the award, or that they are appealing on a point of law. To bring an appeal then either all parties must consent to the appeal or the court must grant leave to appeal (s.69 of the Arbitration Act 1996). The court will generally only grant leave following arbitration where the question of law could substantially affect the rights of the parties involved in the case or the decision of the arbitrator is obviously wrong, or the issue is one of general public importance and the decision is open to serious doubt.

Figure 8.4 Alternative dispute resolution

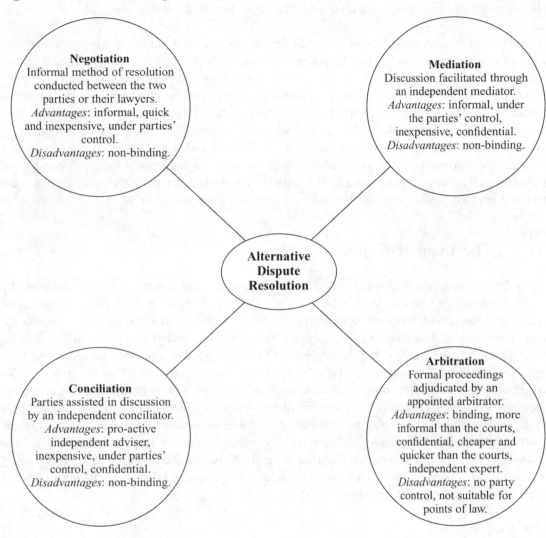

8.11 Tribunals

Operating alongside the courts are found a number of tribunals, each specialising in their own different area. Many of these are well known by the public, for example the Employment Tribunal and the Asylum and Immigration Tribunal, as they feature regularly in the media. Headlines such as 'Employment Tribunal award an employee dismissed due to her pregnancy £2.3 million in compensation', or 'Asylum and Immigration Tribunal refuse to allow a mother of five children to stay in the UK', can be found on the daily newspapers, and the British public has a basic understanding about the work of such tribunals. However, what is not overly known is the fact that there are over 70 different tribunals, each focusing on a different area and dealing with a variety of specialised matters, and that they deal with nearly one million cases per year.

The tribunal system arose out of the need for members of the public to have recourse to a panel of impartial persons who had the power to review administrative decisions taken by either governmental departments or by private bodies, where they did not have the grounds for the commencement of traditional legal action. Tribunals are essentially administrative in nature and they are an important element of the justice system as they help to ensure that any perceived unjustness is fairly assessed and remedied where appropriate. There are also a number of domestic tribunals (such as the General Medical Council and the Football Association) that regulate professional conduct in a number of different professions. Overall tribunals are invaluable as they help to alleviate a high volume of potential cases from the more formal court arena and provide justice and fairness where otherwise there might be none.

8.11.1   The Leggatt Report

In May 2000, a review of effectiveness and work of the tribunal service was commissioned by the government. The review was headed by Sir Andrew Leggatt, a former Lord Justice of Appeal, and the review reported its findings in March of 2001 under the title of *Tribunals for Users: One System, One Service*. The Leggatt Report recommended that the Lord Chancellor should assume responsibility for the fragmented tribunal service and that there should be a single, over-arching structure that would give an individual access to all of the tribunals. To provide effective and independent administration of the individual tribunals the report further recommended that a Tribunals Service should be set up so that the individual tribunals were easy to access and navigate and so that the service and approach offered was of the highest quality whilst being responsive to the user. To achieve this the Report proposed that the Tribunal Service should be grouped into nine separate divisions, the first eight divisions dealing with the disputes between the citizen and the state, and the ninth to deal with disputes between parties. The suggested nine divisions were:

- Immigration
- Social Security and Pensions
- Land and Valuation
- Financial
- Transport
- Health and Social Services
- Education
- Regulatory Matters
- Employment (disputes between parties)

The government then produced the White Paper *Transforming Public Services: Complaints, Redress and Tribunals* in July of 2004, which set out their proposals for implementing the recommendations from the Leggatt Report. The result of the White Paper and the catalytic Leggatt Report was that in April 2006 the Tribunals Service came into force. The Tribunals Service is a government executive agency of the Ministry of Justice with the purpose of providing administrative support to the main central government tribunals. At present they have responsibility for 27 central government tribunals, such as the Asylum and Immigration Tribunal, the Charity Tribunal, the Employment Tribunal, the Gender Recognition Panel, the Mental Health Review Tribunal and the Pensions Appeal Tribunal, to name but a few, and it is envisaged that as the Service becomes more established that they will assume responsibility for more of the 40 or so other outstanding tribunals.

To ensure that all of the tribunals are run effectively and fairly the tribunal system is overseen by the Administrative Justice and Tribunals Council (formerly the Council on Tribunals), who is an independent non-departmental public body, which is charged with the supervision and review of the constitution and workings of tribunals.

8.11.2 Tribunal hearings

Tribunals are normally either headed by a single judge, or by a panel of three (of whom the chair will be legally qualified and the other two will be experts in the respective field). For example, in the Asylum and Immigration Tribunal it is usual to find a solo judge sitting to hear the hearings, whilst hearings at the Mental Health Review Tribunal will be conducted by a panel of three consisting of a judge and either two mental health experts, or one mental health expert and one lay person. Each tribunal has its own set composition appropriate to the matter is deals with and there is no uniformity within the tribunal service as a whole.

Hearings held within the tribunal service are normally an informal and rather relaxed affair with there being no formal rules on the production of evidence or the course of the case. The primary focus of a tribunal is to ensure that justice is done and therefore it will allow both parties to present their case in the most appropriate manner for this to be achieved. The only real exception to this rule is that the Employment Tribunal is more formal than most tribunals in nature and the proceedings within this tribunal closely resemble those found within the traditional court system.

In the majority of cases the parties themselves will present their own cases and it is unusual to find legal representation present at a tribunal. The main reason behind this is that it is difficult to secure legal aid for a tribunal hearing, with the only exception to this rule really being found where there is an issue concerning the applicant's liberty or human rights (i.e. within the Asylum and Immigration Tribunal, the Employment Tribunal and the Mental Health Review Tribunal etc.).

8.11.3 Appeal from the tribunal service

There is a right of appeal from most tribunals but it will depend on which individual tribunal a person is appealing from as to the route that will be taken. There are certain tribunals, such as the Employment Tribunal, that has its own appeal route by way of the Employment Appeals Tribunal, or the Asylum and Immigration Tribunal from which an appeal can be lodged with the Immigration Appeals Tribunal. Beyond this in-house appeal system lies the traditional route of appeal to the Court of Appeal, but this must be with leave to appeal and the grounds of appeal must be based on a point of law (as opposed to simply being against the decision taken by the tribunal). The decision of a tribunal is also open to judicial review in the High Court where it is believed that the court has acted ultra vires.

Figure 8.5 Advantages and disadvantages of tribunals

Advantages	Disadvantages
Specialist knowledge of the bench or panel	Mistakes made due to the speed of the hearings
Informal nature of the hearings	Impartial (due to being overseen by the Ministry of Justice and wider government)
Inexpensive (compared to traditional legal proceedings)	Lack of case precedent (cases decided on their individual facts)
Cases are dealt with quickly and efficiently	Often full reasoning for a decision is not provided
The majority of hearings are private (besides the Employment Tribunal) and therefore receive little publicity	Lack of legal aid and/or award of costs in the majority of cases

8.12 Summary

(a) The parties to a civil claim are normally known as the claimant (the person bringing the claim) and the defendant (the person defending the claim). The names can change depending on the focus of the proceedings as in an appeal the party appealing would be named the 'appellant', of if they were making an application then they would be called the 'applicant'.

(b) The burden and standard of proof in a civil claim is that the case must be proven by the party bringing the claim on the balance of probabilities. This means that they must show that it is more likely than not that the facts are as they assert them to be.

(c) An extensive review of the civil justice system, *Access to Justice,* was completed by Lord Woolf in 1995. The conclusion and recommendations of the Woolf Report lead to an overhaul of the civil justice system by the introduction of the Civil Procedure Rules (CPR). The main objective of the CPR is found in the overriding objective and this is to ensure that all cases are dealt with justly. The CPR also introduced extended case management powers for the judiciary so that they can achieve the overriding objective.

(d) The Woolf Reforms introduced a 'track system' into the civil courts. Claims under £5,000 are now dealt with by way of the 'small claims' track. The 'fast track' deals with claims between the value of £5,000 and £15,000 (or over £50,000 in a personal injury case) and the 'multi-track deals with claims over £15,000 (or £50,000 for personal injury) and the more complex claims.

(e) To further aid the overriding objective, the Woolf Report introduced the concept of pre-action protocols, which aim to identify the main issues in a case prior to the commencement of formal action and to potentially aid early settlement wherever possible. There are a number of template protocols for different causes of action (i.e. personal injury and judicial review) but where the cause of action does not fall under one of the set protocols then the parties are still expected to follow the spirit of the pre-action protocols.

(f) Part 36 offers are a method of trying to achieve an early settlement in the case. A party may put forward the basis of what they are prepared to settle the claim for (or what they are prepared to accept in settlement) and if this offer is then not matched or beaten in the courts then the party will be penalised by the allocation of costs for not accepting the original offer. Part 36 offers can be used tactically to force a settlement.

(g) There are a number of ways to settle a claim besides the judge in the case deciding the outcome. Settlement can occur by way of default judgment (where the defendant fails to respond to or defend the claim), summary judgment (where there is no realistic prospect of success or a valid claim, and judgment on admission can occur where the defendant accepts liability for at least part of the claim in full and final settlement of the whole claim.

(h) Judgments can be enforced in a number of ways by the court. A writ or warrant of execution can be issued where outside agents (bailiffs) will be requested to attend the debtor's premises and recover property to the value of the outstanding judgment. A third party debt order can be imposed so that the judgment value is recouped directly from a third party who owes the debtor money. A charge can be placed over a debtor's house in lieu of the debt and then sale of the property can be forced to realise the debt, or an attachment of earnings order can be made whereby the value of the judgment is directly claimed from the debtor's earnings.

(i) There are a number of other ways to resolve a dispute that do not include resorting to the traditional court system—these are known as alternative dispute resolution or ADR. ADR can occur by way of negotiation (between the two parties), mediation (with the help of a facilitator), conciliation (where by a third party actively encourages settlement) and arbitration (where the parties agree to a third party adjudicating on the issues). Each method has its own advantages (cost, speed and privacy etc.) but they also carry with them a number of disadvantages as well (non-binding, potential for no settlement etc.).

(j) Tribunals work alongside and compliment the main court system. There are over 70 different tribunals and they deal with almost one million cases per year. Tribunals are mainly administrative in nature and they provide a forum for a party to challenge a decision taken that they would not be able to pursue in the courts.

8.13 Self-test questions

1. The party name of a person appealing against a judicial decision is the:

   (a) claimant
   (b) plaintiff
   (c) appellant
   (d) applicant

2. The overriding objective of the Civil Procedure Rules is that cases should be dealt with:

   (a) justly
   (b) efficiently
   (c) inexpensively
   (d) proportionately

3. A case involving a claim for the sum of £13,500 will be heard on/in the:

   (a) small claims track
   (b) fast track
   (c) multi-track
   (d) magistrates' court

4. The passing down of summary judgment means:

   (a) that the case had no realistic prospect of success
   (b) that the defendant admitted the claim
   (c) that the claimant withdrew their case
   (d) that the claim was settled out of court

5. Conciliation means that:

   (a) the parties decide the matters between themselves
   (b) the parties are aided in their decision making by a third party
   (c) the matter is decided for the parties by a third party
   (d) a judge determines the outcome prior to trial

8.14 Further reading

N. Andrews, "A new civil procedural code for England: party-control 'going, going, gone' " [2000] C.J.Q. 19(Jan), 19–38.
J. Baldwin and R. Cunnington, "The crisis in enforcement of civil judgments in England and Wales" [2004] P.L. Sum. 305–328.

V.R. Handley, "Changing the burden of proof" [2007] J.P.I. Law 1, 35–48.

T. John, "Plus ça change?" [2006] 156(7241) N.L.J. 1413.

R. Jordan, "The Woolf is all claws and no bite" [2007] 151(32) S.J. 1078.

M. Partington, "Alternative dispute resolution: recent developments, future challenges" [2004] 23 C.J.Q. (Apr), 99–106.

S. Prince, "Mediating small claims: are we on the right track?" [2007] C.J.Q. 26 (Jul), 328–340.

G. Richardson and H. Genn, "Tribunals in transition: resolution or adjudication?" [2007] P.L. Spr, 116–141.

A.A.S. Zuckerman, "CPR 36 offers" [2005] 24 C.J.Q. (Apr) 167–184.

9   The Criminal Justice System 1

9.1   Introduction

The chapter title of 'The Criminal Justice System' is a broad title that does not really allude to its specific focus. The reason for this is that the criminal justice system itself is a wide and varied structure that has many different facets to it. There is no better title to encompass the various areas that are found within this area of law as the criminal justice system requires detailed consideration of a myriad of issues, such as how the decision to prosecute is made and how criminal offences are classified, through to what, if any, bargains the defendant can make in respect of their sentence. This chapter will now consider the more salient pre-trial topics within this system and the remaining issues (at trial) will be dealt with in the following chapter.

Figure 9.1 The progression of a criminal case

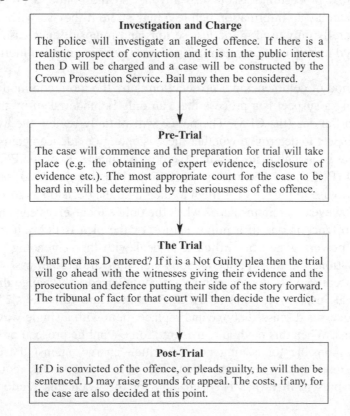

Investigation and Charge
The police will investigate an alleged offence. If there is a realistic prospect of conviction and it is in the public interest then D will be charged and a case will be constructed by the Crown Prosecution Service. Bail may then be considered.

Pre-Trial
The case will commence and the preparation for trial will take place (e.g. the obtaining of expert evidence, disclosure of evidence etc.). The most appropriate court for the case to be heard in will be determined by the seriousness of the offence.

The Trial
What plea has D entered? If it is a Not Guilty plea then the trial will go ahead with the witnesses giving their evidence and the prosecution and defence putting their side of the story forward. The tribunal of fact for that court will then decide the verdict.

Post-Trial
If D is convicted of the offence, or pleads guilty, he will then be sentenced. D may raise grounds for appeal. The costs, if any, for the case are also decided at this point.

9.2   Commencing a prosecution

The criminal justice system really comes into play upon a suspect being charged by the police for the alleged commission of an offence. How and why the police decided to charge that particular suspect is outside the remit of this text, so the analysis of the process will begin by consideration of the commencement of a prosecution.

Currently there are two ways in which a prosecution against a suspect can be commenced. The first is called 'laying an information' and this involves a prosecutor (usually a police officer with the authority of a senior officer) laying (or placing) information before a magistrate, which contains details of the alleged offence and the suspect's involvement in it. If the magistrate is satisfied that the information provided sufficiently incriminates the suspect then they will issue a warrant or 'summons' in respect of them. A summons basically requires the suspect to attend the court so as to answer the offence alleged against them. If a person is prosecuted by way of a summons then they will generally be aware of the impending possibility of being prosecuted, as the police will most likely have already spoken to them about the alleged offence. Many road traffic offences are prosecuted by way of a summons and it is more than likely that most people will know someone who has, at some point or other, been prosecuted in this manner (although they may be unwilling to admit it). This method of commencing criminal proceedings is open to anyone, so the police, a prosecutor or even a private individual can lay an information before a magistrate if they so wish. The laying of an information is generally only used in the less serious and minor offence cases, but technically it could be employed to begin the proceedings in a case involving a much more serious offence, such as murder.

The second method of commencing a prosecution is by the more commonly known way of 'charging'. Charging a suspect is a process that can only be undertaken by the police and the Crown Prosecution Service (the CPS). The police will initially review the evidence that they have against the suspect to determine whether there is enough evidence against them to initiate proceedings. If there is enough evidence then the police, under s.37 of the Police and Criminal Evidence Act 1984 (PACE) (as amended by the Criminal Justice Act 2003), are now generally required to refer the case to the CPS for them to then take the decision as to whether to charge or not. There are however, certain instances when the police themselves can charge the suspect, such as when the offence is one of a minor nature, or the plea is likely to be guilty and the magistrates' court powers would be sufficient to deal with the sentencing, although as CPS officers are now stationed in most police stations then they are able to assist in this decision.

The law and procedure on how proceedings are commenced will change dramatically when s.29 of the Criminal Justice Act 2003 (CJA 2003) comes into force as s.29 will effectively remove the two processes discussed above and replace them with a single way of commencing criminal proceedings. When this method comes into force a public prosecutor (as defined under s.29(5)) will be responsible for issuing both a written charge against the defendant, and a requisition, which requires the person to attend the named magistrates' court to answer the written charge. At present there has been no date set for when this section will come into force.

9.2.1   The Crown Prosecution Service

As can be summarised from above the CPS are the primary agency responsible for deciding to charge an individual with a criminal offence. The CPS was created by way of the Prosecution of Offences Act 1985 (POA 1985) and, under s.3(2)(a) of the POA 1985, they are charged with the responsibility of taking over the conduct and control of nearly all cases instituted by the police. The CPS was established following concerns that the police (who at that time conducted all prosecutions 'in house') were not independent of the process. Therefore it appeared that many cases were going to court with little or no hope of a conviction; not a satisfactory state of affairs.

The decision to prosecute an individual for a criminal offence is a serious step to take, as even the least serious offence can still have implications for all involved. To enable the CPS to make informed judgments as to when it is appropriate or not to initiate proceedings s.10 of the POA 1985 required that the Director or Public Prosecutions (who is the head of the CPS) to provide the CPS with a Code which contained guidance on the general principles they should apply when making such decisions; this is known as The Code for Crown Prosecutors. If the police are to charge the suspect then they will also refer to this Code to determine whether prosecution is appropriate or not.

9.2.1.1   The Code

The test that prosecutors will apply when determining whether or not to prosecute an individual is known as 'The Full Code Test' and is found at para.5 of the Code. The Full Code test is split into two distinct stages. The first part is known as the 'evidential' stage and the second part is the 'public interest' test.

The evidential stage

To satisfy this first stage the CPS must be sure that there is a 'realistic prospect of conviction'. This test is an objective one and it concerns looking at the available evidence and deciding whether the trier of fact (the jury, judge or magistrates) would be *more likely than not* to convict the defendant of the alleged offence. This however, is not the same test employed by the criminal courts (the test of beyond reasonable doubt) when deciding whether or not the defendant *is guilty* of the offence.

For a prosecutor to determine whether there is a realistic prospect of conviction, they must ask themselves two questions; these being:

- Can the evidence be used in court?
- Is the evidence reliable?

The first question relates to the admissibility of the evidence against the defendant. If the evidence is not allowed to be used in court, maybe due to the way in which it was obtained (for example the arrest of the suspect was unlawful, or the confession relied upon was beaten out of the suspect), then there may be no admissible evidence against the defendant and therefore any prosecution will be futile. If the evidence is useable and admissible in court then the second consideration needed to be undertaken by the prosecutor is to decide how reliable the evidence is. The Code lists five points that a prosecutor may take into account when deciding this question, and this may involve them taking into account the defendant's age or mental ability, the credibility of defendant's explanation or a witness' background etc. For example, if the defendant gives an innocent explanation of events and the evidence supports this explanation then there is little likelihood that there will be a realistic prospect of conviction.

If there is no admissible or reliable evidence then the intended prosecution must stop here and the charges against the defendant should be dropped. Only if the evidential test is positively satisfied should a prosecutor then go on to consider the public interest test.

The public interest stage

In 1951 Lord Shawcross, who was the then Attorney-General, made the classic statement on public interest:

> It has never been the rule in this country—I hope it never will be—that suspected criminal offences must automatically be the subject of prosecution.
>
> (House of Commons Debates, vol.483, col.681, January 29, 1951.)

If the evidential test is satisfied then that still does not mean that a prosecution will automatically follow. For a prosecution to continue then the prosecutor must determine whether it would be in the public interest for the individual to be prosecuted for the alleged offence. To decide this, the prosecutor must look at the factors for and against prosecution, and then balance these up carefully and fairly. To help prosecutors with this decision the Code lists a number of common factors both for and against prosecution; these factors are not an exhaustive list and which, if any, factors should be taken into account will be dependent upon the individual facts of each case.

For example, prosecution in respect of the more serious offences will be likely to be needed in the public interest if:

- a conviction is likely to result in a significant sentence;
- a conviction is likely to result in a confiscation or any other order;
- a weapon was used or violence was threatened during the commission of the offence;
- the offence was committed against a person serving the public (for example, a police or prison officer, or a nurse);
- the defendant was in a position of authority or trust;
- the evidence shows that the defendant was a ringleader or an organiser of the offence;
- there is evidence that the offence was premeditated;

- there is evidence that the offence was carried out by a group;

- the victim of the offence was vulnerable, has been put in considerable fear, or suffered personal attack, damage or disturbance;

- the offence was committed in the presence of, or in close proximity to, a child;

- the offence was motivated by any form of discrimination against the victim's ethnic or national origin, disability, sex, religious beliefs, political views or sexual orientation, or the suspect demonstrated hostility towards the victim based on any of those characteristics;

- there is a marked difference between the actual or mental ages of the defendant and the victim, or if there is any element of corruption;

- the defendant's previous convictions or cautions are relevant to the present offence;

- the defendant is alleged to have committed the offence while under an order of the court;

- there are grounds for believing that the offence is likely to be continued or repeated , for example, by a history of recurring conduct;

- the offence, although not serious in itself, is widespread in the area where it was committed; or

- a prosecution would have a significant positive impact on maintaining community confidence.

Whereas, the factors where prosecution would be less likely to be needed include:

- the court is likely to impose a nominal penalty;

- the defendant has already been made the subject of a sentence and any further conviction would be unlikely to result in the imposition of an additional sentence or order, unless the nature of the particular offence requires a prosecution or the defendant withdraws consent to have an offence taken into consideration during sentencing;

- the offence was committed as a result of a genuine mistake or misunderstanding (these factors must be balanced against the seriousness of the offence);

- the loss or harm can be described as minor and was the result of a single incident, particularly if it was caused by a misjudgement;

- there has been a long delay between the offence taking place and the date of the trial, unless the offence is serious, the delay has been caused in part by the defendant, the offence has only recently come to light; or the complexity of the offence has meant that there has been a long investigation;

- a prosecution is likely to have a bad effect on the victim's physical or mental health, always bearing in mind the seriousness of the offence;

- the defendant is elderly or is, or was at the time of the offence, suffering from significant mental or physical ill health, unless the offence is serious or there is real possibility that it may be repeated;

- the defendant has put right the loss or harm that was caused (but defendants must not avoid prosecution or diversion solely because they pay compensation); and

- details may be made public that could harm sources of information, international relations or national security.

So if the CPS were faced with the case of a 79-year-old man who had stolen a bottle of milk from his local corner shop they may, after trawling through the common public interest factors for and against prosecution, be likely to reach the conclusion that very little public interest would be served by him being prosecuted for the theft of a bottle of milk; the court would be likely to impose a nominal sentence, there was no weapon or violence used and the defendant is elderly etc. However, it is likely that they would change their mind if the facts were that the man was a persistent offender and this was the fifteenth time he had been arrested for shop lifting in the past four months. The factors for prosecution here would be that there are grounds for believing that the offence is likely to be continued or repeated (for example, by a history of recurring conduct, the defendant's previous convictions or cautions are relevant to the present offence), and a prosecution would have a significant positive impact on maintaining community confidence. Therefore the factors for prosecution would probably outweigh the factors against prosecution.

Whether to prosecute or not is determined by balancing the facts, and factors of the individual case. Just because there are more ticks against the list of factors against prosecution does not necessarily mean that the prosecution should not go ahead. It could be more in the public's interest to prosecute and then these potentially mitigating factors against would be raised at sentencing if the defendant is convicted.

As well as deciding whether an alleged offender should initially be prosecuted, the CPS are also responsible for continuously reviewing the case right up until the point of trial. The evidence and the facts of a case are not always static and new evidence may come to light at any time. The CPS should regularly review each case by reference to the Full Code test, to ensure that the prosecution is still appropriate. By undertaking such reviews the CPS will also be able to identify any areas in the case where the evidence is weak, and by doing so they may be able to advise the police as to where to focus their investigations.

9.2.2 The selection of charges

The CPS are in most cases, responsible for determining which is/are the most appropriate charge(s) to be levied against the alleged offender. To ensure that they do so they are required, under para.7 of the Code, to select charges that:

- reflect the seriousness and extent of the offending;

- give the court adequate powers to sentence and impose appropriate post-conviction orders; and

- enable the case to be presented in a clear and simple way.

This means that they will not always charge the individual with the most serious possible offence, but with the offence that they feel is the most suitable in the circumstances. An example of this could be that, following a drunken Friday night street brawl where a number of people sustained injuries, the police wish to charge a participant in the fight with a s.18 grievous bodily harm with intent offence (the most serious non-fatal offence against a person which can result in a term of life imprisonment), whereas the CPS feel that a s.47 actual bodily harm offence (which is much less serious and can be dealt with by the magistrates' court) would be more appropriate once they have considered the evidence. The CPS could have the choice of charging with the more serious offence but they may decide that, when taking into consideration the Full Code Test and the factors set out in para.7 of the Code (above), that the lower offence is more appropriate and that there will be a realistic prospect of conviction with this lower offence than with that of the more serious one. The CPS will also be responsible for reviewing, and possibly amending, the offence charged if new evidence comes to light.

Figure 9.2 Commencing a prosecution

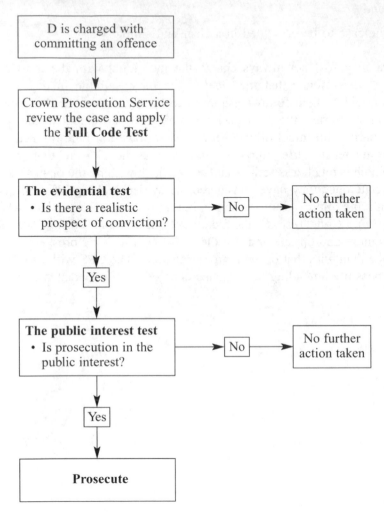

9.3 Alternatives to prosecution

Returning back to scenario above of the 79-year-old man and the theft of a bottle of milk, if the CPS decides that prosecuting him is not in the public interest then it does not mean that he will necessarily just get away with the offence that he has committed as the CPS have available to them a number of alternatives to formal prosecution. If there were not these alternatives then many offences would go unpunished and this could result in more individuals being tempted to commit crime due to the lack of sanctions and, as a result, there could be a further potential loss in public confidence with the criminal justice system as a whole. So what are these alternatives to prosecution?

The alternatives to prosecution are:

- cautions (adults)
- reprimands and warnings (juveniles)
- fixed penalty notices

9.3.1 Cautions

Cautions come in two different forms, either a simple caution or a conditional caution.

9.3.1.1 Simple cautions

Simple cautions are governed by the Home Office Circular 30/2005 and are therefore a non-statutory means of disposal. The aims behind a simple caution are to deal quickly and simply with less serious offences, to divert offenders from appearing in the criminal courts and to reduce the likelihood of re-offending. The main questions to ask are whether a simple caution is appropriate on consideration of the facts of the case and if so, whether a simple caution will be effective when taking into account the aims behind this form of caution.

A simple caution may be viewed as appropriate if the offender is over the age of 18, they have made an admission of guilt in relation to the offence, there is sufficient evidence to warrant a prosecution and it is in the public interest to dispose of the matter by such a caution.

Simple cautions will generally be administered at a police station and the person receiving the caution must consent to it. A caution must be entered onto the Police National Computer and may be citied in any subsequent criminal proceedings and must be disclosed to potential employers if requested. There is also the potential for a person to still be prosecuted for the offence after receiving a caution, although this is generally unlikely. This form of disposal would be the most appropriate for our 79-year-old shoplifter.

9.3.1.2 Conditional cutions

A conditional caution is a method of statutory disposal and is dealt with by ss.22 to 27 of the Criminal Justice Act 2003 (CJA 2003). Section 22(2) defines a conditional caution as:

> a caution which is given in respect of an offence committed by the offender and which has conditions attached to it with which the offender must comply.

The conditions are required to fall into one or both of two categories:

- rehabilitation (treatment for drug or alcohol dependency, anger management classes, restorative justice etc.)
- reparation (making good any damage caused, restoring stolen goods, paying modest finanical compensation etc.)

The conditions must however be *appropriate, achievable and proportionate*. The key to determining whether a Conditional Caution should be given is that the imposition of specified conditions will be an appropriate and effective means of addressing an offender's behaviour or making reparation for the effects of the offence on the victim or the community. The police are generally responsible for the administering of a conditional caution but they themselves have no discretion as to the decision to use a conditional caution as a method of disposal, under s.23 this responsibility falls to the prosecutor (the CPS).

For a conditional caution to be viewed as appropriate the defendant must first have attained the age of 18. If this is the case then the five requirements under s.23 need to be satisfied. These five requirements are:

- there is evidence that the offender committed the offence (a realistic prospect of conviction);
- the offender has admitted the offence;
- the prosecutor has decided that a conditional caution is appropriate;
- the offender must have the effect of the conditional caution explained to them;
- the offender must consent to the conditional caution.

The whole idea behind the use of a conditional caution is that prosecution may not be in the best interest of the public, whereas the imposition of a condition may be. If the defendant is a drug user who has just started stealing to fund their habit then the journey through the criminal justice system may be very detrimental to their well-being, this could result in their further reliance upon drugs, which in turn could mean that they commit more crime to sustain their habit; in other words it could become a vicious circle. However, if that defendant is given a conditional caution with the condition of attending treatment for drug dependency, instead of being prosecuted then they may be able to break their drug habit, not commit further crime and become a positive member of society. If the defendant subsequently breaches the conditional caution they can then be prosecuted for the original offence and therefore justice will be done. A defendant must always consent to the caution, and by agreeing to a caution they are formally admitting guilt to the offence charged. If the defendant in any way disputes their involvement with the alleged offence then a caution would not be appropriate and the CPS would have to consider whether prosecution was a viable option, by reference to the Code as discussed above.

9.3.2 Reprimands and warnings

So far the simple and conditional cautions considered above can only be administered to adult offenders, but sadly in this world there are also a high number of young offenders, so appropriate sanctions for them also need to be available. The Crime and Disorder Act 1998 introduced under s.65, a young person's equivalent to cautions by way of reprimands and warnings, which apply to those aged 17 and under. A young person can be disposed of in this way if:

- there is evidence that a child or young person committed the offence;
- there is sufficient evidence against the defendant;
- they make admissions as to the offence;
- they have not previously been convicted of any offence;
- it would not be in the public interest to prosecute.

As can be seen this criteria is basically the same as for adult cautions. The only difference is that a child will receive a reprimand if they have not previously been warned or reprimanded. For a second offence it will be a final warning, and for a third offence they will be prosecuted. The police do have the discretion to warn or prosecute for a first offence if they deem the offence to be serious enough and a final warning will come with conditions attached, such as requiring the young person to attend at least one session at a local Attendance Centre.

9.3.3 Fixed penalty notices

The final alternative to prosecution is the issue of a fixed penalty notice. Fixed penalty notices are generally thought as synonymous with road traffic offences, such as speeding etc. The offender is issued with a penalty notice that requires a set monetary amount to be paid in order to discharge any liability to be convicted of the offence that the notice relates to. Fines can range from about £50 up to £300 depending on the offence in question. Most people only equate fixed penalty notices with motoring offences but they can in fact be prescribed for a number of different offences such as being drunk in a public place, trespassing on a railway, criminal damage, selling alcohol to children and knowingly giving a false alarm of fire. A person who receives a notice can request to be tried for the offence instead of making an admission by payment. However, if a fixed penalty notice is ignored then, after a set time (normally 21 days from issue of the notice), a further fine, which is a sum equal to one and a half times the original fine, will then be issued.

9.4 The court hierarchy

There are two main functions of the courts within the criminal jursidiction; these are either as courts of first instance or as appellant courts. The structure of the court system is such that there is not really a clear distinction between those courts that are first instance courts and those that have an appellant jurisidiction.

Courts of first instance are those courts that hear and decide the original case, they have evidence adduced and witnesses called. In criminal matters they will be determining the guilt or innocence of the defendant. Appellant courts are those courts that hear cases on appeal. This means that the case has already been determined by a court of first instance but that one party to the case is then disputing the decision made by that court. The issue of appeals is dealt with in detail in chapter 13 and therefore it is only intended at this point to give an overview of the courts and their respective jurisdiction.

273

9.4.1 The magistrates' court

The magistrates' court is a court of first instance and it is often viewed as being at the bottom of the court hierarchy. The magistrates' court can hear a number of civil matters (certain family proceedings, and often issues concerning licencing applications etc.) but its main jurisidiction is concerned with criminal matters. The magistrates' court hears the majority (approx 98 per cent) of criminal cases at first instance although all cases will pass through the magistrates' court, albeit very briefly. The magistrates' court has the power to hear all cases involving summary offences; these offences being the least serious criminal offences. However the more serious cases are also briefly entertained by the magistrates' court. Either-way offences (explained below at 9.5.2) have a preliminary hearing in the magistrates' court to determine the venue of the trial (this is known as an allocation hearing and greater detail on this procedure can be found at 10.1), and even the most serious (indictable) offences, such as murder and rape, will be first presented at the magistrates' court so as to be formally sent to the Crown Court for trial.

The magistrates' courts are presided over either by magistrates or by a district judge. Magistrates are lay people who have volunteered their time to come and sit at the court in a judicial capacity. In general they are not legally qualified and they hold the official title of 'Justices of the Peace', although they are commonly referred to as magistrates. A district judge is a legally qualified appointed member of the judiciary, and they were known until recently, as stipendary judges.

9.4.2 The Crown Court

The Crown Court is both a court of first instance and an appellant court. In its role as a first instance court it will hear trials on indictment (and those either-way offences deemed too serious for the magistrates' court, or where the defendant has elected trial by jury (see 10.1.2)), and will in some cases sentence on either-way cases sent up from the magistrates' court. The court, when sitting as a court of first instance is comprised of a judge and a jury. The function of the judge is to direct upon the law, whereas the jury are the tribunal of fact who will determine the guilt or innocence of the person being tried. When the court is acting in its appellant function the Crown will hear matters on appeal from the magistrates' court. The judicial personnel who preside over the Crown Court can vary from case to case, as all the High Court judges, Recorders and Circuit Judges have the jurisdiction to sit with the Crown Court. Occasionally magistrates will also sit in the Crown Court alongside a judge when a matter is being heard on appeal from the magistrates' court.

9.4.3 The Administrative Division of the High Court

The Administrative Division of the High Court, formerly known as the Divisional Court of the Queen's Bench Division, is a court that has both civil and criminal jursidiction. In respect of its criminal remit it has the power to hear cases on appeal from the magistrates' court by way of case stated. This form of appeal can be made by either the prosecution of the defence and is explained in further detail in 13.2.2.1.3. The High Court is part of the Supreme Court of England and Wales, which also consists of the Court of Appeal and the House of Lords.

9.4.4 The Court of Appeal (Criminal Division)

The Court of Appeal is a court of an appellant function and it has the power to hear and determine cases on appeal in respect of either the conviction or the sentence from the Crown Court, references made by the Attorney-General, and referrals by the Criminal Cases Review Commission. The Court also has civil jurisdiction under the Court of Appeal (Civil Division). The Civil Division is headed by the Master of the Rolls, and the Criminal Division by the Lord Chief Justice and the judges of the court are known as the Lord or Lady Chief Justices of Appeal. The Court of Appeal (Criminal Division) originally started out life in 1848 as the Court for Crown Cases Reserved, this then changed to the Court of Criminal Appeal in 1907, and finally the court became the Court of Appeal (Criminal Division) in 1966.

9.4.5 The House of Lords

The House of Lords is the final court of appeal for England and Wales. It is the highest judicial court in the land and it mainly hears appeals from both the Court of Appeal and the High Court. To appeal to the House of Lords, leave to appeal (or permission) must be obtained from either the court being appealed from, or from the House itself and the appeal must be based on a point of law of general public importance. The judges who sit in the House are known as Lords of Appeal in Ordinary, and are more commonly referred to as the Law Lords.

The House of Lords, as we know it now, will disappear in October 2009 when the Supreme Court of England and Wales (as established by the Constitutional Reform Act 2005 (CRA 2005)) comes into effect. The House of Lords will be taken over by the Supreme Court but its functions, jurisdiction and composition will generally remain the same, the main difference will be that any new judge appointed will not receive an automatic peerage or the right to sit in the House of Lords.

9.4.6 The Privy Council

The Privy Council, or the Judicial Committee of the Privy Council if using the full title of the court, is the final appeal court for several Commonwealth countries, UK overseas territories and the British Crown dependencies (such as Jersey and Guernsey). The court is composed of the House of Lords judges but it does not deal directly with domestic cases. An example of the Commonwealth countries that have the right to appeal to the Privy Council include Antigua, Trinidad and Tobago, Jamacia and Mauritius. It used to be that all Commonwealth countries had the right to appeal to the Privy Council, but over time a large number of the countries have established their own court of final appeal which has reduced the reliance upon the Privy Council.

In 1875 Canada established its own Supreme Court and abolished appeals to the Privy Council, in 1978 Sri Lanka abolished its remit to the Privy Council for criminal cases, in 1997 Hong Kong established the Court of Final Appeal thereby removing its need for reference, and in 2003 New Zealand abolished its right to appeal to the court. The nations of the Caribbean community are currently pushing for their right of appeal to be abolished in favour of the Caribbean Court of Justice, but so far this has not been successful.

Figure 9.3 Criminal court hierarchy

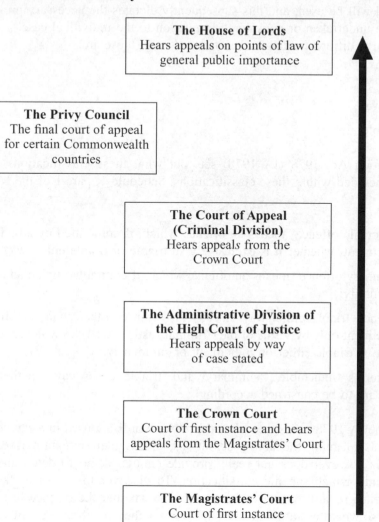

9.5 Offence classification

In England and Wales there are two forms that a trial in criminal proceedings may take; there is either a trial on indictment or a summary trial. Summary trials are heard by a magistrates' court, and will be presided over by either a bench of three lay justices of the peace (magistrates (see Chapter 5 for further details as to who magistrates' are) or a single district judge. Trials on indictment are heard in the Crown court before a judge and a jury.

One of the main determining factors as to whether the case will be tried on indictment or heard summarily will be the actual offence that the defendant has been charged with. Each offence falls into a specific offence classification and this classification will then establish which method of trial will be used, and this subsequently dictates the necessary pre-trial procedures that need to be undertaken or considered in relation to the individual case.

There are three different offence classifications, and these are:

- summary

- either-way

- indictable

The Interpretation Act 1978 (IA 1978) sets out what these classifications mean and what offences are included within these classifications. Schedule 1, para.1 of the IA 1978 provides that:

(a) 'indictable offence' means an offence which, if committed by an adult, is triable on indictment, whether it is exclusively so triable or triable either-way;

(b) 'summary offence' means an offence which, if committed by an adult, is triable only summarily;

(c) 'offence triable either-way' means an offence, other than an offence triable on indictment only by virtue of the Criminal Justice Act 1988 which, if committed by an adult, is triable either on indictment or summarily;

and the terms 'indictable', 'summary' and 'triable either-way', in their application to offences, are to be construed accordingly.

Section 5 of the IA 1978 states that when the above words are used in a statute then they must be construed as meaning the above definitions, unless their intention is contrary to these meanings. This however does not really provide enough detail to determine which specific offence falls into which specific classification. To discover the offence classification of an individual offence regard first needs be given as to whether the offence has been created by statute (and if so what the statute says about it) or whether the offence is one found at common law.

9.5.1 Summary offences

Summary offences are generally the least serious of all of the criminal offences. A summary offence as stated above, will normally only be tried in a magistrates' court and the level of the seriousness of a summary offence is reflected by the magistrates' sentencing powers. The maximum penalty that can currently be imposed by a magistrates' court is either a six-month term of imprisonment (rising to 12 months maximum for cases involving more than one offence) or a £5,000 fine. The word 'currently' is used here as, under s.154 CJA 2003, the sentencing powers of the magistrates' court have been increased to a maximum custodial sentence of 12 months (24 months for cases involving more than one offence); the idea behind these increased sentencing powers is that the magistrates' courts will be able to then deal with a greater number of cases, but these powers are not yet in force and there is no prospective date of when they will be introduced. Summary offences are created by statute and the Act and offence in question will provide details of the maximum penalty that can be imposed upon conviction for the offence. If the statute sets out that the maximum penalty is either six months' imprisonment or a £5,000 fine then the offence can be taken to be summary. Some examples of summary offences are:

- common assault
- driving whilst disqualified
- taking a motor vehicle without the owner's consent

9.5.2   Either-way offences

Either-way offences are generally viewed as hybrid offences. They can either be tried summarily or on indictment and this decision will be dependent on the facts of the individual case and the seriousness of the offence committed. It appears that they are in fact a derivative of the indictable only offence classification, because when (according to s.5 of the IA 1978) a statute speaks of an indictable offence but does not provide further detail, then it must be taken to be referring to an indictable only *or* an either-way offence because both can be tried on indictment.

Whether an offence is an either-way offence or not, can be discovered in one of two ways. The first is by reference to the statute if the offence is one created statutorily. If the statute sets out that the maximum penalty is *either* punishable by a penalty for summary conviction *or* by a penalty for an indictable conviction, then the offence is triable either-way. If the offence is not one created by statute (so a common law offence) then reference should be made to the Magistrates' Courts Act 1980 (MCA 1980) Sch.1, as this schedule contains a list of offences which are triable-either-way.

The more commonly known offences that appear on the Schedule are offences such as assault occasioning actual bodily harm under s.47 of the Offences Against the Person Act 1861 (OAPA 1861), or the offence of theft under the Theft Act 1968 (TA 1968), but the Schedule also contains a number of more obscure offences, such as the one found at number 13 of the schedule (making false representations etc., with a view to procuring the burning of any human remains) or the one at number 11 (damaging submarine cables). The majority of the offences listed under Sch.1 are old offences (some very old) ranging from 1751, but there are no offences listed later than 1971 in the Schedule. The reason behind this is not that no new either-way offences have been created since this date, but rather that when such an offence is created the penalties for the offence are drafted directly into the statute and therefore the offence does not require being added to the Schedule.

Obviously there are only two forms of trial, summary and on indictment, so when dealing with an either-way offence a decision needs to be made as to which court the case will be heard in. The procedure and realities of this process are discussed at 10.1.

9.5.3 Indictable offences

Indictable only offences are seen as being the most serious types of criminal offence that can be committed. They are so serious that they can only be heard in the Crown court in front of a judge and a jury and they have the potential to carry heavy sentences, which can be as serious as life imprisonment. All common law offences, such as murder, are generally only triable on indictment, unless they are specifically listed in Sch.1 of the MCA 1980. If it is an offence created by way of statute, then, if the maximum penalty is beyond the powers of the magistrates' court, then it is an indictable offence.

Indictable only offences are further split down into four different categories called classes. In Class 1 the most serious indictable only offences are listed, and these include murder, treason, genocide and torture etc. Class 2 indictable only offences include manslaughter, rape, infanticide, sex with a girl under the age of 13, piracy and mutiny; and then Class 3 and 4 contain the remaining indictable only offences such as wounding with intent or robbery or assault with intent to rob.

The alleged commission of indictable only offences and the subsequent trials on indictment are regularly reported by the media, and therefore the public can be forgiven for thinking that most of the crimes dealt with by the criminal justice system are in fact very serious indictable ones. In reality though only a small number of crimes committed are indictable only, and the approximate figure of cases tried on indictment is 2 per cent of all criminal cases, meaning that the remaining 98 per cent are tried summarily. This can be looked at in one of two ways and, the way in which an individual will choose to view it will depend upon their perception of society and the media. The first approach to interpreting these figures could be to decide that the media over report and sensationalise the most serious offences committed and therefore, as a result, the public have a distorted perception of the crime levels and the nature of the crimes committed in the UK. The flip side of this, and the second way in which these figures can be viewed, is that there are in fact a substantial amount of indictable only offences committed and, if this is the case, then there consequently must be a phenomenal amount of less serious and petty crimes occurring within this country on a very regular basis.

9.6 Bail

Bail can be granted by both the police (under PACE) and by the courts. This text will only focus on court bail, but be assured that police bail is very similar to court bail, so the understanding of court bail will automatically bring with it the ability to understand police bail.

9.6.1 What is bail?

The phrase 'being on remand' is often bandied about in everyday conversation and in the media, but what does this mean? Most people make the assumption that if a defendant is 'on remand' then they are locked up in a prison cell for 23 hours per day, but it does not just mean this, it can also mean being released from custody on bail. Bail is where a defendant is released from the custody of the court (or the police), so that they can go home and sleep in their bed and go to work etc., but that they are under a requirement to surrender back into the custody of the court at a future time. Essentially bail is a promise by the bailee to return to the court when they are told to do so, and not to commit any further offences whilst on bail.

Bail can be granted for the time in between hearings pre-trial (so the time between a preliminary hearing and a PCHM, or between a PCMH and the trial) and it can also be granted post-conviction if a pre-sentence report is pending so as to enable the court to sentence appropriately. Bail hearings are generally heard by the magistrates' court and this court can deal with any bail issues relating to all offence classifications at first instance. A point to note is that in summary offence cases where the defendant has been brought to the court by way of a summons and has not previously been remanded in custody, bail does not necessarily need to be considered. The Crown court can hold bail hearings and grant bail in cases where the defendant has been committed or sent for trial or sentence in the Crown, or the defendant has been remanded into custody pending trial on a summary offence or upon conviction and pending an appeal. The High Court has very limited powers in relation to granting bail and can only grant it where the defendant is appealing a conviction by way of case stated. The Court of Appeal can also grant bail, but this is extremely rare and only really occurs in relation to retrials, such as in the case of Sion Jenkins who was re-tried twice for the alleged murder of his stepdaughter Billie-Jo (see 13.2.2.2.1 for further details of this case).

9.6.2   The presumption of bail

The granting of bail is governed by the Bail Act 1976 (BA 1976) and s.4 sets out that the defendant is afforded a statutory presumption in favour of being granted bail under subs.(1). This presumption though only applies to defendants who appear before either the magistrates' court or the Crown court (so not applicable to police bail) and it only applies prior to conviction. After conviction (whilst waiting for sentence) the court have the discretion to grant bail but there is no automatic presumption of it being granted. This presumption of bail has been statutorily removed in certain circumstances, such as where the defendant has been charged with murder, attempted murder, manslaughter, rape or other specified sexual offences and they have previously been convicted of such an offence (s.25 of the Criminal Justice and Public Order Act 1994 (CJPOA 1994)), although the court does retain a discretionary right to grant bail in these cases where the court is satisfied that there are exceptional circumstances to justify the granting of bail.

There are a number of issues for consideration that are raised by the statutory presumption under s.4. The statutory presumption to bail means that prolific offenders, like a burglar for example, are always to be granted bail, regardless of how many times they have offended. Another issue that needs to be considered is whether alleged murderers or rapists, who have not previously been convicted of such an offence, will automatically get bail. It would seem unfair that an alleged rapist against whom there is overwhelming evidence, should then be allowed back into society whilst their case is pending due to a statutory presumption. However, simply denying them bail outright because they may have committed a heinous crime could conversely breach their human right of being innocent until proven guilty. So how does the court deal with issues such as these?

Schedule 1, para.2 of the Bail Act 1976 sets out the exceptions to the general presumptions of bail. There are three reasons set out in para.2 as to why the granting of bail can be refused. These are if the court is satisfied that there are substantial grounds for believing that the defendant, if release on bail would:

(a) fail to surrender to custody, or

(b) commit an offence whilst on bail, or

(c) interfere with witnesses or otherwise obstruct the course of justice, whether in relation to himself or any other person.

When considering these grounds in relation to the refusal of granting bail the court must take into account the seriousness of the offence that the defendant has been charged with, the defendant's character, any antecedents (this means previous convictions) they may have, if they have been through the court process before what their previous bail record was like, the strength of the evidence against them, the defendant's associations and ties with the community and any other relevant considerations. The court must have *substantial grounds for believing* that the defendant would fall into one of these exceptions. A hunch based on no or little evidence that the defendant might disappear whilst on bail will be insufficient to rebut the presumption to bail, there must be a justifiable reason as to why bail has been withheld and this reason must be able to stand up to scrutiny as the right to liberty is a fundamental right under the European Convention of Human Rights (ECHR) and this refusal could be seen to breach this right.

The paragraph also sets out that just one of the conditions must be satisfied for the presumption of bail to be withdrawn, however in practice the courts often require two of the conditions being fulfilled in the case before they refuse to grant bail. One of the reasons behind this seems to be that if all defendants who were at risk of committing an offence whilst on bail were simply remanded into custody then the prison system would become even more over-loaded than it is at the minute, about 40 per cent of offenders arrested are already on bail at the time of arrest, and the prison system would simply not be able to cope if they were all refused bail.

Schedule 1 also includes other situations in which the courts are allowed to refuse to grant bail. These include circumstances such as where the court is satisfied that the defendant should be kept in custody for his own protection or if he is a child or young person, for his own welfare, or the fact that he is already serving a custodial order, or that they do not at that time have enough information to make an informed decision. The right to bail will also be removed if the defendant has already been released on bail for the offence but has then subsequently breached the bail conditions, has attempted to abscond, or has committed further offences whilst on bail.

The CJA 2003 recently amended the Bail Act 1976 and introduced a new provision in an attempt to tackle the growing drug related crime issues which are currently occurring within our society at present. This new provision can be found under s.6B of the Act and this section states a defendant may be declined bail when:

- the defendant is over 18 years of age;

- they have tested positive for Class A drugs;

- they have been charged with a drug offence or the crime was completely motivated by drugs; and

- the defendant declines to take up the offer of a 'relevant assessment' in respect of their drug taking.

The purpose of this newly added exception is to try and address the problems caused by drugs and drug taking as by agreeing to treatment the defendants retain their liberty and receive help and support to address their drug habit, which in turn will hopefully reduce the drug related crime rate.

9.6.3   The conditions of bail

It is not always the case that if a defendant receives bail then they can just disappear off and do what they like until their next court appearance. Bail can come in two forms, either unconditional or conditional. Unconditional is exactly as it sounds—without any conditions attached—so in this instance the defendant will be allowed to go and live their life as normal until the next court date. The only provisos being that they turn up on time for their next court hearing and do not commit any further offences.

Conditional bail though is where the court imposes conditions upon the defendant, which the defendant is then obliged to keep. These conditions may be the reporting to a police station weekly, twice weekly or even daily, it may require the defendant to be under house arrest (not leaving the house at all) or they may impose a curfew between, say, between the hours of 11 pm and 7 am. The defendant may be electronically tagged or ordered to stay away from a particular geographical location, the courts may even say where they must live, which could range from the defendant's own house, to their parents' house to even a bail hostel, depending on the circumstances. Conditions will be imposed that are suitable for the individual facts of the case.

The purpose of the conditions is to prevent the defendant re-offending or absconding whilst on bail and it was argued in the case of *R. v Mansfield Justices Ex p. Sharkey* [1985] Q.B. 613 that conditions to bail should only be imposed where there were substantial grounds for believing that an offence would be committed whilst the defendant was on bail if the conditions were not imposed, in effect mirroring the reasoning behind the refusal of bail found in Sch.1. The case of *Sharkey* arose in relation to the miners' strikes in the mid 1980s. The majority of miners were on strike and the nine applicants had been involved in the picketing of collieries in the East Midlands. The nine applicants were arrested whilst picketing and were charged with threatening. The justices, when considering granting bail to each applicant had regard to the numerous outbreaks of disorder on the picket lines and, in order to prevent the commission of a further offence by the applicant whilst on bail, decided to act in this case as they had acted in the case of other miners, by imposing the condition that each applicant did 'not visit any premises or place for the purpose of picketing or demonstrating'. On their application for judicial review Lord Lane C.J. stated that:

> In the present circumstances the question the justices should ask themselves is a simple one: "Is this condition necessary for the prevention of the commission of an offence by the defendant when on bail?" They are not obliged to have substantial grounds. It is enough if they perceive a real and not a fanciful risk of an offence being committed.

Thereby the court set out that a substantial risk of an offence being committed, or the defendant absconding is not required. All that is required is an affirmative response to the fact that the conditions are 'necessary'. To what they must be necessary for can be found under s.3 of the Bail Act, which set out that the reasons for necessity are:

(a) to secure that he surrenders to custody,

(b) to secure that he does not commit an offence while on bail,

(c) to secure that he does not interfere with witnesses or otherwise obstruct the course of justice whether in relation to himself or any other person,

(ca) for his own protection or, if he is a child or young person, for his own welfare or in his own interests,

(d) to secure that he makes himself available for the purpose of enabling inquiries or a report to be made to assist the court in dealing with him for the offence,

(e) to secure that before the time appointed for him to surrender to custody, he attends an interview with an authorised advocate or authorised litigator, as defined by s.119(1) of the Courts and Legal Services Act 1990.

An application can be made to vary the conditions imposed under s.8 of the Bail Act 1976. If a defendant moves address from the one he is bailed to he will need to apply to have the condition of the address he lives at changed. The defendant may change jobs whilst on bail and this may mean he is unable to report to the office station at the scheduled times or he may need to enter a banned geographical location for work purposes etc. An application can also be made by the prosecution to impose conditions onto what was originally unconditional bail.

9.6.4 Sureties

The Bail Act 1976 abolished the need for the defendant himself to provide recognisance (money or security) in an effort to secure his release on bail, but this concept still exists today in relation to 'sureties'. A surety is someone who effectively acts as a sponsor for the defendant. The surety agrees to put up a certain amount of money and an item of security (such as their house) to ensure that the defendant is released from custody. This act is called 'standing bail' and the courts take it very seriously as if the defendant breaches their bail and fails to attend at the next court date the surety may forfeit their recognisance.

The courts will generally fix a set amount for the bail and this could range from a few hundred pounds to £100,000 depending on the seriousness of the case and the level of flight risk the defendant is perceived to be. The court, before agreeing to the surety standing bail, must be convinced that the proposed surety understands the commitment they are undertaking and that they are fully aware of the consequences if the defendant breaches their bail. The court will also investigate the surety's character, financial resources, previous convictions and their relationship with the defendant before they agree to the surety standing bail.

If the surety does stand bail but the defendant does not attend court at their next court date then the court may waive the forfeiture if the surety can show that they tried to ensure that the defendant attended court. If the defendant breached their bail and the surety then refused to pay the forfeit the surety can be held in contempt of court and could receive a maximum of a 12-month custodial sentence.

Sureties only feature occasionally in bail hearings and are not a pre-requisite of being granted bail.

9.6.5   Refusal of bail

If the magistrates refuse to grant a defendant bail then they are required to produce a certificate stating so. Initially a defendant is allowed two attempts to secure bail; if he is refused on his first application then he can make a further application at a subsequent hearing. However, once he has made two unsuccessful bail applications the court are not obliged to hear any further applications, they will generally only do so when it appears that there has been a change in circumstances in respect of the defendant or the case. These changes in circumstances need not be huge, something as simple as the defendant now having a suitable address they can be bailed to, or a change in the strength of the prosecution case against him may be sufficient to persuade the court to rehear the application and potentially grant bail.

Another option open to the defendant upon refusal of bail by the magistrates is to make an application to the Crown Court under s.81 of the Supreme Court Act 1981 (SCA 1981). Under such an application the Crown Court will hold a full bail hearing within 48 hours of the refusal by the magistrates.

The prosecution are also entitled to appeal against the granting of bail by the magistrates where the offence the defendant is charged with is an imprisonable one. The prosecution are required to notify the court of their intention to appeal bail at the end of the initial bail hearing and again this appeal will be heard within 48 hours of the bail being granted.

9.6.6   Breach of bail

So what happens if a defendant breached their bail? Maybe they failed to report to the police station at their scheduled time, or perhaps they were spotted in a pub which they had been banned from going into.

If the defendant breaches their bail conditions then they can be rearrested and brought before the court. Breaching bail conditions is not viewed as the commission of an offence so there will be no separate penalty for the breach. However, the court may view the breach as a sign that the defendant has no regard or respect for the court and therefore, under s.7 of the BA 1976, they may revoke their bail and remand them in custody for the remainder of the time before their case comes to trial.

If the defendant breaches their bail by failing to appear at court at the allotted time' then this carries with it much more serious consequences. Failure to appear is an offence under s.6(1) Bail Act 1976, however, failing to appear will not be classed as a criminal offence if the defendant has a reasonable excuse for why they did not surrender into custody at the required time. The onus will be upon the defendant to show this reasonable excuse. If the defendant does have a reasonable excuse then they must still surrender themselves to the court as soon as is practicable under s.6(2) and explain this excuse to the court.

A normal part of the working day in the criminal courts is dealing with cases where defendants have breached their bail conditions by failing to attend court. A surprisingly large number of defendants fail to appear at court and lawyers will often find themselves taking phone calls from their clients in which the defendant proceeds to tell them that they are not at court for such reasons as 'their taxi did not turn up', 'they haven't got enough money to travel to court', 'they're ill' or that they 'simply got their court dates muddled up'. Often the court will accept these reasons (they will require proof such as a doctors note) and they will either grant an extension to the bail until the next court hearing, or alternatively they may issue a 'warrant backed for bail', which means that the defendant will be arrested and then, if their reasons for non appearance are accepted, re-bailed. Occasionally, when the offence does not carry with it a custodial sentence, the court may decide to continue on and try the defendant in their absence.

When a defendant fails to attend and there is no explanation provided then the court will issue a 'warrant not backed for bail'. This means that the defendant will be arrested and brought before the courts at the earliest opportunity. Once this has occurred it is likely that further bail will be refused and that the defendant will be remanded in custody. If the defendant is then prosecuted for a Bail Act offence, then, under s.6, they may receive a maximum of a three months prison sentence or a £5,000 fine from the magistrates' court, or a maximum of a 12-month prison sentence or an unlimited fine if bailed from the Crown Court. The court guidelines advise that offenders should generally be given a custodial sentence for this offence.

9.6.7 Bail and human rights

It is argued that bail breaches a fundamental human right under art.5 of the ECHR. Article 5 states that:

Everyone has the right to liberty and security of person.

Obviously being remanded in custody is an encroachment upon this right to liberty and freedom. However, art.5 is not an absolute right as there are qualifications to it in certain circumstances.

Article 5(1) sets out the qualifications that can result in the setting aside of this right. These qualifications include the lawful detention after conviction, after non-compliance with a court order, or to bring a person before a court on reasonable suspicion of having committed an offence. Subsections (b) and (c) are particularly relevant to the issue of bail and if the right is abrogated under subsection (c) then art.5(3) must be complied with, which states:

> Everyone arrested or detained in accordance with the provisions of paragraph 1.c of this article shall be brought promptly before a judge or other officer authorised by law to exercise judicial power and shall be entitled to trial within a reasonable time or to release pending trial. Release may be conditioned by guarantees to appear for trial.

The main two factors that must be balanced when considering bail in relation to the rights under the Convention is that of the issue of public interest against the issue of the presumption of innocence. Everyone is presumed innocent until found guilty so how can the detention of an innocent person be justified? The only ground upon which such detention can be justified on is that the defendant needs to be detained in an effort to protect the public. This detention does have limits and a person cannot be detained indefinitely as was decided in the case of *A v Secretary of State for the Home Department; X v Secretary of State for the Home Department* [2004] UKHL 56; [2005] 3 All E.R. 169. In *A* the appellants were all foreign nationals who had been certified by the Secretary of State as suspected international terrorists. They could not be deported since that would in the circumstances have involved a breach of their Human Rights so they were detained without charge or trial in accordance with the derogation from art.5 of the ECHR as permitted by the Human Rights Act 1998 Order 2001; the Order having been enacted to deal with the perceived terrorist threat from Al-Qaeda after the terrorist attacks in the US on September 11, 2001. They successfully appealed to the House of Lords who stated their detention was unlawful and a breach of their human rights.

Figure 9.4 The bail process

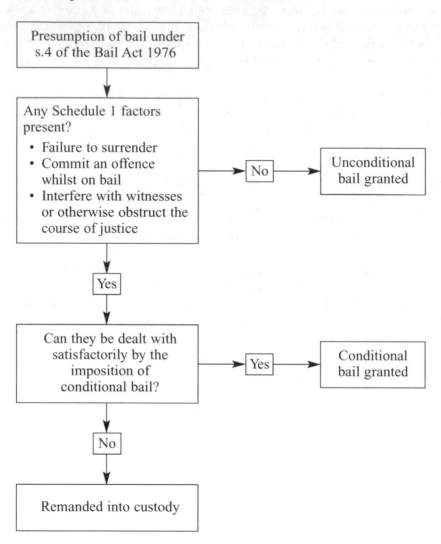

9.7 Summary

(a) The Crown Prosecution Service (CPS) are the primary agency concerned with charging and prosecuting offenders. In most cases the CPS will determine the appropriate charge, although the police may decide this in certain minor cases.

(b) To determine whether prosecution is appropriate prosecutors must refer to the Full Code test to decide whether there is a realistic prospect of conviction and whether the prosecution would be in the public interest.

(c) The alternatives to prosecuting an offender are to issue them with a caution (either simple or conditional), a reprimand or a warning (if the offender is a young person) or a fixed penalty notice.

(d) Criminal courts can either be a court of first instance, an appellant court or both. The court hierarchy spans from the magistrates' court as the lowest court in the land, to the House of Lords as the final court of appeal.

(e) How and where an offence is tried will be dependent upon the offence classification. Offences are categorised as either summary, triable either-way or indictable. Summary offences include the less serious offences and are tried in the magistrates' court. Either-way offences become either triable summarily or upon indictment following a mode of trial hearing. Indictable offences include the most serious criminal offences and are tried upon indictment in the Crown Court.

(f) Court bail may be granted at any point pending trial, as well as post trial pending sentencing and there is a presumption in favour of the defendant being granted bail. Bail may either be unconditional or with conditions attached. The granting of bail may be refused where it is believed that the defendant is likely to fail to surrender, may interfere with witnesses or commit an offence whilst on bail.

(g) If conditional bail is granted but then breached this does not impose further criminal liability but it can result in the bail being revoked and the defendant being remanded into custody. If a defendant fails to surrender at an allotted time then they will commit a bail act offence, which can result in a separate sanction to that of the offence that they are on bail for.

9.8 Self-test questions

1. The Crown Prosecution Agency will commence a prosecution where:
    (a) it is in the public interest to do so
    (b) there is a realistic prospect of conviction
    (c) it is in the public interest to do so and there is a realistic prospect of conviction
    (d) the prosecutor believes that the defendant is guilty

2. The term a 'realistic prospect of conviction' means:
    (a) that the trier of fact would find the defendant guilty
    (b) that the trier of fact might find the defendant guilty
    (c) that the trier of fact would be more likely than not to convict the defendant
    (d) that the trier of fact will find the defendant guilty beyond reasonable doubt

3. The final appeal court for England and Wales is:

    (a) the Privy Council

    (b) the Court of Appeal

    (c) the Administrative Division of the High Court

    (d) the House of Lords

4. An either-way offence can be tried in:

    (a) the Crown Court

    (b) the magistrates' court

    (c) either the magistrates' or Crown Court, depending on the seriousness of the offence

    (d) the county court

5. The presumption of bail can be rebutted where the defendant would:

    (a) fail to surrender to custody

    (b) commit an offence whilst on bail

    (c) interfere with witnesses or otherwise obstruct the course of justice

    (d) any of the above

9.9 Further reading

A. Ashworth, "Bail: human rights—European Convention on Human Rights 1950, Art.5(3)" [2007] Crim. L.R. Jan, 63–65.

I.D. Brownlee, "The statutory charging scheme in England and Wales: towards a unified prosecution system?" [2004] Crim. L.R. Nov. 896–907.

I. Brownlee, "Conditional cautions and fair trial rights in England and Wales: form versus substance in the diversionary agenda?" [2007] Crim. L.R. Feb. 129–140.

S. Cammiss, " 'I will in a moment give you the full history': mode of trial, prosecutorial control and partial accounts" [2006] Crim. L.R. Jan. 38–51.

C. Hamon, "Taking the CPS into the 21st century" [2006] 103(36) L.S.G. 15.

A. Mimmack, "Statutory charging—the nationwide scheme" [2006] 10(4) M.C.P. 5–7.

S. Nicholls, "Statutory charging—the implications for the defence" [2006] 10(4) M.C.P. 8–9.

S. O'Doherty, "The changing of the guard: CPS charging" [2004] 168(44) J.P. 848–850.

J. Rozenberg, "Out to cause harm" [2008] 105(03) L.S.G. 14.

"Sentencing for Bail Act offences". (Editorial) [2007] Crim. L.R. Aug. 589–590.

R. Suff, "Transforming performance on diversity at the CPS" [2006] 159 E.O.R. 14–20.

N. Taylor, "Conduct of judge: judge critical of time estimate—judge refusing to continue bail" [2008] 4 Crim. L.R. 299–300.

10 Criminal Justice System 2

In this chapter we will consider the remaining salient issues in relation to the criminal trial process, such as the appropriate trial venue for an either-way offence, the issues that can arise within the criminal justice system in relation to pleas and plea-bargaining, as well as what happens during the course of a trial.

10.1 Either-way offences

Either-way offences, as described earlier at 9.5.2, are a hybrid offence, and are somewhere in between a summary offence and an indictable only offence. They do not have a set home as do summary offences (the magistrates' court) and indictable only offences (the Crown Court), but of course they must end up at one of these courts so that the defendant can be tried for the alleged offence. How this is determined will now be considered below.

10.1.1 Plea before venue

As stated previously all cases initially pass through the magistrates' court, even if it is only briefly whilst on their way through to the Crown Court. With an either-way offence the first court hearing to take place in the matter is known as a 'plea before venue hearing', and this is heard at the magistrates' court. This hearing is the earliest point at which the defendant's plea can be formally taken and it is effectively a preliminary hearing where no matters of substantive law will be heard. To illustrate the procedure involved in determining the trial location of an either-way offence the below case study will be referred to.

CASE STUDY

Bertie Bunting is a 26-year-old drug addict. He has been charged with burglary under s.9 of the Theft Act 1968. It is alleged that he entered 73 Birrell Road, a residential property, at approximately 3:10 a.m. and stole a number of items of jewellery, including a Rolex watch valued at £7,000 and a diamond ring worth £4,000. Bertie already has one previous conviction for burglary.

Section 17A of the MCA 1980 contains the procedure on how a plea before venue hearing should be conducted. At the hearing the charges will be put before the defendant, so in the above case Bertie would have the charge and particulars of the offence of burglary put to him. The form of words used would be something along the lines of:

Clerk: 'Are you Bertie Bunting of 1A Main Street, Nonchester?'

Bertie: 'Yes'

Clerk: 'Bertie Bunting, you are charged with burglary contrary to s.9 of the Theft Act 1968. The particulars of the offence are that on the 2nd February 2007 at 3:10 a.m. you entered 73 Birrell Road and stole a diamond ring and a rolex watch. How do you plead to this indictment, guilty or not guilty?'

It would then be explained to him (the defendant) that if he pleaded guilty at this point then he would then be dealt with summarily and the magistrates may pass sentence without hearing any evidence. If however, the magistrates' court felt that their sentencing powers were insufficient (see 5.9 for details as to the magistrates' sentencing powers) for the case then Bertie could still be committed to the Crown for sentence under s.3 of the Powers of Criminal Courts (Sentencing) Act 2000 (PCC(S)A 2000) and then be sentenced as if he had been tried on indictment (so the full range of sentences which could be imposed at the Crown Court for the offence would be available to the court in respect of him). After this has all been explained to him in language that he can understand, he will then be asked to indicate his plea of either guilty or not guilty. If the defendant refuses to enter a plea, or his plea is equivocal, then a not guilty plea will be entered on his behalf by the court (s.17A(8)).

10.1.2   Allocation hearing (mode of trial)

If the defendant chooses to enter a not guilty plea then the next step is for a 'mode of trial' hearing to be conducted in order to determine which court (the magistrates' or the Crown) will hear the case. The CJA 2003 has changed the title of these proceedings from a 'mode of trial' hearing to an 'allocation hearing', but many practitioners will still refer to them as a 'mode of trial' hearings.

The procedure for the determining the mode of trial is set out extensively in the MCA 1980, between ss.17A to 21. Section 19 provides the statutory factors that the magistrates should bear in mind when determining whether the case should remain in the magistrates' court or be committed to the Crown Court for trial. Section 19(3) sets out that when considering whether the offence is more suitable for summary trial or for trial on indictment, the court should have regard of those factors such as:

- the nature of the case
- the circumstances of the offence
- whether the magistrates' court has sufficient sentencing powers and
- any other circumstances that appear to the court to be relevant

The magistrates also have access to the National Mode of Trial Guidelines 2004, (which can be found in the *Consolidated Criminal Practice Direction* [2002] 2 Cr. App. R. 35 at Pt 5, para.V.51); to further help them deliberate as to which court is the most appropriate to hear the trial. If the court reaches the decision that the case is suitable to be dealt with summarily then the procedure under s.20 of the MCA 1980 must be carried out. This section requires the court to firstly inform the defendant of the fact that the case is deemed appropriate in seriousness to be dealt with by the magistrates' court, and at that point the defendant can then either consent to a summary trial or refuse this and elect to be tried by the Crown Court. This is often described as the 'right to elect trial by jury' and it is quite a controversial and heavily criticised procedure of the criminal justice system, the criticisms of which we will consider in a moment.

Either-way offences are offences that are allocated to the appropriate court depending on the nature and circumstances of the offence and the other factors noted in s.19. Offences such as theft or assault occasioning actual bodily harm are either-way offences and there can be a wide range and difference between the levels of seriousness of these offences in individual cases. For example, take the offence of theft; theft can be the stealing of two chocolate bars from a local corner shop with a low value to the tune of £1, but the same offence can also be committed by the stealing of £200,000 from the defendant's employer. It is the same offence, charged under the same statutory provision, but with greatly varying degrees of seriousness. Another example can be seen with the offence of actual bodily harm under s.47 of the Offences Against the Person Act 1861 (OAPA 1861); this may be committed by causing a bruise to someone's arm or it could be that the victim sustains a broken nose, again varying degrees of seriousness of the same offence. In the more serious cases the magistrates' court will hand over jurisdiction to the Crown Court for a trial on indictment, but in the less serious cases, where the magistrates feel that they are capable of dealing with the case the defendant can still elect to have his case heard before a jury in the Crown Court if he so chooses. There are two sides to the argument that arises in relation to the right to elect a trial by jury, the first is that everyone has the fundamental right of having a fair trial (as stated in art.6 of the ECHR) and that if a defendant wishes to have his case heard before 12 of his peers then he should be allowed to exercise this right. The alternative side to the argument, and the reason why this provision attracts such criticism, is that a jury trial for a low level theft, such a the £1 worth of chocolate above, is completely disproportionate in time, expense and resources to the actual seriousness of the offence committed. By allowing a defendant to elect a trial by jury in these kinds of cases it can be argued that doing so amounts to an abuse of the system, which could ultimately lead to the criminal justice system becoming overloaded and ineffective.

Under s.20 MCA 1980 the defendant also has the right to ask for an indication of sentence before deciding upon whether to consent to a summary trial or elect for a Crown Court trial. The only indication that the court is permitted to give in these circumstances is as to whether the sentence will be custodial or non-custodial. The court are not obliged to give such an indication if they feel it would be inappropriate to do so and the indication given may have an impact on how the defendant decides to proceed.

10.1.3 Burglary and criminal damage

There are special rules relating to the either-way offences of burglary and criminal damage in relation to the mode of trial hearings. If the burglary is the third burglary committed by the defendant since November 1999 then under s.111 of the PCC(S)A 2000 it was envisaged that a custodial sentence of three years would be imposed. However this section has not yet come into force and so currently the magistrates' court receive regular updates from the Sentencing Guidelines Council advising them as to how to deal appropriately with cases of burglary. If the case is viewed as being beyond the scope of the magistrates' sentencing powers then the defendant must be sent to the Crown Court for trial on indictment by way of s.51 of the Crime and Disorder Act 1998 (CDA 1998). Section 51 formally sets out the fact that any defendant charged with an offence triable only on indictment will be sent to the Crown court for trial, but this also applies to either-way offences. Sending for trial is a simple administrative process.

In respect of the offence of criminal damage contrary to s.1 of the Criminal Damage Act 1971, if the value of the item damaged is less than £5,000 then the case must be tried summarily and the defendant cannot elect trial in the Crown Court. If the damage was however caused by fire, or the damage inflicted is worth over £5,000 then the normal mode of trial proceedings must be undertaken.

If we now relate these provisions to the case study of Bertie, then as this is only the second burglary that Bertie has been charged with the magistrates would not need to consider the provisions under s.111 of the PCC(S)A 2000. They would therefore need to consider the statutory factors found in s.19 of the MCA 1980; these being the nature of the offence, the circumstances of the offence, their sentencing powers and any other relevant circumstances. The burglary was of a domestic nature and it occurred during the night time when the homeowners were likely to be asleep in bed, plus the items stolen were also of a high value. So should the case be sent to the Crown Court or can the magistrates keep jurisdiction of it? To decide this, the magistrates would refer to the National Mode of Trial Guidelines, and as a result it would be likely that they would decide to commit the offence to the Crown Court for trial. The reason for this decision is that under the guidelines (specifically the paragraph entitled Burglary: Dwelling House) there are detailed a number of factors which may indicate that the offence should be tried on indictment, the two factors relevant to Bertie's case are:

(b)   entry at night of a house which is normally occupied, whether or not the occupier (or another) is present; and

(f)   the unrecovered property is of a high value.

Please note though that these are just guidelines and that the magistrates are not obliged to follow them if they do not want to do so. The decision as to whether or not to keep or commit a case is at their discretion and this decision is mainly dependent on whether or not they feel that they have sufficient sentencing powers to deal with the matter. It would be unlikely that they would commit the case to the Crown Court simply because the burglary happened during the night, there would need to be more to the offence than this one factor which would take the required sentence upon conviction out of their remit.

If the magistrates in Bertie's case decide that the case is suitable for trial on indictment and intend to commit him to the Crown Court Bertie loses all power to elect a summary trial in the magistrates' court. Once the magistrates have decided that the case is not suitable for summary trial, due to the fact that they have insufficient sentencing powers, the case must be committed to the Crown and the defendant no longer has any say in the matter. To allow him to then elect a summary trial would be perverse as, if this were allowed and he was then convicted after a trial, the magistrates would not be able to impose a just and appropriate sentence.

10.1.4   The committal process

If the magistrates' court do decline jurisdiction of a case then it must be committed to the Crown so as to be heard on indictment (this process would also need to be undertaken if the defendant has elected to be tried in the Crown). The legislation, which deals with committal proceedings, is currently found under s.6 of the MCA 1980. Under s.6 there are two forms that the committal proceedings can take, s.6 provides that:

(1) A magistrates' court inquiring into an offence as examining justices shall on consideration of the evidence—

(a)   commit the accused for trial if it is of opinion that there is sufficient evidence to put him on trial by jury for any indictable offence;

(b)   discharge him if it is not of that opinion and he is in custody for no other cause than the offence under inquiry;

but the preceding provisions of this subsection have effect subject to the provisions of this and any other Act relating to the summary trial of indictable offences.

(2) If a magistrates' court inquiring into an offence as examining justices is satisfied that all the evidence tendered by or on behalf of the prosecutor falls within section 5A(3) above, it may commit the accused for trial for the offence without consideration of the contents of any statements, depositions or other documents, and without consideration of any exhibits which are not documents, unless—

(a)   the accused or one of the accused has no legal representative acting for him in the case, or

(b)   a legal representative for the accused or one of the accused, as the case may be, has requested the court to consider a submission that there is insufficient evidence to put that accused on trial by jury for the offence;

and subsection (1) above shall not apply to a committal for trial under this subsection.

Hidden within the legal terminology are two methods by which a defendant can be committed to the Crown for trial. The first can be found in s.6(1) of the Act. This form of a committal requires the court to hear the evidence against the defendant so as to determine whether there is a case against the defendant that warrants putting them on trial before a jury; this is known as a 'long' committal and its occurrence is quite rare. The second form of a committal can be found under s.6(2) and this is where the court commit the defendant without any consideration of the oral evidence as they are satisfied that there is a prima facie case against the defendant; this is known as a 'short' committal and is the most commonly used form of committal proceedings. The most important factor to consider when committing a case is that there is a prima facie (on the face of it) case against the defendant; a committal under subs.(2) means the court has accepted there is one and a committal under subs.(1) means that the court requires this fact to be shown.

10.1.5   The short style committal

A short style committal occurs where the court are satisfied that there is a prima facie case against the defendant and that they are not required to consider any oral evidence to determine this. During the committal proceedings (either short or long) the defendant should at all times be present (s.4(3) MCA 1980) unless it is not practicable for the evidence to be tendered in their presence due to their disorderly conduct or they cannot be present due to health reasons but they are legally represented and have consented to the evidence being tendered in their absence. This form of a committal is really a paper based administrative exercise as the evidence is presented to the bench by the prosecution by way of a 'committal bundle', but the magistrates are not required to read it.

The format the hearing should take is detailed in r.10.2 of the Criminal Procedure Rules (CrimPR), which sets out that the defendant will be asked by the court as to whether they wish to make a submission that there is insufficient evidence against them (which is otherwise known as a submission of no case to answer) and, if they do not and the evidence tendered in the committal bundle is all correct and they have legal representation, then the case will be committed to the Crown Court.

The evidence that should be contained in the committal bundle is such evidence as set out by s.5A(3) of the MCA 1980 and this usually consists of written statements as described under s.5B.

10.1.6   The long style committal

The longer style committal can be described as something much closer to what most people imagine a court hearing to be like. This form of a committal is set out in r.10.3 of the CrimPR, and will be undertaken if the defendant is either not legally represented or wishes to make a submission of no case to answer. At the beginning of the hearing the charge against the defendant will be read out, although he is not required to enter a plea at this point. Then the prosecution will tender their evidence to show that there is a case to answer by the defendant. The prosecution will not call live oral testimony but will instead present their evidence relevant to the offence under s.5A(3), this may mean that they read out statements or show the court relevant documents. The prosecution do not need to present all of their evidence, just simply enough to show that there is a prima facie case against the defendant and the court here is not interested in determining the (in)admissibility of any of the evidence adduced, if there are issues surrounding the evidence then the trial court will deal with them if the case is committed. The defence will then put forward their submission of no case to answer and then the prosecution will be presented with a final opportunity to make representations regarding this submission.

Following hearing from both sides the court will then deliberate until they have made a decision as to whether or not to commit. If the court feels that a prima facie case has not been made out against the defendant then they can discharge the proceedings. Discharging the proceedings is not the same as acquitting the defendant, as if discharged the prosecution may re-charge him later after collecting more evidence. The magistrates can also commit the defendant for trial on a lesser or alternative charge if they feel that there is a case against them in respect of this.

A long style committal will generally be used where the defendant does not have legal representation; as in these circumstances a committal which involves the consideration of the evidence by the court will help to ensure that the defendant is not prosecuted unnecessarily and, that the welfare of the defendant and the justice system (in terms of costs and resources etc.) is protected. In today's society it is very unlikely for a defendant to reach a stage in the proceedings, such as a committal hearing, without legal representation. Legal representation is usually sought at the police station or at the very latest on the commencement of court proceeding, and therefore long style committals are very rare within the criminal courts.

10.1.7 A few further points to note

There are a few other points that you may wish to be aware of in relation to committals. The first is the committal proceedings can be conducted by a single magistrate under s.4(1) of the MCA 1980. The second is that if, after a mode of trial hearing which resulted in the magistrates declining jurisdiction, evidence at the committal hearing then indicates that the matter is not as serious as it was first thought to be, then under s.25(3) of the MCA 1980 the bench can suggest that it returns to the magistrates' court to be dealt with summarily. If all parties to the proceedings are agreeable with this then, as long as the defendant consents, the matter can be retained by the magistrates' court. The next point to note is that, once the defendant has entered a not guilty plea and a summary trial for the offence has begun, the magistrates still have the option, under s.25(2), to commit the trial to the Crown Court if, after hearing the prosecution case, they feel that the matter is more serious than first thought and that their sentencing powers will be insufficient.

If we return one more time to the case study of Bertie then it would appear on the face of it that there is a case against Bertie and therefore a short style committal with no consideration of the evidence under s.6(2) of the MCA 1980 would be the most appropriate method of committal.

The final point to make is that if a defendant has been charged with an either-way offence *and* a summary offence, and the defendant either elects trial at the Crown or he is committed to the Crown then the linked summary offence will also be heard in the Crown under s.41 of the Criminal Justice Act 1988. However, if he then pleads guilty or is found guilty of the summary offence after trial the Crown can only sentence him as if it were a summary offence.

10.1.8 Magistrates' court v Crown Court

If the magistrates feel that they have sufficient sentencing powers to deal with a matter summarily the defendant will then need to make a choice as whether to remain in the magistrates' court or elect trial on indictment, but what are the factors that they will need to take into account when making this decision?

- **Conviction rates**

  The magistrates' court are believed to have a higher conviction rate, convicting in approximately 90 per cent of cases, whereas there is believed to be a higher chance of acquittal by a trial before a jury. This may be due to the composition of the triers of fact in each forum. The selection process for magistrates tries to ensure that the bench is representative of society but it is limited by the number and type of people who volunteer to become magistrates. A jury is randomly selected from the electoral role which offers a greater chance that the jury will be reflective of society.

- **Delay**

  Cases proceed with more speed through the magistrates' court. You may have to wait up to nine months before the case can be heard in the Crown, whereas in the magistrates' the case may only be waiting a few weeks or months. A lengthy delay in the case will often be very stressful to those involved in the case, such as the defendant, the vicitm, witnesses and their families. Summary trial will resolve the matter more quickly. However, from the defendant's point of view delay may be advantageous as witnesses are less likely to appear for the trial, and the reliability of their evidence will be undermined by the passage of time.

- **Publicity**

  Generally cases that are heard in the Crown Court will command more media attention than those heard in the magistrates' court, which again can be very stressful for all parties involved. The publicity may have a detrimental effect on the defendant's quality of life both personally and professionally.

- **Legally qualified**

  The Crown Court has the advantage of the fact that the case is overseen by an experienced criminal judge who should be able to deal with any evidential issues as they arise. The jury will also generally be excluded from the hearing when points of law are raised so as not to be prejudiced by such matters. In the magistrates' court the bench are not legally qualified, although they are advised by a legal advisor. Also if points of law are raised then the bench are (at times) required to deal with them and this may inadvertently have a prejudicial effect on their decision.

- **Sentencing powers**

  Although the magistrates' courts are believed to have a higher conviction rate they also have lesser sentencing powers than the Crown Court. By electing to have their case heard by a jury the defendant will be running the risk of receiving a much harsher sentence if eventually convicted.

Figure 10.1 Either-way offences

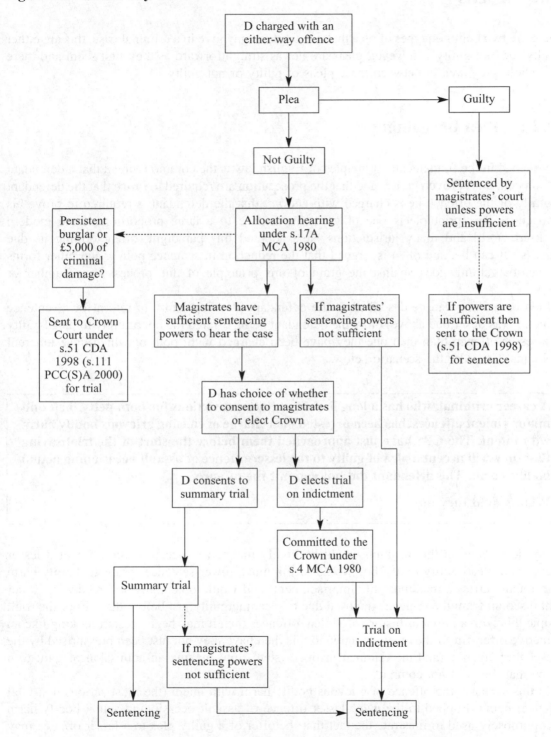

10.2 Pleas

There are two common types of plea that a defendant may give in a criminal case, this are either 'guilty' or 'not guilty'. However, pleas are not as straightforward as they first seem and there is a whole grey area in between these pleas of guilty or not guilty.

10.2.1 Plea bargaining

Entrenched in the fundamental principles of English law is the common thread that a defendant is 'innocent until proven guilty' and that the prosecution are required to *prove* that the defendant is guilty of the offence he is charged with and *not* that the defendant is required to prove his innocence. This principle is one of great importance to a large proportion of the modern civilised world and many jurisdictions have adopted this paradigm, often terming it 'due process.' It can be, and often is, argued that the reduction in sentence policy, and other forms of plea-bargaining goes against the grain of this principle of due process in a number of ways.

Plea bargaining can be described as the defendant pleading guilty in return for a sentence reduction (as described above) or by the defendant being offered the opportunity to plead guilty to a lesser offence than then one they have been charged with; both of which have inherent problems. Consider the scenario below.

A career criminal, who has a long list of previous convictions for both petty theft and minor violent offences, has been arrested on a charge of causing grievous bodily harm with intent. The CPS have just approached them before the start of the trial saying that they will accept a plea of guilty to the lesser offence of assault occasioning actual bodily harm. The defendant did not commit the offence.

What would they do?

Many defendants in this position would be highly inclined to accepted the offer of a lesser charge and plead guilty to it. They would face a much lower sentence (grievous bodily harm with intent carries a maximum life imprisonment) and would potentially still receive a 10 per cent discount from the sentence imposed due to pleading guilty just before the start of the trial; couple this with a previous history of violent offences then it may begin to start looking like an attractive offer. But if they were to agree to this then have they not just been pressurised by the prosecution agency (and the criminal justice system) into making an admission of guilt to a crime that they did not commit?

In this scenario the offence of grievous bodily harm with intent (the most serious non-fatal offence) being dropped to the *much* lesser offence of assault occasioning actual bodily harm was purposely used to illustrate the fact that the offer of a guilty plea to a lesser offence may seem like an attractive proposition, even when it is actually a cover for the fact that the prosecution do not have enough evidence available to reach the required standard of proof necessary for the more serious offence. A criticism that can be made of plea-bargaining is that the offer of a plea to a lesser offence may simply be a way of the CPS attaining their conviction targets, particularly in weak cases. It could be quite easy to spot this motive when the two offences are considerably different in respects of severity, but what if the offered offence was only slightly less serious (so in the above scenario maybe grievous bodily harm under s.20 OAPA 1861 (s.18 without the offence requirement of intent)), would such a motive be so easy to spot?

This tactic by the prosecuting agencies is sometimes described as 'over-charging'. Over-charging can be described as the prosecuting agency deciding to press ahead with a charge of a more serious nature than the facts of the case warrant. Such as charging an individual with an offence of s.18 OAPA 1861 offence of grievous bodily harm with intent in a case that warrants at the very most, a charge of assault occasioning actual bodily harm under s.47 OAPA 1861 (as in the scenario above). By over-charging a defendant and then offering a plea to a lesser offence the CPS manage to secure a conviction and fulfil their target goals.

Obviously the CPS and the police do not work in a vacuum and there are other arms to the criminal justice system that will to some degree, have an effect or some input into the issue of plea-bargaining; the main one being the judiciary.

The case of *R. v Turner* [1970] 2 Q.B. 321 was one of the first cases to deal directly with the issue of plea-bargaining and judicial involvement. Following the judgment in this case the judiciary were only allowed a very limited involvement in the process of plea-bargaining. In the case the appellant was told by his counsel that the judge had indicated a custodial sentence should he be convicted following a not guilty plea. However, if he pleaded guilty, a non-custodial punishment would ensue. Turner changed his plea from not guilty to guilty. On appeal Lord Parker C.J. stated, in relation to the issue of plea-bargaining, that:

> . . . counsel on both sides may wish to discuss with the judge whether it would be proper, in a particular case, for the prosecution to accept a plea to a lesser offence.
>
> It is of course imperative that so far as possible justice must be administered in open court. Counsel should, therefore, only ask to see the judge when it is felt to be really necessary and the judge must be careful only to treat such communications as private where, in fairness to the accused person, this is necessary. The Judge should, subject to the one exception referred to hereafter, never indicate the sentence, which he is minded to impose. A statement that on a plea of Guilty he would impose one sentence but that on a conviction following a plea of Not Guilty he would impose a severer sentence is one that should never be made. This could be taken to be undue pressure on the accused, thus depriving him of that complete freedom of choice which is essential.

In essence he was saying that the judiciary should not become involved in any questions concerning plea-bargaining, especially in relation to the issue of sentencing, because if they were to do so it could be seen as undue pressure being exerted over the defendant. The only exception to this rule was that a judge could indicate the type of sentence they were minded to impose if the type of sentence would be the same regardless of whether the conviction resulted from a guilty plea or upon conviction after trial.

Even after the clear guidelines laid down in *Turner* a number of legal and academic professionals were still of the opinion that the judiciary should be more actively involved in the concept of plea-bargaining. One of the strongest arguments for greater judicial involvement was that the more directly involved the judiciary were within this area of law then less opportunity would be presented for an abuse of the fundamental principle of due process. This state of affairs however, continued on as settled principle for 25 years until the 2005 case of *R. v Goodyear* [2005] 1 W.L.R. 2532, where the issue of judicial involvement in plea-bargaining was revisited.

In the case of *R. v Goodyear* Lord Woolf C.J. concluded that the principles set down by *Turner* were no longer satisfactory in today's legal culture. He gave consideration to the fact that counsel were entitled to give opinion and advice (the basis of which was drawn from their own experience and court knowledge) to the defendant upon the possible sentence that they may receive, but that the judge who would ultimately have a much more certain and clear idea as to the likely sentence could not intimate such, even if requested to by the defendant. In his deliberations over this point Lord Woolf C.J. stated:

> Therefore, a somewhat strange situation developed that although the defendant's decision about his plea could properly be informed by the views of counsel about the sentence the judge would be likely to pass (provided always that he, counsel, had not participated in any discussions with the judge) it had simultaneously to be made ignorant of the judge's own views, even if the defendant wanted to know them. That position requires examination. In any event, the further question remains whether it continues to be appropriate to proceed on the basis that clear, and if necessary strong, but inevitably incompletely informed advice from counsel, about the advantages which would accrue from and the consequences which would follow an early guilty plea is permissible, while an intimation of these matters initiated by the judge should always, without more, be deemed to constitute improper pressure on the defendant, and therefore prohibited.
>
> In our judgment, there is a significant distinction between a sentence indication given to a defendant who has deliberately chosen to seek it from the judge, and an unsolicited indication directed at him from the judge, and conveyed to him by his counsel. We do not see why a judicial response to a request for information from the defendant should automatically be deemed to constitute improper pressure on him. The judge is simply acceding to the defendant's wish to be fully informed before making his own decision whether to plead guilty or not guilty, by having the judge's views about sentence available to him rather than the advice counsel may give him about what counsel believes the judge's views would be likely to be. [. . .] Accordingly it would not constitute inappropriate judicial pressure on the defendant for the judge to respond to such a request if one were made.

Following the guidelines laid down in *Goodyear* the judge in a case can now, in prescribed circumstances, give an advanced indication of sentence. These circumstances are that:

(a) the defendant must have voluntarily requested such an indication from the judge;

(b) the judge must give an indication of the maximum sentence if a plea of guilty were tendered *at the stage at which the indication is sought* [emphasis added];

(c) the factual basis of the plea must be agreed between the two parties;

(d) once an indication has been given it is binding upon the court.

The judge of course, retains an unfettered discretion to refuse to give an advanced indication of sentence, if they are of the opinion that it would not be appropriate to do so under the circumstances. The decision by the judge to refuse to give such an indication may arise due to a variety of reasons, such as the defendant already being under pressure or that the defendant may not have fully appreciated that he should not plead guilty unless he is in fact guilty. The judge may also choose to reserve his indication until he feels that it is appropriate to give one. For example if the prosecution and defence have not agreed the factual basis of the case (for the purposes of sentence indication) then the judge would be likely to reserve comment until this was decided between the parties, as this is obviously likely to have an effect on the maximum sentence he is minded to impose.

Despite the clear guidelines and safeguards laid down in *Goodyear* there is still a wealth of legal and public opinion that is strongly opposed to the idea of plea-bargaining. It can be argued that by allowing a judicially advanced indication of sentence there is the potential for it to undermine the judicial function of the criminal justice system. By defendants pleading guilty to receive a lesser sentence it could be argued that they are avoiding the full consequences of their actions, which in turn is unfair upon the victims of the crime; potentially justice is not being seen to be done, in neither their eyes or in the eyes of the public. Nor can an innocent person pleading guilty to a crime they have not committed, which is still a realistic possibility even despite the safeguards laid down in the *Goodyear*, be said to be the sign of a completely effective and healthy criminal justice system.

10.2.2   Fraud trials

Very recently (reported in *The Times*, April 4, 2008), a formalised concept of plea-bargaining, or rather 'plea-negotiation' has been proposed for fraud cases. Under the plea-negotiation system a prosecutor could put forward a specific sentence or range of sentences to the defendant on the indication that he wishes to plead guilty. If the defendant is agreeable to the proposed sentence then the matter would be put forward to the judge for consideration. The judge would not have to accept the offered plea agreement and could, if they so wished, require the defendant to stand trial, or they could propose a tougher sentence that they felt was more appropriate. Neither the defendant nor the court would be under any obligation to accept or agree to any proposal from the prosecutor. The benefit of such a system would be that very complex fraud trials would not need to go forward to a lengthy and costly hearing and that jurors would consequently be relieved of the need to sit on such demanding cases.

10.2.3 Guilty pleas

A defendant will enter a guilty plea when they admit that they were the person who committed the offence. It is essentially a full and frank admission of their guilt and an agreement as to the facts of the offence put forward by the prosecution.

There may be a number of reasons why a defendant decides to plead guilty to an alleged offence. It may be that there is overwhelming evidence against the defendant, such as a number of credible eyewitnesses to the offence, or that there is undisputable forensic evidence. Alternatively the defendant may simply be the type of person who knows and admits that they did wrong, is full of remorse and is willing to accept the inevitable consequences of their actions. The law however, also provides some incentives for a plea of guilty from a defendant. Section 144 of the CJA 2003 sets out that a reduction in sentence due to a guilty plea can be considered by the court if they feel that it is appropriate in the circumstances. To determine whether such a reduction is appropriate in the circumstances the court is directed (under s.144) to look at:

(a) the stage in the proceedings for the offence at which the offender indicated his intention to plead guilty, and

(b) the circumstances in which this indication was given.

The general rule has been that if a defendant enters a guilty plea at the earliest opportunity (normally at the first court hearing) then they will be afforded a reduction in their sentence to reflect this fact. However as the case continues to draw nearer to trial before a guilty plea is entered then a lesser reduction will be furnished upon the defendant to reflect this fact, to the point that if a defendant pleads guilty on the day of the trial he may be unlikely to receive any sentence reduction at all; his chance to redeem himself by the entering of such a plea will be viewed as having long passed. Essentially there is a progressive loss of mitigation. The court, under s.144(b), is also required to consider the circumstances in which the indication was given. If it appears that the defendant refused to plead guilty until an irrefutable case against him was shown by the prosecution then he may be viewed as having been simply backed into a corner and had no other option but to plead guilty; in these circumstances the courts are less likely to look upon the guilty plea in a sympathetic light and therefore the defendant may not receive the full sentence reduction that could be granted in the circumstances.

Traditionally the maximum percentage reduction has been about 33 per cent (one third of the sentence), this percentage then decreasing down to the point of 10 per cent depending (amongst other things) on the timing of the guilty plea in relation to the start of the trial. However, very recently the Sentencing Guidelines Council (SGC) conducted a review of the sentence reduction policy and produced definitive guidelines, which are now effective in all cases where sentencing occurs on or after July 23, 2007.

The SGC have set out a recommended approach to be used when applying the sentence reduction principle. The court are firstly required to decide the sentence for the offence(s) by taking into account any aggravating or mitigating factors, as well as any other offences that have been formally admitted so as to be taken into consideration in respect of sentencing. The court, once having decided the full sentence, must then apply a sliding scale to determine the appropriate level of reduction. The sliding scale ranges from one third (1/3) where the guilty plea was entered at the first reasonable opportunity (as was the case prior to the review), reducing to a recommended one quarter (1/4) when the trial date has been set, and then down to a recommended one tenth (1/10) for a guilty plea entered just prior to or after the commencement of the trial. The SGC guidelines state that:

> The level of reduction should reflect the stage at which the offender indicated a <u>willingness to admit guilt</u> to the offence for which he is eventually sentenced.

This recommended approach is little different to the way in which sentencing reductions were decided prior to the review. The guidelines have, however, introduced a new concept in relation to the withholding of a reduction in part when the prosecution case is overwhelming against the defendant. The guidelines state that:

> Where the prosecution case is overwhelming, it may not be appropriate to give the full reduction that would otherwise be given. Whilst there is a presumption in favour of full reduction being given where a plea has been indicated at the first reasonable opportunity, the fact that the prosecution case is overwhelming without relying on admissions from the defendant may be a reason justifying departure from the guideline.

If the prosecution case is overwhelming then a recommended reduction of only 20 per cent is likely to be given even if the admission was made at the first reasonable opportunity. If a court now wishes to deviate away from this recommendation and give the full one-third discount then they must (under the guidelines) state their reasons for doing so.

The review also considered what was meant by the term 'first reasonable opportunity' and it concluded that it may be considered to be the first time that the defendant appears in court, but it could also be (especially in relation to indictable offences) that it was reasonable to have expected an indication of willingness to admit guilt to occur at an earlier opportunity, such as during interview at the police station.

There are numerous advantages for providing a defendant with a reduction in sentence in return for a guilty plea, such as it removes the need for a trial, it shortens the whole criminal process between charge and sentence, it helps to preserve and save on resources and costs, and it prevents victims and witnesses having to go through the ordeal of a trial. By being able to provide such an incentive to plead guilty the courts are able to help in alleviating the burden upon the criminal justice system, which in turn allows the time and resources to deal with other cases in a more efficient and expeditious manner.

One of the criticisms that can be made against the policy of sentence reductions for a guilty plea is the argument that this system potentially places unfair pressure upon a defendant to plead guilty to an offence, even when they may not have committed it. This issue falls under an area of the law known as 'plea bargaining'; plea-bargaining is a highly controversial and heavily criticised aspect of the criminal justice system.

10.2.4 *Newton* hearings

Occasionally a situation may arise where the defendant does admit that he committed the offence, but that the way in which he committed it was not as the prosecution allege. To illustrate what this means let us look at the facts of the case study below.

CASE STUDY

Alfie is 20 years old and has never been in trouble with the police before. He has been charged with the offence of assaulting a constable in the execution of his duty under s.89 of the Police Act 1996 following a night out on the town. It is alleged that PC Short was attempting to arrest Alfie's friend, Frank, for urinating in the street when Alfie tried to stop him from carrying out the arrest by pushing PC Short, spitting in his face and calling him a 'pig'.

Alfie has been charged with the summary offence of assaulting a police officer in the execution of his duty contrary to s.89 of the Police Act 1996

Alfie has decided to plead guilty to the offence of assaulting a police officer in the execution of his duty. Alfie admits that he pushed PC Short and called him a pig, but the prosecution are also alleging that Alfie spat in the officer's face. Alfie denies this element of the facts. The issue as to whether Alfie spat in the police officer's face or not will have an effect on the sentence that he receives following his guilty plea (as it severely aggravates the offence), therefore this is an issue that needs to be decided. To determine that facts that he should be sentenced upon the court are required to hold what is know as a *Newton* hearing, following the principles set out by Lord Lane C.J. in case of *Newton* (1983) 77 Cr. App. R. 13.

A *Newton* hearing involves the judge or magistrates listening to the evidence called by either side and then making a decision as to the facts upon this evidence. This may involve calling witnesses for either side, such as other police officers or other people present at the scene of the incident. The prosecution are required to prove their version of the events beyond reasonable doubt and any element of doubt will be afforded to the defendant (unless the defendant's version is completely implausible *R. v Hawkins* (1985) 7 Cr. App. R. (S) 351). *Newton* hearings are not just confined to summary offences and may be used in relation to both either-way and indictable offences. They are an important part of the judicial process in ensuring that justice is administered effectively and that the sentence imposed is representative and relative to the crime that has been committed.

10.2.5   Equivocal pleas

A guilty plea by a defendant must be unequivocal for it to be accepted by the court. This means that it cannot be ambiguous, in that it raises a possible defence, such as self-defence or provocation, or that the defendant does not understand the charges or case against him. A few examples of what could be classed as an equivocal plea are:

- "Yeah, I'm guilty, I punched her three times in the face, but it was only 'cos she wouldn't leave me alone. I'd told her to get off but she wouldn't, she just kept coming back at me again and again". (Possible defence of self-defence)

- "I plead guilty to the murder of my daughter. I wasn't thinking straight at the time because I had post-natal depression and I thought social services were coming to get her, I really thought she was better off dead than in care. Now I've recovered from this illness and I realise what I did was wrong so, yes, I'm guilty". (Possible defence of diminished responsibility)

- "I admit that I went into the house and stole old Mrs Brown's savings from her teapot in the kitchen but I wouldn't have normally done something like this, I'm not a bad person really, it's just because they said they'd kill my little brother if I didn't". (Possible defence of duress)

If a plea is equivocal then the judge in the case is duty bound to raise the issue of what may be a potential defence and request the case to be adjourned so discussions can take place with the defendant and so that a new plea of not guilty can be entered into the court. If it becomes apparent that the defendant does not understand what they are pleading guilty to then the court must also enter a not guilty plea on their behalf.

   If the defendant refuses to enter any plea at all then, under s.6 of the Criminal Law Act 1967 (CLA 1967) the court must enter a plea of not guilty on the defendant's behalf. This was the situation that arose in the 2006 trial of Saddam Hussein for crimes against humanity, genocide and war crimes. Saddam Hussein challenged the legitimacy of the court that was trying him and refused to enter a plea to the charges against him, as a result the court were obliged to enter a plea of not guilty on his behalf. Even though this was at international level the principle was still exactly the same. If a person does not unequivocally plead guilty then they are entitled to have the case against them proved to the requisite standard of proof.

10.2.6   Not guilty

If a defendant pleads not guilty to the charges brought against them then the case will proceed to trial. This means that the prosecution are required to prove the case (meaning each element of the actus reus and mens rea) to the requisite criminal standard as well as disproving any defence that they may raise (also to the same standard). In a criminal trial the required standard is that the prosecution must prove the case against the defendant beyond reasonable doubt.

Figure 10.2 Pleas

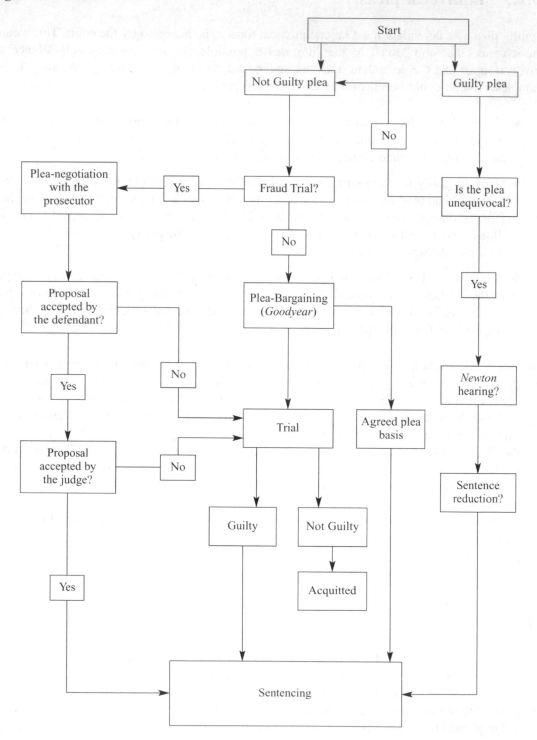

10.3 Course of trial

10.3.1 Burden of proof

One of the most fundamental principles of the English law is that a defendant is innocent until proven guilty. This is known as the 'presumption of innocence' and it is defined within art.6 of the European Convention of Human Rights and Fundamental Freedoms (ECHR), art.6 states that:

(1) In the determination of his civil rights and obligations or of any criminal charge against him, everyone is entitled to a fair and public hearing within a reasonable time by an independent and impartial tribunal established by law. Judgement shall be pronounced publicly by the press and public may be excluded from all or part of the trial in the interest of morals, public order or national security in a democratic society, where the interests of juveniles or the protection of the private life of the parties so require, or the extent strictly necessary in the opinion of the court in special circumstances where publicity would prejudice the interests of justice.

(2) Everyone charged with a criminal offence shall be presumed innocent until proved guilty according to law.

(3) Everyone charged with a criminal offence has the following minimum rights:

(a) to be informed promptly, in a language which he understands and in detail, of the nature and cause of the accusation against him;
(b) to have adequate time and the facilities for the preparation of his defence;
(c) to defend himself in person or through legal assistance of his own choosing or, if he has not sufficient means to pay for legal assistance, to be given it free when the interests of justice so require;
(d) to examine or have examined witnesses against him and to obtain the attendance and examination of witnesses on his behalf under the same conditions as witnesses against him;
(e) to have the free assistance of an interpreter if he cannot understand or speak the language used in court.

It is at art.6(2) that the presumption of innocence is set out. What this means is that no defendant in a criminal case will be viewed as being guilty of the offence charged until this fact has been determined by a court of law. This overall burden of proof in a criminal case rests with the prosecution and the prosecution must prove that a defendant is guilty of the offence; as the Latin maxim states '*necessitas probandi incumbit ei qui agit*', which when translated, means 'the necessity of proof lies with he who complains'. Lord Sankey V.C. confirmed the existence of the doctrine of the presumption of innocence at common law, in the case of *Woolmington v DPP* [1935] A.C. 462, where he famously stated:

Throughout the web of the English criminal law one golden thread is always to be seen, that it is the duty of the prosecution to prove the prisoner's guilt subject to what I have already said as to the defence of insanity and subject also to any statutory exception. If, at the end of and on the whole of the case, there is a reasonable doubt, created by the evidence given by either the prosecution or the prisoner, as to whether the prisoner [committed the offence], the prosecution has not made out the case and the prisoner is entitled to an acquittal. No matter what the charge or where the trial, the principle that the prosecution must prove the guilt of the prisoner is part of the common law of England and no attempt to whittle it down can be entertained.

The standard of proof required to be evidenced by the prosecution in a criminal case is that the defendant is guilty 'beyond reasonable doubt'. What this means is that the prosecution must prove their case so that the jury is 'sure' that the defendant committed the offence alleged. Any element of doubt in the minds of the triers of fact must be afforded to the defendant. The Judicial Studies Board provides the judiciary with specimen directions for directing the jury, and the specimen direction in relation to the burden of proof reads as follows:

How does the prosecution succeed in proving the defendant's guilt? The answer is—by making you sure of it. Nothing less than that will do. If after considering all the evidence you are sure that the defendant is guilty, you must return a verdict of 'Guilty'. If you are not sure, your verdict must be 'Not Guilty'.

If the defendant is relying on a specific statutory defence or the common law defence of insanity then they will hold the burden of proof in respect of the one issue (the prosecution will still retain the burden to prove the case overall against the defendant). Where a defendant does bear the burden of proof in relation to a specific issue then the standard required to be shown by him is 'on the balance of probabilities'; what this means is that the defendant must show that it is more likely that what he is alleging is true as opposed to what the prosecution are alleging. Quite often this lower standard of proof is quantified into a numerical form and is set out at 'greater than 50%' (there is no equivalent way to quantify 'beyond reasonable doubt'). In all civil matters the standard of proof is at this lower level of 'on the balance of probabilities'.

The rationale for the burden of proof, for it being placed upon the prosecution and set at such a high standard, is reasoned by Paul Roberts in his article 'Taking the burden of proof seriously' [1995] Crim. L.R. Oct, 783–798, where he states:

The burden of proof checks and constrains the power of the state to intervene in the lives of individuals and their families in the far-reaching and sometimes catastrophic ways sanctioned by the machinery of criminal justice.

The reason that the overall burden of proof is placed upon the prosecution and not the defence really comes down to the issue of fairness. In many cases the defendant's liberty is at stake and it would be unjust to require the defendant to prove that he was innocent of the offence, especially when the prosecution have infinite resources available to them to prove a person's guilt, whereas the defendant has very limited resources available to him to prove his innocence, and the resources he does has access to will undoubtedly be controlled by his finances.

10.3.2   The criminal trial process

The majority of criminal trials will be held in open court, this means that persons who are not directly involved with the case, i.e. members of the public, can enter the court at any time and watch the proceedings. Actually going along to the court for a morning and watching part of a criminal case is excellent experience and is well worth considering, as some of the cases are fascinating (be warned some proceedings can be just the opposite and be extremely boring), and the knowledge that can be gained by watching the experts at work is often invaluable. Sometimes the courtroom will be closed to the public and the hearing will be *in camera*, this means that the proceedings are private and that only those with a direct interest in the case will be permitted to be present in court. Hearings are normally *in camera* in family proceedings (for obvious reasons), in the Youth Court, and an adult criminal case will occasionally be heard *in camera* where there is sensitive material being heard.

10.3.3   The prosecution case

The prosecution will always open the case as they are the ones who are bringing the proceedings against the defendant and therefore they must show that there is a case for the defendant to answer. The prosecution will normally begin their case with an 'opening speech'; this is a speech setting out the allegations against the defendant, and it will provide a summary of the evidence that the prosecution intend to call, the details of the relevant law they are relying upon (although they should qualify this with an acknowledgement that the judge in the case will direct them further on the law), and a brief conclusion of what they will (hopefully) have proven by the end of their case. The prosecution will then call their first witness.

Witness examination will occur in the following order:

Figure 10.3 The order of witness examination

Examination-in-chief	Prosecution
Cross-examination	Defence
Re-examination	Prosecution

The prosecution will normally call their main witness first. They will ask them a number of questions by way of examination-in-chief, so as to elicit their version of events from them. There are rules and regulations regarding the types of questions that a party can ask of their own witness. When a party is conducting examination-in-chief it means that they can only ask their witness non-leading questions; questions which do not put words into the mouth of the witness, but are intended to enable the witness to tell their story in their own words. Examples of non-leading questions are:

"Tell me where you were on the night in question."

"What did you see?"

"What happened next?"

The whole purpose of non-leading questions is for the witness to say what they actually witnessed. The party calling them will lead them through their evidence, often stopping and asking them to expand points, if counsel feels that something has been missed or has not been given enough attention. If however, the witness fails to mention crucial evidence and does not 'come up to proof' then there is little that the party can do to remedy the situation in those circumstances. Even if the witness provided damning evidence in their police statement, if they do not repeat it in court it will not become part of the evidence in the case.

Once the prosecution have finished their examination-in-chief then the defence are provided the opportunity to question the witness. The style of questioning employed by the defence here will be entirely different to that of the prosecution. In questioning the other side's witness the defence can use a method of questioning known as 'cross-examination'. Cross-examination involves counsel challenging the witness' testimony and putting the defence case to them. Examples of questions used within cross-examination are:

"Do you like a drink Mrs X? Did you have a couple too many on the night in question? Isn't it really the case that you were upstairs throwing up in the bathroom at the time of the alleged offence and that you never saw what really happened?"

"How good is your eyesight? Do you wear glasses? Isn't it entirely possible that you are mistaken in your identification of the defendant due to your poor eyesight?"

"I put it to you that you are lying and that you never saw the defendant at the time that you say you did."

Cross-examining a witness, as can be seen by the examples given above, is not really about allowing the witness to tell the court what happened (they have already done this under examination-in-chief), but it is rather about picking holes in the testimony of the witness and trying to find the weak points so that their credibility is lowered (or even destroyed) in the eyes of the triers of fact.

Once the defence has cross-examined the witness they may then be re-examined by the prosecution so that the prosecution can effectively undertake a method of damage limitation; clarifying the points that came out during cross-examination and getting the witness to expand further on any new information that has come to light. The prosecution are not obliged to re-examine a witness, and they maybe of the opinion, when taking all things into consideration, that there is either no need to re-examine the witness, or that re-examination will only compound an already bad situation. At the conclusion of the witness' evidence the judge or magistrates may wish to ask them a number of further questions, possibly in an effort to seek further clarification on a matter, and occasionally a jury may wish to ask a question. When the jury do ask a question they do not do so orally but rather hand a note to the judge (by way of the court clerk) that sets out their question. The judge will then consider whether the question is allowable, and if so they will ask the witness the question on behalf of the jury. This sequence of events will then be repeated for all of the prosecution witnesses.

After the prosecution have set out their case and have presented all their evidence the trial then arrives at a point informally known as 'half time', or more formally as the 'close of the case for the prosecution'. It is at this point that the defence has the opportunity to make a submission to the court that the prosecution have not established a prima facie (or on the face of it) case against the defendant. This submission is called a 'submission of no case to answer' and it is a request to the judge that the case be stopped at this point and the defendant be acquitted as, if the prosecution have not established a case against the defendant, then they have no need to defend themselves. The test that the court must consider when deliberating on a submission of no case to answer is contained in the case of *R. v Galbraith* [1981] 1 W.L.R. 1039 and can be found p.1042 where Lord Lane C.J. stated:

> How then should the judge approach a submission of 'no case'?
>
> (1) If there is no evidence that the crime alleged has been committed by the defendant, there is no difficulty. The judge will of course stop the case.
> (2) The difficulty arises where there is some evidence but it is of a tenuous character, for example because of inherent weakness or vagueness or because it is inconsistent with other evidence. Where the judge comes to the conclusion that the prosecution evidence, taken at its highest, is such that a jury properly directed could not properly convict upon it, it is his duty, upon a submission being made, to stop the case.

A submission for no case to answer must be made in the absence of any jury in the case, because if they were aware of it and the submission was not accepted then they may become prejudiced by the knowledge of such a submission and consequently they may then find it difficult to place the correct amount of weight on the prosecution evidence. If the court accepts the submission then that is the end of the case and the defendant will be formally acquitted of the charges made against him. If the submission is not accepted then the case will move onto the second half where the defence then presents their case.

The first point to mention in relation to the presentation of the defence case is that the defendant does not have to give evidence if he does not want to. All persons are deemed as being competent to give evidence in criminal proceedings (s.53(1) Youth Justice and Criminal Evidence Act 1999 (YJCEA 1999) but a defendant cannot be compelled (forced) to give evidence as s.1(1) of the Criminal Evidence Act 1898 states:

> A person charged in criminal proceedings shall not be called as a witness in the proceedings except upon his own application.

This means that if the defendant wishes to sit in the dock and simply watch and listen to the proceedings he is completely entitled to do so. There may be a variety of reasons why the defendant does not wish to give evidence, however the main one is that once he is in the witness stand he will not only give his side of the story, but he will also be cross-examined by the prosecution. This is something that the defendant may wish to avoid as cross-examination could potentially result in him further incriminating himself, or if he has numerous previous convictions then, by putting himself on the stand these convictions may become admissible in court; both of which could have disastrous consequences for his case. However if the defendant decides to omit to give evidence then this can also have a negative effect on his case as, under s.35 of the Criminal Justice and Public Order Act 1994 (CJPOA 1994), the court or the jury in determining the defendant's guilt, may draw adverse inferences from his failure to testify. The defendant must be warned that such inferences may be drawn if he refuses to give evidence or answer any questions asked of him.

If the defendant does decide to give evidence then, under s.79 of the Police and Criminal Evidence Act 1984 (PACE 1984), he should give evidence before any other defence witness as s.79 provides:

> If at the trial of any person for an offence—
>
> (a) the defence intends to call two or more witnesses to the facts of the case; and
> (b) those witnesses include the accused,
>
> the accused shall be called before the other witness or witnesses unless the court in its discretion otherwise directs.

The rationale behind this provision is so as to prevent the defendant tailoring their evidence to that of the other defence witnesses. By giving his evidence first it is believed that the defendant will be as truthful in his evidence as he can and he will not amend his evidence to fit in with the other witnesses in the case.

The questioning of the defence witnesses will take the same format and style as that of the prosecution witnesses but simply in reverse, so counsel for the defence will undertake the examination-in-chief and the prosecution will conduct the cross-examination. After all the defence witnesses have been called both sides, the prosecution and the defence, will deliver their closing speeches to the jury. The prosecution will go first, summing up their evidence and setting out their case; the defence are then afforded the last word on the matter, this is again a summary of the evidence but with the edge of an emotive speech as to the defendant's innocence.

Finally the judge will sum up the evidence and provide guidance and direction on the law to the jury (guidance on the law is provided by the legal adviser in the magistrates' court (see 5.8)). The judge's role in the case is an objective one, he must not give extra weight to either side's case, but he can comment on the credibility of the evidence where he feels it is appropriate to do so. The judge's role is to guide the jury through the minefield that is the criminal law and to direct them so that they can make sense of the law and relate it to the case that they are trying. Once the judge has summed up the evidence the jury are then required to retire and consider the evidence in detail before returning their verdict on the case (for further discussion on juries and jury deliberation see Chapter 7).

Figure 10.4 Pre-trial process

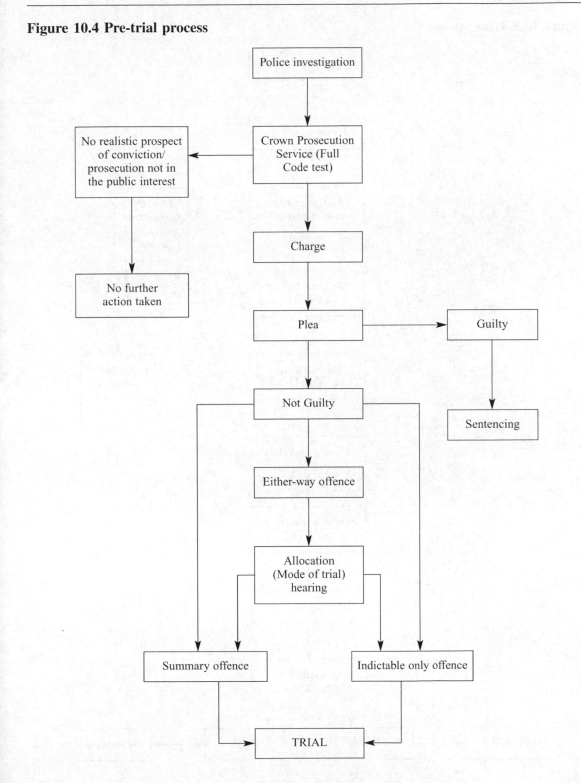

Figure 10.5 Trial process

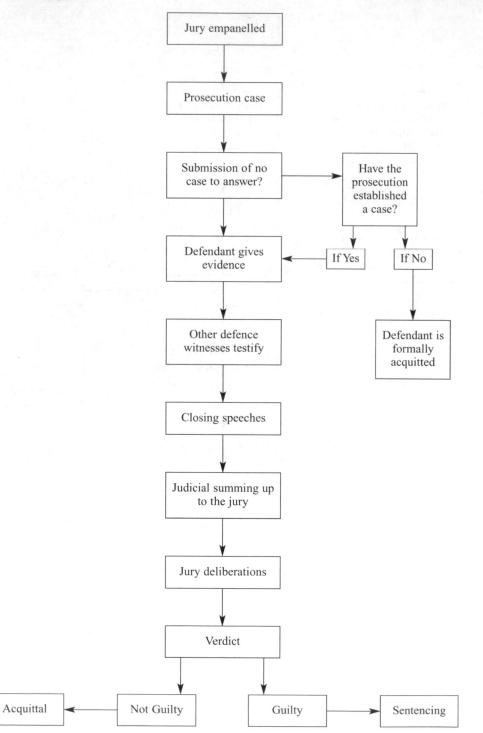

10.4 Summary

(a) An either-way offence is a hybrid of a summary offence and an indictable only offence. It can be tried either summarily or upon indictment. Common either-way offences are assault occasioning actual bodily harm under s.47 OAPA 1861 and theft under the Theft Act 1968.

(b) To determine the appropriate venue for an either-way offence the magistrates' court will hold an allocation hearing (otherwise known as a Mode of Trial hearing). If they have sufficient powers to sentence the defendant then they may decide that they can hear the case, if they do not have sufficient sentencing powers then they will send the case to the Crown for trial. The magistrates will refer to the National Mode of Trial Guidelines 2004 for guidance.

(c) If the magistrates' court feel that they can keep jurisdiction of the case then the defendant must agree to this. Otherwise they can elect for their case to be heard in the Crown Court before a judge and a jury.

(d) If the offence involved over £5,000 of criminal damage, or the defendant is a persistent burglar then the case will be sent directly to the Crown Court.

(e) If the magistrates hear the case but decide upon hearing the facts that their sentencing powers are insufficient then they can commit the defendant to the Crown Court for sentence.

(f) A defendant can either plead guilty or not guilty to charges alleged against them. If they plead guilty then the plea must be unequivocal, if the plea is determined as equivocal then a not guilty plea will be entered into court on the defendant's behalf.

(g) If a defendant considers pleading guilty to an offence then they are permitted to ask the judge to indicate the maximum sentence they would be minded to impose at that time. The defendant must request such an indication voluntarily so as to avoid any improper pressure being imposed upon them.

(h) Where the defendant pleads guilty to an offence but the facts of the case are not agreed between the prosecution and the defence the court can order a *Newton* hearing to determine the facts upon which to sentence.

(i) In a criminal case the defendant is afforded a presumption of innocence (art.6 ECHR) in that the prosecution must prove the defendant's guilt as opposed to the defendant having to prove their innocence.

(j) The standard of proof in a criminal trial is 'beyond reasonable doubt', unless it is placed on the defendant in relation to specific issue (insanity or a statutory defence), in which case it is then 'on the balance of probabilities'.

(k) The prosecution open the case and call their witnesses first. They must succeed in establishing a prima facie case against the defendant. At the close of the prosecution case the defence can make a 'submission of no case to answer', which, if accepted by the judge, will mean that the defendant is formally acquitted of all charges.

(l) The defence will then present their case. If the defendant is to be called as a witness they will be called before any other defence witness. The defendant does not have to give evidence but if they do not adverse inference may be drawn from their silence.

(m) After the defence case both sides will present a closing speech for the jury, with the defence being afforded the final word. The judge will then sum up the evidence for the jury and direct them on the law before they retire to consider their verdict.

10.5   Self-test questions

1. A defendant who has pleaded not guilty to an either-way offence:

   (a) always has the choice to elect a jury trial
   (b) never has the choice to elect a jury trial
   (c) has the choice to elect a jury trial if the magistrates deem the case suitable to be heard in the magistrates' court
   (d) has the right to refuse jury trial if the magistrates decide to send the case to the Crown Court

2. If a defendant pleads guilty to an offence they:

   (a) always receive a full sentence discount
   (b) never receive any sentence discount
   (c) will be able to choose their sentence discount
   (d) may receive a sentence discount that is commensurate with the timeliness of the plea

3. A *Newton* hearing is used to determine:

   (a) the guilt of the defendant
   (b) the facts that the defendant will be sentenced upon
   (c) the defendant's sentence
   (d) the facts of the case

4. An equivocal plea is where the defendant:

   (a) provides an ambiguous guilty plea
   (b) provides an ambiguous not guilty plea
   (c) provides an unambiguous guilty plea
   (d) provides an unambiguous not guilty plea

5. In a criminal trial the overall burden of proof is:

    (a) on the defendant to prove their innocence beyond reasonable doubt

    (b) on the defendant to prove their innocence on the balance of probabilities

    (c) on the prosecution to prove the defendant's guilt beyond reasonable doubt

    (d) on the prosecution to prove the defendant's guilt on the balance of probabilities

10.6 Further reading

A. Ashworth and M. Blake, "The presumption of innocence in English criminal law" [1996] Crim. L.R. 306.

European Commission Green Paper on the Presumption of Innocence: *http://eur-lex.europa.eu/ LexUriServ/LexUriServ.do?uri=CELEX:52006DC0174:EN:NO*.

P. Farmer, "Procedure: pleading guilty but disputing the facts" [2004] 8(8) M.C.P. 19–20.

P.R. Farmer, "Practice and procedure: discretion to change election for summary trial" [2003] 7(7) M.C.P. 15–16.

A. Herbert, "Mode of trial and magistrates' sentencing powers: will increased powers inevitably lead to a reduction in the committal rate?" [2003] Crim. L.R. May, 314–325.

J. Morton, "If I ran the criminal justice system" [2006] 70(2) J. Crim. L. 93–96.

J. Morton, "Pleas please me" [2005] 69(4) J. Crim. L. 277–279.

J. Phillips, "Reducing delay in the criminal courts of England and Wales" [2007] Com. Jud. J. 17(2) 20–25.

R. Powell, "It"s easy to plead guilty . . . " [2004] 8(7) M.C.P. 14–17.

P. Roberts, "Taking the burden of proof seriously" [1995] Crim. L.R. 783.

J. Spencer, "The danger of convicting the innocent" [2004] N.L.J. (September 17, 2004).

K. Spencer, "A Good year for auld habits—formalising the practices of plea-bargaining" [2007] 11(5) Bar Review 175–178.

V. Tadros and S. Tierney, "The presumption of innocence and the Human Rights Act" [2004] 67(3) M.L.R. 402.

P.W. Tague, "Tactical reasons for recommending trials rather than guilty pleas in Crown Court" [2006] Crim. L.R. Jan. 23–37.

D.A. Thomas, "Sentencing: advance indication of sentence—new procedure" [2005] Crim. L.R. Aug. 659–664.

M. Zander, "Please m'lud, how long will I get?" [2005] 155(7175) N.L.J. 677.

M. Zander "Why oh why do magistrates commit so many cases to the Crown Court?" [2003] 153(7079) N.L.J. 689.

11 Funding

The funding of legal services has been in an almost constant state of flux for the past 60 years. Just as everyone must abide by the laws of the land there is the ideal that everyone should also be able to access the justice system when they need to do so. In fact access to legal justice is a fundamental human right under art.6 of the ECHR (the right to a fair trial). However access to legal services can be a costly affair, as all of those involved in the case (the solicitors, the barristers, the administrative staff, the judges and the court, to name but a few) must be paid for their services and therefore the cost implications of a case can be quite large. The Woolf Report (*Access to Justice* (1995)) identified that the average cost for litigation involving a medical negligence claim was £38,252 and for an average personal injury claim costs could mount to £20,413. This chapter will not consider the issues of funding in minute detail, as an entire book could be written on this subject alone, but it will consider the development of the funding system for legal services within England and Wales, the main issues that have arisen in respect of it and it will set out the state of the funding system at present.

11.1 The unmet legal need

The legal system of England and Wales prides itself on that the fact that it provides access to justice for all. However just as everyone has the right to buy an expensive racing car or go on a round the world trip does not mean that everyone is actually able to treat themselves to these items, the same can be said in respect of the equality of access to justice. Not every person that requires legal services is able to access them and this sector of society has become known as the unmet legal need.

There may be many reasons behind why an individual who needs to access the legal system is not able to do so. Research commissioned by the Legal Services Commission and undertaken by Pascoe Pleasence (*Causes of Action: Civil Law and Social Justice*, Second Edition, LSRC Research Paper No.14 (2006)) identified a number of the reasons as to why this unmet legal need exists. The main findings of the research were that:

- People thought that nothing could be done to resolve the situation and therefore did not attempt to access legal services.

- People thought that taking action would make no difference to the situation, often due to lack of knowledge as to the help, advice and potential remedies available.

- People thought that for a variety of reasons there was no need to take any action; such as no wrong had been committed or that the wrong was not that serious and did not warrant any legal action being brought.

- There was uncertainty as to individuals' rights. Due to a lack of knowledge and education potential claimants were not aware of what they were entitled to bring an action for.

- There was uncertainty as to where to get help. Even though many people lived within a few miles of legal representation (solicitors or Citizen's Advice Bureaus etc.) they did not know where to begin looking so as to access such advice.

- Concerns were present as to the psychological, economic or social consequences of resolving the situation.

- Concerns as to the potential cost of any action were apparent. There is a general view that all litigation is very expensive and therefore out of the normal person's reach

- A number of people were scared to take any action. Either due to the potential repercussions of commencing legal proceedings from other individuals or due to the fact that many people viewed the legal profession as personally unapproachable.

11.2 Public funding

Prior to 1949 there was virtually no public funding for people who were involved in or wished to bring litigation. If a person wanted to bring a claim then they had to find the money themselves to pay for its costs and only limited representation was provided for those charged with a criminal offence under the Poor Prisoners Defence Acts 1903–1930. This was obviously an unsatisfactory state of affairs as many people were denied justice purely due to the fact that they were not rich enough to undertake litigation. In 1945 a government review undertaken by the Rushcliffe Committee was the catalyst that began to change and shape the public funding of legal services as the concept of the Welfare State in general was introduced (access to medical services and educational facilities for all etc.) and this was to also encompass the introduction of public funding for legal services. The Rushcliffe Report recommended that the funding system (or its non-existence) for legal expenses needed a radical overhaul and that access to justice was just as important as access to medical services etc. The Report recommended that:

- Legal aid be made available in all courts.

- Legal aid should not just be limited to the poor but should also be available to those of more moderate means.

- The level of legal aid available to an individual should be assessed by way of a means test.

- A merits test should also be employed to assess the appropriateness of the litigation and funding.

- The legal aid costs should be borne by the state but administered by the legal profession.

- All lawyers providing legal aid services should be adequately rewarded for their services.

The essence of the Rushcliffe Report was that public funding for legal services should be 'demand led and never cash limited'. The government broadly accepted these proposals and in 1949 under the Legal Aid and Advice Act the first legal aid services were established. Legal aid as a concept quickly became an entrenched and fundamental right within the justice system and by the 1980s the system had developed into six clearly defined limbs under the enactment of the Legal Aid Act 1988 (this Act also established the Legal Aid Board who were charged with managing the scheme and maintaining a legal aid fund). The distinct limbs of the legal aid system were:

Legal advice and assistance scheme—This form of legal aid was otherwise known as the 'Green form' scheme and was applicable to both criminal and civil matters alike. A person entitled to aid under this scheme would receive up to two hours worth of work and this work could involve the provision of advice and the drafting of documents, but it did not cover representation at court.

Assistance by way of representation—This limb of the legal aid provided cover for the conduct of and representation in proceedings in either the courts or the tribunal system. It was essentially an extension of the legal advice and assistance scheme but its application was limited in its use (it could not be used in defamation cases) and eligibility was subject to a means test.

Civil legal aid—This scheme allowed the cost of legal advice and representation in court to be covered regardless of whether the individual in question was defending or bringing the claim. Eligibility for this limb of the legal aid scheme was subject to means testing.

Criminal legal aid—Again this covered the cost of legal advice and representation in court and was subject to a means test.

Duty solicitor scheme (police stations)—This scheme provided free access to legal representation for anyone detained by the police regardless of whether they had been arrested or not. Solicitors worked on a rota so that access to a solicitor would always be available. The provisions of these services were not subject to any form of means or merit testing and were essentially free for all. This scheme is still available under the new public funding scheme (discussed below).

Duty solicitor scheme (magistrates' courts)—Similar to the police station duty solicitor scheme above, solicitors were available at the magistrates' court to provide legal services to any unrepresented defendants. Again there were no means or merit testing for the provision of these services and the scheme is still available under the new public funding scheme.

Figure 11.1 The six limbs of legal aid

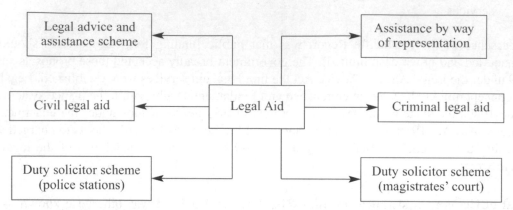

The legal aid scheme worked extremely well for a considerable length of time but as litigation became more common and the crime rates began to increase the strain placed upon the legal aid system began to become untenable. The government attempted to stem the amount of money that was being ploughed into the legal aid system as, despite the fact that each individual scheme had its own terms and conditions of eligibility, the annual legal aid bill was still mounting up into millions of pounds (in 1997 the legal aid bill totalled £1,477 million). The government introduced severe cuts into the funding available and tightened up the eligibility criteria but these moves provoked widespread criticism that the government was reducing the equality of access to justice as only those who were very poor or very rich were able to access the justice system. In 1997 Sir Peter Middleton, on the invitation of the Lord Chancellor, undertook a review of the system in his report *Review of Civil Justice and Legal Aid: A report to the Lord Chancellor* (1997). The report considered the state of the legal aid system as it was then and made recommendations as to how it should be reformed. The three main problems identified by the review were:

- the rapidly growing costs of the scheme and the lack of satisfactory mechanisms for controlling that growth

- the inability to target resources on priority areas and thereby address areas of unmet need within existing resources and

- poor value for money

The main principles proposed by the review were that

Legal aid should be the servant of civil justice, not its master. In particular, legal aid should work with the grain of the justice system and be organised in a way that reinforces its objectives. It should contribute to ensuring that disputes are settled in the best forum, and to the efficiency with which they are handled [. . .] It is reasonable and legitimate for the Government to reach a decision on how much legal aid the country can afford, and to put a legal aid system in place which enables it to adhere to that decision. The issue is not whether to limit expenditure, but how to devise a legal aid scheme under which decisions about resources, priorities and targeting are taken in a transparent and accountable way.

Essentially the report recommended a change to the underlying philosophical theory that underpinned the whole legal aid system. The proposed change involved a move away from a demand-led system and the establishment of a finite funding service that was more cash limited. Following the publication of the Middleton Report the government then drafted the White Paper, *Modernising Justice*, Cm.4155 (1998), which largely embraced the reforms suggested by the earlier report and the end result was the enactment of the Access to Justice Act 1999 (AJA 1999).

11.2.1 Access to Justice Act 1999

The introduction of the AJA 1999 had the effect of a radical overhaul of the legal aid system. Under s.1(1) the Legal Services Commission (LSC) was established and the old Legal Aid Board abolished. The LSC is now charged with the responsibility of administering the legal aid system in England and Wales and it currently has a budget of £2 billion to do so. The LSC governs the legal aid by the provision of two separate schemes:

- **Community Legal Services (CLS)**—this provides advice and legal representation for people involved in civil cases.

- **Criminal Defence Service (CDS)**—this provides advice and legal representation for people facing criminal charges.

Under the old legal aid scheme legal representatives would simply make an application to the Legal Aid Board for funding on an individual client basis. The LSC has replaced this system and now if a defendant or litigant in a matter wishes to receive public funding then they must approach a firm of solicitors who hold a contract (is franchised) with the LSC for the provision of civil or criminal work.

11.2.1.1 Community Legal Services

The CLS is a network of LSC-funded advice providers who have the aim of helping people to protect their civil rights. It was set up under s.1(2)(a) of the AJA 1999 and its statutory responsibility under s.4(1) is to promote the availability of a range of services and to secure access to those services so as to effectively meet individual needs. Section 4(2) sets out the services it offers as including:

(a) the provision of general information about the law and legal system and the availability of legal services,

(b) the provision of help by the giving of advice as to how the law applies in particular circumstances,

(c) the provision of help in preventing, or settling or otherwise resolving, disputes about legal rights and duties,

(d) the provision of help in enforcing decisions by which such disputes are resolved, and

(e) the provision of help in relation to legal proceedings not relating to disputes.

The CLS can be used to fund:

- initial advice and assistance with any legal problem (the old green form scheme)
- a solicitor who can speak on someone's behalf at court hearings without formally representing them
- help and advice on family disputes, including assistance with family mediation
- legal representation in court proceedings

As there is only a limited annual fund for the provision of such services only certain types of work can receive CLS funding and to ensure that appropriate cases received this funding the Lord Chancellor directed that the LSC should give top priority to child protection cases and cases where the client is at real and immediate risk of loss of life or liberty. After that cases involving social welfare issues, domestic violence proceedings, other child welfare matters and proceedings against public authorities alleging serious wrongdoing, abuse of position or power or significant breach of human rights should then take priority over all other cases. A number of different types of causes of action have been excluded completely from CLS funding and these are listed in Sch.2 of the 1999 Act. The Schedule lists cases involving conveyancing issues, boundary disputes, the making of wills, matters of trust law, defamation or malicious falsehood, matters of company or partnership law, and other matters arising out of the carrying on of a business as being prohibited from receipt of public funding.

So as to enable effective liaison between the organisations offering legal help and advice services under the CLS (such as local councils, Citizen Advice Bureaus, law centres and other not for profit advice organisations) the Commission has set up the Community Legal Services Partnerships so that the organisations have a forum in which to communicate and discuss issues relating to local funding matters.

An individual will be eligible to receive CLS funding if they pass both of the means and merits tests employed to determine eligibility. To be eligible in respect of the means test an individual's gross monthly income cannot exceed £2,530, and they must not have more than £8,000 in savings. These figures are reviewed on a yearly basis and are often increased in line with the cost of inflation etc. The merits test makes an assessment as to the merits of the individual case and to do this factors such as the likely prospect of success, the potential benefit to the client and the likely cost to the CLS will be considered along with the possibility as to whether the litigation could be funded by any other method.

11.2.1.2 Criminal Defence Service

The funding of criminal cases has recently undergone a great deal of change in the past year or so and it has been the focus of considerable controversy and debate, both in the media and the professional legal world. Most defendants who appear before the criminal courts are of limited means and therefore unlikely to be able to pay for their criminal defence privately. To ensure that such a defendant receives a fair trial (as required under art.6(3) ECHR) the State will, in most circumstances, provide the defendant with publicly funded access to legal representation. The funding received by the defendant is commonly known as a Representation Order and the funding is provided by the Criminal Defence Service (CDS), as set up under s.12 of the AJA 199 and governed by the LSC.

The Criminal Defence Service Act 2006 has introduced a number of changes in respect of the way that cases are funded and currently a defendant's eligibility to receive public funding is determined on the court in which he is to be tried in. If the defendant is to be tried in the magistrates' court then they will undergo a two-stage test to decide whether they are eligible for a representation order. The first part of the test is a means test, and the second part a merits test. However if the defendant is to be tried on indictment in the Crown Court then he will only have to satisfy the merits test. If the defendant is successful in his application for a representation order then the order will cover all of the proceedings, from the preparation for trial to the end of the appeal process.

A means test is used to assess whether the defendant has the means to pay for his defence privately or if he can be granted a representation order. The means test is comprised of two elements:

- an initial assessment

- a full means test

The initial assessment will consider the defendant's weighted gross annual income and is undertaken to determine whether the defendant is either automatically eligible or ineligible for public funding, or to determine whether a full means test will be required. If the defendant's gross annual income is below £12,007 then they will automatically qualify for a representation order; if their gross annual income is above £21,487 then the defendant fails the means test and will be required to fund the proceedings privately. If the defendant's income falls in between these two figures then a full means test will be required to decide upon their eligibility. The defendant's income from all sources (minus state benefits) will be taken into account in this initial assessment and this may then be weighted by taking into account their partner's income if they have one (unless there is a contrary interest to this such as the partner is the victim, prosecution witness or a joint defendant) and any dependent children they happen to have.

The full means test will calculate the defendant's disposable income and will take into account the defendant's housing costs, maintenance payments, child care fees, income tax and national insurance contributions, as well as their annual living allowance. If after calculating all of above the defendant is shown to have a disposable income exceeding £3,270 then they will be deemed as ineligible for public funding.

Even if the defendant passes the means test this does not automatically mean that he will secure a representation order, as he will still be required to satisfy the merits test. If the defendant has satisfied the means test in a case being tried summarily, or if the case is to be tried on indictment then they will have to show it is in the interests of justice to grant a representation order.

Schedule 3, para.5 of the Access to Justice Act 1999 (AJA 1999) sets out the circumstances where the merits test will be deemed to have been satisfied. It states that it will be in the interests of justice to grant a representation order where:

- the individual would, if any matter arising in the proceedings is decided against him, be likely to lose his liberty or livelihood or suffer serious damage to his reputation;

- the determination of any matter arising in the proceedings may involve consideration of a substantial question of law;

- the individual may be unable to understand the proceedings or to state his own case;

- the proceedings may involve the tracing, interviewing or expert cross-examination of witnesses on behalf of the individual; and

- it is in the interests of another person that the individual be represented.

This list is not wholly exhaustive and there may be other factors in a case that mean it is in the interests of justice to warrant the issuing of a representation order. If the defendant fails the means test then there is no right to appeal this decision. However, if such a situation were to occur then the defendant could request that a hardship review be undertaken, especially if they have a high level of outgoings not factored into the initial calculations or if the cost of defending the case is likely to be beyond the average level for such a case. If, after initially being refused public funding, a defendant's personal circumstances change then they are entitled to request that their means be re-assessed based on the new circumstances. If the defendant fails the merits test then they are permitted to appeal to the court on this point and request that the decision be reconsidered.

Duty solicitor schemes have remained almost exactly the same as before the reforms and free legal advice (without the need to undergo a means and/or merits test) is still available at police stations and in the magistrates' courts. However since 2005 the CDS has been piloting a new telephone advice service (CDS Direct) for people detained at police stations for less serious offences, such as drink driving offences, non-imprisonable offences, breaches of bail and warrants. The scheme was expanded in February 2008 from only providing advice in duty solicitor matters to then being permitted for solicitors to take on client work and, due to the high success rate on initial evaluation of the scheme, the scheme was rolled out nationally on April 21, 2008. The benefits of CDS Direct are that the speed of providing free advice at police stations has been dramatically increased as instead of having to wait for a couple of hours until a duty solicitor can attend the station the CDS Direct advisers are (in 99 per cent of the cases) able to phone the police station within 30 minutes of receiving the initial call requesting legal advice. As a result there has been a significant reduction in the waiting time for legal advice and the time spent by the client in detention has also been greatly reduced as on the whole matters can be dealt with quickly and efficiently. This has then cumulated in a better use of the taxpayer's money as overall costs have been reduced and consequently the money saved can be directed to the more serious and deserving cases.

Figure 11.2 Public funding

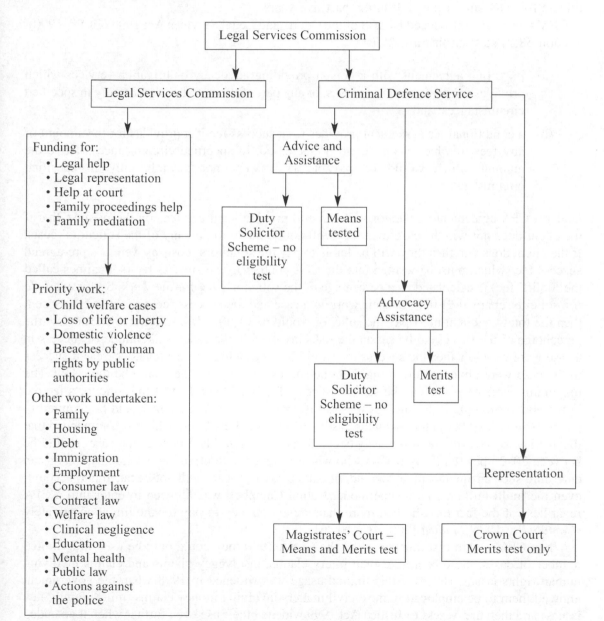

329

11.3 Conditional fee agreements

When an individual wishes to, or needs to bring litigation but they are not eligible for public funding, and nor can they afford to pay the costs privately they may be able to enter into a conditional fee agreement (CFA) with a solicitor so that the legal costs in the case are covered. A CFA is often described as a 'no-win, no-fee' agreement and they have become more popular in recent times due to the frequent daytime TV adverts offering this service to help people litigate for 'any slip, trip or fall in the past five years'.

CFA's were first introduced by s.58 of the Courts and Legal Services Act 1990 (CLSA 1990). Section 58(2) sets out that a CFA is:

(a) [...] an agreement with a person providing advocacy or litigation services which provides for his fees and expenses, or any part of them, to be payable only in specified circumstances; and

(b) a conditional fee agreement provides for a success fee if it provides for the amount of any fees to which it applies to be increased, in specified circumstances, above the amount which would be payable if it were not payable only in specified circumstances.

Under a CFA agreement a solicitor will agree to provide legal services on the premise that if the client does not win the case then they will not be liable to pay any of the solicitors' costs. If the client does win then they will be liable to pay the solicitors' costs as well as a pre-agreed success fee (which must be written into the CFA contract). The success fee (sometimes called the 'uplift' fee) is calculated as a percentage of the solicitor's fee for the work. So for example if a solicitor charged £1,000 for their work in a case and the success fee was set at 50 per cent then the total the client must pay the solicitor would be £1,500. The solicitor will calculate the percentage of the success to be set on the risks involved in the case; if likelihood of success in a case were very low then the success fee would be set as a high percentage, whereas if success in the case were almost a sure thing then the success fee percentage would be quite low. The maximum percentage that can be set as a success fee is 100 per cent of the solicitor's fee (so in the above example if the success fee was 100 per cent then the client would be required to pay the solicitor £2,000 if they won the case), however the Law Society have recommended that the average success fee set (obviously depending on the individual facts of the case) should be between 20–25 per cent. Any person who wishes to undertake litigation covered by CFA's can enter into such an agreement and an individual's personal means will not be taken into account; even the multi-million pound supermodel Naomi Campbell was allowed to enter into a CFA regardless of the fact that she had more than enough money to pay for the litigation privately (*Campbell v MGN Limited* [2005] UKHL 61).

When CFA's were first introduced by the CLSA 1990 they could only be used in a limited number of cases, these being personal injury claims, insolvency claims and claims involving human rights issues. However this limited usage was widened in 1998 when the government allowed them to be employed in most civil matters involving money claims (minus family law issues) and then the Access to Justice Act 1999 widened their use even further when it amended the CLSA 1990 by inserting s.58A into the 1990 Act. Section 58A sets out that CFA's can now be used to fund any legal proceedings except those involving criminal proceedings or family proceedings.

On the face of it CFA's appear to be a very simple and attractive way of solving the funding issue as the individual is not dependent on receipt of public funding so as to gain access the justice system; if they lose they pay nothing and if they win they are only obliged to pay the solicitor a little extra so as to thank them for a case well done. However if the CFA system is investigated a little further then this simplistic view is not such a true representation of it. Issues as to costs arise when a client loses a case. The traditional stance taken by the courts is that the losing party is liable to pay the winning party's costs in the case. Therefore even if the losing party is not liable to pay their own legal costs they will be responsible for paying the other sides legal costs, which could amount to a hefty sum of money. Also when preparing a case a solicitor will often incur extra costs that are outside of their own fees. These are known as disbursements, and a common disbursement that can be incurred in a claim is the preparation of an expert's report. If an expert (say a doctor) is required to write a report on the injuries suffered by the claimant in the case then they will expect to be paid a fair fee for doing so. The solicitor does not factor in such expenses into his own fee agreed with the client and therefore the client is liable to pay this disbursement regardless of whether they win or lose the case. So as to avoid having to pay out personally for all of these extra costs an individual who agrees to fund litigation by way of a CFA should be advised to take out insurance (known as 'after-the-event' insurance) to cover any further expenses incurred. After-the-event insurance is similar to any other insurance premium (car, buildings or contents) and the underwriter of the insurance will assess the risks involved in the claim to determine the premium that is required to be paid. If the insured person is then unsuccessful in their claim the insurance company will then pay for any of the costs that they are liable for.

The further issue that arose in respect of CFA's was that the winning party was still liable to pay the solicitor's success fee and after-the-event insurance premium out of their own money (the solicitors' basic costs being paid by the losing party as per the norm). This seemed to be an unsatisfactory state of affairs, as the winning party would normally have to use part of the damages awarded to them in the case to pay these costs. This was argued to be unjust as the damages awarded were to compensate the party for their losses incurred due to the cause of action and not for funding litigation. This issue was considered by the House of Lords in the case of *Callery v Gray* [2002] UKHL 28.

In *Callery v Gray* the claimant suffered minor injuries in a road traffic accident and, on first instructing solicitors to claim damages from the defendant, entered into a CFA, with an agreed success fee of 60 per cent. Shortly thereafter, and before the defendant's response to the claim was known, the claimant also paid a premium of £350 for after-the-event insurance to cover the risk of any liability for costs he might incur if the claim failed. The claim settled quickly without the issue of proceedings and the defendant agreed to pay the claimant damages and reasonable costs. The district judge ruled that a success fee of 40 per cent was reasonable and could be recovered as part of the claimant's costs and that the cost of the insurance premium was also recoverable. The defendant appealed to the Court of Appeal, which upheld the district judge's decision. The court stated that in modest and straightforward claims following road traffic accidents it would normally be reasonable for a claimant to enter into a conditional fee agreement and take out after-the-event insurance when he first instructed his solicitor and, that where a reasonable premium and a reasonable success fee were agreed each was recoverable from the defendant if the claim succeeded or was settled on terms that the defendant pay the claimant's costs. The court also concluded that the maximum reasonable success fee in such a case was 20 per cent.

On further appeal to the House of Lords the House held, whilst dismissing the appeal, that it was pre-eminently the responsibility of the Court of Appeal, not the House of Lords, to supervise the developing practice of the use of conditional fee agreements and after-the-event insurance, as the House could not respond to changes in practice with the speed and sensitivity of the Court of Appeal, and accordingly it was inappropriate for the House to interfere with the rulings which that court had given in the instant case.

The principle that was developed by this case is that the losing party (or rather their insurance company if they have taken out after-the-event insurance) are liable to pay all reasonable costs incurred by the winning party and that these reasonable costs can include the other side's solicitor fees, any success fee agreed so long as it is of a reasonable amount, and any premium paid out for after-the-event insurance obtained. Considering the potential level of costs that the losing party could be liable for, remembering to take out after-the-event insurance at the earliest point possible seems to be a rather prudent step to take.

The final point to note in relation to CFA's is that they are different to the American system of funding litigation known as a 'contingency fee agreement'. Contingency fee agreement's work on the same basic 'no-win no-fee' premise but with contingency fees, the success fee claimed by the lawyer upon winning the case is based on a percentage of the damages awarded. Contingency fees are illegal in the UK as it is thought that they provide the lawyer with a far greater financial interest in the case than is healthy. If a solicitor were to be paid a percentage of the damages awarded there would be the possibility that unethical lawyers may exaggerate the facts of the claim so as to increase the damages payable, or that they may only take those cases where the return was to be lucrative, which would then have the effect of denying parties with a minor claim being able to secure legal representation and gain access to justice.

11.4 *Pro bono* work

The Latin term '*pro bono publico*' (shortened to *pro bono*) translates as meaning 'for the public good' and the term is used to describe legal work that is conducted for free. There are a number of organisations that will conduct litigation on behalf of an individual without charge where the individual cannot secure any form of funding to otherwise undertake the work. The Free Representation Unit (FRU) is one of the largest *pro bono* providers in England and Wales. It was set up in 1972 and is now a registered charity and they provide free representation in cases heard in the Employment Tribunals, social security appeals in the Social Security and Child Support Appeals Tribunals and some immigration and criminal injury compensation cases. The volunteers who undertake the cases for the FRU are law students and legal professionals in the early stages of their careers and currently there are approximately 270 volunteers registered with the FRU willing to undertake such work. As well as registered charities such as the FRU there are many other organisations that offer *pro bono* work. Citizen's Advice Bureaus and many Law Schools at universities up and down the country also offer free legal advice (although they do not usually provide legal representation for formal hearings) and it is an excellent and worthwhile forum for potential lawyers to gain experience at advising real clients in real cases.

11.5   Summary

(a) Within the English legal system there is an unmet legal need where members of the public, for a variety of reasons, are not accessing the legal services available to them. These reasons vary from an unawareness that any wrong has been committed, to concerns over the costs implications of litigation and the fact that the legal profession is viewed as unapproachable.

(b) Public funding for legal proceedings began in 1949 with the introduction of the Welfare State. Legal Aid was available for a number of different legal services (such as advice or representation in court). Eligibility for public funding was determined in most cases by way of a means and/or merits test.

(c) The Access to Justice Act 1999 abolished the old style legal aid and introduced the Legal Services Commission (LSC) who are now charged with overseeing and administrating the provision of funding for both civil and criminal matters.

(d) The Community Legal Services (CLS) is the limb of the LSC that is responsible for the control of public funding in civil matters. Eligibility for funding under the CLS is determined by way of means and merit testing.

(e) The Criminal Defence Service (CDS) also act under the provisions of the LSC and it is responsible for control of public funding in criminal matters. Eligibility for funding is generally determined by either means and/or merit testing although the duty solicitor schemes are still free for all.

(f) A conditional fee agreement (CFA) is a private method for paying for legal costs. A 'no-win no-fee' agreement is made between the solicitor and the client on the understanding that if the case is successful the client will be liable to pay the solicitor's costs and a further success fee, which is calculated on a percentage basis of the basic legal fee.

(g) After-the-event insurance should be obtained when entering into a CFA as this will cover an individual for any extra costs incurred or it will pay the other sides' costs if the individual loses the case.

(h) *Pro bono* work is free legal work carried out by a number of organisations on a voluntary basis.

11.6   Self-test questions

1. Public funding was originally:

    (a) cash limited
    (b) demand fed
    (c) demand limited
    (d) cash fed

2. The Access to Justice Act 1999 introduced the:

    (a) Legal Services Committee
    (b) Legal Funding Committee
    (c) Legal Services Commission
    (d) Legal Funding Commission

3. A defendant who wishes to receive public funding for a trial in the Crown Court will have to satisfy:

    (a) a means test
    (b) a merits test
    (c) a means and merits test
    (d) nothing as criminal representation is always publicly funded

4. The success fee in a Conditional Fee Agreement is a calculated percentage of:

    (a) the damages awarded in the case
    (b) the public funding granted for the case
    (c) other sides' costs
    (d) the solicitors' costs

5. A Conditional Fee Agreement can be used to fund:

    (a) divorce proceedings
    (b) criminal proceedings
    (c) child care proceedings
    (d) personal injury proceedings

11.7   Further reading

K. Ashby and C. Glasser, "The legality of conditional fee uplifts" [2005] C.J.Q. 24(Jan) 130–135.

R. Clayton, "Public interest litigation, costs and the role of legal aid" [2006] P.L. Aut. 429–442.

A. Gore, "Access to justice in personal injury cases" [2006] J.P.I. Law 2 189–198.

A. Hogan, "Conditional fees: problems solved and problems yet to come" [2006] J.P.I. Law 1 40–60.

A. Hogan, "Costs—new law and practice" [2007] J.P.I. Law 1, 94–108.

C. Regan, "Legal aid reform—the next steps" [2008] 105(01) L.S.G. 10.

R. Smith, "Love me tender?" [2008] 158 (7314) N.L.J. 425.

K. Underwood, "CFAs, success fees and after-the-event insurance" [2001] 3 J.P.I. Law 272–279.

M. Zander, "A bit more time please" [2008] 158(7311) N.L.J. 349–351.

M. Zander, "Where are we heading with the funding of civil litigation?" [2003] C.J.Q. 22 (Jan) 23–40.

12 Sentencing

12.1 Introduction

Throughout various chapters of this book we have worked our way through almost the entire criminal trial process. The point we come to consider now is the point in time where the defendants have been either convicted or acquitted and the witnesses and the viewers in the public gallery may have gone home either satisfied that the criminal justice system seems to work or, alternatively, horrified that justice has not (in their eyes) been done. However, the verdict being delivered by the jury is not the final instalment in the case as there are still a few final issues to be determined, namely sentence (if the defendant has either pleaded guilty or been found guilty) and the possibility of an appeal (after either conviction or acquittal).

As a student of law it is important to be aware of the various penalties and punishments that can be imposed by the courts as the legal process does not just stop at the courtroom door. This penultimate chapter will explore the sentences that may be imposed in the criminal courts, as well as the issues that commonly arise in respect of sentencing. This may not seem as exciting or glamorous as the actual trial process but it is an issue of equal importance; especially to a defendant, who will undoubtedly want to know whether they will be sentenced to a term in prison or if they will simply get a number of hours of unpaid work as a means to pay their penance.

12.2 Types of sentence

The sentencing options available to the court, i.e. the types of sentence that could be imposed, were originally governed by the Powers of the Crown Court (Sentencing) Act 2000 (PCC(S)A 2000). However, the introduction of the highly influential Criminal Justice Act 2003 (CJA 2003) has since taken over on these matters and sentencing now falls mainly under the proviso of this statute. There are a number of different types of sentences available to the court, but the first sentence that most people would think of if they were asked to write a list of available sentences would be imprisonment or a custodial sentence (it matters not how it is termed (unless it is a younger offender who would serve a term of 'detention' as opposed to 'imprisonment'), as this is often seen as the most serious sentence option available to the courts. Custody is the main sentence that is reported in the media in relation to criminal trials, and so most lay people are familiar with, at the very least, the concept of it; custody is also the form of sentence that the majority of defendants will want to try and avoid at all costs. Other sentencing options that may have been considered could include non-custodial sentences such as unpaid work, drug rehabilitation orders and fines etc. There are in fact four general categories of sentence that can be split down further to cover the numerous more specific forms of sentencing. These four general categories are:

- custody
- community sentence
- financial penalties
    - fines
    - compensation
- other (including bind overs and deferred sentences)
    - absolute discharges
    - conditional discharges

And yes, discharges, even absolute ones, as surprising as it may seem are a form of sentence, as will be explained later in this chapter.

Each type of sentence, and each specific sentence within a type, has various rules governing whether it will be an appropriate and imposable sentence for the individual case in question. Obviously a life sentence cannot be imposed for a crime of petty theft, nor can a cold-blooded contract killer be given an absolute discharge after a conviction for murder. What will now be considered is how an appropriate and commensurate sentence is decided, as well as what the rules are that prevent a judge from handing out life sentences willy-nilly because they do not like the look of the defendant or because he is a prolific repeat offender of petty crimes. However, before we move on to consider the individual sentences and their application it is useful here to take a moment to stop and consider the aims of sentencing to discover whether there is more to the idea of sentencing an individual than simply punishing the offender.

12.3   Aims of sentencing

If a person on the street were asked to write another list, but this time the list detailed what they believed the main aims of sentencing to be, then it is guessed that they would write down something along the lines of the main aim of sentencing being to punish the proverbial 'bad man', or to make the offender pay for their crimes and to repay society and the victim for whatever offence they have subjected them to. If the list were to include any of the above then it would have certainly pinpointed one of the possible aims of sentencing, that being the punishment of the offender; but if the list had included similar words or phrases to those above, such as 'pay for their crimes' or 'repay society and the victim' etc., then they would have actually identified more than one aim of sentencing. There are, in fact, a number of aims of sentencing and the aim that will be focused upon (the *priori*) will depend very much on the individual crime, the circumstances of the crime and the parties involved in the crime. As a general rule the aims of sentencing can be listed as such:

- punishment of the offender
- reparation (making amends personally or financially)

- reform/rehabilitation of the offender
- protection of the public
- crime reduction

Consider the following short examples and attempt to state the main aim(s) of the sentences imposed.

A. **Eric (aged 16) has been convicted of ten separate counts of indecently assaulting young children. He has been sentenced to detention at Her Majesty's pleasure.**

B. **Frank has been convicted of spraying malicious graffiti on an elderly lady's house. He has been sentenced (by the imposition of a referral order) to clean off the graffiti and to make a formal apology to the victim.**

C. **Gary has been convicted of possession of a Class A drug and an imitation firearm. He has been sentenced to two years in a young offenders institution, where there are the facilities for him to possibly receive drug and alcohol dependency treatment.**

Whilst working through these short illustrative examples it is hoped that the realisation that there does not just have to be one aim behind the chosen sentencing option would have occurred. An individual sentence, depending on the type of sentence imposed, can actually cover two or even more of these aims depending on the circumstances.

In example A, Eric has been sentenced to detention at Her Majesty's pleasure; the aims of this sentence could be said to be both a punishment (Eric has been deprived of his liberty for the foreseeable future) and a way of protecting the public (as he is detained indefinitely he will not be able to assault any more young children). In fact, if Eric were to have access to appropriate treatment whilst he were in custody then the sentence could possibly be said to even have the aim of reforming and rehabilitating him.

In example B, Frank has been requested to clean off the graffiti and apologise to the victim. By undertaking these two actions Frank will be making two acts of reparation (firstly by making amends to the victim by putting right the damage he has caused and secondly by making the apology), and there will also be an element or aim of reform behind the sentence as well. By having to apologise to the victim of his actions and therefore seeing firsthand the effect his actions have had upon another, it would be hoped that this would have the effect of reforming his character so that he does not commit a similar offence again. This method of sentencing by way of a referral order has been made quite popular by the courts in recent years when sentencing young offenders because, as stated above, it is hoped that the young offenders, by carrying out such acts of reparation, will then be turned away from travelling further down the route of a criminal life.

Finally in example C, Gary being sentenced to a young offenders institution, which has drug and alcohol treatment facilities, has more than one aim. The first could be said to be the rehabilitation of the offender: placing Gary into such a unit where he will be able to access appropriate treatment will potentially mean that he could overcome any drug or alcohol dependency issues that he may have. In the short term the aim of the sentence could also be to reduce the amount of crime being committed in the locality by the removal of an individual who is involved with both drugs and firearms. Considering the current climate in the UK in respect of violent and drug related crime, this may be a factor that is taken into account by many of the judiciary whilst they are determining similar cases to this.

Each of the sentences above had aims behind them, but, as it can be see, it is not just a matter of course that the outright punishment of the offender will be the principal aim. An individual's ideas about the aims behind each sentence may have differed slightly or even completely to those set out above and there probably is no determinative correct answer to which aims are the most predominant in each scenario. The aims act as a form of guidance for the courts when they are required to determine the appropriate sentence in an individual case.

12.4   Assessing the seriousness of the offence

As well as considering the aims of the sentence one of the fundamental principles behind determining an appropriate sentence is that the sentence should never be more severe than the seriousness of the offence warrants. How, then, do the courts determine the seriousness of the offence in such a way as to assess the severity of the sentence? How do they determine whether Gary, in the example above, should be given two years' detention or two months' detention? Consistency of sentence for similar crimes is an important issue to the courts and all of those involved in the criminal justice system. The system would become unworkable if the judiciary were allowed to make arbitrary decisions as to type and length of sentence; the necessary certainty that the public requires and relies upon in the criminal justice system would disappear. Imagine how the lay person would react if, upon conviction for the offence of drunk driving, they were told that their sentence (whether custodial or a fine) would all depend on whether the judge had had his lunch-time glass of port or not. Society would be in uproar and any remaining confidence in the criminal justice system would crumble.

To help determine the appropriate sentence the courts will look to a number of sources. The first step (as stated above) is to establish the seriousness of the offence, and the authority that deals with this element is the CJA 2003, namely ss.143, 145 and 146. Under these sections there are a number of factors that the court are required to have in mind when deciding on the seriousness of the offence for sentencing purposes. Under s.143 the court must consider the offender's culpability in committing the offence and any harm that the offence caused, may have caused or could forseeably have caused. They are also permitted to take into account, as an aggravating factor, any previous convictions that the offender may have (whether the conviction arises from a UK court or from within another jurisdiction), and if the offence was committed whilst on bail then this fact will also be treated as an aggravating factor. Further, if the offence was motivated by any religious or racial bias or had an element of hostility relating to either sexual orientation or disability then, under ss.145 and 146, the presence of this factor will require the court to increase the sentence imposed to a level that they feel appropriately reflects the seriousness of the offender's actions.

The statutory provisions under the CJA 2003 do go some way to assisting the court when determining sentence, but they do not provide the in-depth guidance that a normal everyday working court would require. If a magistrate faced with a case of assault had to determine what would be a suitable sentence on the facts of the case in front of them, based only upon the provisions in the CJA 2003 they would immediately run into difficulty. How would they know what the starting point of the sentence should be? Three months' custody? Six months? Would a community sentence be more appropriate? It may be thought that experience would guide the bench as to where they should begin in their considerations, and this assumption would not be wrong, but for the sake of consistency and certainty, more than experience alone must be employed when identifying the starting point for the sentencing of specific offences.

The CJA 2003 also provided for the creation of the Sentencing Guidelines Council (SGC). The SGC was established with the primary aim of providing sentencing guidelines for all criminal offences. It is envisaged that they will eventually set out the sentence starting point for each offence, and then detail any aggravating and mitigating factors that the court must take into account when deciding whether the sentence should be increased or decreased. The Sentencing Advisory Panel is the body that then issues the sentencing guidelines once they have been created. Obviously the SGC have only been in existence for a relatively short period of time and there are many thousands of criminal offences on the statute books, therefore only a limited number of sentencing guidelines have thus far been produced, and at present the courts are still heavily reliant on the methods of determining appropriate sentence that they used prior to the creation of the SGC.

Traditionally if an offender has been convicted of a statutory offence then the relevant statutory provision may provide some assistance in determining the sentence. However, statutes invariably only set out the maximum sentence that can be imposed by the court for the offence in question; they do not set out the minimum or recommended sentence. Consequently the statute will only go so far in providing some assistance to the court in this matter, and of course, consideration must also be given to the fact that not all offences are laid down in statute. Currently there are two methods employed by the courts to determine this difficult and very important issue of appropriate sentence, and which of these two methods will be used will depend on the level of the court (magistrates' or Crown) dealing with the case.

12.5   The magistrates' court

When the issue of determining the appropriate sentence arises in the magistrates' court the bench will turn to the guidance provided in the Magistrates' Court Sentencing Guidelines (MCSG). The MCSG set out the offences that the magistrates deal with regularly and frequently within the adult criminal courts. They provide a sentencing structure, which sets out how to establish the seriousness of each case and determine the most appropriate way of dealing with it. The guideline sentences are based on a first-time offender being convicted after pleading not guilty. The guidelines speak of reaffirming the principle of 'just deserts' so that any penalty must reflect the seriousness of the offence for which it is imposed and may take into account the personal circumstances of the offender. They must always start the sentencing process by taking full account of all the circumstances of the offence (such as any relevant aggravating and mitigating factors) and make a judicial assessment as to which category of seriousness the offence falls into. The magistrates are required to consider in every case whether:

- a discharge or a fine is appropriate;
- the offence is serious enough for a community penalty;
- it is so serious that only custody is appropriate.

To fully understand how the MCSG work in practice we will now return to two of our case studies (see Chapter 10), namely Alfie and then Bertie. We will look at Alfie first and work on the assumption that he was convicted after trial in the magistrates' court of assault of a police officer contrary to s.89 of the Police Act 1996 and it was determined at trial that Alfie had spat at the police officer in question. Figure 12.1 is a copy of the MCSG for the offence of assaulting a police officer, for illustrative purposes.

As can be seen, the guidelines set out that the maximum sentence that can be imposed by the magistrates for this offence can be either a level 5 fine (meaning up to £5,000), or a six-month custodial sentence. The guidelines require the court to consider every possible sentence from a discharge up to custody depending on how serious they deem the offence to be after taking into account the facts of the case, including aggravating and mitigating factors. The suggested entry point for this offence is custody. It appears from the facts that there are two of the aggravating factors present, those being that Alfie both spat at the officer and showed gross disregard for police authority by calling the officer a 'pig'. There is also a potential mitigating factor present in the case as Alfie's behaviour could be termed as impulsive action. The magistrates could also consider other points, such as the fact that Alfie is still quite young, and he may have shown remorse for his actions (although he has not pleaded guilty so could not be described as overly remorseful) etc. It is likely that Alfie would find himself facing a custodial sentence of at least a few months, or being required to pay the police officer he assaulted some form of compensation.

Now consider the guidelines (found in Figure 12.2) that would be referred to in Bertie's case.

The entry point guideline in the MCSG for this offence requires the magistrates to begin by considering whether their sentencing powers are sufficient enough to deal with the matter appropriately. To determine this they again must look to the aggravating and mitigating factors in the case. Bertie committed the burglary at night, when it is likely that the homeowners were present, and stole items of a high value (the watch and the ring). Looking at the MCSG then the magistrates' powers of sentence (in this instance a level 5 fine or six-month custodial sentence) are insufficient and the guidelines set out that the court should commit to the Crown for sentence. The magistrates would simply not be able to sentence appropriately in this case.

Figure 12.1 Sentencing guidelines—assaulting a police officer

Police Act 1996 s.89 Triable only summarily Penalty: Level 5 and/or 6 months	**Assault on a police officer**

CONSIDER THE SERIOUSNESS OF THE OFFENCE
(INCLUDING THE IMPACT ON THE VICTIM)

IS DISCHARGE OR FINE APPROPRIATE?

IS IT SERIOUS ENOUGH FOR A COMMUNITY PENALTY?

GUIDELINE: → IS IT SO SERIOUS THAT ONLY CUSTODY IS APPROPRIATE?

THIS IS A GUIDELINE FOR A FIRST-TIME OFFENDER PLEADING NOT GUILTY

+ CONSIDER AGGRAVATING AND MITIGATING FACTORS AND THE WEIGHT TO ATTACH TO EACH −

for example	**for example**
Any injuries caused Gross disregard for police authority Group action Premeditated Spitting *This list is not exhaustive*	Impulsive action Unaware that person was a police officer *This list is not exhaustive*

If racially or religiously aggravated, or offender is on bail, this offence is more serious
If offender has previous convictions, their relevance and any failure to respond to previous sentences should be considered – they may increase the seriousness. The court should make it clear, when passing sentence, that this was the approach adopted.

TAKE A PRELIMINARY VIEW OF SERIOUSNESS, THEN CONSIDER OFFENDER MITIGATION

for example
Age, health (physical or mental)
Co-operation with police
Evidence of genuine remorse
Voluntary compensation

CONSIDER YOUR SENTENCE

Compare it with the suggested guideline level of sentence and reconsider your reasons carefully if you have chosen a sentence at a different level. Consider a reduction for a timely guilty plea.

DECIDE YOUR SENTENCE
NB. COMPENSATION – Give reasons if not awarding compensation

Source: Magistrates' Court Sentencing Guidelines, page 15

343

Figure 12.2 Sentencing guidelines—burglary (dwelling)

Burglary (dwelling)	Theft Act 1968 s.9 Triable either way – see Mode of Trial Guidelines Penalty: Level 5 and/or 6 months

CONSIDER THE SERIOUSNESS OF THE OFFENCE
(INCLUDING THE IMPACT ON THE VICTIM)

IS DISCHARGE OR FINE APPROPRIATE?
IS IT SERIOUS ENOUGH FOR A COMMUNITY PENALTY?
IS IT SO SERIOUS THAT ONLY CUSTODY IS APPROPRIATE?
GUIDELINE: → *ARE YOUR SENTENCING POWERS SUFFICIENT?*

THIS IS A GUIDELINE FOR A FIRST TIME OFFENDER PLEADING NOT GUILTY

⊕ CONSIDER AGGRAVATING AND MITIGATING FACTORS AND THE WEIGHT TO ATTACH TO EACH ⊖

for example	for example
Force used or threatened Group enterprise High value (on economic or sentimental terms) property stolen More than minor trauma caused Professional planning/organisation/execution Significant damage or vandalism Victim injured Victim present at the time Vulnerable victim *IF ANY of the above factors are present you should commit for sentence.*	First offence of its type AND low value property stolen AND no significant damage or disturbance AND no injury or violence Minor part played Theft from attached garage Vacant property *ONLY if one or more of the above factors are present AND none of the aggravating factors listed are present should you consider NOT committing for sentence.*

If racially or religiously aggravated, or offender is on bail, this offence is more serious
If offender has previous convictions, their relevance and any failure to respond to previous sentences should be considered – they may increase the seriousness. The court should make it clear, when passing sentence, that this was the approach adopted.

TAKE A PRELIMINARY VIEW OF SERIOUSNESS, THEN CONSIDER WHETHER THE CASE SHOULD BE COMMITTED FOR SENTENCE, THEN CONSIDER OFFENDER MITIGATION

for example
Age, health (physical or mental)
Co-operation with police
Evidence of genuine remorse
Voluntary compensation

CONSIDER COMMITTAL OR YOUR SENTENCE

Compare it with the suggested guideline level of sentence and reconsider your reasons carefully if you have chosen a sentence at a different level.
Consider a reduction for a timely guilty plea.

DECIDE YOUR SENTENCE
NB. COMPENSATION – Give reasons if not awarding compensation

Source: Magistrates' Court Sentencing Guidelines, page 18

Even if a case, such as Bertie's, is tried by the magistrates' court the court still reserves the ability to commit the case to the Crown Court for sentence if they feel that their sentencing powers are not sufficient, and they are even forced to do so in certain situations (as illustrated by Bertie's case above). This committing for sentence can occur if the offence was originally an either-way offence and the magistrates retained the jurisdiction of the case with the defendant's consent. The magistrates derive their power to commit a case for sentence from s.3 PCC(S)A 2000. This power is a necessary one as occasionally it is the situation that all the facts to a case are not apparent during the initial court hearings and the real seriousness of the offence only transpires during the actual course of the trial. If the court were not afforded the power to commit in such instances then they would not be able to impose an appropriately termed sentence and therefore the criminal justice system would be seen to have within it a major flaw. By providing this course of action the courts can ensure that appropriate justice is therefore done. It can of course only be undertaken when an offence is an either-way offence, or there are several offences, one of which is an either-way one (see 9.5.2 and 10.1 for details on either-way offences).

Finally, whenever the court hands down a sentence they are required, under s.174 CJA 2003, to provide their reasoning for the sentence imposed in addition to the aims of such a sentence. This is to ensure that the sentence is commensurate to the seriousness of the offence and to ensure that the magistrates have taken all relevant and necessary factors into account in their deliberations upon sentence. As is explained in the final chapter on Appeals, this requirement to provide full reasoning for the sentence imposed can be crucial for determining whether the sentence was appropriate and, if not, the reasoning will provide the grounds for any subsequent appeal.

The Revised Magistrates' Court Sentencing Guidelines 2008 come into effect on August 4, 2008 and will apply to all relevant cases appearing for allocation hearings or for sentence. They will also supersede the Mode of Trial Decisions (Part V.51) Practice Direction. Students are advised to ensure they source the latest (2008) copy.

12.6   The Crown Court

The Crown Court, at present, do not have their sentencing guidelines contained in any one text but instead rely upon Court of Appeal (Criminal Division) decisions to guide them in determining appropriate sentence, as well as advice from the Sentencing Advisory Panel in respect of certain offences. Judgments that contain sentencing guidance are normally reported in the Criminal Appeal Sentencing Reports, and an edited version of useful judgments can also be found in criminal law practioner texts, such as *Archbold* and *Blackstones*, as well as a number of other specialised sentencing texts.

To illustrate exactly how the Court of Appeal sets out such guidelines it is useful to look at a couple of judgments produced by the court. The case of *Millberry* [2003] 1 W.L.R. 546, for example, sets out in response to the Sentencing Advisory Panel's advice on the revision of the current sentencing practice for offences of rape some very clear guidelines as to how an appropriate sentence should be determined in rape cases.

The Court indicated that rape almost invariably called for an immediate custodial sentence. They broadly agreed with the principal suggestions of the Panel that the guidelines should deal explicitly with the question of sentencing levels for relationship rape and acquaintance rape, as well as stranger rape. They also agreed that the same guidelines should apply equally to male and female rape, and that anal rape should be treated similarly to vaginal rape. The Court also considered that the offender's culpability, especially in relation to the victim's behaviour, or historic cases, where the event was reported many years after it occurred, would be relevant.

In general the Court laid down guidelines that the normal starting point of five years should apply where there were no aggravating features. If there were certain aggravating factors, such as the rape of a child, a vulnerable victim, the rape was racially aggravated or due to the victim's membership of a vulnerable minority, or if the rape was committed by a man who was knowingly suffering from a life threatening and sexually transmittable disease, then the starting point to be adopted would be eight years' imprisonment. Fifteen years' imprisonment was thought to be a suitable starting point where the case involved a campaign of rape on either the same or multiple victims and, finally, an automatic life sentence would be appropriate where the offender already had a conviction for a serious offence under s.109 PCC(S)A 2000.

The case of *Millberry*, therefore, is a very useful tool for the court to turn to when they are required to determine the seriousness of the offence and decide the appropriate sentence in rape cases.

In respect of other offences there are many Court of Appeal judgments dealing with numerous offences and setting out relevant guidelines. If a student were to use one of the online legal databases and search with the term 'sentencing' and their chosen offence then it would undoubtedly return a suitable and contemporary case to use as guidance.

For example by inputting the search terms of 'sentencing' and 'supply of Class A drugs with intent' the case of *Attorney-General's Reference No.20 of 2002 (Oliver Alex Birch)* [2003] 1 Cr. App. R. (S) 58 would be found. Here the court provided guidelines on the appropriate sentence for offenders who have committed the offence of possessing a Class A drug, with a street value of between £6,000 and £12,000, with intent to supply. The court in this case held that the usual range of sentence for an offence of this kind was three to four years' imprisonment and that only in the most exceptional cases could such a case result in a non-custodial sentence.

If the terms 'sentencing' and 'aggravated burglary' were used then the case of *Attorney-General's Reference (No.101 of 2001)* [2002] EWCA Crim 86 would be displayed. This case involved the offences of grievous bodily harm, robbery and aggravated burglary. The defendant had stabbed an 83-year-old man in his own home and then demanded money following a forced entry. He also slashed a married couple, who were in their sixties, with a razor blade while demanding money after having called at their home. The Attorney-General stated that when the violent attacks were on elderly victims in their own homes then the deserved sentence would be one in double figures (a commensurate sentence being one of ten years' imprisonment), and if the case involved issues of public protection then a longer commensurate term of 14 years' imprisonment would be more appropriate.

As stated above, it is intended that the SGC will eventually produce guidelines for all criminal offences, but until that occurs the Crown Court will continue to rely upon the many Court of Appeal decisions to help them determine the seriousness of the offence and the appropriate sentence to impose. As each case will have its own individual facts therein does lie a certain danger that the courts will not always sentence consistently in every case and every year there are a number of appeals based on the grounds that the sentence is either too lenient or too harsh (depending of course on the party bringing the appeal (see Chapter 13 for further detail on appeals)). However as the law stands at present, reference to previous sentencing precedent is the most effective method for the Crown Court to determine the appropriate level of sentence, and if the SGC do manage to eventually produce guidelines then these guidelines will still carry with them an inherent possibility of inconsistency as they will only ever be guidelines as the courts will never be faced with two offences with an identical set of circumstances.

12.7   Other factors

In addition to the sentencing guidelines discussed above there are also a number of other factors that the courts regularly take into account when deciding upon sentence—these include things such as pre-sentence reports, victim impact statements, personal offender mitigation and other offences that are to be taken into consideration.

12.7.1   Pre-sentence reports

Pre-sentence reports, commonly known as PSRs, are reports compiled by the Probation Service after consultation with the offender. They are primarily aimed at assisting the court in their quest to determine the most appropriate sentence for the offender in question. To help the court with this deliberation the PSR focuses on a number of different elements, such as the offence itself, the offender's culpability, their attitude towards their actions (i.e. if they are remorseful about or unconcerned about their offending), the offender's personal circumstances such as their history, education, employment, health, previous convictions, risk of re-offending, and any other relevant matters that the probation officer feels are pertinent. Often the PSR will also contain a recommendation that the offender be sent for psychiatric or medical reports. The report will not usually specify an exact sentence but will detail those sentences that the probation officer feels the offender is most suitable for. For example, it would not recommend a community order with the requirement of attending a drug and alcohol treatment programme for an offender who is teetotal, but it may consider that this would be a suitable and appropriate sentence for a drug addict who has expressed a desire to undergo rehabilitation.

The governing statutory provision for the obtaining of PSRs is s.156 CJA 2003. Under s.156 the court are obliged to obtain a PSR whenever they are minded to:

- impose a custodial sentence or
- impose a community order with requirements

Under subs.(4) the court are not required to obtain a PSR in situations where they are of the opinion that it is not necessary, such as if the offence carries with it a mandatory life sentence (although a PSR may be helpful in identifying the minimum term to be served), or if the offence can only be dealt with by way of a fine etc. In essence a PSR will not be necessary when the sentence is already pre-determined irrespective of the offender's personal circumstances and consequently the PSR would not have any effect on the proceedings. It is normal practice, however, to order a PSR, and they are a rather routine request within the criminal court system. A full PSR (allowing the sentencer all options) will take approximately three weeks to compile, however a fast delivery or oral PSR (allowing the sentencer to impose a community penalty and below) is done either on the day of, or within a day of, conviction. The offender's sentencing hearing will be adjourned until the expected availability date of the report.

12.7.2   Victim impact statements

Victim impact statements (VISs) are a relatively new phenomenon within the criminal justice system and as such do not appear within criminal proceedings with the same regularity as PSRs. However, as time goes by they will become very much the norm in assisting the court with sentence determination. A VIS allows the victim of the offence to voice their thoughts and feelings about the offence to the court. The victim will detail how the offence has affected their life and how they view the offender. This statement may have one of two effects upon the court when they consider it in relation to offence seriousness and appropriate sentence in that, depending on its contents, they may view it as an aggravating, or a mitigating, factor.

A VIS could be taken into account as an aggravating factor if the victim of the offence sets out the negative ways in which the offence has affected and is possibly still affecting their life. If a victim, after being subjected to the offence of rape or a violent street robbery, states that they are terrified to leave their house, walk to the shops alone, still have nightmares and have to take medication to cope with life on a day to day basis, then the court will take this into account as an aggravating factor when considering the appropriate sentence. If, however, the victim to the offence states that they forgive the offender, that they are not suffering any long lasting detriment as a result of the offence and that they wish the offender to be dealt with leniently, then the court may take this into account when considering any mitigating points in relation to the offence.

One point to question here is really how much input the victim should have into the offender's sentence. It is submitted that in the majority of cases a VIS will be quite helpful to the court as they will be able to assess the level of the harm caused by the offender, but if the prosecution and conviction of an offender was more malicious in nature (imagine a jilted ex-partner alleging rape in an effort to seek revenge) then a VIS could further compound a rather bad situation and possibly increase a sentence that maybe should not have been imposed in the first place. The extent of the reliance upon and the effects of VISs is something that can only really be speculated upon at this present time, but it is certainly an area of criminal procedure to keep an eye on in the future.

12.7.3   Personal offender mitigation

Personal offender mitigation (POM) has some common elements to a PSR, in that the court considers the offender's personal circumstances and situation when coming to the conclusion as to what is to be an appropriate sentence. POM is generally raised at the point of oral advocacy in the case known as the 'plea-in-mitigation'. A plea-in-mitigation will be presented, during the sentencing hearing proceedings, to the court by the defence counsel. The aim of a plea-in-mitigation is to minimise the severity of the sentence that the offender receives, by putting forward the personal circumstances and feelings of the offender (i.e. remorse as to their involvement in the offence). By doing so it is hoped that the court will, to a degree, empathise or sympathise with the defendant and therefore impose a less onerous sentence. POM will focus on the individual concerned in the instant case. So, for example, if, at the age of 45, the offender has been convicted of the offence of fraud then the court will not be interested, in respect of considering sentence, to learn that the defendant came from a broken home and spent three years in foster care; this would be likely to be viewed as an irrelevant sob story. However, if the offender has been convicted of an offence, such as theft, and the court learns, through the POM, that she is a single mother with four young dependent children and no family support system to care for the children if she is imprisoned, then the court may be more minded, if possible on the facts, to impose a non-custodial sentence to avoid the children being taken into care. Nevertheless, the court is not obliged to take into consideration any personal mitigation but they are duty bound however to consider all aggravating and mitigating circumstances of the offence itself.

12.7.4 Offences taken into consideration

In the English court system the general rule is that an offender is only sentenced upon the offences that they have been convicted of. However, there is one exception to this rule. This exception only occurs when the offender in question requests that the court, when they come to the point of considering sentence, takes into account other offences that the offender has committed, but has not been formally convicted of. These offences are termed as 'offences taken into consideration', or TICs. This may seem to be quite a strange concept to understand when first introduced to it, but there is logic behind the principle.

TICs can be beneficial to both the prosecution and the offender in a case. The principle behind TICs is that an offender requests the court to take into account any other offences that they have committed and made admissions to when determining sentence. It may be the case that the offender has been convicted of four dwelling house burglaries but also asks the court to take into account a further twelve burglaries when deciding sentence. By doing so the prosecution (and police) benefit as it has the result that another twelve burglaries are 'solved' and so can be struck off from the unsolved crime statistics. The offender also benefits as it means that, although their sentence will be increased in the immediate instance so as to take into account the other offences, the offender will not subsequently be prosecuted and convicted separately of the offences that have been TIC.

For an offence (or offences) to be taken into consideration the offender must first admit to the offences and then they must be set down in a schedule which is signed by the offender and then entered into court. Once in court the offender will then be asked to confirm and consent to the schedule so that they can be formally TIC'd. Guidance on how the court should then deal with the TICs in relation to sentence (particularly in relation to weight) is provided in the case of *R. v Miles* [2006] EWCA 256, by Sir Igor Judge:

> In relation to offences taken into consideration, we have these observations: the sentence is intended to reflect a defendant's overall criminality. Offences cannot be taken into consideration without the express agreement of the offender. That is an essential pre-requisite. The offender is pleading guilty to the offences. If they are to be taken into account (and the court is not obliged to take them into account) they have relevance to the overall criminality. When assessing the significance of TIC's, as they are called, of course the court is likely to attach weight to the demonstrable fact that the offender has assisted the police, particularly if they are then able to clear up offences that might not otherwise be brought to justice. It is also true that cooperative behaviour of that kind will often provide its own very early indication of guilt, and usually means that no further proceedings at all need be started. They may also serve to demonstrate a genuine determination by the offender (and we deliberately use the colloquialism) to wipe the slate clean, so that when he emerges from whatever sentence is imposed on him, he can put his past completely behind him, without having worry or concern that offences may be revealed as that he is then returned to court.
>
> As in so many aspects of sentencing, of course, the way in which the court deals with offences to be taken into consideration depends on context. In some cases the offences taken into consideration will end up adding nothing or very little to the sentence which the court would otherwise impose. On the other hand, offences taken into consideration may aggravate the sentence and lead to a substantial increase in it. For example, the offences may show a pattern of criminal activity that suggests careful planning or deliberate rather than casual involvement in a crime. They may show an offence or offences committed on bail, after an earlier arrest. They may show a return to crime immediately after the offender has been before the court and given a chance that, by committing the crime, he has immediately rejected. There are many situations where similar issues may arise. One advantage to the defendant, of course, is that once an offence is taken into consideration, there is no likely risk of any further prosecution for it. If, on the other hand, it is not, that risk remains. In short, offences taken into consideration are indeed taken into consideration. They are not ignored or expunged or disregarded.

TICs do not fit into the normal English legal system pattern of the offender having to be formally convicted of an offence to be sentenced upon it, but it is a very useful and often productive procedure when employed by the courts.

12.8   Custodial sentences

Custodial sentences are the most severe form of sentence that a court can impose. The pronouncement of a term of imprisonment means that the offender will be deprived of their liberty and right to freedom for a set period of time. Not only does a custodial sentence affect the offender detrimentally in a physical sense, but it can also have a substantial impact on the offender and their family in the emotional, financial and social sense. It may well be the case that the offender is the only person in gainful employment within the family and that their removal for a period of time could have significant consequences upon the financial well being of the rest of the family. Alternatively, if the offender has children then their absence may result in emotional hardship for the children who have temporarily lost their parent. Society in general also looks unkindly upon those who have been convicted of a criminal offence, and as such the offender and their family, who will be left to deal with the public, will also be faced with the stigmatisation that a spell in custody can often carry. Therefore, the imposition of a custodial sentence is an action only taken by the courts where they feel that, on the facts of the case, it is absolutely necessary to do so.

To determine when to impose a custodial sentence the courts will refer to the guidance laid down in s.152 of the CJA 2003 as to when to impose a custodial sentence. Section 152(2) provides the details of the test that the court must apply when deciding whether or not to impose custody. Section 152(2) states that:

> The court must not pass a custodial sentence unless it is of the opinion that the offence, or the combination of the offence and one or more offences associated with it, was so serious that neither a fine alone nor a community sentence can be justified for the offence.

Simply because a custodial sentence can be imposed for a certain type of offence does not then mean that it will always be imposed in every case. So how does the court determine whether custody is necessary or if a fine or community order could be justified instead? How does the court reach such a decision, especially in those cases where there is a very fine line between the possible imposition of custody and the choice of another, less serious sanction. The statute itself is silent on this matter but the courts have laid down valuable advice on how to determine this question in the case of *R. v Howells* [1999] 1 W.L.R. 307.

The court, by way of the judgment given by Lord Bingham C.J., sets out that there are five points that should be taken into account when considering custody in a borderline case:

> In deciding whether to impose a custodial sentence in borderline cases the sentencing court will ordinarily take account of matters relating to the offender.
>
> (a) The court will have regard to an offender's admission of responsibility for the offence, particularly if reflected in a plea of guilty tendered at the earliest opportunity and accompanied by hard evidence of genuine remorse, as shown (for example) by an expression of regret to the victim and an offer of compensation.
>
> (b) Where offending has been fuelled by addiction to drink or drugs, the court will be inclined to look more favourably on an offender who has already demonstrated (by taking practical steps to that end) a genuine, self-motivated determination to address his addiction.
>
> (c) Youth and immaturity, while affording no defence, will often justify a less rigorous penalty than would be appropriate for an adult.

351

(d) Some measure of leniency will ordinarily be extended to offenders of previous good character, the more so if there is evidence of positive good character (such as a solid employment record or faithful discharge of family duties) as opposed to a mere absence of previous convictions. It will sometimes be appropriate to take account of family responsibilities, or physical or mental disability.

(e) While the court will never impose a custodial sentence unless satisfied that it is necessary to do so, there will be even greater reluctance to impose a custodial sentence on an offender who has never before served such a sentence.

The guidance from this case then is that the handing down of a custodial sentence should only be done where it is *absolutely necessary* and can be *justified*. Further, the sentence imposed should not be any longer than is required to satisfy the penal purpose of the sentence. So what forms of custodial sentences can be given and in what circumstances?

12.8.1 Life imprisonment

This is probably the best-known custodial sentence and is often viewed by the media and the public as the most controversial in its application, as it is often quoted that 'life' does not actually mean 'life'. Essentially there are two types of life sentence: discretionary and mandatory. Discretionary life can be imposed by a court for common law offences, and where the maximum specified in the statute pertaining to the offence is life.

However, when an offender has been convicted of the offence of murder the courts are statutorily obliged, under s.269 CJA, to impose the penalty of life imprisonment. This sentence means that the judge in the case has no discretion as to impose any other type or length of sentence. Life imprisonment is the only penalty that can be imposed on an offender who is convicted of murder and is aged 21 years or over. Although the judge has no discretion as to the type of sentence in these cases they do, however, have a certain element of discretion as to the minimum term that the offender must serve (the starting point) before being eligible to be released on licence. Being released on licence means that the defendant will then serve the remainder of their term out of prison, with an impending possibility of returning to serve the remainder of the full term in custody if they commit another offence whilst on licence.

Section 269 and the relevant Sch.21 of the CJA 2003 set out the starting point that must be imposed in relation to a mandatory life sentence depending on the circumstances of the offence; these starting points range from the whole life sentence down to one of 12 years depending on the individual facts of the case.

A whole life term should be imposed (under Sch.21, para.4) where the offence falls into one of the following categories:

(a) the murder of two or more persons, where each murder involves any of the following—

   (i) a substantial degree of premeditation or planning,
   (ii) the abduction of the victim, or
   (iii) sexual or sadistic conduct;

(b) the murder of a child if involving the abduction of the child or sexual or sadistic motivation;

(c) a murder done for the purpose of advancing a political, religious or ideological cause; or

(d) a murder by an offender previously convicted of murder.

A number of high profile murderers such as Myra Hindley, Rosemary West, Roy Whiting and very recently Levi Bellfield have received 'whole life' sentences (or their equivalent pre-2003), which means that they will stay in prison for the entirety of their lives. Only a very limited number (approximately 30) of these whole life sentences have been imposed since their introduction.

A starting point of 30 years will be imposed (under Sch.21, para.5), where the offence involved:

(a) the murder of a police officer or prison officer in the course of his duty;

(b) a murder involving the use of a firearm or explosive;

(c) a murder done for gain (such as a murder done in the course or furtherance of robbery or burglary, done for payment or done in the expectation of gain as a result of the death);

(d) a murder intended to obstruct or interfere with the course of justice;

(e) a murder involving sexual or sadistic conduct;

(f) the murder of two or more persons;

(f) a murder that is racially or religiously aggravated or aggravated by sexual orientation.

The Soham murderer, Ian Huntley, received a sentence with the recommendation that he should serve at least 40 years before being considered for parole. He was convicted prior to the 2003 Act, however his appeal joined a backlog of cases waiting for the decision on the role of the Home Secretary in relation to mandatory life sentences (see below), and therefore the appeal judge was able to increase his tariff to one of 40 years.

If the offence does not fall into any of the above categories then the minimum starting point is 15 years, unless the offender is under the age of 18 at the time of the offence and if this is the case then the starting point will be a minimum of 12 years' imprisonment.

A quick point to note with the minimum starting point before release is that it is only a starting point. The judge can then take into account any case-specific mitigating or aggravating factors and adjust the starting point accordingly. The imposition of a minimum time that the offender must serve before being considered for release on licence does not also mean that they will be automatically released when they have served this time; the fact of their release will then be determined by the Parole Board who will decide if the offender is suitable to serve the remainder of their time in the community, although they will remain 'on licence for life'.

The whole 'life does not mean life' discussion has been very much in the public eye over recent years. Historically the Home Secretary had the power to impose a minimum tariff for those convicted of an offence carrying with it a life sentence. This power came very much to the attention of the media in the case of the two child killers, Thompson and Venables, who had been convicted of murdering toddler James Bulger in 1993, as the then Home Secretary, Michael Howard, set the minimum tariff that they should serve at 15 years. Thompson and Venables appealed against the decision to set a minimum tariff, submitting that this was beyond the powers of the Home Secretary. Upon hearing the case (*R. v Secretary of State for the Home Department Ex p. Venables and Thompson* [1998] A.C. 407) the House of Lords held that the actions of the Home Secretary had been unlawful and that he was not permitted to impose minimum sentences in respect of juvenile offenders; this decision was then later confirmed by the ECHR (*V v United Kingdom* (1999) 30 E.H.R.R. 121). This was the start of erosion of the government's powers over being able to determine sentence in life imprisonment cases.

In 2002 the powers to determine minimum sentence in respect of adults convicted of offences carrying with them a life sentence was also stripped away from political control, due to a challenge made by Anthony Anderson. Anderson had been convicted in 1988 of two murders; at the time of sentencing the judge in the trial recommended that he should serve at least 15 years. Six years later the then Home Secretary, Michael Howard, increased the minimum term that Anderson would have to serve before being considered for release to 20 years. Anderson then appealed the decision to the House of Lords (*R. v Secretary of State Ex. p. Anderson* [2002] UKHL 46) who allowed his appeal, holding that it was unlawful for a politician to set a minimum tariff to be served, Lord Bingham of Cornhill commenting:

> The conclusion that the Home Secretary should play no part in the fixing of convicted murderers' tariffs makes for much greater uniformity of treatment than now exists. The tariff term to be served by a discretionary life sentence prisoner is already determined by the trial judge in open court [. . .] and the Parole Board decide whether it is safe to release the prisoner at the end of that tariff term. The Home Secretary has no role.

The fact that certain murderers, in fact the majority of murderers, including those who are as notorious as Ian Huntley and Mark Goldstraw (who killed his 16-year-old ex-girlfriend and her family by a premeditated arson attack and was recommended a minimum tariff of 35 years), do not receive full life sentences has been the subject of much debate and often outrage by both the media and the public alike. The fact that politicians can no longer interfere with these sentences does seem to mean that such offenders are free from being used as a political pawn for personal or party gain which, it is submitted, can only be a good thing for the interests of justice. However, there is the other side of the coin to also consider, this being that the law cannot make any exceptions for those convicted of murder who have mitigating circumstances (e.g. a parent who kills their severely disabled child in a 'mercy killing'). If such an offender can not have their conviction reduced to one of manslaughter then they will face a life sentence regardless of the circumstances of the offence. They will be convicted as a murderer and serve as a murderer. When the two extremes, and all the shades of grey in between, in respect of cases of murder are compared, the question that begs to be asked is just how fit for purpose such a 'rigid' sentencing structure is.

12.8.2 Fixed term sentences

Certain offences carry with them a mandatory minimum sentence as fixed by statute. Examples of such sentences can be found on the statute books under s.110 of the PCC(S)A 2000, which imposes a minimum sentence of seven years' imprisonment on a third conviction of Class A drug trafficking, or under s.111 of the PCC(S)A 2000 which imposes a minimum sentence of three years' imprisonment on the third conviction of domestic burglary (although this section is not yet currently in force). Such fixed term sentences are clearly laid out in statute and the courts must follow the recommendations unless they are of the opinion that upon the circumstances of the offence it would be unjust to do so.

12.8.3 Suspended sentences

Under s.189 of the CJA 2003 the court can, in certain circumstances, impose a suspended sentence upon an offender. This means that the offender will remain out of custody but will have the suspended sentence hanging over their head, which it is hoped will work as a deterrent to committing any further offences during the foreseeable future. To impose a suspended sentence the custodial sentence must be between 28 and 51 weeks and it can then be suspended for between six months and two years.

The CJA 2003 now also requires the offender to comply with set requirements whilst they are under the suspended sentence. These requirements are the same as for community orders (see below). If the offender refuses or fails to comply with the requirements imposed then the suspended sentence is activated and the offender can be required to serve the remainder of his prison term actually in custody.

12.8.4 Offenders aged between 18 and 21 years

Where an offender is between the ages of 18 and 21 years there are special provisions relating to where such an offender can serve a term of detention. Section 89 sets out that an offender who is aged between 18 years and 21 years cannot be committed to prison. At present an offender aged 18–20 years old will serve their custodial sentence in a young offenders institution, as directed by s.91 PCC(S)A 2000. However, once they turn 21, they will be transferred to an adult prison to serve out the remainder of their sentence. This is set to change at some point in the future as s.61 Criminal Justice and Court Service Act 2000 abolishes the requirement for offenders in this age category to be detained in a young offenders institution. When this section is eventually brought into force offenders who fall into this age category will simply be sent directly to adult prison to serve out the entirety of their tariff.

12.8.5 Detention at Her Majesty's pleasure

The term 'detention at Her Majesty's pleasure' is effectively the equivalent of a life sentence for a juvenile offender (this is what Thompson and Venables above were sentenced to). An offender is detained at Her Majesty's pleasure when they are aged between 10 and 17 and have committed the offence of murder. As there is no determination of the minimum time required to be served (otherwise known as the starting point) the flexibility is then present to allow the offender to be released when it is felt that it would be suitable to do so. A judge can, if so minded, impose a minimum time to be served if they believe it to be appropriate in the circumstances. Refer back to the commentary above for further discussion of this matter.

12.8.6   Home detention curfews

Under s.246 of the CJA 2003 an offender can be released early from prison to serve the remainder of their sentence in their own home. This concept is different to that of being on licence (see below) as the offender is still very much seen as serving a custodial sentence. The offender will be required to comply with curfew requirements and be electronically tagged at all times until the sentence expires. The creation of this novel way to serve out a sentence has resulted from the severe over-crowding that has occurred in prisons over the past few years. The prison governor will decide which prisoners they feel are suitable for home detention curfews and the discretion to choose an appropriate candidate rests solely with them.

12.8.7   Release upon licence

Under the CJA 2003 an offender who has been sentenced to more than 12 months' imprisonment can be released upon licence to serve out the remainder of their sentence in the community. The offender is normally released on licence after serving half of their full sentence. If the offender re-offends whilst on licence then they will be returned to custody to serve the remainder of their original sentence as well as any subsequent sentence for the latter offence.

12.8.8   Consecutive and concurrent sentences

If the offender has been convicted and given a custodial sentence in respect of more than one offence then the court can decide whether to run the sentences concurrently, which means that they run at the same time as each other, or whether to run them consecutively, which means that the offender will serves the sentences one after another. To determine whether to run the sentences consecutively or concurrently the court must take into consideration the totality of the sentences imposed. Section 153(2) of the CJA 2003 sets out that:

> The custodial sentence must be for the shortest term (not exceeding the permitted maximum) that in the opinion of the court is commensurate with the seriousness of the offence, or the combination of the offence and one or more offences associated with it.

To illustrate what is commensurate with the seriousness of the offence, consider the following example.

Wilf has been convicted of ten counts of theft and has been sentenced to six months for each respective count. If these sentences were to run consecutively to each other then Wilf would be facing a custodial sentence that totalled five years. It is likely that this totality would be completely disproportionate to the seriousness of the offences. Whereas, if they were run concurrently so that he only served six months in prison, this is likely to be far more proportionate to the seriousness of the offence; this is known as the 'totality principle'.

12.8.9 Is it serious enough for custody?

To help the courts determine whether the offence is of such a serious nature that custody should be imposed the SGC have, in their guideline entitled 'Overarching Principles: Seriousness', set out the approach that the courts should now adopted under the CJA 2003. The flow chart below (Figure 12.3) details the considerations the courts should undertake.

Figure 12.3 Considerations to be undertaken by the court when considering custody

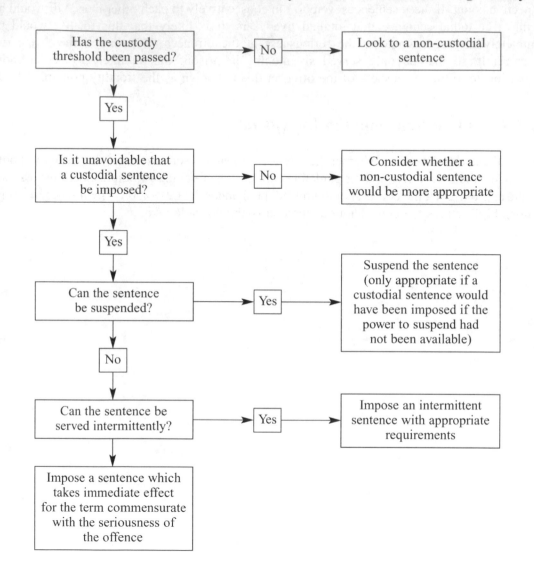

12.9 Non-custodial sentences

If the custody threshold has not been passed in the case then the court are required to consider which non-custodial sentence would be appropriate to impose.

The non-custodial sentences currently available to the courts are:

- community sentences
- financial penalties
- discharges and other disposals

12.9.1 Community sentences

Until very recently the courts were able to impose a number of different individual community orders, depending on the circumstances of the offence and the offender. This was to ensure that the offender received an appropriate and commensurate sentence tailored to them. For example if the offender was a drug addict then they could impose a community service order (unpaid work within the community), or a drug and alcohol treatment programme order so as to try and ensure that the offender received appropriate help to reduce the risk of them re-offending.

Under the CJA 2003 the imposition of individual community orders was abolished and replaced with the ability to impose a single generic community order with certain requirements added on, the requirements being made up of what were the individual orders prior to the CJA 2003, plus a number of new orders. The change in the way that community sentences worked was to allow the court to have access to the whole range of orders available so that the sentence could really be tailored to the offender.

Section 177 sets out 12 different types of order that may be imposed upon a person aged 16 or over who has been convicted of an offence. The court has the option to impose any one or more of the following types of order:

(a) an unpaid work requirement

(b) an activity requirement

(c) a programme requirement

(d) a prohibited activity requirement

(e) a curfew requirement

(f) an exclusion requirement

(g) a residence requirement

(h) a mental health treatment requirement

(i) a drug rehabilitation requirement

(j) an alcohol treatment requirement

(k) a supervision requirement

(l) in a case where the offender is aged under 25, an attendance centre requirement

As with the imposition of a custodial sentence, the courts are also required to be mindful of the threshold test, under s.148 CJA 2003, in respect of community sentences. Section 148 sets out that a community sentence should only be passed if the court are of the opinion that the offence(s) are serious enough to warrant such a sentence; again the sentence must be proportionate and commensurate to the crime committed (how this is decided will be considered below). In addition to this s.148 states:

> (2) Where a court passes a community sentence which consists of or includes a community order:

    (a)   the particular requirement or requirements forming part of the community order must be such as, in the opinion of the court, is, or taken together are, the most suitable for the offender; and

    (b)   the restrictions on liberty imposed by the order must be such as in the opinion of the court are commensurate with the seriousness of the offence and one or more offences associated with it.

12.9.2   The requirements

(a) Unpaid work

This requirement is defined by s.199 CJA 2003. A probation officer will organise for the offender to work on a suitable project within the local community for between 40 hours and 300 hours (the exact amount of time to be fixed by the court) and to be completed within 12 months of the sentence being passed. The work will normally take place during the week but can occasionally take place at weekends (so as to allow for people in full time employment) and the type of work undertaken (gardening, painting, litter collecting etc) will depend upon the schemes that the probation office have running at that time.

(b) Activity requirement

Under an activity requirement order the offender must (as directed by s.201 CJA 2003) participate in the activities specified in the order. The number of days that the offender is required to participate in a certain activity must not exceed the maximum of 60 separate days and the types of activities required have behind them the purpose of reparation and may take the form of day centre attendance, education or contact between the offender and the victim of the crime.

(c) Programme order

Section 201 requires the offender to attend a specified place and take part in a programme accredited by the Secretary of State. For example, an offender who has been convicted of drink driving may be required to attend a Drink Impairment Drivers programme to address their behaviour and avoid them re-offending.

(d) Prohibited activity requirement

This order (under s.203) requires the offender to refrain from a specified activity on specified days or during a specified period. So if the offender has a history of committing violent offences whilst drunk the order may prevent them drinking alcohol for a set period of time, or if the offender was involved with football hooliganism then the order may prohibit them from attending certain football matches.

(e) Curfew requirement

A curfew order under s.204 requires the offender to remain in a specified place (normally their home address) for between two and 12 hours in any 24-hour period. To ensure that the offender remains at the set address they will wear an electronic tag, which sends out signals to the central monitoring service via a telephone line. If the offender leaves the address within the curfew hours then the monitoring service will alert the police so that they can check on the offender's whereabouts. Curfew orders are normally imposed to stop the offender re-offending; if the offender is in the habit of committing burglaries at night then being under curfew will hopefully curtail their criminal activities. However, this is not a failsafe method as occasionally there are technical problems with the electronic tag, which results in the tag not properly transmitting to the tracking system and the offender then being arrested for breaking curfew even though they were actually within the specified premises during the curfew hours.

(f) Exclusion order

Under s.205 the offender is barred from entering a specified place or locality for a period of up to two years. This again is monitored electronically with the offender wearing a tag, and the places could include premises such as football stadiums (e.g. for the football hooligan above), or public houses (e.g. for the offender who becomes violent when drunk). As with curfew orders there can occasionally be problems with the electronic tagging equipment.

(g) Residence order

The offender (under s.206) may be required to reside at a certain address. However, the court cannot specify a hostel or other institution, unless it has been recommended by the probation office as a suitable address.

(h) Mental health treatment requirement

This order is aimed at rehabilitating an offender who is suffering from a mental illness. The offender (under s.207) must submit, during a specified period, to treatment by or under the direction of a registered medical practitioner or a chartered psychologist (or both, for different periods) with a view to the improvement of the offender's mental condition. For this order to be imposed by the courts the offender must consent to the treatment and the court must believe that the offender requires and will be susceptible to the treatment.

(i) Drug rehabilitation requirement

Under s.209 the offender must submit to treatment that has the aim of reducing or eliminating the offender's dependency on or propensity to misuse drugs. The offender will normally be required, at specified points during the order, to provide bodily samples so that it can be ascertained if he has been taking drugs. The courts may only impose a drug rehabilitation order if they are satisfied that the offender is dependent on or has a propensity to misuse drugs, and that his dependency or propensity is at such a level that he requires and will be susceptible to treatment. The order must last a minimum of six months.

(j) Alcohol treatment order

This order is very similar to the drug rehabilitation order in (i) above but for persons dependent on alcohol as opposed to drugs. The order (under s.212) has the aim behind it of reducing or eliminating the offender's dependency on alcohol. Such an order must be imposed for at least six months, and the courts must be certain that the offender is dependent on alcohol to the point that he requires treatment, and that he will be susceptible to treatment.

(k) Supervision order

This order is what was known as a probation or community rehabilitation order prior to the introduction of CJA 2003. Under this order the offender is placed into the supervision of a probation officer. The offender must attend set meetings with the probation officer in an attempt to rehabilitate the offender. The order must be for a period of between six months and three years and is governed by s.213.

(l) Attendance centre requirement

Where the offender is aged 25 or under, an attendance centre requirement under s.214 will be open to the court as an option. The offender may be required to attend an attendance centre for anywhere between 12 and 36 hours, but they may only attend the centre for a period of no more than three hours per day. The offender will take part in a number of activities whilst at the attendance centre, such as first aid courses and lectures on the effects of their crimes.

12.9.3   How to determine the appropriate requirement

Deciding upon which order is the most appropriate for a particular individual may be very easy to do on the facts of the case (i.e. a drug addict who has been convicted of possession of drugs with an intent to supply would probably benefit from a drug treatment order). However, not all cases are as easy to pinpoint, and just because an order is an obvious choice it does not necessarily mean that it is the right one to impose.

To decide on the appropriate community sentence the courts may look to a number of sources. Section 142 of the CJA 2003 sets out the main purposes behind sentencing and s.148 gives the courts the guidance that a community order should not be imposed unless it is both suitable for the offender in question and the recommended order is commensurate with the seriousness of the offence.

The SGC also provides the courts with valuable advice in relation to how to determine the appropriate sentence and requirements by way of the SGC guidelines, '*New Sentences: Criminal Justice Act 2003*'. The SGC states that when deciding which requirements to include, the court must be satisfied on three matters, these being:

- that the restriction on liberty is commensurate with the seriousness of the offence;

- that the requirements are the most suitable for the offender; and

- that, where there are two or more requirements included, they are compatible with each other.

The guidelines also advise the court to keep firmly in mind the possibility of a breach of the sanctions when they pass sentence for the original offence. To reflect the seriousness of an offence, they are required to ensure that the requirements chosen are demanding enough for the offender but equally are not so demanding that they would 'set an offender up to fail' and therefore end in an inevitable breach of the sentence.

The SGC sets out that the guiding principles of community sentences are proportionality and suitability, stating that:

> Once a court has decided that the offence has crossed the community sentence threshold and that a community sentence is justified, the initial factor in defining which requirements to include in a community sentence should be the seriousness of the offence committed.
>
> There should be three sentencing ranges (low, medium and high) within the community sentence band based upon seriousness. It is not intended that an offender necessarily progress from one range to the next on each sentencing occasion. The decision as to the appropriate range each time is based upon the seriousness of the new offence(s). The decision on the nature and severity of the requirements to be included in a community sentence should be guided by:
>
> (i) the assessment of offence seriousness (LOW, MEDIUM OR HIGH);
> (ii) the purpose(s) of sentencing the court wishes to achieve;
> (iii) the risk of re-offending;
> (iv) the ability of the offender to comply; and
> (v) the availability of requirements in the local area.
>
> The resulting restriction on liberty must be a proportionate response to the offence that was committed.

As can be seen, the imposition of a community sentence is to be taken with the same degree of seriousness and responsibility that the imposition of a custodial sentence demands. Just because this type of sentence is below custody in the sentencing hierarchy it does not mean in any way that it is a lesser sentence and therefore the courts are required to give it the same amount of consideration as they do to other sentences.

12.9.4 Enforcement

Before the introduction of the new range of sentences under the CJA 2003 the old community sentence was often seen as the 'soft option' by the media and the public as enforcement was lax and little was done to punish the offender for a breach. Now under Sch.8 of the CJA 2003 the enforcement and breach of a community sentence is taken very seriously, and the court **must** take action against the offender if the breach is admitted or proven.

There are two ways in which a community sentence can be breached. The first is by the offender failing to comply with the requirements of the order(s); the second is by way of the offender committing further offences whilst being the subject of a community sentence. If the offender breaches the sentence in either of these ways then the courts have the power to deal with the breach in a number of different ways. The courts can:

- impose further requirements upon the offender

- revoke the order(s) and re-sentence the offender for the original offence(s) where they can then impose a prison sentence not exceeding six months

The Probation Service will issue a first and final warning, as a means of encouraging the offender to comply with the requirements, before the offender is brought back before the court. When the courts are faced with a breach of a community sentence they will take into account the efforts that the offender has made in attempting to fulfil the requirements imposed, so as to check that the original order was suitable for the offender in question and to see what further options are available. The imposition of custody for the breach of a community sentence should only be used as a last resort. However, often it is found that a vicious circle begins to occur with repeat offenders, as each time they fail to comply with the sentencing requirements they are brought back before the court where the court is likely to impose further requirements for the offender to comply with. As the offender was not able to comply with the original requirements then it is unlikely that they will do any better with the new requirements and they will end up failing to comply with any requirements, which will result in them being brought back into court, and so on.

12.10   Financial penalties

12.10.1   Fines

Both the magistrates' court and Crown Court have the ability to impose a fine upon an individual convicted of an offence; in fact the imposition of a fine is one of the most common methods of disposal in the magistrates' court. A fine can be imposed for any offence except those specified by law (i.e. murder). The courts will look at imposing a fine as punishment where it is felt that the offence is not serious enough to warrant the imposition of a custodial or community sentence. Section 164(2) of the CJA 2003 requires that the fine is fixed to reflect the seriousness of the offence and the court (under subs.(1)) must enquire into the financial circumstances of the offender before fixing the fine amount; obviously ordering an offender who lives on benefits to pay £75,000 in fines would be a completely pointless exercise.

The Crown Court have the benefit of being able to impose any level of fine that they feel is appropriate in the circumstances—even a fine exceeding £1 million pounds can be given as long as they believe that it reflects the seriousness of the crime committed and is proportionate. Essentially the Crown Court are not limited in the amount of fine that they can impose.

The magistrates' court (limited to imposing fines of up to £5,000) can find guidance on how to assess the level of fine to impose in a way that reflects the seriousness of the offence in the MCSG. Fines in the magistrates' court are set by way of certain levels. The level is the maximum fine that can be imposed in respect of the individual offence. If reference is made back to the guidance given by the MCSG on the offence of assaulting a police officer it can be seen that the maximum fine that can be imposed is one that is level 5 on the scale; the offence of criminal damage, when tried summarily, carries with it a maximum fine of level 4, whereas the offence of trying to enter a football ground whilst drunk only carries with it the maximum statutory fine of level 2. Each offence that can be dealt with by way of a fine will carry with it a maximum fine that can be imposed in respect of it. So how do these fine levels equate to monetary figures? The fine scales in the magistrates' court are shown below in Figure 12.4.

Figure 12.4 Magistrates' court fine scale

Level of fine	Maximum amount of fine
Level 1	£200
Level 2	£500
Level 3	£1,000
Level 4	£2,500
Level 5	£5,000

This scale obviously sets out the maximum fine that is possible for an offence, but it does not set out the recommended or most suitable level of fine for an offence. The reason for this is hopefully quite clear, this being that the most suitable level of fine will depend upon the circumstances of the offence and the offender.

To determine the exact fine amount the magistrates will consider the seriousness of the offence by taking into account any aggravating or mitigating factors and then assign it a level of seriousness on the scale of A to C (C being the most serious and A the least serious). This level of seriousness combined with the court's knowledge of the offender's financial circumstances, following the enquiry under s.164, will then determine the level of fine to be imposed. Levels A to C have the following meanings:

Figure 12.5 Level of fine to be imposed

Level of seriousness	Level of fine to be imposed
Level A	50% of the defendant's weekly income
Level B	100% of the defendant's weekly income
Level C	150% of the defendant's weekly income

Obviously not every defendant will have the spare cash to be able to pay the fine to the court outright, so if a defendant is not able to pay the fine as one lump sum the court can direct that he pay the fine by way of instalments. A Fines Collection Order will be made at the same time as fixing the fine, which delegates certain powers to administrative staff to collect the fine. If the defendant then defaults on a payment the court can enforce the fine by way of making an Attachment of Earnings Order (or a Deduction of Benefits Order if the defendant is on certain benefits). The court also has the option of increasing the fine on default of payment or enforcing the sale of the offender's vehicle to meet the payment of the fine. The court can also issue a distress warrant, allowing bailiffs to enter the offender's home and remove goods to the value of the outstanding amount. As a last resort the court can impose detention within the court building or, in more serious circumstances, custody in respect of an unpaid fine. These powers can only be used if the offender is either already serving a custodial sentence, they have the means to pay the fine immediately but are refusing to do so, or the offender has wilfully refused or culpably neglected to pay the fine.

12.10.2   Compensation

Under s.130 PCC(S)A 2000 the court is under a duty to consider compensation in every case where loss, damage or injury has resulted from the offence. The Crown Court has the power to impose an unlimited compensation order on the offender but the magistrates' court is limited to imposing a maximum compensation order of £5,000. The purpose of compensation in the criminal courts is to compensate the victim for their losses or injuries. There are two types of compensation that the court must consider for loss. The first is known as 'special damages', and includes compensation for any financial loss sustained as a result of the offence, such as the cost of repairing the damage or any loss of earnings incurred. The second type of loss is known as 'general damages'. These general damages include compensation for the pain and suffering of the injury itself and for any loss of facility that has occurred as a result of the offence.

When calculating the compensation to be awarded the court will again take into account the circumstances of the offender (their means and ability to pay any compensation together with any offer of compensation they may have already made). If the offender does not have sufficient means to pay both a fine and a compensation order then the compensation will take precedence. The MCSG gives guidance on the level of fines that should be imposed for certain types of personal injury.

If the court is minded to not award a compensation order then they are required to state their reasons as to why not. Figure 12.6 lists examples of the level of fine that should be imposed for common injuries.

Figure 12.6 Levels of fines imposed for common injuries

Type of injury	Level of fine
Graze—depending on size	Up to £75
Black eye	£125
Finger: fractured little finger, recovery within month	£1,000
Loss of front tooth	£1,500
Wrist: closed fracture, recovery within month	£1,500
Leg or arm: closed fracture of tibia, fibula, ulna or radius, recovery within month	£1,500

12.11 Discharges

Discharges are at the bottom of the sentencing hierarchy in respect of seriousness and are the final form of sentence to be considered in this chapter. Discharges are governed by s.12 PCC(S)A 2000 and they come in two forms: a conditional discharge and an absolute discharge.

12.11.1 Conditional discharge

Apart from fines, a conditional discharge is the most common form of disposal within the magistrates' court. A conditional discharge is where the offender is discharged on the condition that they will commit no further offence within the time set by the court (up to a maximum of three years). When an offender is given a conditional discharge the court will explain to him that as long as he does not re-offend within the period of the conditional discharge then no further action will be taken in relation to the matter. If, however, the offender does re-offend and is convicted within the period of the conditional discharge then he will be brought back to court and the discharge will be revoked. This then means that the court will not only sentence him for the new conviction but that they will also revisit the previous offence and re-sentence on that matter as well. Conditional discharges are often passed down in the magistrates' courts for those offenders who are first time offenders and have committed a minor offence. The aim behind this type of discharge is to deter the offender from committing another offence in the future.

12.11.2 Absolute discharge

An absolute discharge is where the offender is formally convicted of the offence but then no punishment is imposed and they are discharged from the courts without further action. This type of discharge is only really used when the offence is one of a trivial nature and the offender, although technically guilty, was found to be morally blameless, or where the court is showing its displeasure with the police and/or the CPS for their handling of the case. They are quite a rare occurrence in the courts as it is not often in today's society that the court finds stood before it a defendant who is not morally responsible for their own actions and the resulting consequences, or that the law enforcement agencies have acted so reprehensibly.

12.11.3 Bind overs

If an offender receives a 'bind over' then they are formally 'bound over to keep the peace'. This essentially means that if they are to re-offend within a set time then they will be punished for breaking their bind over, as well as for the new offence committed. Again this is another method of trying to ensure that an offender does not re-offend.

12.12 Summary

(a) There are four broad categories of sentence that can be imposed upon a criminal conviction: custody, community sentences, financial penalties and other (including discharges). The most appropriate sentence for the offence and offender in question should be the one that is ultimately imposed.

(b) The aims of sentencing can be seen to be the punishment of the offender, deterrence, reparation, reform and rehabilitation, the protection of the public and an effort to reduce crime. Any sentence imposed upon an offender will have one or more of these aims.

(c) The sentence that is imposed must reflect the seriousness of the offence. It must be proportionate and appropriate in the circumstances.

(d) To determine the seriousness of the offence the courts can turn to guidelines issued by the Sentencing Guideline Council, the Magistrates' Court Sentencing Guidelines and appellate court decisions. The courts will also take into consideration other factors such as pre-sentence reports and victim impact statements when assessing the seriousness of the offence.

(e) Custodial sentences should only be imposed where the custody threshold has been passed. There are a number of different types of custodial sentences ranging from life imprisonment down to a suspended sentence.

(f) The court can impose a community sentence when the community threshold of 'serious enough' has been passed, but where the offence is too serious for disposal by a lesser sentence. Community sentences have 'add on' requirements, such as unpaid work or a prohibited activity order, so that the sentence can be tailored to suit the offender's circumstances.

(g) Financial penalties (such as fines or compensation) and discharges (either absolute or conditional) can be imposed by the courts in situations where custody or a community sentence would not be not appropriate.

12.13   Self-test questions

1. The main aim of sentencing is:

   (a) to punish
   (b) to reform
   (c) to protect the public
   (d) all of the above

2. The magistrates' court, when considering sentence, will:

   (a) always start by considering whether a custodial sentence is appropriate
   (b) always start by considering whether a community sentence is appropriate
   (c) always start by considering whether a fine or a discharge is appropriate
   (d) always start by imposing a custodial sentence

3. The Crown Court are guided in their sentencing by:

   (a) the House of Lords
   (b) the Court of Appeal
   (c) the Privy Council
   (d) other Crown Court cases

4. Adherence to the totality principle means that a sentencer should:

   (a) impose the maximum sentence possible for the offences in question
   (b) impose the minimum sentence possible for the offences in question
   (c) take into account the overall level of seriousness of the offences and sentence proportionally to this
   (d) impose whatever level of sentence they feel like based upon their personal opinions

5. The maximum fine that can be imposed by the magistrates' court is:

   (a) £10,000
   (b) £5,000
   (c) £1,000
   (d) £500

12.14 Further reading

J. Cooper, "The Sentencing Guidelines Council—a practical perspective" [2008] 4 Crim. L.R. 277–286.

J.V. Roberts, "Aggravating and mitigating factors at sentencing: towards greater consistency of application" [2008] 4 Crim. L.R. 264–276.

S. Shute, "Who passes unduly lenient sentences? How were they listed?: a survey of Attorney-General's reference cases 1989–97" [1999] Crim. L.R. Aug, 603–626.

M. Wasik, "Going around in circles? Reflections on fifty years of change in sentencing" [2004] Crim. L.R. Apr. 253–265.

M. Wasik, "The status and authority of sentencing guidelines" [2007] 39 Bracton L.J. 9–18.

M. Wasik, "Sentencing guidelines in England and Wales—state of the art?" [2008] 4 Crim. L.R. 253–263.

13 Appeals

13.1 Introduction

In his report *Access to Justice* (1996), Lord Woolf wrote that there are two main purposes of appeals. The first is the private one of doing justice in individual cases by correcting wrong decisions. The second is the public one of engendering public confidence in the administration of justice by making those corrections and in clarifying and developing the law. Although the Report was focused on the civil law jurisdiction this comment is also applicable to the criminal forum. When Lord Justice Auld conducted his *Review of the Criminal Courts* (2001) he referred to Lord Woolf's comments and added that the main criteria of a good criminal appellate system are that:

- it should do justice to individual defendants and to the public as represented principally by the prosecution;

- it should bring finality to the criminal process, subject to the need to safeguard either side from clear and serious injustice and such as would damage the integrity of the criminal justice system;

- it should be readily accessible, consistently with a proper balance of the interest of individual defendants and that of the public;

- it should be clear and simple in its structure and procedures;

- it should be efficient and effective in its use of judges and other resources in righting injustice and in declaring and applying the law; and

- it should be speedy.

It is with these points in mind that this final chapter will now explore the different possibilities of appealing within the criminal and civil system. If, in a criminal case, a defendant has been convicted of an offence, or in a civil claim a finding has gone against the defendant, then the possibility of an appeal will be of extreme importance to them. In this chapter we will consider the different routes of appeal within the criminal and civil jurisdiction: where the case originated and which court will hear the appeal, the procedures that need to be followed, as well as the issues that can be appealed upon. Whilst progressing through this chapter bear in mind the criteria set out by Lord Justice Auld, and consider whether these criteria have been successfully achieved by the present appeal system.

13.2 Criminal appeals

Criminal appeals can be a complicated matter depending on a variety of factors such as what court the decision is being appealed from, the party bringing the appeal and what the ground for the appeal is.

13.2.1 Prosecution appeals

The issue of appeals especially in relation to the criminal courts have, over recent years, been the subject of numerous discussions and debates. This is especially true following recent changes in the law such as the fact that the prosecution can now appeal against an acquittal since the abolishment of the long-standing principle of *autrefois acquit*, which is more commonly known as the rule against double jeopardy. The prosecution has the limited possibility to appeal a decision by the routes set out below, and they can also use the process of appealing by way of 'case stated', which is explained in more detail at 13.2.2.1.3.

13.2.1.1 Attorney-General's references

Issues of precedent

An appeal by the prosecution by way of an Attorney-General's reference (the Attorney-General is the chief law officer of the Crown in England and Wales) can occur in one of two ways. The first of these is where the prosecution, after the acquittal of the defendant following a trial on indictment, refers a point of law to the Court of Appeal for it to give its opinion. The power for the prosecution to appeal in this manner is governed by s.36 of the Criminal Justice Act 1972 (CJA 1972) and Part 74 of the Criminal Procedure Rules (CrimPR). No matter what the outcome of the appeal, even if the Court of Appeal hold that the trial court applied the law incorrectly, the defendant in the case will remain acquitted. The purpose of an Attorney-General's reference is simply so that the law can be clarified in anticipation of future cases, or in other words, so that binding precedent can be set down.

Unduly lenient sentence

The second way in which an Attorney-General's reference can be made is under s.35 and s.36 of the Criminal Justice Act 1988 (CJA 1988). Section 36 applies where the prosecution wishes to appeal against an 'unduly lenient sentence' set by the Crown Court. Section 35 sets out that the provisions to appeal against an unduly lenient sentence can be used where a sentence is passed upon a person for an offence triable only on indictment, or for an offence of a description specified in an order under that section. Upon review of the sentence the Court of Appeal has the power to leave the sentence imposed by the Crown Court or to quash the original sentence and to substitute it with a new one that they feel is more appropriate. If the Court of Appeal is minded to quash the original sentence in these circumstances then it is likely that they will then impose a heavier sentence.

So what then is meant by the term 'unduly lenient sentence'? Surely most victims to a case will view the sentence imposed as 'unduly lenient'? The phrase 'they should have locked him up and thrown away the key' is often voiced in general conversation; should the victim's or the victim's family's view be taken into account here? What about the prosecution or the police who investigated the crime? They will often be displeased with the sentence handed down. Is it their views that will be taken into account when deciding if a sentence is too lenient? Obviously the prosecution will be disputing the length of the sentence imposed, that is why the reference has been made, but their views will not be the driving force behind the court's ultimate decision. The Court of Appeal in *Attorney-General's Reference (No.4 of 1989)* [1990] 1 W.L.R. 41 set out what they viewed as the correct approach to be taken when considering whether a sentence imposed was in fact too lenient. Lord Lane C.J. stated, at page 46, that:

> A sentence is unduly lenient, we would hold, where it falls outside the range of sentences which the judge, applying his mind to all the relevant factors, could reasonably consider appropriate.

It is not a decision that should be made on emotion or the simple facts of the case, but with regard to reported cases, and to the guidance given by the Court in guideline cases. What will be viewed as unduly lenient by one person could well be viewed as unduly harsh by another. A rounded and objective view of all the factors should be taken into account in deciding whether a sentence is really too lenient.

Although the prosecution are afforded this method of appeal they will not be able to revert to it in every case where they feel slightly aggrieved by the sentence. Leave to appeal (permission to appeal) must be obtained and even where the prosecution are granted leave to appeal it does not necessarily follow that the sentence will be increased upon appeal. The court is generally reluctant to interfere with the trial judge's decision because, if it were to constantly interfere with lower court rulings, it would be highly likely that the public would quickly lose confidence with the whole justice system. In the case of *Attorney-General's Reference (No.5 of 1989)* (1990) 90 Cr. App. R. 358 the Court of Appeal, by way of the judgment delivered by the Lord Chief Justice, stated that the court would only interfere in a sentencing decision where there was an error of principle in the case and public confidence in the judicial system would be damaged if the original sentence were to stand.

An issue that does arise with an appeal brought this way is that it is possible for the offender to feel as though they have been sentenced twice for the same offence. Court proceedings, even after the offender has been found guilty, will still be a nerve wracking experience, and the court are aware of the potential effects that a further review of sentence may have upon the offender, especially when there is a high chance that their sentence will be increased. In many instances the court will mitigate the increased sentence to recognise the detrimental effect the further proceedings had upon the offender. In the case of *Attorney-General's Reference (No.1 of 1991)* [1991] Crim. L.R. 725 the court increased the sentence to seven years from five years. Whilst giving judgment they indicated that they felt a minimum sentence of eight years would have been appropriate on the case facts, but to allow for the offender's added anxiety by the appeal they would mitigate this by reducing the sentence by a year. In murder cases however, the court are barred from mitigating the new sentence by way of s.272 of the CJA 2003.

Any increase in sentence can also mean that the offender is remanded into custody from an original non-custodial sentence. This is what happened in the case of *Attorney-General's Reference (No.5 of 1989)* above. The defendant in the case had caused death by reckless driving and had been originally sentenced to two years' probation, with the condition of attending a 60-day behaviour course, and he was disqualified from driving for three years. On appeal by the prosecution on the grounds that the sentence was unduly lenient the defendant was sentence to 21 months in a young offender's institution.

13.2.1.2 Terminating rulings

Under s.58 CJA 2003 the prosecution may appeal against a judicial decision which has had the effect of terminating the proceedings against the defendant. The ruling that is being appealed can have occurred at any point in the trial up until the point that the judge begins to sum up the case. Examples of rulings that may effectively terminate proceedings are ones such as a ruling that there is no case to answer, or the judge refuses to allow the admission of crucial evidence against the defendant.

There are two possible procedures for an appeal on this point; one is the expedited route and the other is the non-expedited route. Under s.59 if the judge decides to follow the expedited route he can order an adjournment in the case whilst waiting on the outcome of the appeal, whereas under the non-expedited route the judge (again under s.59) has the option to either order an adjournment or discharge the jury whilst waiting on the outcome of the appeal. Which route they take will be dependent on the action that they feel to be more appropriate in the circumstances.

In respect of such an appeal the Court of Appeal have three possible options to consider: they may confirm, reverse or vary any ruling made to which the appeal relates. If the court decides to reverse or vary the ruling then this must be because either the ruling was wrong in law, wrong in principle or unreasonable. If it does decide that the decision was not a correct one then there are three possible outcomes that may occur in respect of the trial. The court may order, on a decision to reverse or vary a terminating ruling, insomuch as:

- proceedings for that offence be resumed in the Crown Court;
- a fresh trial takes place in the Crown Court for that offence;
- the defendant be acquitted of that offence.

If the court confirms the Crown Court judge's decision in respect of the ruling then the defendant will be acquitted of the offence in question.

13.2.1.3 Abolition of double jeopardy

The abolition of the rule against double jeopardy (more formally known as the common law doctrine of *autrefois acquit*) has proved controversial in recent years. The old rule of law was that if a defendant was acquitted of an offence then they could not be re-tried for it at a later point. The reasoning behind this was one of due process; that the defendant did not have to worry about constantly being chased by the law and that there was finality to the proceedings, which reduced the potential for abuse of process and safeguarded the liberty of individuals. This meant that if a defendant was lucky enough to be tried for a crime they had committed and be acquitted, they could then boast about their exploits or even write a book about it as they faced no fear of further prosecution. The rule against double jeopardy was a doctrine spanning back into the roots of the common law, and was firmly entrenched in not just the UK legal system, but in many other legal systems around the world such as France, Germany and even Japan.

The racially motivated murder of Stephen Lawrence in April 1993 began the wheels of change to the longstanding doctrine of the common law. Stephen Lawrence was stabbed to death whilst waiting for a bus home, five suspects were arrested but no conviction ever resulted from these arrests. Stephen's family privately prosecuted the suspects, but the case against two of the suspects was dropped before trial due to lack of evidence and the other three men were acquitted after trial, again due to lack of sufficient evidence (the judge ruled that evidence identifying the suspects was inadmissible). The family of Stephen Lawrence then made a complaint to the Police Complaints Authority, alleging that the investigation into their son's death had been conducted incompetently due to the alleged racism of the investigating police officers. The Police Complaints Authority exonerated the officers involved but a public inquiry was ordered. The result of the public inquiry was the *Macpherson Report*, which alleged that the initial investigation into Stephen's murder had involved fundamental errors and that the police were institutionally racist. The report made a number of recommendations, one of these (recommendation no. 38) being that consideration should be given to allow the Court of Appeal to prosecute after an acquittal where fresh and viable evidence is presented.

The Law Commission in their report, *Double Jeopardy and Prosecution Appeals* (Law Com No.267 (2001)), which followed on from the recommendation made in the *Macpherson Report*, put forward the proposition that the rule against double jeopardy should be abrogated in the case of acquittals in murder cases, and Lord Justice Auld in his *Review of the Criminal Courts* took this point further, stating that where

> a guilty man has probably been wrongly acquitted [. . .] that the public interest requires the matter to be re-opened

The government heeded this recommendation for reform on the law, and the introduction of the CJA 2003 dramatically changed this area of law by abolishing the rule against double jeopardy for certain crimes. If a defendant is acquitted of an offence the prosecution can now, in certain circumstances, appeal against the acquittal under ss.75 and 76 of the CJA 2003, and a re-trial can be ordered. Such an appeal will be entertained if there is:

- new (not adduced in the original trial) **and** compelling evidence of the acquitted person's guilt; and

- it is in the public interest to re-try the accused.

There are currently 30 qualifying offences in which the rule against double jeopardy has been abolished—these include murder, rape, manslaughter, kidnapping, certain drug and sexual offences, war crimes and terrorism offences. The Director of Public Prosecutions, Sir Ken McDonald QC, stated (BBC News April 3, 2005) that only a handful of cases per year are likely to be retried under the new rule, and only one case has been tried so far.

On September 12, 2006 Billy Dunlop was re-arraigned for the murder of Julie Hogg. In November 1989 Julie was attacked in her own home, murdered and then hidden behind the bath panel in her flat, where her mother found her body three months later. Dunlop had already been tried twice for the offence but each time the jury could not decide on a verdict and so he was formally acquitted. Later on he confessed to the murder to a prison officer while he was serving a seven year sentence for an unrelated attack. He was subsequently charged with perjury, as at the time re-trying him for murder was not an option due the rules against double jeopardy. After the abolition of the rule against double jeopardy for murder cases, fresh charges were laid against Dunlop for the murder of Julie Hogg to which he pleaded guilty.

13.2.1.4 Acquittals tainted by intimidation

The final way in which the prosecution can appeal is under s.54 of the CPIA 1996. Here the prosecution can appeal against an acquittal where a person has been convicted of intimidating a juror in order to effect an acquittal. The appeal is made to the High Court and they will allow such an appeal where it appears to the court that it is likely that, but for the interference or intimidation, the acquitted person would not have been acquitted. So far this provision has not been used in practice.

Figure 13.1 Prosecution appeals

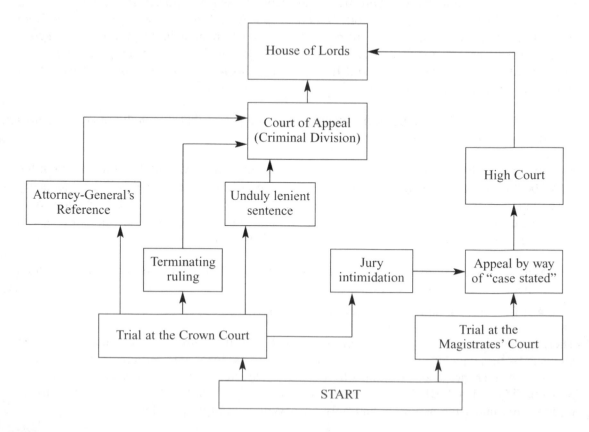

13.2.2 Defence appeals

There are a number of ways in which the defence can appeal, and the court from which the defendant is appealing as well as the reasoning behind the appeal will determine the most appropriate method of appeal.

13.2.2.1 Appeals from the magistrates' court

13.2.2.1.1 Re-opening a case

Following a conviction in the magistrates' court by way of either a conviction after trial or on a guilty plea, the defence may be presented with the ability to appeal under s.142 of the MCA 1980. Section 142 involves the defence requesting that the case be re-opened in order to rectify a mistake made in the original proceedings. The case will be heard by a differently constituted bench to that which heard the original trial; obviously if there is an allegation of an error in the original trial the original bench could not be seen to be objective enough to deal with the matter. By hearing the appeal in this manner the magistrates' court has the option of varying or rescinding the sentence imposed in the original trial. The court is permitted to allow the appeal when it appears to the court that it would be in the interests of justice to do so. This type of appeal can often be a quicker route than appealing to the Crown Court (see below) and is mainly used where the defendant has been convicted of an offence in their absence or if the original court made an obvious error in the case.

13.2.2.1.2 Appeals to the Crown

After conviction the defendant in the case can appeal to the Crown Court by way of s.108 of the Magistrates' Court Act 1980, as supplemented by Pt 63 of the Criminal Procedure Rules 2005. When using this route the appeal must be based upon either a question of law or a question of fact. When the defendant was convicted after trial, the appeal can be against conviction *or* sentence. However where the defendant has pleaded guilty, then the appeal may only be against sentence.

The defendant does not need to obtain leave (otherwise known as permission) to appeal from the magistrates' court to the Crown Court under s.108, as the right to appeal truly exists as a 'right' and the defendant is afforded the benefit of an automatic appeal if they wish to go down this route. The Crown Court will undertake a complete re-hearing of the case under a procedure known as a 'trial *de novo*' (new trial). The evidence in the case will be re-heard, and the witnesses who appeared at the original trial will be recalled. Even though the case is re-heard in the Crown Court, there will not be a jury present to deliberate on the matter. The composition of the bench that will hear the appeal consists of a judge, who is normally either a circuit judge or a recorder, and two magistrates, neither of whom will have sat in the original trial. The judge will direct and rule on the law but the overall decision as to the issue on appeal will be decided by way of a majority decision.

The Crown Court will have the option of either confirming, varying or reversing the original decision (or any part of it) by the magistrates' court, or remitting the case back to the magistrates' court with an opinion of how the matter should be disposed with. If the defendant chooses to proceed with this form of appeal then they need to be warned that the Crown Court has the power to increase the original sentence given by the magistrates; however, the Crown Court cannot exceed the maximum sentencing powers allowed by the magistrates' court for the offence in question.

This process of allowing the defendant a complete rehearing of the case, or a 'second bite of the cherry' so to speak, was criticised by Lord Justice Auld in his 2001 Review of the Criminal Courts. Lord Justice Auld stated that this right of appeal had its origins in the general lack of confidence in the impartiality and competence of the old 'police courts' and that, due to the development of the abilities and knowledge of the magistrates' courts over recent times by way of training and the provisions of legal advisors in the court etc., their new standing and function bear little resemblance to the courts of old. He concluded that "it is hard to see what is left of the original justification for permitting another tribunal, even one presided over by a judge, to re-hear the case" (Chapter 10, para.17). It can be argued that this conclusion is erroneous as the magistrates' court, although a highly respectable and worthwhile tribunal, is still only composed of lay-people who have volunteered to help in the distribution of justice, and who are only aided by a legal advisor whose advice they can decide to ignore if they so wish. It would be unfair for a defendant to be denied the opportunity for his case to be reheard by a legally qualified tribunal where it is felt that the original decision was made in error; to deny this, it could be argued, would be to breach the defendant's right to a fair trial under art.6 of the European Convention of Human Rights and Fundamental Freedoms. The very low number of appeals brought about in the manner is also an argument for the retention and continuation of such a process. Even Lord Justice Auld acknowledged this point, commenting that less than one per cent of magistrates' court decisions are appealed in this way. Surely then this very limited use of the procedure indicates that it is a process that is only used when appropriate and therefore only when it is necessary for justice to be done?

Once the defendant's case has been reheard and decided upon by the Crown Court they are not afforded any further form of appeal, except by way of 'case stated' under s.28 Supreme Court Act 1981. For an appeal to be made by way of case stated from the Crown Court the basis of the appeal must be that an error was made in law by the court. If the appeal by way of 'case stated' is allowed to progress then it will be treated as any other appeal by way of 'case stated' from the magistrates' court, as described below.

13.2.2.1.3 Appeal by way of 'case stated'

An appeal by way of 'case stated' can be made under s.111 MCA 1980 and it is an unusual form of appeal as *both* the prosecution and defence can appeal by way of it (s.111(1)). This means that defendants who have been acquitted may then find themselves subject to an appeal, even though they have been found by a court of law to be innocent. In such a situation the purpose of the appeal by the prosecution is not to try and have the defendant convicted of the offence, but rather to try and have the law settled so that it is clear for future cases. An appeal under this process is from the magistrates' court direct to the Administrative Court of the Queen's Bench Division of the High Court (previously known as the Queen's Bench Divisional Court). Once an appeal is made in this manner then all grounds for appealing to the Crown Court in the case are lost (s.111(4)); often it is better to begin by appealing to the Crown Court, and if that proves unsuccessful, then appealing by way of this method (as stated above).

The grounds of an appeal by way of case stated can be either that the magistrates were:

- wrong in law; or
- exceeded their jurisdiction.

The court from which the appeal originates from (normally the magistrates' court but possibly the Crown Court) are then required to 'state their case' to the High Court, which effectively means that they must set out to the court their reasoning for the decision. The High Court will then decide whether they did in fact exceed their jurisdiction or if the decision was made in error of the law. This method of appeal only works in relation to cases heard in the magistrates' court (or from the Crown Court after appeal from the magistrates' court) as they are the only court of first instance who are required to set out the reasoning behind their decision when they deliver their verdict. On trial in the Crown Court the jury are not required to provide details of their deliberations, but are simply required to hand down their verdict of either guilty or not guilty, therefore the Crown Court would not be able to 'state their case' to a High Court as they simply would not have the details necessary to be able to do so.

The appeal must be lodged within 21 days of the decision being delivered (s.111(2)). This form of appeal does not carry with it an automatic right to appeal and therefore the party wishing to bring the appeal must request leave to do so. This leave will normally be requested from the court that made the decision that is to be the subject of the appeal (s.111(1)). There is a potential difficulty with this process in that by requesting that the court states the matter to a higher court, and then by them doing so, it may be perceived that the court is being asked to admit that they were (or at least might have been) wrong in their original decision. Nobody likes to be wrong, so consequently is there not the danger that the leave will always be refused? Under s.111(5) the justices (magistrates) can refuse to state a case if they believe that the application is 'frivolous'. What is meant by the term 'frivolous' was explored by the Court of Appeal in the case of *R. v North West Suffolk (Mildenhall) Magistrates' Court* [1998] Env. L.R. 9, where the court held that the meaning of frivolous was that an application was 'futile, misconceived, hopeless or academic'. If the justices do refuse the application on the basis that it is frivolous then they must give full reasoning as to why they have found in this way.

If leave to appeal is granted then the High Court will consider a written 'statement of the case'. This written statement will include a number of questions that the party appealing wishes the court to decide upon; normally these questions have been agreed in advance between the appellant (the party appealing) and the respondent (the party responding to the appeal). No evidence is called as the appeal is not a re-hearing of the case but rather a more paper based exercise in legal argument, and the case will be heard by at least two High Court judges. There are a number of options open to the court in respect of determination of such an appeal and they can affirm, reverse or amend the magistrates' original decision, or they can remit the case back to the lower court with an opinion that the court should acquit, convict or re-hear the case against the defendant. There is a further option of appeal from the High Court direct to the House of Lords in these matters (under s.1 Administration of Justice Act 1960), but only if the point of law is one of general public importance and leave to appeal is granted by them.

13.2.2.1.4 Judicial review

The issue of judicial review is governed by Pt 54 of the Civil Procedure Rules 1998 (CPR), and these are applicable even when the content of the review is criminal in nature. Judicial review can occur when the jurisdiction of the court is called into question due to the fact that the court acted illegally in respect of its powers (*ultra vires*), failed to follow the correct procedure or acted unreasonably. Judicial review is considered in further detail at 13.4.

13.2.2.2 Appeals from the Crown Court

Under s.1 of the Criminal Appeal Act 1968 (CAA 1968), and Pt 68 of the CrimPR, a defendant can appeal from the Crown Court to the Court of Appeal against conviction or sentence after trial, or upon sentence only where they pleaded guilty to the offence. The first hurdle that needs to be dealt with in an appeal of this nature is the securing of leave to appeal. This can be granted by either the original trial court or the Court of Appeal, although the preferred court to seek leave from is the Court of Appeal. The application for leave to appeal is made by way of written application and this is then decided by way of a review of the application by one judge. If the leave is granted and the appeal proceeds to court the case will be heard by a panel of appeal court judges. Normally the panel will consist of three judges, but occasionally for the more notable cases a 'full' court of five judges may sit.

13.2.2.2.1 Appeals against conviction

An appeal against conviction will be brought where the defendant believes that they should not have been convicted following the original trial. Many (if not most) defendants will probably say that they should not have been convicted and will still be protesting their innocence long after the end of the trial. If a defendant is convicted then one of their first comments may well be 'can we appeal?' So for what reasons can a defendant appeal, and on what grounds can an appeal against conviction be allowed? Why are the appellate courts not swamped with appeals from every disgruntled defendant who has been convicted?

Section 2 of the CAA 1968 states that the Court of Appeal shall:

> allow an appeal against a conviction if they think that the conviction is unsafe; and . . .
> shall dismiss the appeal in any other case.

The Court of Appeal is only permitted to allow an appeal if they believe that the conviction is 'unsafe', and in all other instances the appeal must be dismissed. Therefore leave to appeal will only be granted where it seems that there is a question mark over the reliability of the conviction. The concern as to whether the conviction is safe or not will arise from within the facts of the original trial. Common grounds for appeal against conviction are either that the trial judge misdirected the jury, evidence was either wrongly admitted or excluded, or there were errors in either counsel's or the judge's conduct. Whatever the reason, there must be present the possibility that the ground for appeal has led to the conviction potentially being unsafe; the one thing that the appeal will not focus upon is the guilt or innocence of the defendant in question.

To determine whether a conviction is unsafe or not the court will consider the question of whether they *personally* believe that the conviction is unsafe. It is a subjective test and each individual judge in the court must consider it. To help the court determine whether the appeal should be allowed on this ground or whether it should be dismissed, the court will hear arguments from counsel on both sides and, if relevant, they also have the discretion to hear new evidence under s.23 CAA 1968. Section 23 sets out that the court are entitled to hear fresh evidence in an appeal if, and only if:

- the evidence appears to the Court to be capable of belief;

- it appears to the Court that the evidence may afford any ground for allowing the appeal;

- the evidence would have been admissible in the proceedings from which the appeal lies on an issue which is the subject of the appeal; and

- there is a reasonable explanation for the failure to adduce the evidence in those proceedings.

The provisions under s.23 have been under scrutiny in numerous appeals, with the question being asked, in what circumstances should new evidence really be allowed to be adduced? In the case of *R. v TS* [2008] EWCA Crim 6 the Court of Appeal were faced with a request to adduce new evidence of a recently diagnosed medical condition. In *TS* the appellant had been charged and convicted of the rape of his estranged wife. At trial the judge, when directing the jury, stated that in the case of a rape there might be room for misunderstanding on the defendant's part in a situation where a woman did not make clear that she was not consenting, but in the instant case there was no room for doubt or misunderstanding. The appellant was later diagnosed with Asperger's syndrome, which had the effect of him being liable to misunderstand the signs, and even straightforward indications, of those with whom he comes into contact. At appeal the court viewed the doctor's evidence as being capable of belief, that it would have been admissible at trial, and was covered by a reasonable explanation for the failure to adduce it at trial. On balance they came to the conclusion that the appellant's conviction was unsafe and therefore that the appeal should be allowed.

However, just because there is new evidence that was not adduced at trial does not mean that the evidence will automatically be adduced. In the case of *R. v Hill* [2008] EWCA Crim 76 the appellant had been convicted of murder. The facts of the case were that Hill had been out drinking with the victim, a known homosexual, on the day of the murder. He returned to the victim's flat where he fell asleep in a chair. Hill then awoke to find the victim undoing his trousers with the intention of sexual activity. Hill then lashed out and killed the victim by way of strangulation. After the conviction Hill appealed on the basis that he had been sexually abused as a child and that it was a flashback to this that caused him to kill the victim. No evidence of the sexual abuse had been raised during the original trial. The evidence may have been capable of belief, and therefore it may have afforded a ground for allowing the appeal as it would have been relevant to the defence of provocation and the evidence would have been admissible at the original trial, however the evidence was held not to be admissible by the

381

appeal court as there was no reasonable explanation for Hill having failed to advance evidence of this abuse at the original trial. Lord Justice Hughes stated that:

> It is of central importance to the law that a person charged should advance whatever material is available to him at trial. This court will not ordinarily so exercise its powers to admit fresh evidence as to permit a defendant to change his account after trial in order to run a different defence on appeal, in the absence of the witnesses and of the jury.

The court therefore took the view that fresh evidence should only be adduced in an appeal where it is relevant and pertinent to the issues under review and that it really could not have been adduced at the earlier hearing. The principle to be taken away is that an appeal should not be used as a method by the appellant to try and raise another defence, in order to have a second chance of being acquitted of the offence.

One problem that arises out of the use of the word 'unsafe' in s.2 is the question of what to do where there is a procedural irregularity in the case, but the defendant is guilty of the offence in question. The appellant courts have had to consider this issue on more than one occasion, and their approach to this dilemma can be seen in the case of *R. v Mullen* [1999] 2 Cr. App. R. 143. In *Mullen* the court held that the meaning of 'unsafe' in s.2 of the CAA 1968 was broad enough to permit the quashing of a conviction on the sole ground that it was unsafe because of abuse of process prior to trial. In the case, British authorities had obtained the appellant's deportation from Zimbabwe by unlawful means for the purposes of putting him on trial. By so doing they had encouraged unlawful conduct in Zimbabwe and had acted in breach of public international law. The certainty of guilt could not displace the essential feature of this type of abuse of process, namely the degradation of the lawful administration of justice. The court, in making this decision, had to take into account the gravity of the offence and balance it against the failure to adhere to the rule of law. They stated that for a conviction to be safe it must be lawful, and where it resulted from a trial which should never have taken place it could not be regarded as safe. They allowed the appeal against conviction despite the fact that the defendant was guilty of the offence. The conclusion that can be drawn from this decision is that the court was of the opinion that it is more satisfactory for a guilty person to be released due to a procedural irregularity than their conviction upheld, regardless of their guilt.

The courts' own opinion of how the case would have been decided at trial should also not be a considered factor in their deliberations of whether a conviction is unsafe or not. In the case of *R. v Pendleton* [2001] UKHL 66 the appellant had been convicted of a murder committed 14 years previously. The appellant had made admissions to the police during interview but had not given evidence in the original trial due to his counsel's doomed view about the strength of the admissions in the jury's eyes. On referral by the Criminal Cases Review Commission (explained below at 13.2.2.2.4) the Court of Appeal dismissed the appellant's appeal against conviction, even though they heard fresh evidence from a psychologist that raised serious doubts about the reliability of the statements the appellant had made to the police. The court was of the opinion that the new evidence did not put a 'flavour of falsity' on the admissions made and they found it inconceivable that the accounts given by the appellant were imagined or invented. The House of Lords then granted them leave to appeal and they considered the actions of the Court of Appeal in the case, holding that the conviction was unsafe and that:

In holding otherwise the Court of Appeal strayed beyond its true function of review and made findings which were not open to it in all the circumstances. Indeed, it came perilously close to considering whether the appellant, in its judgment, was guilty.

The Court of Appeal had acted outside of their remit by considering the facts of the case and the defendant's guilt as opposed to considering the safeness of the conviction by undertaking a review of the case. What they should have considered was whether the psychological evidence, if presented at trial, would have affected the decision of the jury to convict, and if they were of the opinion that it would have done then they should have allowed the appeal. This principle has been confirmed in later cases such as *Newcombe* [2007] EWCA 2554.

An issue that has arisen a number of times within the courts is the relationship between the words 'unsafe' in s.2 and 'unfair' in art.6(1) ECHR. On first sight it would be logical to assume that if a case breaches the right to a fair trial under art.6 then it must also be 'unsafe' under the test employed by s.2. Unfortunately, case law would seem to indicate otherwise. In *R. v Togher* [2001] 3 All E.R. 463 the Court of Appeal followed the logical thought process that if there was a breach of art.6 then the result would be that the conviction was also unsafe. The ECHR confirmed this approach in the case of *Condron v UK* (2001) 31 E.H.R.R. 1, where they implied that where there was an unfair trial the conviction should always be quashed. However the domestic courts in *R. v Davies, Rowe and Johnson* [2001] 1 Cr. App. R. 115 and *R. v Williams, The Times,* March 30, 2001 came to the conclusion that a breach of art.6 would not automatically lead to a finding that the conviction was unsafe, but would rather require the court to consider the fairness of the trial as a whole. The approach taken in *Togher* would seem to be the most sensible decision, because if the defendant has been denied the right to a fair trial how could the resulting conviction be safe? However, the issue will need to arise before the courts again before it can be said with complete certainty which is the correct approach to adopt.

If the Court of Appeal finds that the defendant's conviction is unsafe then they have a number of options open to them. They may quash the conviction and acquit the defendant, quash the conviction and order a re-trial, find the defendant guilty of an alternative offence (e.g. allow the appeal against conviction for murder but then find the defendant guilty of the offence of manslaughter instead), allow part of the appeal, or dismiss the appeal completely. One thing that they cannot do however is increase the original sentence imposed by the court of first instance.

The Court of Appeal's powers to order a retrial in a case have been expanded over recent years. Prior to 1989 the court only had the statutory power to order a retrial in one specific instance, this being that the appeal had been allowed due to fresh evidence being received by the court. In all other cases the appellant who successfully managed to demonstrate the unsafeness of his conviction was acquitted completely, irrespective of the fact that there was overwhelming evidence as to his guilt. In 1989 the Criminal Justice Act 1988 amended the law under the CAA 1968. Section 7(1) of the CAA 1968 now provides that the Court of Appeal has a general discretion to order a retrial whenever they allow an appeal against conviction under s.2(1) of the CAA 1968 and the interests of justice require the appellant to be retried. The new trial must not be for a completely different offence but only for (a) the offence of which he was convicted at the original trial and in respect of which his appeal is allowed, (b) an offence of which he could have been convicted at the original trial on an indictment for the first-mentioned offence, or (c) an offence charged in an alternative count of the indictment in respect of which the jury was discharged from giving a verdict in consequence of his being convicted of the first-mentioned offence.

A well-reported retrial that gained considerable media attention was that of Sion Jenkins (*R. v Jenkins* [2004] EWCA 2047) where the Court of Appeal allowed Jenkins' second appeal in respect of his conviction for the murder of his 13-year-old foster daughter, Billy Jo Jenkins. The court ordered that Jenkins stand trial again for her murder after new evidence came to light that cast doubt on the safety of his first conviction. Jenkins then underwent two more trials for the alleged murder. In both trials the jury could not agree on a majority verdict and eventually in February 2006 Jenkins was formally acquitted of the murder.

The point to remember in respect of the Court of Appeal's power to order a retrial is that it is not under a duty to order a retrial as this is a discretionary power and it may instead simply choose to quash the conviction. The decision not to retry an appellant may occur for a number of different reasons and these could include factors such as that the alleged crime took place many years ago and that the re-calling of witnesses and evidence would be difficult or even impossible, or that the case was heavily covered in the press and that consequently there would be a real risk that the appellant would not receive a fair trial (imagine that Ian Huntley was to be re-tried for the Soham murders—there would be little chance that any jury convened would not be prejudiced in some way or another).

13.2.2.2.2 Appeal against sentence

A defendant can appeal against the sentence imposed by the court on the grounds that the sentence is either:

- wrong in law
- wrong in principle
- manifestly excessive

The Court of Appeal has the option of either dismissing the appeal, quashing the sentence or imposing a new sentence in substitution of the one in question. If the court is minded to impose a new sentence then they are permitted to impose any sentence that can be imposed by the Crown Court in the matter.

13.2.2.2.3 Appeal to the House of Lords

Appeals can be made directly from both the Divisional Court (under s.1 of the Administration of Justice Act 1960) and the Court of Appeal (under s.33 CAA 1968) to the House of Lords. Leave to appeal is required in both circumstances and the appeal will only be heard if a point of law of general public importance is certified.

13.2.2.2.4 Criminal Cases Review Commission

There are strict time limits in which an appeal can be brought (generally 21 days after the decision that the appeal relates to has been handed down). Once these time limits have expired then the case is out of the court system (unless leave out of time is granted) and this then leaves the possibility that there are defendants who remain in custody despite the fact that their conviction may be unsafe and that a miscarriage of justice may have occurred. The Criminal Cases Review Commission (CCRC) was created by the Criminal Appeal Act 1995 (CAA 1995) as an independent body with the primary purpose of reviewing such cases. The CCRC does not decide the appeal but simply refers the case to the appropriate court for review. The CCRC can review and investigate any case where there is a suspected wrongful conviction and/or sentence, whether the case was tried summarily or on indictment, or where there has been a finding of not guilty by reason of insanity. Most of the cases that the CCRC deals with are the more serious cases that have been tried on indictment as due to the low sentencing powers of the magistrates' court, it is very rare for a person who has been convicted of a summary offence to be detained for long enough for the CCRC to become involved.

The CCRC will refer a case to the Court of Appeal where, in the case of a conviction, it considers there is a real possibility that the conviction would not be upheld because of an argument or evidence not raised at the trial or on appeal; or in the case of a sentence, it considers there is a real possibility that the sentence would not be upheld because of an argument on a point of law, or information not raised at the trial or on appeal (s.7(2) CAA 1968). The Commission is really there to help safeguard against miscarriages of justice occurring since no matter how many provisions and procedures are put in place miscarriages of justice will occur due to reasons such as unfairly obtained confessions and abuse of police powers, the wrongful identification of the defendant, witnesses perjuring themselves in court and bad trial tactics. The decision to review a case can be made on the Commission's own initiative or the case could be referred to them by an application from the convicted person. The Commission have a large caseload of referred cases to work through. To date there have been 10,627 applications made to the Commission (279 of these they inherited from the Home Office when they started work in 1997), there are currently 223 cases waiting for review, and 462 cases under review. The Court of Appeal has heard 356 cases referred by the CCRC out of which 246 convictions were quashed, 107 were upheld and three were reserved. In total so far the CCRC have reviewed 9,943 cases since their beginnings in 1997 (figures correct as of February 29, 2008; source: Case Library at http://www.ccrc.gov.uk).

Figure 13.2 Defence appeals

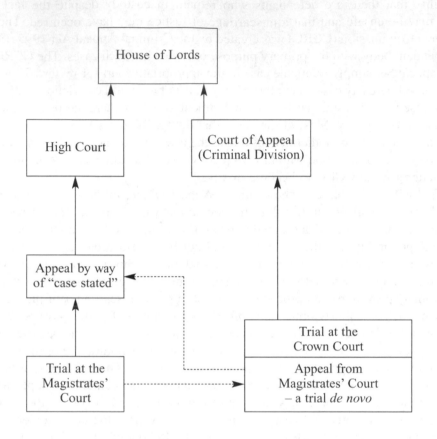

13.3   Civil appeals

The appeals system within the civil jurisdiction of the courts is a far more simplified affair than that found within the criminal court system. Prior to the introduction of the Access to Justice Act 1999 (AJA) and the Civil Procedure Rules 1999 (CPR) there were two common forms of appeal; the first was a complete rehearing of the case, where the parties would again present their full case to the court, with evidence and witnesses etc, and where new evidence and issues could also be presented. The second was a review of the previous case decision, where the appeal court would examine the decision and decision making process of the lower court in the matter. Under the old system the 'right to appeal' was mainly an automatic right, which meant that parties could lodge an appeal to a decision without having to prove the merits of the proposed appeal.

The right to an automatic appeal, although generally viewed as a positive for those using the appeal system (especially those who lost a case), certainly led to a large number of unmeritorious appeals. The effect of such a right meant that cases were not dealt with effectively or expeditiously; a claimant who was successful in their claim would have the threat of the decision being appealed by the disgruntled defendant. Alternatively a defendant who was vindicated at first instance would often have to face the possibility of being chased through the courts once more as the claimant appealed the decision, and hoped that they would be more successful the second time around. Parties to a claim would face further months of uncertainty and the courts became overrun with numerous appeal cases, which created delays and unnecessary costs for all involved.

One of the main aims of the introduction of the CPR was to ensure that justice was done and that cases were dealt with fairly, effectively and expeditiously. Civil appeals are now governed mainly by Pt 52 of the CRP (although the AJA 1999 contains statutory provisions on the matter as well), which provides comprehensive guidance on what can be appealed, under what circumstances an appeal will be allowed to progress and how an appeal will go forward. Two of the main differences between civil appeals pre the CPR and civil appeals under the CPR are that now there is no longer an 'automatic' right to appeal, and that there is no longer the option for a rehearing of a case, except in very limited circumstances (as set out under r.52.11).

Permission to appeal in a civil matter will only be granted in certain circumstances (as provided for under r.52.3 of the CPR). Rule 52.3(6) sets out that permission to appeal will only be given where:

(a)   the court considers that the appeal would have a real prospect of success; or

(b)   there is some other compelling reason why the appeal should be heard.

The introduction of such a limitation on the possibility of appealing is an effort to stop vexatious litigants continuing on with a claim, or appealing a decision where the case itself does not merit such actions. The main focus of the courts when deciding whether or not to grant permission to appeal is generally based on subsection (a), and the court has to be convinced that there is a really good reason for allowing a person to continue on to an appeal (maybe the judge erred in law etc.), and that the case really does have the merit to continue. The courts can grant permission for a general appeal against the overall decision in a case, or they may also decide, when granting the permission to appeal, that the appeal is limited to certain issues in the case as opposed to against the overall decision.

As permission is now required in all but the most unusual cases, the normal procedure is for the party seeking permission to appeal to apply to the court against whose decision they are appealing (known as the 'lower court') for permission. This may seem a rather strange concept as it could be thought unlikely for a judge to grant a party permission to appeal against their own decision, but this does seem to be the most sensible approach for the courts and system to take. The majority of judges do not take an application to appeal as a personal slight against their judicial capabilities and will grant the permission if the benchmark found in r.52.3(6) is, in their opinion, satisfied. It is logical for the court that has heard the case to consider whether an appeal is appropriate since they will be in full possession of the facts of the case and will have the adequate in-depth knowledge required to make such a decision quickly and appropriately, without the need for further extended recourse to precious court resources. However if permission to appeal is refused by the lower court and the party making the application is of the opinion that the court was wrong in its conclusion to refuse, then they may make a further application to the court to which the appeal would be made (known as the appeal court). This application must however be made within 21 days of the initial refusal (again so that the case is dealt with both expeditiously and fairly, as required by the overriding objective).

As stated above, if permission to appeal is granted then the appeal will normally take the form of a review of the lower court's decision. This review will generally be a legally based exercise, where counsel for the parties make submissions to the courts on the relative merits or flaws of the appeal, and will not involve the hearing of any oral or new evidence.

An appeal in a civil case will only be allowed in two situations (both detailed under r.52.11(3)) and these are either that the earlier decision was:

- wrong, or

- unjust

A decision will be seen to be wrong where the appeal court, after having reviewed the previous hearing, reaches the conclusion that they would have decided the appeal differently. A decision will be viewed as being unjust when the appeal court considers that there was a serious procedural or other irregularity in the previous proceedings. If this is their conclusion then the court is not criticising the overall decision of the deciding court, they are simply saying that, due to the irregularity etc, the decision cannot stand in the interests of justice.

When considering a case on appeal, the appeal court is afforded a variety of powers under r.52.10. These powers are provided so that the court can deal with the case at hand in the most appropriate and effective way, dependent on the individual case facts and requirements.

Under r.52.10(2) the court can:

(a) affirm, set aside or vary any order or judgment made or given by the lower court

(b) refer any claim or issue for determination by the lower court

(c) order a new trial or hearing

(d) make orders for the payment of interest

(e) make a costs order

Civil appeals are generally a rather straightforward affair, but there is one interesting distinction that really separates the workings of a civil appeal from that of a criminal appeal, which is that civil appeals do not go to the next court in the hierarchy, but that they actually go to the next judge in the hierarchy. This is an individual foible of the civil appeal system and it can be quite confusing to work out where an appeal will actually lie so below is a brief chart to aid in the understanding of the appeal routes.

388

Figure 13.3 Routes of appeal (civil)

Appeal from	Appeal to
District judge in the county court	Circuit judge
District judge in the High Court	High Court judge
District judge on the small claims/fast track	Circuit judge
Circuit judge on the fast track	High Court judge
High Court judge	Court of Appeal
Multi-track cases (when a final decision)	Court of Appeal

Occasionally an appeal from a High Court judge will not be heard by the Court of Appeal but will 'leap frog' up to the House of Lords by virtue of the provisions set out in the Administration of Justice Act 1969 (AJA 1969). The provisions under this Act allow the Court of Appeal to be bypassed in situations where there is a point of law of general public importance that relates to the construction of an Act or statutory instrument, or the judge in the case is bound by a previous court decision, and all the parties to the case agree to the appeal proceeding to the House of Lords. This is a rarely used statutory provision.

There is one more point to note about civil appeals that sets them apart from the criminal system, this being that there is generally only one appeal per case. The idea is that once an appeal has been determined that is the end of the matter, unless one of the criteria under r.52.13(2) is satisfied. Rule 52.13(2) sets out that a further appeal will only be allowed if the court considers that the appeal would either raise an important point of principle or practice, or that there is some other compelling reason as to why it should be heard by the Court of Appeal. Again the introduction of this restriction on the ability to appeal was focused on the stemming of the number of unmeritorious appeals that were present in the civil courts before the introduction of the new rules under the CPR and the AJA 1999. The introduction of such restrictions does not mean that it is impossible for a further appeal, but rather that such a further appeal will only be allowed where it is truly required.

13.4 Judicial review

As briefly mentioned above, there is another form of 'appeal' open to the parties of a case which is known as 'judicial review'. The term 'appeal' is set in quotes above as judicial review is not so much a traditional form of appeal but is rather a supervisory function as it allows the decisions and actions of a court to be reviewed. The process of judicial review will only be given a brief mention here as the process can be found detailed in great depth in other law texts that focus more upon the administrative aspects of the legal system.

Part 54 of the CPR governs the process of judicial review and r.54.1(2) sets out that a claim for judicial review is

. . . a claim to review the lawfulness of

   (i) an enactment; or

   (ii) a decision, action or failure to act in relation to the exercise of a public function.

An application for judicial review is made to the High Court, and the application is for the court to determine whether the public body in question has acted ultra vires, or beyond their powers. Section 6 of the Human Rights Act 1998 (HRA 1998) sets out what is classed as a public body and it includes any court or tribunal and any persons whose functions are of a public nature. This may then include bodies such as the police, the prison service, healthcare trusts and even universities.

13.4.1 Who can make an application for judicial review?

For a person to be eligible to bring a claim for judicial review they must have what is known as *locus standi* in that they have a 'sufficient interest in the matter to which the application relates' (s.31(3) SCA 1981). What then is a sufficient interest in a claim? In the case of *R. v Secretary of State for the Environment Ex p. Rose Theatre Trust Co* [1990] 2 W.L.R. 186 during the development of a building site in London there was discovered what was believed to be the remains of the Rose Theatre, which had seen the first performances of works by Shakespeare and Marlowe. A group of archaeologists and actors joined together to form the Rose Theatre Trust Company, which had the main aim of preserving the remains and making them accessible to the public. The Trust applied to the Secretary of State for the Environment for the theatre to be listed in the Schedule of Monuments but the Secretary of State, whilst acknowledging the remains were of national importance, declined to list them and in his decision letter gave his reasons for doing so, one being that in his view the site was not under threat. The Trust applied to the High Court for a judicial review of the decision but the High Court dismissed the application as it was believed that the Trust did not have a sufficient interest in the claim. Schiemann J., whilst addressing the issue of *locus standi*, stated that for an applicant to be successful in his application for judicial review:

> The challenger must show that he 'has a sufficient interest in the matter to which the application relates.' The court will look at the matter to which the application relates—in this case the non-scheduling of a monument of national importance—and the statute under which the decision was taken (in this case the Act of 1979) and decide whether that statute gives that individual expressly or impliedly a greater right or expectation than any other citizen of this country to have that decision taken lawfully. We all expect our decision makers to act lawfully. We are not all given by Parliament the right to apply for judicial review.

The Trust, although interested in the case, simply could not show a sufficient enough interest in the matters to be granted leave (as judicial review is a form of appeal leave has to be granted in the normal way) to proceed with a judicial review of the Secretary of State's decision.

13.4.2   The grounds for judicial review

There are three possible grounds for bringing an appeal for judicial review, as set out by Lord Diplock in the case of *Council of Civil Service Unions and Others Appellants v Minister for the Civil Service Respondent* [1985] A.C. 374 at 410. Lord Diplock stated that:

> Judicial review has I think developed to a stage today when without reiterating any analysis of the steps by which the development has come about, one can conveniently classify under three heads the grounds upon which administrative action is subject to control by judicial review. The first ground I would call 'illegality', the second 'irrationality' and the third 'procedural impropriety'.

By illegality it is meant that the body in question has no right or power to make the decision they have; they have effectively acted ultra vires. An example of this would be a Local Council deciding that everyone who lived in the locality must dress in black at all times or face a £70 penalty—they would have no power to make such a decision and would be acting unlawfully if they started fining people.

The second ground of irrationality is commonly referred to as 'Wednesbury unreasonableness' following the case of *Provincial Picture Houses Ltd v Wednesbury Corporation* [1948] 1 K.B. 223. Wednesbury unreasonableness is said to occur where the decision made is "so outrageous in its defiance of logic or of accepted moral standards that no sensible person [. . .] could have arrived at it" (per Lord Diplock in *Council of Civil Service Unions and Others Appellants v Minister for the Civil Service Respondent*). The standard of the test employed under Wednesbury reasonableness has been criticised for being too strict, in that if the decision is not completely outrageous, but just a little outrageous, then the decision will be deemed as being legal. In the case of *Smith and Grady v UK* (2000) 29 E.H.R.R. 493, the European Court of Human Rights criticised the use of Wednesbury unreasonableness by the UK court. The case involved four applicants who had all been discharged from the armed forces for being homosexual, they had applied for judicial review of the Ministry of Defence's decision and their appeals were dismissed. They appealed to the House of Lords and then to the ECHR on the basis that their discharge constituted an infringement of their right to respect for their private lives and discrimination under the European Convention on Human Rights 1950 art.8 and art.14 respectively. They also contended that an application for judicial review in the UK did not afford them an effective domestic remedy as required under art.13. The ECHR held that their art.8 rights had been infringed and that the applicants did not have access to an effective domestic remedy as required by art.13. They further commented that the test of irrationality (or Wednesbury unreasonableness) formulated by the domestic courts had been set at such a level that the UK courts were precluded from even considering whether the alleged interference with private lives could be justified on the basis of social need, national security or public order. These were matters that constituted the very essence of the court's considerations under art.8 and the test under English law had been set at such a high level the court was precluded from considering such issues. It may be that the best route for the courts to take would be to move away from the strict irrationality test and look towards considerations of proportionality, which is now commonly referred to by the courts in other areas outside judicial review when they are considering the balancing of domestic law with European law.

13.4.3 Remedies

Under an application for judicial review the courts have available to them three prerogative orders:

- A quashing order. This order annuls the original order and returns events to the situation prior to the making of the decision that has been annulled.

- A mandatory order. This order sets out what the public body *must* do to rectify matters.

- A prohibiting order. This order prevents the public body from taking a certain course of action.

The court also has available to them the full range of other remedies, such as injunctions (although the same effect can be achieved by way of a prohibiting or mandatory order) and, in extremely rare cases, the award of damages. The final point to note in relation to judicial review is that the prerogative remedies are discretional and the court need only impose them where they feel they are appropriate in the circumstances.

13.5 Summary

(a) Both the prosecution and defence may have the opportunity to appeal a decision in a case. The prosecution have the power to appeal against acquittals by way of an Attorney-General's reference, against a terminating ruling or an acquittal due to juror intimidation, and since the abolition of the rule against double jeopardy in 2003 they can now re-try an acquitted defendant for certain specified offences.

(b) The defence have a number of routes to appeal open to them depending on the court of first instance. If appealing from the magistrates' court the defence may request that the case be re-opened, they may appeal to the Crown Court, or by way of case stated to the Divisional Court and they can bring a judicial review if challenging the jurisdiction of the magistrates' court.

(c) From the Crown Court the defence can appeal against conviction and/or sentence after trial, or just against sentence after a guilty plea. An appeal against conviction will be allowed where the original conviction is felt by the court to be unsafe. If the route to appeal is barred due to time limitations then the Criminal Cases Review Commission may investigate the case and refer it back to the courts.

(d) There is limited scope to appeal in a civil case. The right to appeal is no longer automatic and there is to only be one appeal per case. Permission to appeal must be granted and the next judge in the hierarchy as opposed to the next court normally hears a civil appeal.

(e) Judicial review is a more a supervisory function than an appellate function of the High Court. An interested party can make an application for judicial review against a public body where they believe that that body has acted *ultra vires*. The court may then use its prerogative powers to remedy the situation.

13.6 Self-test questions

1. A prosecution appeal against an unduly lenient sentence goes to the:

   (a) House of Lords
   (b) Court of Appeal
   (c) High Court
   (d) Privy Council

2. A prosecution appeal against an acquittal tainted by intimidation goes to the:

   (a) House of Lords
   (b) Court of Appeal
   (c) High Court
   (d) Privy Council

3. If after an appeal from the magistrates' court to the Crown Court for a trial *de novo* the defendant still wishes to appeal he can do so by:

   (a) appealing to the Court of Appeal
   (b) appealing to the Court of Appeal by way of case stated
   (c) appealing to the High Court
   (d) appealing to the High Court by way of case stated

4. In a civil claim an appeal from the decision of a district judge in the High Court would go to:

   (a) a circuit judge
   (b) a High Court judge
   (c) the Court of Appeal
   (d) the House of Lords

5. The term 'Wednesbury unreasonableness' means that:

   (a) the judge was unreasonable on a Wednesday
   (b) the judge who was unreasonable was called Wednesbury
   (c) the judge made a decision with which the appealing party disagreed
   (d) the judge made a decision that was completely outrageous

13.7 Further reading

K. Kerrigan, "Miscarriage of justice in the magistrates' court: the forgotten power of the Criminal Cases Review Commission" [2006] Crim. L.R. Feb, 124–139.

L.H. Leigh, "Lurking doubt and the safety of convictions" [2006] Crim. L.R. Sep, 809–816.

D.C. Ormerod, "Criminal Cases Review Commission: change of law case" [2007] Crim. L.R. May, 383–387.

R. Pattenden, "Prosecution appeals against judges' rulings" [2000] Crim. L.R. Dec, 971–986.

"Rethinking appeal and review in criminal proceedings" [2008] 3 Crim. L.R. 3 175–176 Ed.

S. Sedley, "The sound of silence: constitutional law without a constitution" [1994] 110 L.Q.R. (Apr) 270–291.

R. Smith, "Human Rights and the UK Constitution: can Parliament legislate irrespective of the Human Rights Act?" [2006] 6(4) L.I.M. 274–281.

J. R. Spencer, "Does our present criminal appeal system make sense?" [2006] Crim. L.R. Aug, 677–694.

J.R. Spencer, "Quashing convictions for procedural irregularities" [2007] Crim. L.R. Nov, 835–848.

14   Self-test question answers

Chapter 1:   Introduction to the English Legal System

1. The 'English legal system' encompasses:

   (a) England
   (b) England and Scotland
   (c) England and Wales
   (d) England, Scotland and Wales

   The correct answer is (c)

2. Parliamentary sovereignty means that Parliament is:

   (a) supreme to any other law-making body in the UK
   (b) supreme to any other law-making body in Europe
   (c) supreme to any other law-making body in the world
   (d) supreme to any other law-making body in the universe

   The correct answer is (a)

3. Equity developed due to failings in:

   (a) the civil law system
   (b) legislation
   (c) the European Union
   (d) the common law

   The correct answer is (d)

4. If the House of Lords reject a Bill on two successive occasions then:

   (a) the Bill is dropped
   (b) the Bill returns for a third passing through the House of Commons
   (c) the Bill bypasses the need for House of Lords' approval and receives Royal Assent
   (d) the Bill has to be re-drafted entirely

   The correct answer is (c)

5. Delegated legislation is:

   (a) superior to primary legislation
   (b) inferior to primary legislation
   (c) equal to primary legislation
   (d) subordinate to primary legislation

The correct answer is (c)

Chapter 2:   Judicial Reasoning

1. Persuasive precedent can come from:

   (a) the Privy Council
   (b) academic commentary
   (c) lower courts
   (d) all of the above

The correct answer is (d)

2. The Court of Appeal can depart from one of its own previous decisions when:

   (a) it does not agree with the decision
   (b) the decision is made *per incuriam*
   (c) the decision is *res judicata*
   (d) it wants to develop the law

The correct answer is (b)

3. The term 'reversing' means:

   (a) the facts of the case are different
   (b) the court declares a previous case as bad law
   (c) the court changes the outcome of the instant case
   (d) the court changes its own mind

The correct answer is (c)

4. To avoid an absurd result a judge will employ which technique of statutory interpretation:

   (a) the literal rule
   (b) the golden rule
   (c) the mischief rule
   (d) the purposive rule

The correct answer is (b)

5. Which source below is not an extrinsic aid to interpretation:

   (a) case law
   (b) *Hansard*
   (c) another Act of Parliament
   (d) the *Noscitur a Sociis* rule

The correct answer is (d)

Chapter 3:   How to Find the Law and Use It

1. Authoritative case law can be found:

   (a) online
   (b) in the library
   (c) in a journal
   (d) all of the above

The correct answer is (d)

2. The case name *Charleston v DPP* means that:

   (a) Charleston is appealing and the DPP is the defendant
   (b) the DPP is appealing and Charleston is the defendant
   (c) Charleston is being prosecuted by the DPP
   (d) the Attorney-General is clarifying a point of law upon Charleston's conviction

The correct answer is (a)

3. The citation [2000] 5 Q.B. 202 means:

   (a) the case was the 5th case reported for the Queen's Bench Division for 2000
   (b) the case was the 202nd case reported for the Queen's Bench Division for 2005
   (c) the case was reported in the 5th volume of the Queen's Bench Reports for 2000 at page 202
   (d) the case was the 202nd case reported in the 5th volume of the Queen's Bench Reports for 2000

The correct answer is (c)

4. The All E.R. reports are:

   (a) the most authoritative law reporting series
   (b) the least authoritative law reporting series
   (c) published by the ICLR
   (d) commercially published

The correct answer is (d)

5. The most commonly used title for legislation is the:

   (a) chapter number
   (b) short title
   (c) long title
   (d) preamble

   The correct answer is (b)

Chapter 4:   The Legal Profession

1. The body that represents solicitors in England and Wales is the:

   (a) Legal Services Commission
   (b) Law Society
   (c) Solicitors Regulation Authority
   (d) Legal Complaints Service

   The correct answer is (b)

2. Barristers are called to the:

   (a) Bar
   (b) Bench
   (c) Cloth
   (d) Inn

   The correct answer is (a)

3. Queen's Counsel are otherwise known as:

   (a) satins
   (b) velvets
   (c) silks
   (d) God

   The correct answer is (c)

4. Barristers can refuse to take a case because:

   (a) they do not like the client
   (b) they are disgusted by the nature of the case
   (c) they suspect the defendant to be guilty
   (d) they are inexperienced in the area of law involved

   The correct answer is (d)

5. The higher rights of audience for solicitors were introduced by the:

(a) Administration of Justice Act 1985
(b) Courts and Legal Services Act 1990
(c) Access to Justice Act 1999
(d) Legal Services Act 2007

The correct answer is (b)

Chapter 5:   Magistrates

1. The maximum length of time that a magistrates' court can impose a custodial sentence for an offence is:

(a) 6 months
(b) 12 months
(c) 24 months
(d) they cannot impose custodial sentences

The correct answer is (a)

2. Magistrates can sit in the:

(a) Youth Court
(b) Family Court
(c) Crown Court
(d) all of the above

The correct answer is (d)

3. Magistrates are appointed on their:

(a) political views
(b) sentencing policies
(c) personal qualities
(d) physical appearance

The correct answer is (c)

4. Once trained, magistrates are appraised:

(a) annually
(b) every three years
(c) every five years
(d) never

The correct answer is (b)

5. Magistrates are expected to sit in court for a minimum of:

(a) 10 days per year
(b) 26 half-days per year
(c) 52 half-days per year
(d) 100 days per year

The correct answer is (b)

Chapter 6:   The Judiciary

1. The most superior type of judge in England and Wales is the:

(a) Lord Chancellor
(b) Circuit Judge
(c) Lord Justice of Appeal
(d) Lord of Appeal in Ordinary

The correct answer is (d)

2. The Lord Chancellor is now:

(a) the Head of the judiciary
(b) the Head of the Ministry for Justice
(c) a Speaker in the House of Lords
(d) a member of the judiciary

The correct answer is (b)

3. Judges used to be appointed by way of:

(a) secret soundings
(b) secret ballots
(c) open competition
(d) automatic promotion

The correct answer is (a)

4. Judges are now appointed by:

(a) the Commissioner for Judicial Appointments
(b) the Judicial Appointments Commission
(c) an election process
(d) the Judicial Appointments Committee

The correct answer is (b)

5. The Supreme Court will incorporate the:

    (a) Court of Appeal and House of Lords
    (b) Court of Appeal and Privy Council
    (c) House of Lords and Privy Council
    (d) House of Lords

The correct answer is (c)

Chapter 7: Juries

1. To be eligible to sit as a juror a person must be:

    (a) registered on the electoral roll
    (b) between the ages of 18 and 65
    (c) have lived in the UK for at least three years
    (d) own their own property

The correct answer is (a)

2. A person is disqualified from serving as a juror for ten years if they have:

    (a) been cautioned by the police
    (b) received a speeding ticket
    (c) received a community sentence
    (d) been declared bankrupt

The correct answer is (c)

3. Routine jury vetting involves checking a juror's:

    (a) credit score
    (b) employment history
    (c) professional qualifications
    (d) criminal record

The correct answer is (d)

4. An individual's right to sit on a jury can be challenged on the grounds that:

    (a) they look like they will convict the defendant
    (b) a witness in the case knows them
    (c) the defendant lives in the same town as them
    (d) the jury is unrepresentative

The correct answer is (b)

5. Section 8 of the Contempt of Court Act applies to:

(a) the court
(b) the defendant
(c) the prosecutor
(d) any person who discloses details of the jury room deliberations

The correct answer is (d)

Chapter 8:   The Civil Justice System

1. The party name of a person appealing against a judicial decision is the:

(a) claimant
(b) plaintiff
(c) appellant
(d) applicant

The correct answer is (c)

2. The overriding objective of the Civil Procedure Rules is that cases should be dealt with:

(a) justly
(b) efficiently
(c) inexpensively
(d) proportionately

The correct answer is (a)
(although the answers of (b), (c) and (d) are ways in which this can be achieved)

3. A case involving a claim for the sum of £13,500 will be heard on/in the:

(a) small claims track
(b) fast track
(c) multi-track
(d) magistrates' court

The correct answer is (b)

4. The passing down of summary judgment means:

(a) that the case had no realistic prospect of success
(b) that the defendant admitted the claim
(c) that the claimant withdrew their case

(d) that the claim was settled out of court

The correct answer is (a)

5. Conciliation means that:

(a) the parties decide the matters between themselves
(b) the parties are aided in their decision-making by a third party
(c) the matter is decided for the parties by a third party
(d) a judge determines the outcome prior to trial

The correct answer is (b)

Chapter 9:   The Criminal Justice System 1

1. The Crown Prosecution Agency will commence a prosecution where:

(a) it is in the public interest to do so
(b) there is a realistic prospect of conviction
(c) it is in the public interest to do so and there is a realistic prospect of conviction
(d) the prosecutor believes that the defendant is guilty

The correct answer is (c)

2. The term 'a realistic prospect of conviction' means:

(a) that the trier of fact would find the defendant guilty
(b) that the trier of fact might find the defendant guilty
(c) that the trier of fact would be more likely than not to convict the defendant
(d) that the trier of fact will find the defendant guilty beyond reasonable doubt

The correct answer is (c)

3. The final appeal court for England and Wales is:

(a) the Privy Council
(b) the Court of Appeal
(c) the Administrative Division of the High Court
(d) the House of Lords

The correct answer is (d)

4. An either-way offence can be tried in:

(a) the Crown Court

(b) the magistrates' court

(c) either the magistrates' court or Crown Court, depending on the seriousness of the offence

(d) the county court

The correct answer is (c)

5. The presumption of bail can be rebutted where the defendant would:

(a) fail to surrender to custody

(b) commit an offence whilst on bail

(c) interfere with witnesses or otherwise obstruct the course of justice

(d) any of the above

The correct answer is (d)

Chapter 10:   Criminal Justice System 2

1. A defendant who has pleaded not guilty to an either-way offence:

(a) always has the choice to elect a jury trial

(b) never has the choice to elect a jury trial

(c) has the choice to elect a jury trial if the magistrates deem the case suitable to be heard in the magistrates' court

(d) has the right to refuse jury trial if the magistrates decide to send the case to the Crown Court

The correct answer is (c)

2. If a defendant pleads guilty to an offence they:

(a) always receive a full sentenced discount

(b) never receive any sentence discount

(c) will be able to chose their sentence discount

(d) may receive a sentence discount that is commensurate with the timeliness of the plea

The correct answer is (d)

3. A *Newton* hearing is used to determine:

(a) the guilt of the defendant

(b) the facts that the defendant will be sentenced upon

(c) the defendant's sentence

(d) the facts of the case

The correct answer is (b)

4. An equivocal plea is where the defendant:

   (a) provides an ambiguous guilty plea
   (b) provides an ambiguous not guilty plea
   (c) provides an unambiguous guilty plea
   (d) provides an unambiguous not guilty plea

   The correct answer is (a)

5. In a criminal trial the overall burden of proof is:

   (a) on the defendant to prove their innocence beyond reasonable doubt
   (b) on the defendant to prove their innocence on the balance of probabilities
   (c) on the prosecution to prove the defendant's guilt beyond reasonable doubt
   (d) on the prosecution to prove the defendant's guilt on the balance of probabilities

   The correct answer is (c)

1. Public funding was originally:

   (a) cash limited
   (b) demand fed
   (c) demand limited
   (d) cash fed

   The correct answer is (b)

2. The Access to Justice Act 1999 introduced the:

   (a) Legal Services Committee
   (b) Legal Funding Committee
   (c) Legal Services Commission
   (d) Legal Funding Commission

   The correct answer is (c)

3. A defendant who wishes to receive public funding for a trial in the Crown Court will have to satisfy:

   (a) a means test
   (b) a merits test
   (c) a means and merits test
   (d) nothing as criminal representation is always publicly funded

   The correct answer is (b)

4. The success fee in a Conditional Fee Agreement is a calculated percentage of:

(a) the damages awarded in the case
(b) the public funding granted for the case
(c) the other side's costs
(d) the solicitors' costs

The correct answer is (d)

5. A Conditional Fee Agreement can be used to fund:

(a) divorce proceedings
(b) criminal proceedings
(c) child care proceedings
(d) personal injury proceedings

The correct answer is (d)

Chapter 12:   Sentencing

1. The main aim of sentencing is:

(a) to punish
(b) to reform
(c) to protect the public
(d) all of the above

The correct answer is (d)

2. The magistrates' court, when considering sentence, will:

(a) always start by considering whether a custodial sentence is appropriate
(b) always start by considering whether a community sentence is appropriate
(c) always start by considering whether a fine or a discharge is appropriate
(d) always start by imposing a custodial sentence

The correct answer is (c)

3. The Crown Court are guided in their sentencing by:

(a) the House of Lords
(b) the Court of Appeal
(c) the Privy Council
(d) other Crown Court cases

The correct answer is (b)

4. Adherence to the totality principle means that a sentencer should:

(a) impose the maximum sentence possible for the offences in question
(b) impose the minimum sentence possible for the offences in question
(c) take into account the overall level of seriousness of the offences and sentence proportionally to this
(d) impose whatever level of sentence they feel like based upon their personal opinions

The correct answer is (c)

5. The maximum fine that can be imposed by the magistrates' court is:

(a) £10,000
(b) £5,000
(c) £1,000
(d) £500

The correct answer is (b)

Chapter 13:   Appeals

1. A prosecution appeal against an unduly lenient sentence goes to the:

(a) House of Lords
(b) Court of Appeal
(c) High Court
(d) Privy Council

The correct answer is (b)

2. A prosecution appeal against an acquittal tainted by intimidation goes to the:

(a) House of Lords
(b) Court of Appeal
(c) High Court
(d) Privy Council

The correct answer is (c)

3. If after an appeal from the magistrates' court to the Crown Court for a trial *de novo* the defendant still wishes to appeal he can do so by:

(a) appealing to the Court of Appeal
(b) appealing to the Court of Appeal by way of case stated
(c) appealing to the High Court
(d) appealing to the High Court by way of case stated

The correct answer is (d)

4. In a civil claim an appeal from the decision of a district judge in the High Court would go to:

   (a) a circuit judge
   (b) a High Court judge
   (c) the Court of Appeal
   (d) the House of Lords

   The correct answer is (b)

5. The term 'Wednesbury unreasonableness' means that:

   (a) the judge was unreasonable on a Wednesday
   (b) the judge who was unreasonable was called Wednesbury
   (c) the judge made a decision with which the appealing party disagreed
   (d) the judge made a decision that was completely outrageous

   The correct answer is (d)

INDEX

SA

349.
42
BOY